500th Anniversary Volume

Ḥuldrych Zwingli
writings

Volume One

In Search of True Religion: Reformation, Pastoral and Eucharistic Writings

Translated by
H. Wayne Pipkin

PICKWICK PUBLICATIONS
Allison Park, Pennsylvania
1984

Copyright © 1984 by **Pickwick Publications**
4137 Timberlane Drive, Allison Park, PA 15101

Library of Congress Cataloging in Publication Data

Zwingli, Ulrich, 1484-1531.
　Selected writings of Huldrych Zwingli.

　(Pittsburgh theological monographs ; new ser., 12-13)
　Vol. 2 edited and translated by H. Wayne Pipkin.
　Includes indexes.
　Contents: v. 1. In defense of the reformed faith—v. 2. In
search of true religion, Reformation, pastoral, and
eucharistic writings.
　　1. Reformed Church—Doctrines—Addresses, essays,
lectures. 2. Theology—Addresses, essays, lectures. I Furcha,
E.J. (Edward J.), 1935- . II. Pipkin, H. Wayne. III. Title.
IV. Series.
BR346.A2513　　　1984　　　230'.42　　　84-25454
ISBN 0-915138-58-1 (v. 1)
ISBN 0-915138-59-X (v. 2)

Printed and Bound by Publishers Choice Book Mfg. Co.
Mars, Pennsylvania 16046

PITTSBURGH THEOLOGICAL MONOGRAPHS

New Series

Dikran Y. Hadidian

General Editor

12

SELECTED WRITINGS OF HULDRYCH ZWINGLI
Volume One
In Defense of the Reformed Faith

Dedicated with affection and in gratitude
to the memory of

FORD LEWIS BATTLES
1915-1979

His incisive mind and gentle spirit
transformed drudgery into thanksgiving and
elevated scholarship once more to the place of
a divine science.

H. Wayne Pipkin
Rüschlikon, Switzerland

Edward J. Furcha
Montreal, Canada

CONTENTS

ABBREVIATIONS

ADB	**Allgemeine Deutsche Biographie,** 56 vols. Reprint: Berlin: Duncker & Humblot, 1965.
ANF	**The Ante-Nicene Fathers.** Edited by Alexander Roberts and James Donaldson. 10 vols. Grand Rapids: Wm. B. Eerdmans, 1956.
Blackfriars	Thomas Aquinas, **Summa Theologica.** Blackfriars translation. 60 vols. New York: McGraw-Hill Book Company, 1963ff.
Bullinger	**Heinrich Bullingers Reformationsgeschichte.** Edited by J. J. Hottinger and H. H. Vögel. 3 vols. Frauenfeld: Ch. Beyel, 1838.
EA	**Amtliche Sammlung der ältern Eidgenössichen Abschiede,** Serie 1245-1798. Edited by A. P. von Segesser. Lucerne, Berne, 1874-1886.
Egli	Emil Egli (ed.), **Actensammlung zur Geschichte der Zürcher Reformation in den Jahren 1519-1533.** Zurich: J. Schabelitz, 1879.
Erasmus, Op. Omnia	Erasmus, **Opera Omnia.** Edited by Joannes Clericus. 10 vols. Photoreproduction of 1703 Leiden edition: Hildesheim: Georg Olms, 1961-1962.
Georges	**Ausführliches Lateinisch-Deutsches Handwörtbuch.** 9th edition: Basel: Benno Schwabe & Co., 1951.
Jackson	**The Latin Works of Huldrych Zwingli.** Vol. I edited by S. M. Jackson. New York: G. P. Putnam's Sons, 1912. Vol. II edited by William John Hinke. Vol. III edited by Clarence Nevin Heller. Philadelphia: The Heidelberg Press, 1922, 1929.

Karlstadt, Schriften	**Karlstadts Schriften aus den Jahren 1523-1525.** Selected and edited by Erich Hertzsch. Halle: Max Niemeyer Verlag, 1956ff.
Köhler	Walther Köhler, **Zwingli und Luther.** Ihr Streit über das Abendmahl nach seinen politischen und religiösen Beziehungen. Vol. I: **Die religiöse und politische Entwicklung bis zum Marburger Religionsgespräch 1529.** Leipzig: M. Heinsius Nachfolger, 1924.
LCC	**Zwingli and Bullinger.** Vol. 24 of **Library of Christian Classics.** Edited by G. W. Bromiley. Philadelphia: The Westminster Press, 1953.
Locher	Gottfried W. Locher, **Die Zwinglishche Reformation im Rahmen der europäischen Kirchengeschichte.** Göttingen: Vandenhoeck & Ruprecht, 1979.
LW	**Luther's Works.** Edited by Jaroslav Pelikan and Helmut Lehmann. 55 vols. Philadelphia: Fortress Press, 1955ff.
MGL	J. P. Migne (ed.), **Patrologiae cursus completus,** series graeca. 161 vols. Paris: Migne, 1857-1866.
MPL	J. P. Migne (ed.), **Patrologiae cursus completus,** series latina. 221 vols. Paris: Migne, 1844-1855.
NPNF	**The Nicene and Post-Nicene Fathers.** Edited by Philip Schaff et al. First Series, 14 vols. Grand Rapids: Wm. B. Eerdmans, 1956.
NPNF/2	**The Nicene and Post-Nicene Fathers.** Edited by Philip Schaff et al. Second Series, 14 vols. Grand Rapids: Wm. B. Eerdmans, 1956.
OLD	**Oxford Latin Dictionary.** Oxford: The Clarendon Press, 1968-1982.
Otto	A. Otto, **Die Sprichwörter und sprichwörtlichen Redensarten der Römer.** Reprint: Hildesheim: Georg Olms Verlags-buchhandlung, 1962.
Pauly	**Paulys Realencyclopädie der classischen Altertums-wissenschaft.** Stuttgart: J. B. Metzlersche, 1893ff.
Pelikan I	Jaroslav Pelikan, **The Emergence of the Catholic Tradition.** Vol. I of **The Christian Tradition.** Chicago: The University of Chicago Press, 1971.

Pelikan III	Jaroslav Pelikan, **The Growth of Medieval Theology.** Vol. 3 of **The Christian Tradition.** Chicago: The University of Chicago Press, 1978.
RGG³	**Die Religion in Geschichte und Gegenwart.** 7 vols. 3rd edition: Tübingen: J. C. B. Mohr, 1957.
Strickler	Joh. Strickler (ed.), **Actensammlung zur Schweizerischen Reformationsgeschichte in den Jahren 1521-1532.** Zurich: Meyer & Zeller, 1878.
Quasten	Johannes Quasten, **Patrology,** 3 vols. Utrecht: Spectrum, 1945-1960.
Quintilianus	**The Institutio Oratoria of Quintilian.** Translated by H. F. Butler, 4 vols. London: Weinemann Ltd., 1958ff.
TRE	**Theologische Realenzyklopädie.** Berlin: Walther de Gruyter, 1977ff.
WA	**D. Martin Luthers Werke.** Kritische Gesamtausgabe edited by J. K. F. Knaake, G. Kawerau, et al. Weimar: Böhlau, 1883--.
Wander	Carl Friedrich Wander, **Deutsches Sprichwörterlexikon.** 5 vols. Leipzig: E. A. Brockhaus, 1867-1880.
Wyss	**Die Chronik des Bernhard Wyss 1519-1530.** Edited by George Finsler. Basel: Basler Buch- und Antiquariatshandlung, 1901.
Z	**Huldreich Zwinglis Sämtliche Werke.** Edited by Emil Egli, et al. **Corpus Reformatorum,** vols. 88ff. Reprint: Zurich: Theologischer Verlag Zurich, 1983.

FOREWORD

This volume is an attempt to help overcome a lamentable gap in English language Reformation studies by making available in English for the first time several important Reformation, pastoral and eucharistic writings of Huldrych Zwingli on the occasion of the 500th anniversary of his birth.

This project and its antecedents have a long history. At the end of the nineteenth century a complete edition of the works of Zwingli in English was envisioned by the father of North American Zwingli studies, Professor Samuel Jackson of Union Theological Seminary, New York City. Under his direction a series of translations from the Latin was commissioned and many were carried out by the classical scholar, Henry Preble. Many of these were eventually published in the three volumes of Zwingli's **Works**. Two of these volumes were published after Professor Jackson's death. The materials for a fourth volume of the eucharistic writings of Zwingli lay in Preble's handwritten manuscripts in a metal box in an office in Union Seminary. In the 1960's they were in the office of Professor Robert Handy who told Professor Ford Lewis Battles of their existence.

In 1976 Professor Battles and now Professor Pipkin went to New York where they investigated the Preble materials. It was decided that the materials were valuable, but that they would in fact require substantial revising in order to bring them into alignment with both theological language and the English of the mid-twentieth century. With Professor Handy's permission they were taken, and Pipkin transcribed them into typescript. Copies of these transcripts now lie in Rüschlikon, at Princeton Theological Seminary and at Calvin Theological Seminary. Professor Handy told Professor Battles that it was hoped that the materials could one day be published and that the only restriction was that they be published by responsible scholars. Professor Battles contacted a team of scholars, including the editors of this two-volume set of Zwingli's writings, with the intention of publishing the Preble materials along with the other writings of Zwingli.

The lack of financial support and the press of other projects prohibited the successful conclusion of the plans. When the project was resurrected in 1979 it soon encountered a setback in the untimely death of Professor Battles. It was hoped by the present writers, that it would be possible to carry forth the project to conclusion and to do it in memory of Professor Battles. Fortunately, this has been made possible by the willingness of Dikran Y. Hadidian of Pickwick Publications and by the gracious support of the Emil Brunner-Stiftung of Zurich. The two editors, both former students of Professor Ford Lewis Battles, joined together in the project and are now pleased to be able to make available this selection of the works of Zwingli. We dedicate the two volumes to the memory of our erstwhile mentor, Professor F. L. Battles.

The two editors have worked independently but have made every effort to overcome the distance between them by frequent communication. Edward J. Furcha assumed responsibility for the translating and editing of the **Exposition** in Volume I and for **Divine and Human Righteousness** and the **Preaching Office** in Volume II. H. Wayne Pipkin translated and edited the **Shepherd** and the **Instruction** and carefully revised and edited the eucharistic writings initially translated by Mr. Preble. This latter process was carried out in as painstaking a fashion as possible so that the content of those treatises now reflect, in the editors' opinion, the reforming and theological perspective of Zwingli in a way that the Victorian English of the handwritten manuscripts could not. In addition, the editor of Volume II assumed the responsibility for editing the Preble treatises. Both editors were available to the other for consultation and each has read carefully the work of the other and has made appropriate suggestions.

It was our goal to present translations that were true to their original, but which, in the final analysis, were to be English language documents and not just German or Latin documents with English words. Such was the legacy of Professor Battles as translator and editor. The annotations are intended to provide necessary information for understanding the content of the treatises and we have sought, where possible, to make notice of the classical, patristic, and other sources of the writings. This has been particularly important for the Latin writings of Zwingli, for it is in these that Zwingli the humanist most clearly emerges. Whenever possible we have sought to insert references into the text itself and have done so consistently with scripture references and occasional references to other writings of Zwingli or Luther. We have sought to give reference to many technical expressions and classical allusions by citing standard reference works such as those of Otto, Wander, and the now completed **Oxford Latin Dictionary.** The latter source is often given in the annotations in order to alert the reader to possible classical sources of the person, expression or proverb cited. Whenever possible we have used standard, printed editions. In a few cases, such as Erasmus' Latin Bible translation, published in Basel in 1522, no current edition exists. In these cases the editors have been grateful for the rich resources of the Zurich libraries, which often contain the first edition and, sometimes, the autograph.

It is to be noted that we have not merely taken over the annotations of the critical text, however helpful they have been. Every citation has been personally checked. In this way, we found it possible to correct minor errors and to make other allusions that were not possible at an earlier time. For the most part, however, it must be said that the critical text of the works of Zwingli is a model of historical and theological scholarship and we are grateful for it. Reformation scholars are indebted to several generations of Zwingli researchers who have produced these useful volumes.

In the citation of scripture references the verses have been inserted even though they were not so rendered by Zwingli. Where Zwingli did not cite a scriptural source himself, these have been inserted in brackets.

For the most part, space limitations have prohibited our making extensive bibliographical references. It is believed that the standard bibliographies by Finsler, Pipkin and Gäbler and the fruitful work of Locher make such citations unnecessary in a work of this kind.

Special appreciation is extended to Professor Fritz Büsser and the governing board of the Emil Brunner-Stiftung of Zurich for their grant which helps make possible the publication of this two-volume set.

Edward J. Furcha
H. Wayne Pipkin

ACKNOWLEDGMENTS

Acknowledgments are due to the Faculty of Graduate Studies and Research, McGill University for a research grant in 1982 which enabled the translator and editor of Volume I to complete this manuscript. Thanks are due to the staff of the Staatsarchiv, Zurich for their most helpful cooperation in checking out manuscripts. My family has been supportive of this project through their constant encouragement. A special word of thanks goes to my daughters, Heidi and Lia for typing of the several drafts of this volume. The names of others would swell this note of acknowledgment unduly--may they find their reward in the wide circulation of a significant work of Zwingli whose exposition of the sixty-seven articles provided some of the material for the evolution and growth of the reformed tradition. We would be amiss however if we were to neglect high praise for the efficient manner in which Jean and Dikran Hadidian have made this publication their very own in their commitment to excellence and in their desire to have good sources available in translation.

We have aimed at rendering Zwingli's unique and vigorous style in good English prose without losing the freshness of the original. To aid scholars in tracing the texts of the critical edition of Zwingli's works we have provided page references to Z. The completion of this volume and its companion volume, edited by my esteemed colleague H. Wayne Pipkin, marks the end of an era--may it be the beginning of a new phase in studying Zwingli and his significance for the Church of today.

January 1, 1984

Edward J. Furcha
Montreal, Canada

PREFACE

EXPOSITION AND BASIS OF THE CONCLUSIONS
OR ARTICLES PUBLISHED BY
HULDRYCH ZWINGLI, ZURICH, 29 JANUARY, 1523

To the honorable, prudent, wise mylord prefect, [1] the Council and community of Glarus, longstanding Christians and confederates, this preface by Huldrych Zwingli.

Grace, mercy and peace from God, the Father and our Lord Jesus Christ I extend to you, good, prudent, honorable, wise, faithful, gracious, dear gentlemen, as I present to you the matters which follow herewith:

Since I have now for almost five years preached his gospel with God's help and support in the beautiful Christian city of Zurich for which I have often been grossly maligned (in itself this would have been of little consequence were it not for the fact that it happened at the expense of God's word and honor)--the righteous people of Zurich were unable to tolerate this maligning any longer because they wanted to live by it in future. Hence they asked me to give account of my teaching on the 29th January, 1523 in the presence of all scholars of the city and Canton of Zurich and of the Bishop of Constance and the wider confederacy or wherever they may come from and before the Great Council. I was pleased and happy to obey their summons. And I managed to bring together a number of Articles in a few days--for I did not have much time at my disposal--which I was confident, with God's help, to be able to defend on the specified day. Unfortunately there was less discussion on said day than there should have been. I shall not bother with all the reasons for that now, except to say that the two representatives of the court of Constance, the vicar John Faber and Martin Blansch, preacher at Tübingen, finally stated publicly in the gathering which was held before and after the meal [15] that these Conclusions are not grounded in the gospel of Christ and in the teaching of the apostles and that they are not in line with the truth. These are the very words of the vicar, and Martin Blansch agreed to them fully. Yet in all this they were unable to touch a single Article. Although a lot had taken place in wrangling earlier, they did not want to touch these Articles.

1

This surprised me greatly and I responded; but there is no need of mentioning that here. Thus I was earnestly entreated by many friends of God and driven also by the honor of his word, to prove the bases of these Articles with the help of the clear word of God, that it may become apparent to everyone how undeserved have been the unseemly, unwarranted attacks on these true Articles, some of which are, after all, the very word of Christ. And so I have brought together, as your worthy Wisdom may see, the expositions of these Articles.

Though it would have been perfectly in order for me to dedicate this work to none other than the good people of Zurich from whose wise counsel has come the stimulus for this undertaking which was afterwards followed by many other cities, I decided after careful consideration that they can easily do without this dedication of mine, yes, that they would consider it as received when I dedicate it to you, our faithful and dear Christians and confederates, my gracious lords; especially since not only I but many good, sincere and highly learned servants of Christ preach the word of God unceasingly in that city and in the surrounding area. For we are informed through reliable sources how excellently you have begun to appropriate and keep the word. Now that I might assist your scholars, of which you have a great number, whom I cannot help verbally, I dedicated this my work (to aid them in writing at least) to you, formerly my little flock, but now gracious lords and dear brothers in Christ, so that I may be found to have remembered the faithfulness and honor which were afforded me when I was with you. Also that the [16] quarrels which seem to be current almost everywhere right now and which take place largely because of ignorance of the word of God may be known by everyone--however simple--for what they are, so that the right and true teaching and honor of God may be brought out, looked at, recognized and kept.

For these Articles contain almost all of the major controversies which engage us today, such as the following: what the true nature of the gospel is and whether other doctrines and scriptures are of equal value. How rich and sufficient Christ the Son of God is to recompense for our weaknesses. Whether we are able to do good. Whether ceremonies, dreamed up by people, are meritorious. Whether the pope has his authority and dominion from God or from human beings; whether by virtue of his office he is high priest. Whether the mass is a sacrifice or not. Whether we require a mediator with God other than the Lord Jesus Christ alone. How and why one should pray. Whether the so-called spirituals [clerics] are rightly entitled to their pomp and riches under the cover of the name of Christ. Whether we sin when we refuse to perform the ceremonies which have been invented by people. Whether God is more gracious in one place than in another or at one time than at another. How well hypocrisy pleases God.

Whether gowns, crosses, signs, tonsure are good and pleasing to God. Whether it is in keeping with God's word that in so many places splinter groups and sects have been hatched. Whether priests are forbidden to marry. Whether vows of chastity or any such are pleasing to God. Whether bishops [die hohen bischoff] use the ban rightly and whether, whenever they [17] abuse it, one is bound to submit to it. To what end unlawful possessions are to be used. Whether the teaching of Christ is against [temporal] authority. Whether spiritual authority is based on a commandment of God. Whose it is to protect justice. Whether all persons, be they clerics or not, are bound to obey temporal authority and what the same ought to command. What one owes such authority in return. Of what use prayers and choral singing for money are. How one might eliminate or prevent offences. What an abominable vice it is when priests keep whores openly but do not have wives. Whether perchance someone other than the one God can forgive sins. Through whom and for whose sake he forgives them. Whether God commanded the institution of auricular confession and penance. Whether any one may, like God, hold sins against a person who repents and whether it is possible to forgive sins on payment of a fee. Whether there is such a thing as purgatory and whether, should there be none, it is harmful to pray for the dead. Whether consecration is anything special. What true priests are.

Yes, all these views and many more you will find here; and I gathered them together for the benefit of all Christian people, (provided they want to make use of them), and undertook to publish them in the name of your eminence in the hope that your eminence will, after careful consideration and in all order, gradually correct these public abuses which false teachers have introduced; for we have also given a brief statement on how to eliminate abuses. [2] How happy those would have been who went before us, had they been shown the paths which have opened up of late. How heavily they were pressed by clerics abusing the ban, by courtesans who disregarded their discipline and dared call it "liberty". There were further the many ways of forgiving sins, disputes about seasons and offerings, the oppression through confessional and mass, prayers to Our Lady, the treasures of cathedrals, prebends and yearly church taxes and the wantonness of the pope and all his followers.

Yet when one undertakes to overcome these corrupt practices today with the strong and true word of God, as is only right--for the gospel is of such nature that it heals the broken and releases the prisoner, and preaches the opening of what is closed and their [18] release, Is. 61:1--one finds, nonetheless, some who refuse to accept their salvation, rest and peace. They are like the enslaved Cappadocians who, when they were about to be released and given the chance to set up their own army, answered that they could not be free after all. [3]

However, those who in our day resist the word of God cannot escape it, for wherever it it heard one goes to it with force and it is accepted by the very ones by whom it has been refused, Lk. 16:16. For the faith which is within a person, cannot be detected outwardly. It follows then that one may well persecute the preachers of the same outwardly, but in human hearts faith in Christ remains untouched; it is like sourdough which penetrates the entire dough wherever it is found [cf. Mt. 13:33]. In like manner, a truly believing person is one who knows the salvation, rest and joy of his soul; yes, he carries it with him everywhere he goes and cannot suffer his neighbor to be ignorant of such joy and salvation, as one does in other matters, too, when everyone is anxious that his views become known and useful to others as well. But there is the difference between the Spirit of God which instructs in the faith only and the spirit of our flesh which is always out for itself. Hence a believer does not rest as long as he sees his brother remain in unbelief.

From this we learn that it is impossible to resist the word of God. Therefore, your Wisdom, do not be misled into believing that this word could be resisted, for anyone who undertakes to do so will be humbled by God. It is quite true to say that the word of God confronts everyone; [4] and we are all sinners while the word itself is pure; yes, freer of all worldly temptations than silver and gold are free of impurities after having been purified by fire seven times. Therefore it is not [19] surprising that those who cover up their temptations and sins reject it and shout instead, as Isaiah points out, Is. 30:30, "Preach what we like to hear, etc." But this leads to unexpected harsh punishment. Therefore, says the prophet, "They shall perish on account of their wickedness like a high faulty wall which tumbles down unexpectedly" [Is. 30:13]. Those, on the other hand, who accept it, will be assured of their salvation, as long as they believe in this salvation and acknowledge themselves to be sinners and surrender to the grace of the Lord Jesus Christ. Yes, they are as sure of salvation as if they had been given it under letter and seal. Jn. 3:15.36. Christ himself assures us in Mt. 21:44, "Whoever falls upon the stone which is Christ shall break and upon whomever the stone shall fall, it will crush." This means that whoever sets himself against Christ will destroy himself, for we are not able to overthrow him but will be crushed by him; for Christ punishes and grinds to shreds those who fight him. [5] Or, those fall on Christ who discover in confrontation with him that they are nothing at all; that they are shattered by him. This means that they are brought down and humbled. And he falls on those whom he punishes for their unbelief, like Jerusalem. [6]

Therefore, wise, gracious, dear gentlemen, do not allow the teaching of Christ to be driven out from among you as if it were something new; for it really breaks forth loud and clear today, as it has not done since the time of the apostles. Allow the word of God to be preached clearly among you and God will surely watch over you. And see to it also that you are not the last who in this praiseworthy confederacy accept the returning word of God. Your scholars will undoubtedly be able to show you where the root of the matter may be found. Believe them, for they are able to instruct you in the truth and remember, there is no nation upon earth whom Christian liberty suits better and whom it will be given more peacefully than a praiseworthy confederacy. Hold God and his word before your eyes and he will never leave you. May he keep your land according to his will in his grace and honor. Amen. [20]

I commend to you Valentine Tschudi, [7] pastor at Glarus, Fridoline Brunner at Mollis, [8] John Schindler at Schwanden [9] and George Büntzli at Wesen, [10] pastors all, who teach and preach the gospel of Christ faithfully.

May this my letter find you in the best of health and be commended unto the grace of God.

Given on the fourteenth day of hay month [July] in the year 1523.

Huldrych Zwingli
Always your servant

NOTES

1. A certain Jost Tschudi was prefect of Glarus from 1522 until March, 1524 when he was succeeded by M. Maad. Cf. C. Trümpi, **Neuere Glarner Chronik**, Winterthur, 1774, 702.

2. Zwingli himself had served as priest in Glarus from 1506 to December 1518. From 1516 on a vicar took his place there while he served at Einsiedeln. Cf. G. Heer, **Huldreich Zwingli als Pfarrer in Glarus.** Zurich, 1884, 40. By the same author, **Glarner Reformationsgeschichte.** Glarus, 1900, 25. In a letter to Vadian (June 13th, 1517) Zwingli cites pressure from the French as a reason for the change. However, the reformer never lost interest in this parish though he did not return there as had been hoped by many.
Cf. Z I 74-136. **Von Erkiesen und Freiheit der Speisen.** U. Gäbler, **Ulrich Zwingli**, TVZ, 1975, 403 provides bibliographical details. A useful English translation may be found in M. Jackson, **H. Zwingli**, Putnam, 1901.

3. The reference is to the Cappadocians who rejected the freedom offered to them by the Romans. The incident is reported by Junianus Justinus in **Epitoma Historiarum Philippicarum Pompei Trogi**, lib 38, cap 2.

4. . . . das wort gottes fichtet wider alle menschen." Cf. **Idiotikon** I 663. The term implies a professional preoccupation with something, as well as "to fight someone". Hence, "the word of God confronts everyone."

5. "Falt mit rach". Cf. **Idiotikon** V 88 gives "divine punishment" as a possible meaning.

6. "an denen er ir ungloubnus richt". Cf. **Idiotikon** II 1054.

7. On Zwingli's recommendation Valentin Tschudi was called to be vicar at Glarus, December 1518. He was inducted into the parish in October 1522. In later years Tschudi did not wholeheartedly condone Zwingli's reform stance and distanced himself from the reformer. Cf. G. Heer, **Glarnersche Reformations-geschichte**. Glarus, 1900, 38ff. Additional helpful information is found in Zwingli's **Correspondence**.

8. Brunner had recently become chief minister in the town of Mollis. His ministry there is said to have contributed significantly to the cause of Protestant reform. Cf. G. Heer, op.cit., 40.

9. J. Schindler moved 1526 from Schwanden to Wesen.

10. G. Büntzli was a former teacher of Zwingli in Basel. Apparently he was held in high esteem by the reformer since several works are dedicated to him. Cf. G. Finsler, "Dedikationen Zwingli's", **Zwingliana** II, (No. 6) 1907, 189ff. See also Zwingli's **Correspondence**.

THE EXPOSITION OF THE SIXTY-SEVEN ARTICLES
BY HULDRYCH ZWINGLI

THE FIRST ARTICLE

Everyone who says that the Gospel is nothing without the sanction of the Church, errs and blasphemes God. [1]

I have placed this Article first because those who attack the gospel have often undertaken to attack it, too; but they have always had to withdraw shamefacedly. I am hoping that some day they might be forced to speak of it in my presence on the basis of scripture and not with human prattle which they have so highly exalted that God's word, I fear, has lost almost all its meaning for them. And should this Article overcome them, a great many of their troops would take to flight; these had armed themselves with the following (not without defamation of God), "That the Gospel is nothing without the sanction of the Church". [2] They hurled this [sentence] with such impudence against all who opposed their glory that they hurt themselves with it. Several of these impertinent people even dared to preach, not only that the gospel is nothing without the Church's sanction, but also that, should the gospel not exist at all, the Church could establish laws by which one might be saved. In this--God have mercy on them--they sinned grievously. Since their unsound opinion has thus been exposed, I hoped that they might give heed to the following Articles with all the more diligence.

Like some quarrelsome women they kept deplorably silent at a time when they should have spoken. Yet on matters on which they should be silent they will sharpen their tongues like adders and surpass the frogs even in their croaking. Since, however, several good [3] people who did not hear what they expected to on account of this silence have asked me to publish an exposition of the articles which I had prepared in response, I can no longer refuse them such. Indeed, I am actually driven to do so because some people have rejected them altogether--unheard; they did not want to hear scripture on the matter nor could they point to anything at all that would explain why they rejected even a single one [22] of them. Rather, as is typical of people, they clamored blasphemously without showing why. In such a way Christ was killed. When the Jews were asked what cause they had against him, they did not come up with anything other than their own wantonness; on its strength they wanted to be believed. "Had he not been an evildoer, we would not have brought him to you," [Jn. 18:30].

Therefore I should like all brothers in Christ Jesus to know that I published this Article, supported by the solid foundation of scripture.

First of all, Christ says in Jn. 3:31-33, "Whoever is of the earth, belongs to the earth and speaks of the earth; whoever comes from heaven is above everything and what he has seen and heard he witnesses to, yet no one accepts his testimony. Whoever accepts his testimony has sealed or confirmed that God is truthful." [4] In short, note from these words that the one who comes from heaven, is above everything. But since earthly persons talk of earthly things how can one who is earthly receive what is heavenly? Or how could one verify or judge it? Thus he says that no one accepts his testimony even though he does not speak or testify to anything except what is sure, which is what he has seen and heard. But one who received Christ's testimony, that is, his teaching and proclamation [kundschaft] would have verified that God is truthful. In other words, it becomes unmistakably clear to him--just as sure as by a sealed letter--that God is truthful; for no heart and soul can understand the word of God and his deeds unless it be illumined and taught by God. Whenever that happens, a person becomes so sure, courageous and certain with regard to the word of God that he will depend more surely on its truth than upon any seal and letter. On the basis of the words of Christ, I assert the following then: Everyone who would speak true and as coming from God on the basis of the teaching that comes from heaven, which is the gospel, must have been taught, assured and confirmed by God. Thus it follows similarly that a sure understanding of the gospel depends on no one but on the drawing out and illumination by God alone. For Paul says that carnal or animal nature does not accept the things which are of the Spirit of God [Rom. 8:5]. If then the matter rests with God alone, no one can ever assure another of the gospel, except God.

Secondly, however, Christ says, Jn. 6:44, "No one comes to me unless the Father, who sent me, has [23] drawn him". [5] It must follow then that no one can come to a knowledge of Christ through human instruction, teaching or judgment but solely because the Father draws him. Thus human approval contributes nothing to the knowledge of Christ.

Thirdly, Christ says Jn. 5:39-41, "Search the Scriptures; for you think that you have in them eternal life; and it is they which bear witness to me. But you do not want to come to me that you may have life. I do not accept any human glory". [6] Note, how Christ here points to scripture and not to those who judge scripture. Indeed, scripture itself is to bear testimony to him. But those who remain in unbelief do not permit themselves to be drawn to God but they demand human signs or human attestations just like the Jews. Jn. 5:41 clearly states that Christ does not receive any human glory. The one word is strong enough to overcome all antagonists; would it were firmly held before them. Christ does not receive either human glory or testimony.

Fourthly he says, Jn. 14:26, "The comforting and admonishing Holy Spirit, whom the Father will send in my name, will teach you all things and will renew for you or bring to you all the things I have said to you." Note, "The Holy Spirit will teach you all things." He leaves nothing out, but will teach everything we ought to know of God. He will further recall to you all that I have said to you. If that then is the way it really is, what person then dares teach what the Spirit of God alone can teach?

Fifthly, Jn. 16:13, "But when the Spirit of truth will come he shall teach you all truth." Do you hear, that the Spirit teaches all truth? It must be then that human teaching is not true (inasmuch as it is human; however if it is God's, though uttered by a person, it should not be attributed to a person). For all truth comes from the Spirit of God. Whatever comes from elsewhere is untruth, for every person is prone to lie; God alone is truthful, Rom. 3:4. [24].

Sixth, Jer. 31:33f., "The Lord says, I will put my laws within them and write them upon their hearts; I will be their God and they shall be my people. And no longer shall one teach his neighbor or anyone his brother, saying, "Know the Lord," for they all shall know me, from the least to the greatest." Here you hear that God himself writes his will and his law so clearly upon human hearts that no one will have to learn them from anyone else. For even though a person may expound the word, it is not his word, neither does it move (anyone) unless God illumines the heart and draws it to himself. See also Is. 54:13, "All your children shall be taught by God." The same meaning, Christ, who is truth himself, has set down also in Jn. 6:45, "They shall all be taught by God. Everyone who has heard and learned from the Father, comes to me". To sum up: All who rightly know Christ, are taught by God and not by humans; those hear and learn from the Father, who are illumined and drawn by him in their inward members and hearts.

In the seventh place, Paul did not learn the gospel from

any human being, but by the revelation of Jesus Christ, Gal. 1:12.
[7] Likewise also the other apostles, after they were sent and
commissioned to preach the gospel, did not first decide through
Councils whether they were going to accept the gospel. For when
they were filled with the Holy Spirit on the day of Pentecost,
Peter began, soon after he had been ridiculed by the ignorant
and without advice from others (none such is recorded), to proclaim
the gospel with such certainty that he said after several words
[Acts 2:36], "Therefore let all the house of Israel know assuredly
that God has made Jesus, whom you crucified, both Lord and
Christ". But Paul's coming to Jerusalem to discuss the evangelical
cause with the apostles was not because of doubt, but in order
to assure certain simple minded people who spoke evil of Paul
by saying that he was not one of the proper apostles and that
he had not been with Christ. This may be readily noted when
he says in Gal. 2:6, "Those who thought themselves to be something,
helped me in no way". Thus it follows [25] from above-mentioned
and many other statements of scripture that human beings are
not only incapable of confirming [bevesten] the gospel but they
cannot even understand it without the grace and power of God.
How then are they going to verify the gospel?

At this point they counter with a blunt weapon, saying
that it is true that the gospel must be understood solely through
the illumination of God. If then Christ says [Mt. 18:19], "Whatever
two people on earth agree to ask of God in my name, they will
receive", it must follow then that an entire Council, if it asks
God for understanding of scripture shall be granted the same.
Therefore whatever a Council decides, ought to be commonly
adhered to from then on. Answer: Numbers do not assure certainty
of understanding. This is clearly confirmed in Elijah, Micah, Christ,
Paul and others. They fought alone against great numbers and
overcame. However, I am willing to concede the objection which
you have heard, provided it means that as often as a Council
is gathered in the Spirit of God, it cannot err. [8] But then it
will not know anything other than what God-inspired scripture
points to. [9] And if such a Council, as mentioned above, is gathered in and by the will of God, it would not exalt itself and cry,
"Council, Council," but rather "God, God says this or that". [10]
Whether or not it is gathered in the Spirit of God must be determined by the testing stone [11] as 1 Jn. chapter 4 teaches [1
Jn. 4:1-13], "Beloved, do not believe every spirit but test the
spirits whether they are of God; for every spirit is of God, which
knows, praises, and names the Lord Christ who has come in human
form". (Do you perceive that the divine Spirit orders all confessions
in Christ?) And every spirit that does not confess Jesus Christ
who has become human, nor praises and knows him, recognizing
him to be the sole salvation, is not of God. Look here, if in their
Councils Christ is the one refuge and goal upon which they look,
the one head that leads them, the one honor [26] which they seek,

then they are of the Spirit of God. But if they seek their own advantage, name and honor, everything is of the devil and of unbelief--it seeks its own honor. And even though it were to say publicly, "The Lord Jesus," it does not believe in him and holds nothing by him, as Christ himself has proved to the Jews in Jn. 5:44, "How can you believe who receive honor from one another; but the honor which alone comes from the one God, you do not seek?" On this testing stone, which is Christ, you may examine a person's reputation, counsel and judgment. If it shows Christ, it is of the Spirit of God and does not at all need the terms, "Fathers," "Councils," "customs" and "tradition". If, however, it shows the colors just mentioned, "Fathers," "Councils," etc. it is not of God. For all who seek their own honor, do not bank on God, however wise they may appear to human eyes. Christ cannot lie. Whoever disregards the glory of Christ and seeks his own honor, does not believe; hence 'he is not of God. If that, which the Councils recognize is like Christ when tested over against him, why then do you give it the name of some person? If it is unlike him, why then do you pass it off under the exalted name of God? Note, here you find out what faith is, what the teaching of God, what pretense and the teaching and refuse of people.

These proofs I do not want to render worthless and superfluous by simply adding to their number, for they themselves are sufficient to verify our first Article, which states that "Everyone who says that the gospel is nothing without the sanction of the Church, errs and blasphemes". For what person is there who could authenticate God's thought, mind or meaning, if understanding of the gospel (i.e. all proclamation of God addressed to us), does not rest in human wisdom and understanding, but in the illumination and messages of the Spirit of God? As John teaches [1 Jn. 2:26f.], "These things I have written to you concerning those who deceive you. But the anointing (i.e. illumination and inspiration of the Spirit of God through Christ Jesus who is an inexhaustible source of the ointment), which you received from him, remains in you. And you have no need to be taught by anyone; for as the anointing teaches you about all things, it is the truth and no deceit. And as it has taught you, thus remain in it." Look at this afterthought [12] carefully and all thoughtless [27] words drop off like chaff, such as those which assert that one should have a judge to determine the right understanding of scripture as if one could and should judge the word of God like temporal goods. This despite what John says, "You do not need anyone to teach you, but.... etc." But those who would gladly receive from us honor and possessions would love to expound and distort scripture for us according to their own understanding. They are true enemies of the truth of God. Indeed, they are anti-Christs who appropriate for themselves what is God's alone. For what person has ever become so learned or wise that he could not err in his mind? And no one is sure of any truth except one to whom the same has been made clear and sure in his heart by God. How then can one rely on a person? Let them err as much as they will, they are all vain and subject to sin. [13] We have written more on this in our booklet, **On the Clarity and Certainty of the Word of God.** [14] For this reason then, no more at this point. Regarding Councils, however, more in the **Archeteles.** [15]

NOTES

1. Zwingli begins this defense of the evangelical faith by claiming the right to criticize or stand over against ecclesiastical structures with the aid of the gospel. He directs his argument mainly against those in his city who claim the authority of well-established papal or ecclesiastical courts. Among his opponents were John Faber and J. Murner. At the same time Zwingli wishes to encourage his former flock in Glarus to whom the entire **Exposition** is dedicated.

2. The reformer reacted strongly to Faber's method of working against him after the First Disputation in January, 1523 even though during the Disputation Faber had little to say on the matter under discussion.

3. The term "fromm" is frequently used by Zwingli. Its Latin equivalent is, "iustus, sanctus, innocens". There is also the implication of an ethically upright frame of mind. We translate the term with "good" or "just" not with "pious". Cf. Veronika Günther, **"Fromm" in der Zürcher Reformation.** Aarau, 1955.

4. In keeping with his revolutionary discovery that scripture is authoritatively the word of God, Zwingli quotes biblical texts. He uses the New Testament five times as often as the Old Testament and quotes from the Gospels more often than from any other biblical book.

The hermeneutical principle by which alone he allows himself to be judged is Holy Scripture, inspired by God as being its own judge. However, A. Risch, **Anfänge,** 31 contends that Zwingli does not follow too closely either the Erasmian principle [den Buchstaben verachte, schaue vor allem auf das Mysterium], nor that of Luther [der natürliche Sinn ist Frau Kaiserin]. See also, Ibid., 48ff. and O. Farner, **Zwingliana** III, 12.

5. The place of John 6 in the thought of Zwingli is still a much discussed issue. Opinions differ on whether Zwingli's **Exposition** depends on the ideas of Honius or whether he arrived at his insights independently. A study of the relationship between Honius, Crautwald and Schwenckfeld might yield further insights into this exegetical development. H. Gollwitzer, "Zur Auslegung von Johannes bei Luther und Zwingli", **In Memoriam Ernst Lohmeyer** (ed. W. Schmauch), Stuttgart,

1951, 143-168 offers some helpful suggestions. For a critical discussion of Gollwitzer, cf. C. Gestrich, **Zwingli als Theologe**. ZVZ, Zurich, 1967.

6. Doxa – possible means "honor".

7. Cf. Jean Calvin, **Comm. Ep. Gal.** (on Galatians 1:12).

8. Text "A" contains the marginal statement: "A Council which is gather in the Spirit, does not set up new things, but listens to the Spirit."

9. Theopneustos – Zwingli has been called the theologian of the Holy Spirit. The work of the Spirit of God or Christ is decisive in his understanding of how God continues to work in the church which lives in obedience to the ever-renewing word of God.

10. See Luther's position on this point in his **Address to the Christian Nobility** of 1520 in WA vol. VI, 381-403.

11. The term is "Goldstein". Discussed with reference to Peter in Zwingli's **Archeteles**, Z.I.261.8ff.

12. The term is "Nachhut" whose original meaning is, "additional troops sent for protection or to clean up"; here it simply means, "afterthought".

13. A frequently used term, "präesten", is translated by us as "weakness" or "sin".

14. Cf. **Hauptschriften**, vol. I, 63ff. The sermon is dated Sept. 6, 1522. See also Z.I.328-384.

15. The **Apologeticus Archeteles** of August 1522 is Zwingli's first major apologetic pamphlet. In this work Zwingli presumed to have spoken a decisive word in the controversy on fasting. Cf. Z.I.328-384. The specific section referred to here is on pages 302-306.

THE SECOND ARTICLE

The summary of the gospel is that our Lord Christ, true Son of God, has made known to us the will of his Heavenly Father and has redeemed us from death and reconciled us with God by his guiltlessness.

This Article is so firmly established in the mind of every believer that it would require no exposition were it not for the anti Christian who pretend to be Christ's, but oppose his word.

Firstly, the summary of the gospel is found nowhere more clearly stated than in the second chapter of Luke [Lk. 2:10ff.] in the words of the angel to the shepherds, "Behold, I proclaim to you or assure you of great joy, which is to be to all people; for to you is born today a redeemer, savior, or healer; he is Christ, the Lord".

But Paul carried the matter somewhat further, though in a few words in Eph. 1:3-14; God willing, I wish to bring out their meaning [28] in almost the same few words. "Blessed be the God and Father of our Lord Jesus Christ etc., who from eternity has ordained us, to make us his sons and accept us as his own through Jesus Christ. And he has done this according to his good free will that the honor and glory of his grace be praised and freely proclaimed. By this grace he has made us pleasing to himself, through his beloved Son by whose very blood we have been bought and redeemed. In him our sins have been blotted out according to the riches of his grace which he has so lavishly given us or poured out upon us in all wisdom and understanding. The same God after he has opened to us the mystery of his will according to his free pleasure, has himself decided--when the time was fulfilled--to bring all things together, unite and draw them together under one head--which is Christ. Indeed, he has fore-ordained all things (i.e. all generations of reasoning creatures)--whether in heaven or on earth--in him, (i.e. in Christ), through whom we have been made heirs, by the work of him who does all things according to the counsel of his will that we may laud and praise his honor and the riches of his grace." In these words of Paul is contained the work of Christ, viz. that God has through him drawn us unto himself. This was not because of our merit but because of grace freely given, whose fulness and riches he showed us in order to prod us to know, love and possess him.

I have described all this in fewer words, still, yet set them forth at this point as the clearest and shortest possible explanation of the matter.

True Son of God

That Christ is the true Son of God no one, I trust, will deny. But in order that no one remain befogged on the matter, Jn. 10:34-36 reports clearly on it. Quite intelligibly also: Jn. 3, Jn. 5, Jn. 8, Jn. 14, Jn. 15, Phil. 2, Lk. 1, Lk. 3, Mt. 3, Mk. 1, etc. [Jn. 3:17f, 35f; 5:19-27; 8:35f; 14:9-11; 15:1-8; Phil. 2:6-11; Lk. 1:35; 3:22; Mt. 3:17; Mk. 1:11].

He has made known to us the will of his Heavenly Father.

With this statement, I intended to show that Christ has not only come to save us but also to teach us the true love of God and the works which God demands of us, so that we may learn of him the divine wisdom, and not of ourselves, what is pleasing to God and what he demands of us. All the evangelists' writings are full of this; [29] the loveliest expressions, however, concerning Christian conduct toward the neighbor are all contained compactly in Mt. 5, 6 and 7; those concerning the adoration of God--Jn. 5 and 6 and thereafter in the teaching which Christ delivered after the Supper, beginning with chapter 14.

"And by his guiltlessness has redeemed us from death and reconciled us to God."

This, too, does not need more than a few references to scripture. Thus it is written in 1 Pet. 3:18, "Christ died for our sins once, the righteous and guiltless for the guilty or sinners, that he might turn over or sacrifice to God we who are dead after the flesh, but have been made alive by the Spirit". And again on this matter a little earlier in the second chapter [1 Pet. 2:21-24], "Christ has suffered for us, etc., who never committed a sin, neither has any guilt or lie been found in his mouth, etc.; he who bore our sin in his body on the cross, that we, who were dead on account of sin, may live to righteousness". Paul says in Rom. 3:23-26, "All were sinners and fell short of the honor of God". But they have been made righteous without cost by his grace of redemption which is in Christ Jesus, whom God has given and set as mediator [Begnadiger] or reconciler through his blood. We are to depend on him with certainty by whom he showed his righteousness in blotting out our sins through the longsuffering of God that he might show us his righteousness in this age viz. that we may know him the just [righteous] God and that he might justify everyone who believes in Jesus Christ. And again John the baptizer in Jn. 1:29, "Behold, the lamb of God who takes away the sins of the entire world". Christ himself, in Jn. 6:51, "The bread which I shall give you, is my body for the life of the world". See also the entire chapter of Jn. 10 as well and Rom. 5:1f., "Therefore since we are made righteous by faith, we have peace with God through our Lord Jesus Christ. Through him we have obtained access to this grace through faith. In this grace we stand [30] boasting in it and we hope with assurance that we are children of God". Likewise Col. 1:2, 2 Cor 5:2, and also elsewhere, but described, above all, in the beginning of the gospel of John.

THE THIRD ARTICLE

"Therefore, Christ is the only way to salvation of all who were, are now, or shall be."

The way is Christ who says in Jn. 14:6, "I am the way, the truth and the life". He is the door also by which one has to go in to enter salvation. Jn. 10:9, "I am the door. Whoever shall go through me, shall be saved, etc." That he is the only way and that no one is able to come to God by any other, he himself affirms in Jn. 14:6, "No one comes to the Father but alone by me". Heb. 10:19-22, "Brothers, since we have free assurance of entering the holiest place (heaven is meant by this part of the temple) by the blood of Jesus Christ which living way he has newly opened through the curtain, i.e. his humanity, and since we have a great high priest, set over the house of God, let us draw near with a true heart and a right faith". We note here the way to salvation established for us through the humanity of Christ, i.e. newly sacrificed (which means, in the last times) through him. Now there is only one Christ, one sacrifice, therefore there must be only one way.

"Of all who were, are now, or shall be."

This is apparent from what in the Second Article we have drawn out of the first chapter of Ephesians. There Paul says that it has pleased God to draw together, unite and accommodate under the one head Christ, everything in heaven and on earth (read, all reasoning creatures). [1] Further, Paul says in 1 Cor. 15:22, "As in Adam all have died, so in Christ all shall be made alive". Now in Adam all are dead; thus in Christ all who believe shall be made alive, as the Lord says in Jn. 6:40, "Truly I say to you that everyone who [31] believes in me, has eternal life". In this manner also all believers in God, who were before Christ, did set their hope of coming to God upon Christ. This was pointed out always by Abraham, Jacob, Moses, David and others with specific stories or words and by the prophets. But Christ has expressed it in clear words in Jn. 8:56, "Abraham rejoiced that he was to see and experience my time". Now he

17

has seen or experienced it and is glad. Similarly, Paul in Eph. 2:14, "He is our peace who has made the two things (meaning: the Jews and the gentiles; the ancient fathers and the new converts), one. And in Heb. 11:39f., "The above-mentioned have all been well tested in the faith, yet did not receive the promise, for God has foreseen something better for us, viz. that apart from us they should not be made perfect.

NOTE

1. "Vernünfftigen geschöpfften" or its equivalent is generally used to mean "human beings".

THE FOURTH ARTICLE

"Whoever seeks or points to another door, errs. Indeed, he is a murderer of the soul and a thief."

This Article must not be substantiated with anything other than the clear words of Christ in Jn. 10:1-5, "Truly, truly I say to you, whoever does not enter the sheepfold by the door but goes in elsewhere, is a thief and a murderer; but the one who enters through the door is a shepherd and guardian of the sheep. To such a one the gatekeeper opens the door and the sheep hear his voice. And he calls his sheep by their names and leads them out. And when he has let out his sheep, he goes before them and the sheep follow after him, for they know his voice. A stranger they will not follow, but they will flee from him, for they do not know his voice". This parable Jesus told them but they did not understand why. Then Jesus told them once again, "Truly, truly I say to you that I am the door to the sheep. All those who came before me were thieves and murderers, and the sheep did not listen to them. I am the door. Everyone who enters by me shall be redeemed or saved; he shall go in and out and find pasture. The thief comes for no other reason than to steal and kill. But I have come that they might have life; [32] and that, in abundance. I am the good shepherd, etc." I have given these words at length since they not only confirm this Article but give an example at the same time of a true shepherd and bishop [1] and by contrast also of a false murderer of souls. Read in addition, if you please, Mt. 6; 15:3-20; 24; 2 Pet. 2; Acts 20:29 and similar passages and you will learn to know the true murderers of the soul.

NOTES

1. Bishop is interchangeable with overseer (often limited to the socio-political community) and is intended to mean the office of a senior pastor. There is no understanding here of a monarchical episcopate or of a strictly administrative

19

office. In his pamphlet <u>Der Hirt</u> of March 26, 1524, Zwingli discusses the office of pastor at some length. Cf. Z.III.1-68. The tract represents the written account of a sermon preached in Oct. 1523 during the so-called Second Zurich Disputation.

THE FIFTH ARTICLE

"Therefore, all who regard other teachings equal to or higher than the Gospel, err. They do not know what Gospel is." [1]

The greater part of this Article depends on the conclusions reached in the preceding ones. For if Christ is the only way and door to salvation, nothing can ever be put on equality with or counted alongside him; but more of that later. That I have chided those who have contradicted it by saying that they do not know what gospel is, will become apparent soon and thus the concerns of all will become clear.

Firstly, they hold the gospel to be a law which is grounded in and promoted by human reason. We note that from their words when they say, "Even though there were no gospel, the church could make new laws through which one might be saved as long as one lived by them".

Secondly, they do not regard it high enough; as a result they regard everything contained therein wrongly, lightly or useless if it is contrary to their thinking. One discovers this when they say, "It must be proclaimed in keeping solely with the pope's understanding".

Thirdly, they hold it to be an inadequate law which is not perfect. This, one observes when they say, "Look here, not everything is found in the gospel; but the Fathers have added to it what was lacking". Such like and worse statements they eject. You may sense their animosity toward, indeed, their utter blasphemy of God. [33]

If I were to lay out before them the meaning of things I might as well try to whiten a crow. [2] Had they ever wanted to hear and understand, they could long since have been informed. But they neither read nor hear the truth; for their hearts are darkened. Now to stop them from further offending good Christians, I will expose to them their errors so that they may guard against them--even though the enemies of God will neither read nor hear of God.

21

In order that the healing or medicine be known all the quicker, I will first of all expose the illness or weakness [prästen]. When God created Adam he made him lord over all animals in the air, upon the earth and in the waters, Gen. 1:28, for he was still good then. He placed him in the beautiful garden of Paradise which he had planted, so that he might occupy and work it. He granted him to eat every fruit except that of the tree of the knowledge of good and evil which he forbade him in these words, "Of the tree of the knowledge of good and evil do not eat; for on the day on which you eat of it, you shall die". At this point we must consider Adam's state before the Fall and after the Fall. Adam was originally created with free will so that he might hold to God and his commandments or not, as he willed. [3] You see this by the fact that he made death the penalty for the transgression of the law. Thus life also depended on him just as death did. We have a reference to his free will in the second chapter of Gen. 2:19, "When God brought all kinds of animals before Adam, he gave him the choice to name them as he pleased".

Clearer still is Ecclesiasticus 15:14-17, "God created humankind from the beginning with the free power of decision; he added his commandments and ordained that you might keep them if you wanted to do so, and a faith which is pleasing to God. He has given you fire and water; now you can stretch out your hand to whomsoever you wish. Before humankind is life and death and whatever he desires shall be given him". These words indicate clearly [34] what was the original state of humankind whose nature at that time was still uncorrupted. Now, however, life is no longer in our hands whereas then it was in Adam's hand, as shall be made clear shortly. God says, "At the very hour in which you shall eat of that tree you shall die". It must follow from this that if Adam had not eaten of the tree--i.e. of the fruit of the tree of good and evil--he and his descendants would have remained alive. He would not have had to keep any other commandment, for God would not have given him any other. Rather, had he kept to the will of God and obeyed him, God would have become his guide, reason, spirit and soul. Since, however, he himself wanted to know something--elevating himself with his knowledge-- for that, I think, is the meaning of eating of the tree of the knowledge of good and evil--he and all his descendants in him were condemned to a sure irrevocable [z'steinhertem] death, for the word of God is strong, sure and unchangeable. Now God said, "You shall die if you eat that". He ate and surely died and all his descendants, as indicated in 1 Cor. 15:21 and Rom. 5:12-14. I explain this as follows: He has cast the serpent to the ground; and to this day it creeps along the ground like that. He punished the woman by inflicting on her painful birth; and women to this day bring forth children in severe labor pains. He has forced man to seek his food by the sweat of his brow; to this day he has to conquer the earth through daily toil, etc. He spoke thus, "On the day (or, at the time) you eat of the tree, you will die". They ate; hence they also died. Now if Adam and his descendants are dead, who is to call them back to life? None of them; for they are all on the side of death. And no one who is dead can bring himself back to life. And if everyone is dead in Adam, they are all incapable of bringing themselves back to life. They remain dead until the grace of God's Spirit makes them alive again, as at the first time. For everything which is created has life in him, i.e. in the Son of God and nowhere else, Jn. 1:4. We have now found the defenseless, dead and impotent Adam by which is meant broken, human nature, which, if it had not transgressed the one commandment, would have been led by the Spirit of God at all times, without sorrow, anguish and distress in all honor and joy. [35] This is further shown by his nakedness which before the fall did not concern him at all, but which caused him to blush immediately after the fall--a sign of the fact that as often as a person eats of the tree of knowledge, i.e. whenever he is guided by his own counsel, mind and reason and leaves God, he is brought to nought. And since he transgressed what God prohibited, he turned away from the spirit and grace of God, put himself under the law of God and made himself subject to law and death. Therefore he was forced to live under the law wherein he could not on his own strength come alive; for he was dead. In this we note two marked flaws [prästen]. Firstly, that the person who confidently trusts himself, falls under the law. The other, that keeping the law does not make alive, Rom. 3:19. For such is the property of the Spirit of God alone who is the life of all things.

Now you might say in passing that Christ says, "Whoever does the will of my Father who is in heaven, shall also enter the kingdom of heaven" [Mt. 7:21]. Had Adam done the will of God right after the fall would he not have come to life? The answer is "yes". For the word of Christ, as just stated, does not lie. But there are two problems [prästen]. One, that Adam and his offspring are dead and, as I have now often stated, incapable of bringing anything to life. They were all subject to death and therefore incapable of fulfilling the will of God; they were all under the law, by which sin creeps into us secretly, and in sin. But how can one who is on the side of sin do anything that is pleasing to God? But death proves that all persons are sinners, for death has come to humankind through sin, Rom. 5:5; and where death is there sin is also. And again: Where there is sin, there death is also (let not the simple-minded be confused with regard to Christ. This understanding does not refer to him, since the death which he suffered on our behalf was accepted willingly, etc. More of this later). Thus your objection on the basis of the word of Christ in Mt. 7:21 is well made. Yet Adam and his family were not able to do the will of God. The other problem is, that not [36] only Adam but every creature, however righteous such a one might be, is incapable of its own accord to fulfill the will of God. Perceive this matter as follows: The will of God is an eternal, unerring guideline for everything that is right, true and good. No creature is capable of following this line. For Christ says in Jn. 6:38, "I have come down from heaven, not to do my will, but the will of the Father". And again in Jn. 5:30, "I do not seek my will but the will of my Father". It is readily apparent that these words of Christ were not spoken in his divine person but rather in the person of his human weakness; for as soon as he is true God he has no other will but the will of his Father. But in his human weakness he feared death and desired not to die; nonetheless, he subjected his will, i.e., his human will, to the divine; thus God's will was done. This was not to the detriment of Jesus Christ, but for the better understanding of the holy, immutable, divine will, that we may see how Christ has taken upon himself all our weaknesses in order to heal them. The sum of this is that in the end the will of humankind had to submit in Jesus Christ to the will of God so that whatever is true, right and good may happen. If this is so, how much more impossible will it then be for any creature to fulfill the will of God unless, of course, it can say, "your will be done". If then his will is to be done, our will is nothing, therefore Job says [Job 15:15], "Behold, among his (i.e., God's) righteous ones no one is steadfast, and the heavens are not pure in his sight".

Let me illustrate the will of God through an example: God wants us to love him with our whole heart, mind, strength and soul. The commandment frightens me, for I know that I cannot fulfill it; nonetheless, I have to remain under the law. Place alongside this the guilt and fall of Adam. Since we have become transgressors in him, we are bound to be under the law, yet cannot fulfill it. For when Adam sinned, he withdrew himself from the Spirit of God. Yet where the Spirit of God is not, there you find nothing but death and inability to do good. Yet another example: Not only should I not kill, but I should not even get angry. This, as the former, is impossible for me to observe; yet the law lies heavily upon me. Yet another: Not [37] only am I not to commit adultery, but I should not even desire another's partner. This pinches me, as before. Another: Not only ought I not be stingy, but I should know what I have is not really mine. I am to distribute it, since I am only a steward of it. It pinches me, as before. You will find many such examples if you read scripture diligently. Everyone then, born of human will or of the will of the flesh, is pressed by the law. They can neither put it aside nor fulfill it, nor does God, in keeping with his righteousness, expect such guiltlessness of us. Consider now, if the mercy of God extended its grace to us in such anguish and calamity so that the law did not oppress us but rather delighted us and that whatever we were unable to fulfill would be corrected and recompensed by another, would not that be the best proclamation of which we have ever been made aware? Would not that be the most certain assurance of salvation which has been wrought by God? Look around you at this point and lift up your head and note where the holy gospel shines forth. It takes away all oppression and is, for that very reason, 'euangelion' which means a good, beneficial and sure proclamation.

Now, according to Paul in Rom. 1:16, the gospel is none other than the power of God for the salvation of every believer. Note therefore, "You have heard that no one comes to God unless he does the will of the heavenly Father". To this is added the fact that we cannot fulfill it, partly because we are forever sinners and dead, partly because God's will is so pure, good and just that the fullness of his measure cannot be filled by any creature. Now then, if first of all death, i.e. the veiling of the presence of God which is true death, and the cause of death which is sin, are taken from us, this would have to come solely through the power of life. Thus we find that God's mercy has wrought such strength in that he has made us alive in his Son, though we were once dead; for he is life. Here we have the first part of what the gospel is: the power of God unto salvation. Now to the other: Every believer, in whom the other defect is corrected, which is that the will of God demands so much which is truly good and right that no creature can fulfill the demand. The one Christ alone who is without sin and is equal to God the heavenly Father in goodness, beauty and purity, is [38] able to do his will. And if we are believers, i.e. if we believe the Lord Jesus Christ to be our reconciler etc., we also accept him to be our perfection before God, our salvation, our recompense and propitiation. Now we have actually recognized, I hope, what the gospel is, namely this: Since Adam had turned away from the light and the guidance of God's Spirit and turned to himself, building upon his own counsel to become great and like God he thus brought us and himself under the dominion or enslavement of the law of sin and of inevitable death. From this we could no longer escape because we were carnal, sinners and dead, whatever we undertook to do. No one but God alone was able to overcome the flaw. Hence God in his mercy took pity on us in our misery and plight. He sought to redeem us, not only by a word of his command but by his own natural Son, to reconcile us miserable persons to him. Through him every weakness shall be well and properly healed because, "God is righteous and merciful".

Who is capable of enduring the righteousness of God if he were to judge strictly by it? Or which created being is capable of taking the place of others and do satisfaction for them if in his eyes no one is righteous (as shown earlier)? Yet his righteousness must be satisfied, for it is not lighthearted slovenliness but an eternally lasting uncorrupted sure judgment. Since therefore no created thing was capable of satisfying this divine righteousness, he ordained his own Son to take upon himself our impotence (which in this case, however, did not originate with sin, as it did in our case), and not only did he have him suffer ordinary death, but he made him, who was innocent, suffer the most degrading death on our behalf so that he might redeem us from the cause of death which is sin, thus satisfying the righteousness of God through him, that we might not stand condemned for ever. Rather, since the guiltless Christ was born of the pure virgin Mary without any sin and, in addition, is true God and true Man and an everlasting surety, his unmerited suffering, too, is eternally valid and a ransom for our sin. For if he who suffered on our behalf is very God, as he undoubtedly is, his suffering, too, has to be eternally valid and fruitful, satisfying the righteousness of God in all eternity on behalf of the sin of all persons [39] who trust in it with all sure confidence. Thus God intended to purchase and kindle us in his love by such immeasurable grace, shown to us so that, should his awesome majesty cause us not to love him but rather frighten us, nonetheless, the great lovingkindness of his Son and his good deed would force us to love him and turn to him for all that is good, lest we be considered utter rogues. For what is there that God might refuse to give us if he has given his Son for us? Or who is there whose sins could not be forgiven, if Christ has made payment before God, if we believe this and trust him in full confidence? Lo, this is the sum of the gospel which I have set forth without any testimony of scripture since every believer knows this well and the heretics and half believers even know scripture on the matter, though they might deny it. Nonetheless, I will verify this later in Articles 18, 19 and 60.

> O, gracious, righteous and comforting God. How graciously you have dealt with us thieves and rogues who sought to advance behind your back and break into your kingdom. To what sure hope you elevated us. What great honor you bestowed on us in your Son. Yet we perceive it not. We are ungrateful. We do not believe you.

Further, we note now how God has spoken so clearly to the shepherds through the angel, saying, "Behold, I bring you good tidings of great joy which shall be to all people. To you is born this day a redeemer, a healer, a physician, a restorer of all your weaknesses". Never has the world received more joyous news nor shall it ever receive any news more joyful; for through it all things shall be easy and light for us and that which at one time may have badly frightened and condemned us, is now wholesome. When I spoke earlier about the weight of the law and how we shall never be able to fulfill it, I withheld until now a word about redemption for its full meaning becomes most clear, as follows: When I firmly believe, indeed, know such great salvation to be reserved for me in Christ Jesus, the first commandment no longer burdens me when it says, "you shall love God with all your heart, soul and mind", since I already know [40] I cannot fulfill this; for Christ takes upon himself all my weaknesses. Rather, the commandment leads me to holy awe of the divine grace and assures me inwardly; behold, so high, valid and good is the highest good God that all our desires should be for him alone, to our own greatest advantage. Besides this I am comforted by the good news, "See, whatever you are unable to do, Christ alone will do; he is all in all; he is the beginning and end. Similarly we might speak of other laws such as pertain to anger, adultery, disregard for oneself, self denial and such like, which some people say are more difficult to observe than they were in the Old Testament. But all these laws no longer burden me. Rather, I learn through them firstly, how pure and spotless a treasure God is, when I see him demanding not only that evil deeds be shunned but also that hearts and desires be turned from within to that which is highest and truest, about which he spoke the word, "Blessed are the pure in heart, for they shall see God" [Mt. 5:8]. No one is able to dwell with him except the one who in keeping with his will is free from carnal temptations and desires the pure. And if I were to measure my impotence and find myself incapable of being like that and that no one else, on his own, can be like it either, I also find amidst this anxiety the good news running alongside, "Christ is your salvation; you are nothing and are not capable of anything; Christ is the beginning and end; he is all and able to do all; trust him in your salvation, for everything else will deceive you; for these things cannot be regarded as pure in God's sight and shall not be able to make recompense on your behalf. But Christ the righteous and blameless one, purifies you; he is the righteousness of us all and of all those who have ever been found righteous before God".

Now some meddlesome people of our day might object here that this makes for careless people; for if one relies on Christ for the payment of everything, one will live merrily and sin unchecked, since Christ is to pay for everything. Furthermore, a great many good deeds will remain undone, by which people are accustomed to cancel their sins; and this would be harmful and of disadvantage to the neighbor; for a great deal of almsgiving and many other aids of one's neighbor [41] would cease if everyone were to trust solely in Christ. Answer: Raise what objection you will from your own understanding, it matters little, for this is the sum of the gospel. Whoever abides by it, cares little about what people fear may happen as a result; such a one knows well that everything which is of God must be good and yield good results among people. Who are you to quarrel or dispute with God or to know the reason for his counsel and deeds or to teach him a better way? He wills it to be thus and so. And let every single-minded true believer abide by this answer if he desires to follow strictly the word of God. Let him respond to the crafty, "God says this; I do not care for your objections or your subtleties".

Paul clarifies the matter still further in Rom. 3:3-8 and 6:1-4. I shall quote him here as my second answer. He shows in Romans 3 that although some of the children of Israel might remain in their hardened unbelief, this fact would not harm the believers--for God is truthful. Though one may judge him and demand to know why he forgives so readily or often or so certainly, he would, nonetheless, remain just. In other words, as he promised salvation to all believers, free and without charge, he would always be found true in forgiving those who believe, be they Jews or gentiles. Thereupon some charged Paul with heresy, for it would follow from his teaching that one might say (actually Paul said it), "Well then, let us do evil so that some good may result therefrom". In other words, let us sin and believe in Christ our salvation, so that God, however one may judge him, might nonetheless be found to be true. These Paul rejects rather curtly by saying that such blasphemers deserve condemnation, i.e. those who speak in this manner are children of damnation; they deserve what they get, in part, undoubtedly because they dare to bark their own opinion against God. Secondly, because their objection is not made because they are anxious to promote sinless [42] living but rather so that they might slander the gospel with their ill-intentioned objections as if one could become more evil through it [the gospel].

He deals with this in like manner in Rom. 6. Having clearly stated in chapter 5 that as by one man, Adam, death, sin and condemnation flowed forth to all persons, so by the one Lord Jesus Christ life, grace and righteousness were restored, he now challenges above-named slanderers by stating, "What then shall we say? Shall we remain in sin so that grace may abound? Far be it. For how can we remain in a sinful life if we have died to it? Do you not know, dear brother, that all of us who have been baptized and washed in Christ Jesus have been washed in his death? Then we are buried with him in baptism, so that, just as Christ rose from the dead by the honor of the Father (i.e. the Father revealed his power and honor by raising Christ from death), we too may walk in newness of life, etc." Read the entire chapter and you will soon find [Rom. 6:15-18] the third objection regarding law and grace when he said, "What? Shall we go on sinning, since we are now no longer under the law but under grace?" Answer: Far be it. Do you not know that if you yield yourselves to anyone as obedient slaves, you are slaves of the one whom you obey? If you have become slaves of sin, it will lead to death; if you are obedient to God, it will lead to righteousness. But I give thanks to God, for you were slaves of sin but have become obedient with all your heart in tune with the teaching to which you have been introduced and committed. Now if you have been freed from sin, you have become slaves of righteousness. From these words of Paul we should learn that we need not worry about anyone becoming worse because of the grace of God whose author and originator Christ is, Jn. 1:17, "Grace and truth have been brought by or accomplished through Jesus Christ; especially for those who are drawn by the heavenly Father that they might depend on the salvation and grace of his Son; these fight against sin, since they know full well that they can no longer live in that in which at one time they lay dead for so long. Therefore only those people will make this objection who are still under the law and who have neither tried nor felt the Spirit of God. [43] For where he is, there is no doubt at all about the possibility of evil arising when one depends on the word of God. Christ himself has taught this in Jn. 6:57, "As my living Father sent me, so I live through the Father"(i.e. I live in the Father and for his sake, as he wills). And similarly, immediately following Jn. 6:58, "Whoever eats me, shall live on my account." Christ uses "to eat him" for "to believe in and depend on his word", showing that just as the heavenly Father who is the fountain of life sent him, so he lives through him and in him in such a way that he is doing God's will and not his own human will. Likewise, anyone who surely trusts in his word, would also live in his will; for his word will be in people just as he is in the Father and the Father in him. A similar thing 1 Jn. 4:8 points to, "God is love; whoever remains in love remains in God and God in him." Note that wherever true faith is (a faith, not severed from love, for without a certain hope and love there is no faith), there God is. But where God is, how do I dare worry whether people can sin or become irresponsible?

Now you may say, "But I can see that everyone sins, however holy they claim to be," 1 Jn. 1:8-10. How then can I help not being anxious about sin, since sin leads to damnation? Answer: All these objections arise because you do not rightly know or believe in the gospel. Through it you would know, firstly, that the concern you have about sin is not yours at all but that of the Spirit of God; for you would know with Paul in Rom. 7:14, 18, that we are carnal, given over and sold to sin. He says, "I know that nothing good dwells in my flesh." "And what is born of the flesh," Christ says in Jn. 3:6, "is carnal." Therefore we would not have to be on guard against sin, were it not for the Spirit of God putting us on guard; for without him we can do nothing, Jn. 14:26. You say now, "Nonetheless, there is sin and the righteous people of God are not without wickedness; wherever concern and anxiety for sin may come from." Thus, there is no basis to the statement that those who trust in the word of God do not sin. Answer: Note that Christ condemns the sin of unbelief only, Jn. 16:8ff, "On account of sin [44] the Spirit of God shall punish the world, for they did not believe in me." He says also in Mt. 12:31, "Every sin and disgrace shall be forgiven a person except the sin against the Holy Spirit which is nothing other than unbelief, of which I need not say anything here for lack of space. 1 Jn. 5:16-18 also writes that there is a sin unto death (which is unbelief); for it, no one should pray; but it is also certain that everyone who is born of God does not sin, for he protects himself;

and the evil one (i.e. the devil in all his power), cannot touch him. Who it is that is born of God, he teaches at the beginning of the chapter [1 Jn. 5:1], "Everyone who believes that Jesus is the Christ, is born of God." Thus it follows, lastly, that those who have the Spirit of God in a way that assures them of their salvation in Christ, and who surely trust in his word, do not sin; for not a single sin shall be counted toward their damnation except for the sin of unbelief. However, they are then no longer of God, but have fallen away from him.

One ought to note in this context that the term 'sin' is sometimes taken to mean 'weakness' or 'fallen nature' which again and again tempts us to yield to the temptations of the flesh and is generally referred to as 'infirmity'. Just as the term 'sickness' subsumes all specific aches, diseases, fevers, boils, paralysis, apoplexy, cramps and many other pains which are just like outgrowths of sickness, so we call sin an infirmity from which other distinguishable sins grow like branches; therefore adultery, loose living, self indulgence, avarice pride, envy, jealousy, party spirit, murder are fruits and branches of the infirmity which Paul also calls the flesh in Gal. 5:10 and elsewhere; for these rivulets break out of fallen nature as from a fountain. But that sin, to repeat it again, is called 'infirmity' or 'the flesh' is indicated by Solomon in Prv. 21:4, "The light of the godless is sin"; in other words, where one is rid of and without God, the flesh [45] rules and temptation, born of infirmity, guides. Paul in Rom. 5:12, "Sin has come into the world by one person." Here 'sin' has to mean 'infirmity'. Likewise in Rom. 7:26f., "If I do what I do not want to (according to the inner being), it is not I who brings it about, but sin which dwells in me, which is the inherited infirmity coming from Adam." Everywhere in Romans he generally takes sin to mean infirmity as also in 1 Cor. 15:56 and elsewhere.

Now let us summarize the entire matter. Sin is taken to mean unbelief. Firstly, whoever is found therein, shall not be saved. Secondly, it is the infirmity and defect of fallen nature. Because of this infirmity we are incapable of doing anything of ourselves; for we are children of wrath even though we know of the one true God. However, by the free gift of God we have been redeemed from death and made alive through the Lord Jesus Christ; for he is true life. Sin has been robbed of its power and sting so that it can no longer destroy us; we have been reconciled to God and have become friends, sons and heirs of God from then on. Thus sin and infirmity have been mortified, if we firmly trust in this and believe that they have been forgiven through the Lord Jesus Christ. Thirdly, [sin is taken to mean] the works which grow out of sin like branches. The same are all removed through the Lord Jesus Christ, as it is written in 1 Jn. 2:1, "My sons these things I write to you that you do not sin (note, this says that sin is removed, not the branches). But if someone sins we have an advocate with the Father, Jesus Christ, the righteous one, he is the expiation for our sin, and not for ours only but for that of the whole world." Fourthly, sin is sometimes used to indicate the sacrifice which customarily was made for sin; of that I need not say anything here. In sum, whoever believes he is redeemed by the grace of God through Christ Jesus and is daily cleansed from all outgrowth of sin or infirmity, sins not; for he is not an unbeliever who alone is a condemned sinner.

But it is to be noted here that such believers do not become careless in the honor which they seek, as some evil people maintain, because they trust in Jesus Christ, Rom. 5:3, 5; rather, they become all the more careful and learn to know their infirmities [46] rightly which is to know themselves as dead and incapable of doing anything, except for the grace of God which can do everything. It makes us alive too if we trust in it and give it the same full confidence. And thereafter, the more a person finds himself full of infirmities, the more he is humbled and forced to turn to God, the only salvation. Example: Make a ball of wax and clay. Expose it to the sun and the wax will melt while the clay hardens. Place it in running water and the clay will be washed away while the wax hardens. Another example: Mix wine and water in equal quantities and you will taste immediately that neither of them retain their taste and strength; it remains tasteless until it has been drunk and transformed to blood through digestion. These two examples illustrate how strange human nature is. The first illustrates the combination of body and soul; the second, their respective nature, power and effect. Likewise we note that as long as a person lives, the two are at war with one another; for spirit rebels against flesh and flesh against spirit, so that we are never able to do what we desire, Gal. 5:17. Thus it has to be that all who dwell in the body and who have been conceived in sin must accept throughout life, that their bodies retain their nature just as the water when mingled with wine, struggles to retain its nature. But if, as we indicated above, they recognize their infirmity and do not find comfort and salvation in themselves, that fierce warfare is generated for them which Paul confesses to be present in himself, Rom. 7, when he desires to live in his inner being according to the will of God (i.e. after he who believed in God, was assured of the Spirit and grace of God); for as soon as he began to live thus he sensed another law written in his members; this warred against the law of the Spirit and made him a prisoner under the law of sin even though in his heart, which had been taught and illumined by God, he desired another. This anguish pressed upon him strong enough to make him cry out [Rom. 7:24], "O miserable being that I am. Who is to save me from the body of death?" By "living in the body", which does not end he meant nothing other than a daily dying. But he is soon comforted. He says [Rom. 7:25], "It is the grace of God in Jesus Christ [47] our Lord." Now all true believers experience this warfare. But if they always turn to God through Christ Jesus, they are redeemed by God through Christ so that sin cannot harm them; for at the very moment they turn to God, he has already drawn and moved them. Although he [the believer] knows that we are not without the traces of sin, faith nonetheless brings about that we live in him; thus even our daily sinning works toward the good so that we discover in the process how utterly nothing we are. The more this happens, the more God's Spirit and grace do elevate and protect us from sinning. The more trust in ourselves diminishes, the more trust in God grows; and the more trust in God is in us, the more also the Spirit of God; the more grace, the less sin. Why God has willed us to have such warfare within us is evident in that thereby we are forced by necessity to flee our infirmities and turn to him, Prv. 3:11; Heb. 12:5-11.

Now the fact that more rather than less good is done because of right faith in the gospel, I substantiate, above all, with the help of Scripture whose testimony is sure. And though good Christians may do their good works in such secrecy that no one can see them, the word of God, nonetheless, does not lie. But I shall afterwards indicate also the improvement which is experienced daily. Christ says in Jn. 15:1-5, "I am the vine and you are the branches or shoots. In one who remains in me, I too will remain; he will bear much fruit; for without me you are unable to do anything." Note, firstly what sort of a vine it is from which the shoots must draw their strength: from Christ. Secondly, that Christ works through those in whom he dwells. Look to it that you are in Christ and be bent on that which God works through you. Thirdly, that the works which are not of Christ are of no value at all; for without him we are unable to do anything. Now if everything has to be through him alone, why then do we ascribe anything to ourselves? Where the Spirit of God is, there good works are not neglected; for as he is an everlasting good and the cause and initiator of every good thing, so also where he is, all things are built up and brought about to good effect. Now the objection is wrong which says: "But then no one will do anything good, but will refrain from doing essential daily work even." For where the Spirit of God is, there one knows well that one has to earn one's daily bread in the sweat of one's brow. One also knows [48] that to do good to one's neighbor is the highest possible worship in [the life of] faith. In short, whenever one trusts in God, there God is. And where God is, there one is anxiously set on doing whatever is good.

Jn. 14:15, "If you love me, you keep my commandments." Where God's love is, (which is nothing other than faith, as we said above), there one is intent on doing his will. Where God's love is, there the Spirit of God is also. Where the Spirit of God is, there these virtues emerge which Paul enumerates in Gal. 5:22, "The fruit of the Spirit is love, joy, peace, compliance or patience, gentleness or kindness, goodness, faithfulness or faith, meekness, moderation; these are the genuine Christian virtues." But to run up and down streets to shrines [lit. to the saints], to purchase indulgences, to pray for pay, chant, walk in processions, decorate temple walls and such like innumerable goldmines, invented by humans, is not of God and therefore utter hypocrisy. It is not surprising that these things are less common now; for where the light shines, the darkness vanishes; where the Spirit of God blows, there he clears away all stubble and chaff of hypocrisy and brings forth new bloom. In this I can truly say, whose names I'd rather not mention, what Paul said of the Corinthians [1 Cor. 1:5], the Ephesians [Eph. 1:15], the Colossians [Col. 1:4] and the Thessalonians [1 Thes. 1:3], namely that they increase splendidly (God be eternally praised and thanked), in love of God, peace with the neighbor, the knowledge of the gospel, in humble conduct, divine wisdom, in aid and support of the poor, in moderation of their pride, forgiveness of their enemies and diligence in the teaching of Christ, care for the prisoners of Christ and for the entire Christian community [mengi]. And though they are not pleased by the burning of candles and incense, sacrificing (to the rich priests, I say), endless prayers, vigils, noisome prayers, [huelen], the clanging of the mass, ornate temples, the cowls [49] of theologians, gowns and colors of monks and the well-tailored cassocks of priests, harlotry and drunkenness, games of chance and snobbery [junckherrschafft], they are, however, pleased by everything which is pleasing to God. They reduce the interest rate of their debtors, reward the laborer more richly than he is entitled to claim, welcome to their homes the poor and miserable, practice moderation in games, swearing, buffoonery and generally in all vanity of the times and are intent on preparing themselves for eternal life. Yet, the common vicissitudes of their infirm nature are nonetheless their lot, so that, during this life, they are not without sin. But if they know the same to be forgiven them because of their faith and unwearying trust in Christ Jesus, they become less and less in themselves each day, while God becomes all the greater in them. Where God dwells, nothing evil breaks forth. For example: God led the children of Israel out of Egypt with such providential care that he not only protected them from their enemies but bid them go on when he willed; yet when he bid them stay in one place, they did; and he fed them and gave them water to drink and saw to it that their clothes did not become tattered. Yet they transgressed his commandments by not only yielding to the temptations of the flesh, but by also falling from him through idolatry. Nonetheless, he did not leave them, but again and again granted them his grace. And because of the grace of God, the people of Israel always improved so that when they trusted only in God they were best off. But as soon as they themselves sought to be or know anything they turned away from God, fell into great and fearful vices and became the worse for it; this is attested to in many testimonies. Read the stories of the Old Testament and you will see it to be thus. Read the Prophets and their gravest lament is always that they [the people] turned away from God and left him. All their effort is directed to making people cling to God as to a father.

This is still true to this day. Whoever clings to God with a true heart, though sins (without which no one can be), may afflict him, will have the same corrected by Christ, provided we believe firmly that he is the right medicine. He says so himself in Jn. 11:25f, "I am the resurrection and the life. Whoever believes in me, shall live [50], though he may die. And everyone who lives and firmly believes in me, shall never die."

Now, I believe, everyone understands what the gospel is; he may also have learned whether he has preached the gospel or not. For if he spoke the wholesome words to the people, as drawn from Jn. 11:25f, without clear understanding and an ardent devotion, and admonished them to keep these words and trust in them with all their hearts, he preached the gospel like Caiaphas, who also spoke the truth [Jn. 11:50], "It is good for one person to die on behalf of the people rather than having the entire generation perish," yet did not at all understand the true salvation which he spoke. I will say nothing here of the unlearned scholars who now dare to boast of having always preached the gospel. And if you go about looking up their sleeves for a chapter from Holy Scripture they retort that they do not understand it in the way you do at all. [4] And when you demand their understanding of the same, they turn a wicker basket [5] into a windlass and a pig into a crab, just like the wolf. [6] And when on the basis of scripture you show the correct and natural meaning, they will reply (even though they may know it to be the right and natural meaning), that they will not accept any other meaning than that which the pope and the Fathers have bid them accept. And if you ask them for the meaning of "Christus est caput ecclesie" as recorded in Eph. 1:22 and 5:23, they will reply that Christ is the head of the Church. You then say, "You answered correctly. Why then do you ascribe such to another and make the pope head when it is Christ?" And they will reply, "We are to understand it in the way the pope does." "Then say on, what does 'Christus' mean?" And they will reply, "It means Christ;" for they do not understand enough Greek to know what this fragrant name means. You say, "How can the name Christ be the pope's?" They reply, "The pope wills it thus." And you say again, "If the pope wills it thus, he is the Antichrist, for everyone who calls himself a Christ, is an Antichrist," Mt. 24:5. Now they shout, "Heretic, heretic, out with you, etc." And again you say, [51], "My friend, why have you been taught Latin?" Answer, "That I may understand scripture." You say, "No. You have, as your own words demonstrate, learned so that you may not understand scripture; for whenever I follow the understanding which you confess, you say, "The words need not mean what they say."

Good Christians, forgive me for detaining you for so long with such trifles. I do it that you may not buy a cat in a bag. [7] They got themselves to the point where they are forced to admit that they do not know the meaning of "caput" unless the pope says that it means "head" but they boast to have preached the gospel. I just wonder how they would have understood it had they never seen either pope or councils; and what they know of the two has to be done through scripture. How dare they now know that scripture speaks of the pope without having a report from the pope when they dare not understand the word of God without pope or councils? And those Fathers whom they quote are ambiguous in their meaning. This is where one ends when one does not allow the Spirit of God to be a master and interpreter of his word and when one does not seek understanding with him but rather with humans who are full of lies. I also hope that everyone understood that the gospel comes not from humans, but from the true God and that it cannot be gauged by their own understanding; further, that it is a perfect and flawless teaching unto salvation. From this derive disparaging words such as these: first, that even though there is no gospel at all, one might nonetheless set up the law by which one can be saved; secondly, that one can state it according to the pope's understanding only; thirdly, that it has been improved through the Fathers and that it was in need of such improvement. All these disparagements they will have to drop. They will have to admit that they do not know what gospel is as long as they claim [52] that other teachings are as good as the gospel. [8]

NOTES

1. A detailed discussion of the term "gospel" is given in Article 16 below.

2. Literally: "Rappen lassen sich nicht weiss machen". Leo Jud translates, laterem lavero. Cf. Wander III.1463 No. 7.

3. Earlier than Luther, Zwingli takes exception to the Erasmian understanding of free will. According to some of his interpreters, one may place his "gradual estrangement" from his erstwhile teacher in Zwingli's reformatory phase. Cf. A. Rich, **Anfänge**, 67-70 and elsewhere.

4. The German proverb "Er hat es hinter dem Ärmel" suggests a sly or cunning effort to withhold something. Cf. Wander, I.138, No. 71.

5. The wicker basket was used in kitchens for keeping bowls.

6. The proverb "Er macht aus eme Schüsselkorb en haspel und us ere sou en Chraebs, wie der Wolff" is generally used with reference to an opinionated person. Cf. Wander, IV.252.

7. Literally: "denen waelschen hassen die oren recht besehen moegist". The proverb hints at the tension between French and German Swiss. Whether Zwingli shared such animosity or prejudice is not clear; he uses the proverb effectively, nonetheless.

8. Undoubtedly John Faber is addressed here who expressed such views during the First Zurich Disputation. For a record of proceedings cf. Z.I.479ff; note especially 548-563 for an exchange between Zwingli and Faber.

THE SIXTH ARTICLE

For Christ Jesus is the guide and captain, [1] promised by God and given to the entire human race.

This Article is a support upon which the previous one is firmly built. For if Christ Jesus is promised the human race by God to be a guide and captain, his deeds, teaching and life must, as a result, be above any human counsel so that his name (i.e. his power, honor and strength), as Paul says in Phil. 2:9, is above every other name.

Guide and captain

Is. 55:4, "Take heed, I have given him to the nations as a witness, a leader or captain and a ruler over the heathen." Ez. 37:23-25, in so many other words, "They shall be my people and I shall be their God and my servant David shall be their king and there shall be a shepherd over them all." And shortly thereafter, "And my servant David shall be their sovereign in all eternity." This king, governor and ruler is not David, the father of Solomon and Nathan, for the very same died many years ago, as Peter says in Acts 2:24, but Christ, who alone is eternal king and immortal by his very nature.

Promised by God to the entire human race

God spoke to the serpent which tempted Eve, Gen. 3:15, "I will cause enmity between you and the woman, between your seed and her seed. And her seed shall crush your head." This points to Christ who in his human nature has shown that he shall trample under foot the head of the worm. This is actually shown by the two Hebrew terms 'hu jeschuphcha', "who shall trample under foot" which cannot refer to the woman. And again God promised Abraham from the same seed, Gen. 22:18, "And in your seed shall be saved or blessed [53] all races or nations of the earth." This seed is Christ, Gal. 3:16. And again, Israel spoke not alone of him who was to come in the blessing or promise of Judah, but he also added a sign, Gen. 49:10. Neither the mace (i.e. the king-

37

dom) nor the governor or captain who shall come from Judah's loins shall be taken away from Judah until the one shall come who is to be sent and who shall be the uplifting or consolation of the gentiles or nations. The sign has actually been revealed; for when Christ came into the world, Israel no longer had a prince who ruled in the power of the Jewish kingdom. Moses, too, points to the one who had been promised them; for this reason he cried to God when he was sent to deal with Pharaoh, "Lord, I pray you send the one whom you will," Ex. 4:13. More of this in Deut. 18:15, 18 and Acts 7:37. Isaiah among the other prophets after David points most clearly to Christ. David shows up clearly [2] the most intimate aspects of his life, incarnation, death and resurrection, whose enumeration would take too long at this point.

And given to them.

This the angels made known in the fields of Bethlehem, as did the wise men, Simeon and Hannah, the miracles of Christ, the devils who call him 'son of God' from within the man, the teaching, Nicodemus, the sun, the curtain in the temple, the rocks, the resurrection, ascension, the avenging which swept Jerusalem and destroyed it and many more countless signs. However we shall try, whenever possible, to be brief.

NOTES

1. The term "houptman" is sometimes translated "general".

2. "Vast" means firmly, securely, clearly; in modern German usage its meaning is "almost".

THE SEVENTH ARTICLE

That he is an everlasting salvation and head of all believers who are his body, which is dead and incapable of doing anything; apart from him.

The first part of this Article is the gospel on whose behalf the Son of God has been sent from heaven to be an everlasting salvation and head of all believers. [54]

Salvation

Is. 49:6, "I have set you to be a light unto the gentiles or nations that you might be my salvation (namely, which I shall send to humankind) unto the end of the earth." Christ himself says in Jn. 6:32ff, "This is the true bread of life which has come down from heaven and is to give life to the world." He is the bread, for he is the word and food of the soul of which he speaks throughout the entire chapter. Paul states in Heb. 7:25, "Therefore he is able to make whole unto all eternity; for he himself has gone to God, being alive, that he may speak on its behalf. In the last chapter of Matthew [28:20], "And lo, I am with you to the end of the world."

Head

Paul in Eph. 1:22, "He has subjected all things under his feet and has made him the head of the Church which is his body, etc." And before these words, as we have shown in Article 5, he states that God has willed all things, i.e. all persons, to be brought together in Christ as in one head. Eph. 4:15, "Let us grow in him, acting in true love, to the best of our ability. For he is the head which is Christ, etc." Eph. 5:23, "The man is head of the wife in the same manner in which Christ is head of the Church." Col. 1:18, "He is the head of the body which is the Church." This means that the body of Christ is the Church whose head he is. Woe to those who say they are the head of the Church.

Of all believers who are his body

This has been clearly and strongly proved in earlier expositions. It is Paul who says in 1 Cor. 12:12 in explicit terms, "As
the body is one, yet has many members and since they are all
members, though there are many, likewise it is one body in Christ.
For all of us have been baptized together in one spirit into one
body."

Which, however. is dead and incapable of doing anything apart from him.

In Adam we have all died a definite death, as has been
shown in Article 5. Therefore to this day we are all dead in Adam
and alive only in Christ. 1 Cor. 15:22, "As in Adam all have died,
even so in Christ they shall all be made alive." Rom. 8:10, "But
[55] if Christ is in you, then the body is dead on account of sin
but the spirit lives, on account of justification [rechtwerdens].
Here sin means the weakness out of which the branches grow,
for as long as we live in this world, we are not without weakness;
therefore we are altogether dead. But if we have Christ in us
in a right and believing heart and believe in him, our spirit, which
otherwise is dead, lives in Christ. Without Christ we are incapable
of doing anything, Jn. 15:5, "Without me you are not able to do
anything." He is life. The one who does not have life, is dead.
Consider what an impotent dead body is capable of.

THE EIGHTH ARTICLE

From this follows, first of all, that all who live in the head are members and children of God. And this is the church or communion of saints, a bride of Christ, ecclesia catholica.

Members

How we are members, Paul indicates in Rom. 12:5 and 1 Cor. 6:15, "Do you not know that your bodies are members of Christ?" And in the same epistle in chapter 12 [1 Cor. 12], "These members take their nourishment not from the stomach, as do physical members, but from the head so that all gifts, the office or ministry of the members comes from the head alone" Eph. 4; Col. 2.

Children

Jn. 1:12, "To all who received him, he gave power to become sons of God; indeed to all who believe in his name." Everyone may learn from this that it is God's intention that we be not only called "children of God" but that we rejoice in being his own true children [Gal. 3 and 4] and that we run to him for comfort and help in full confidence, as to a natural father, considering him our own and knowing ourselves to be his own, Rom. 5:2, "We boast in the hope of being sons of God."

And this is the church or communion of saints

It has been argued from of old to this day what and which one is the church. This argument, lamentably, has always come from the desire for power. For several people have [56] sought to give the appearance of being the church so that all things might be administered through them. Since I now undertake to speak of it, I know well that I have to oppose those who speak of it in terms of human prattle; but this concerns me very little indeed; for I do not intend to bring out my word but God's, not human teaching but the meaning of the Spirit of God. I find then that frequently in the Old Testament that which we call "church'

.ed "kahal" or "makhal" in Hebrew, "ecclesia" in Greek and .cio" in Latin. Now among the Germans the term "kirck" or .lch" refers only to the house in which one commonly proclaims the word of God to the gathered people, baptizes, celebrates communion, etc; but this does not fit any of the above-mentioned terms; for kahal, ecclesia, concio do not refer to a temple but only to a gathering, to a communion or community of people. For this reason scripture often uses the term "people" for the term "community." Hence "communion" or "community" is given two fairly closely related meanings in scripture.

First of all, [it refers to] the total gathering of all those who are founded and built upon the one faith in the Lord Jesus Christ. Whoever is in the church or communion cannot be con-demned, for everyone who believes in Christ, has eternal life, Jn. 6:40. Of these Christ speaks in Mt. 16:15. When Christ asked his disciples whom they considered him to be and when Peter answered on behalf of all the others, "You are Christ, the son of the living God", Christ spoke to him once again, "Blessed are you Simon, son of Jonas; for flesh and blood did not reveal this to you but my Father, who is in heaven. And I say to you, you are hard as a rock [a man of the rocks--felserman] and upon the rock (understand here, from which I have derived your name), I shall build my church (which is the communion of all chosen believers), and the gates of hell shall not prevail against it, etc."

The rock is Christ, 1 Cor. 10:4; Mt. 21:42; upon him the church, which is the communion of saints, is built. Consequently, whoever confesses, as did Peter the man of the rocks, that Christ is the Son of the living God, will be unharmed by weapons, fortifica-tions and the power [57] of the devil. This same meaning also, Paul gives to "church" in Gal. 1:13, "I persecuted the church"; this means I persecuted all believers; for Paul did not persecute any temple or a special group of people but all Christians. Likewise in Phil. 3:6. In Heb. 12:18-24, he describes the church actually with this meaning, "You have not come to such a monstrous moun-tain but you have come to Mount Zion and to the place of the living God, to the heavenly Jerusalem and to the countless host of angels and to the communion or church of the firstborn, whose names are written in the heavens and to the judge of all things, God, etc." Here one understands clearly that all the multitudes who come to God through faith, are counted among the first-born, not physically, as Esau, Reuben and Mannasseh believed themselves to be; these were rejected, however, and through them the Jewish race. Rather, all who are in the church or multitude have their names written in heaven, i.e. they are known to God who also adds them to the angelic host and writes down their names. Indeed, all of them, whoever were and shall be, he led home nicely and gracefully as a bridegroom leads home his bride. 2 Cor. 11:2, "I have betrothed you to a man in that I give you to him as a pure daughter of Christ." Likewise in Eph. 5:25-27, "Husbands, love your wives, just as Christ has loved the church or communion, giving himself for her to make her holy, and has washed her with the bath of the water in the word so that he himself may present her an honorable congregation without spot or blemish, and that she may be holy and without reproach." Here we note how greatly Christ has loved his church or communion. We also note who it is, namely those who have been washed with the word in the bath (i.e. the baptism by water). And inasmuch as it remains in Christ, it has no spots or blemishes but is holy and beyond anyone's reproach. Question: Where is the church?" Answer: It is found throughout the earth. Who is it? All believers. If it is a congregation where does it gather? Answer: Here it is gathered by the Spirit of God in hope and there it is united in the one [58] God. Who knows it? God. But are not the bishops who commonly gather at councils that same church? Answer: They are merely members of the church as any other Christians, inasmuch as they have Christ as their head. Now you may say: But they are the visibly represented church. I answer: Holy Scripture knows nothing of this. If you wish, you may draw from human prattle many other names; I am quite satisfied with Holy Scripture alone. By it I am guided. With it, you will have to leave me be and you yourself must be content with it if you are a Christian.

Secondly, the word "church" is used for the special gatherings which we call parishes or ecclesiastical communities. These are always as large a gathering or communion as may gather well and conveniently to hear the word of God together and to be taught. To this day we call them in many places "parishes" from the Greek word "parecia" (paroikia) which means a near or neighborly dwelling. In such cases a given area of some size may gather as may be found suitable. Of this communion or church, Christ speaks in Mt. 18:16, "If he will not be moved by two or three witnesses, go ahead and say it to the church, i.e. to the special community, not to the universal church. Who would want to report to the entire Christian church, united in the spirit only, a person whom one intends to ban? Paul calls ecclesiastical communities, parishes or pastorates, "ecclesias", i.e. communions [communities]; 1 Cor. 1:2, "To the communion which is in Corinth." In the same epistle, chapter 14:34, "Women ought to be silent in church (meaning, parishes or communities) etc; for it ill behooves a woman to talk in the community or parish church." Here it is quite certain that church is taken to mean parish or ecclesiastical community. For there is no other which is more fittingly called a church or general gathering except for the bride of Christ and those who are thus named are members of the general churches which all together make up one church. There are many more instances of both meanings [of the term] in the gospel. But the matter is clear and requires no further exposition. [59]

Wife of Christ, ecclesia catholica

Though I have spoken amply of the church and how it is bride of Christ, I shall quote the words of Rev. 21:2 at this point, so that they may not be overlooked, "I John, saw the new Jerusalem come down from heaven, prepared by God as a bride decked out for the bridegroom." Here John wants to show that the church of which we spoke in the first instance does not become bride of Christ on its own, but that it is called from heaven, prepared and decked out for this by God. The very same partner and bride of Christ is called "ecclesia catholica" in Greek; in German it is known as the "universal gathering" which we call by another name in the Confession of Faith, not altogether falsely but not properly either. We say, "I believe in the holy, Christian church." There the two Greek terms "ecclesia catholica" are found which should actually be translated by the term "universal gathering". Since, however, it is none other than the Church of Christ, i.e. all Christians united in one faith by the Spirit of God, the two words have been translated into the German by "holy, Christian church". Not bad, indeed, though neither the Latins nor the Greeks say it that way in their own language.

Unfortunately, those who are inclined to favor their own position as correct, have tended to use these words to consider themselves the Christian church. Based on these terms, Rome has for a long time now sought to be called the universal Christian church. Some ignorant theologians have allowed this to make such heavy inroads that they tend to answer to this day if you would ask them which is the ecclesia catholica, the Christian church in which we believe: "Ecclesia catholica" is translated "the Christian church" and that is the "Roman church." And if you ask them does "catholicon" mean "Roman" they will say "yes". But they do not really know what kind of term catholicon is, whether it is a cabbage or a stick. [1]

Therefore I shall undertake briefly to make this Article of Faith clear to everyone. The universal gathering which in the Spirit of God is gathered together in one body to be a wedded daughter and bride of Christ and he to be her husband and head, this very one is called in Greek as we noted above, [60] "ecclesia catholica". Now the Latins have taken over these two words from the Greek and use them to this day so that there is no special term for them in Latin. It must not be forgotten either that up to the time of Rufinus who lived around AD 350 these words alone were used in the Confession of Faith without the subsequent term "communion of saints." [2] Of the term "communion of saints" he makes no mention at all, though he explains the Confession step by step. It may be noted from this that the term "communion of saints" was added later and that it explains the term "the holy Christian church". Thus, whenever one says "ecclesiam catholicam" one may get involved in an argument, as has often happened, over what actually constitutes the Christian church. But in order to say it in specific terms for everyone to know what ecclesia catholica means, the term "communion of saints" was added. Now "holy" in this context means as much as "godly" [saintly] for St. Paul called the Christians in his own time "sanctos" which means "godly" or saintly, Rom. 1:7. To the saints at Rome, i.e. the "godly" Christians at Rome. Eph. 3:8, "To me, the least among the saints," i.e. "to me, the least among the 'godly' Christians"; and in many other places. Among the Latins, too, the word "sanctus" means "godly", for Juvenal writes "Egregium sanctumque virum si cerno" etc, whenever I see a noble, "godly" man, it seems as if I encounter a creature, possessed of the sexual characteristics of both man and woman. [3] Thus the "communion of saints" is nothing other than the gathering of "godly" believers or [61] Christians.

For the meaning is nothing which those people erroneously give who claim that "communion of saints" must be understood as the blessedness of those who out of this time have come to God. For soon thereafter we confess that after this life, eternal life will follow, which is known as blessedness. It is not conceivable to express one opinion by two different Articles. Thus the meaning of the Article in the Confession is as follows: I believe that the holy universal or Christian church is the one spouse of God. But this universal church is the communion of all godly, believing Christians. It follows then that the gathering of special persons or bishops--even though the just mentioned bishops may all be in one place--is not the church in which and of which we believe. For in it are all godly Christians who will essentially be gathered by God only after this age; but as long as it is here on earth, it lives in hope alone and does not ever come together visibly; however, in the light of the divine spirit and faith it is always together, even here; only, not visibly. Therefore all those who are not gathered in one pure divine faith and who are not gathered and joined together in the one head Christ, are not in the Christian church. For there is one faith only, as there is one God and one baptism, [Eph. 4:5].

Here everyone may discover for himself whether he is in the church or not. For if he has all confidence, hope and comfort in God through Jesus Christ, he is in the church, i.e. in the communion of all the saints. And if he has the one pure faith of Christ, he has the Spirit of God; for he is one and no one may have two types of faith in the one united Spirit. Therefore all true believers are in one Spirit; they must also have one faith and hope in the one good in which the Spirit instructs them. Then again all those who put their hope in creatures are not in the church or in the multitude of godly Christians; for the one thing which comes from the uniting Spirit of God and which can be understood in him alone, they do not have, which is that the one God is their confidence. Rather they rely on weak, erring and broken persons. For if you ask them whom they give greater credence or why they think they shall be saved, [62] they will say that they have greatest faith in the Fathers and that they shall be saved as long as they remain within the Holy Roman Church. That this is so, is shown by the foolish answer they give. When one says to them: "Do you not lay greater store by the word of God than by the word of the Fathers?" they will say that they are unable to follow the word of God apart from the word of the Fathers. Indeed, they do not dare understand it except through the interpretation of the Fathers; these have to confirm the word of God, as we have amply shown earlier. If now you should find a different teaching in the Fathers than that which is contained in the teaching of Christ and if you abide by that of the Fathers more, it must needs follow that you are not in the church or communion of God but in the church of the Fathers. At that point they retort, "One has to be able to become united through the common voice of the gathered Fathers." Answer: No. One has to be united through the one word of God. For if the Fathers had not been able to overcome Arius and other false teachers by clearly setting against them carefully studied scripture, all the Fathers' wrangling would have been in vain. If then all our knowledge is grounded in the word of God why then do we have to ascribe to Fathers or councils what is God's alone? But if they act or command other than is intended by the word of God, how dare they expect that people will seek their comfort with them or their fabulous stories. Are they God? They say, "no we are not God, but wherever our councils are properly called, there the Spirit of God is and we are a form of the universal church, ecclesia representativa."

To the first: Whether the Spirit of God is with you is demonstrated above all, by whether his word is your guide, and by whether you do nothing except what is clearly stated in the word of God so that scripture is your master and not you, masters of scripture. Secondly, if your judgments and decretals are designed to humble yourselves, to cause you to put away all human prattle and to get you to elevate the word and the honor of God, then one may consider that it is of God. But if you use your minds and hearts as your guideline and if you only work as long as you are not contradicted and your honor, name and title, your riches and glory are not diminished, you then have the spirit that drove the Gerasene pigs into the sea [cf. Mt. 8:32]. Concerning the other, that you are ecclesia representativa, I believe willingly. But show me where you have the name from and where you have been permitted [63] to band together and form decretals which are not in keeping with the word of God. Who has permitted you to load these upon the shoulders of people and to burden their consciences and to say that good is evil and evil is good? Or who has ordered you to count that a sin against people which

God does not count thus and which he has not forbidden? Indeed, I willingly believe that you are ecclesia representativa, i.e. the alleged and false [eingebildet] church and not the true bride and wife of Christ. At this point I have spoken only of the false, avaricious, vain and wanton prelates. Do not be upset by this, righteous man. Those who place themselves under scripture and not above it, are well off. And just so that no one thinks that I have spoken in too derogatory a fashion, you ought to read their own laws [Corpus Juris Canonici, Dist. 8 and 9]. There you will find that scripture alone is to be given total unquestioning faith, even according to their own laws, and that human teaching which they have taught out of ignorance of scripture is to be put away by those who follow and understand it [scripture] aright.

We still have the Roman church to deal with which is called by theologians and canonists alike the universal church with the bishop of Rome being considered a universal head or bishop. On this point it must be noted, as shown earlier, that Christ is the head of the church; ample evidence from Holy Scripture has been given there. But that the bishop or pope of Rome is to be universal head, of that certainly there is no scriptural evidence. Even their own statutes are against this (Corpus Juris Canonici c. 1 Dist. 99). [4] There it is written as follows: The [64] bishop or minister (the Greek term episcopus is translated overseer, guardian or pastor), who sits up front is not to be considered a prince of priests or a high priest or anything of the kind but rather the bishop of the foremost seat. But even the Roman bishop is not to be called a universal bishop. Read the two subsequent Canons [Corpus Juris Can. 2c and 3 Dist. 99]. Note well, godly Christians, how is one to show the tyrant his folly? [5] Not only do they call themselves prince or priest or high priest, but they also pretend to be king, emperor and lord over body and soul of the entire world. And that, when it is clearly stated that the Roman bishop is not to be called a universal bishop. Therefore, all who put their confidence in the Roman church are not in the communion of saints, for the latter put their trust in God alone.

This much for now on the church which, as little as it is, will likely bring a great deal of adverse criticism of this booklet. But unfortunately there is more truth to it than I am able to support by words. But if there is anyone who thinks I have shortchanged him, I will soon give him a long enough account so that the idolatry of the enemies of God will become fully apparent. [65]

NOTES

1. Schlegel or Hammer. Leo Jud translated "an herba an malleus". We use the more general term "stick".

2. Rufinus was born about AD 345 and died about AD 410. Initially he was closely associated with Jerome, but later distanced himself over the question of Origen's orthodoxy. Zwingly undoubtedly means the tract, **Expositio in symbolum apostolicum.**

3. An hermaphrodite having the characteristics of both male and female was seen to be a perfectly balanced person.

4. Corpus iur. can. Dist XCIX 1 pars and 11 pars. See also C 4 & 5 of the same Dist.

5. Cf. the proverb "Einem die Schellen anhaengen" – to make a fool of someone; Wander IV 128 No. 14. How is one to make known the folly of a tyrant?

THE NINTH ARTICLE

It follows secondly, that as the physical members are incapable of doing anything without the head managing them, so it is impossible for anyone in the body of Christ to do anything without Christ, the head.

The first part of this Conclusion is a figure of speech from which the second part follows. This is not to say that the second part gets its meaning from the example but rather that the example or figure of speech gives meaning or clarity to it to simple people. For no parable is capable of proving anything if there is no foundation in scripture, but it may, nonetheless, instruct well.

The first part of this Conclusion is clear to everyone. But the second, namely the observation that no Christian is capable of doing anything without Christ the head, is grounded in the word of Christ who says in Jn. 15:4, "As the branch cannot bring fruit by itself, unless it remain in the vine, so you too (understood is, 'shall not bring fruit'), unless you remain in me. I am the vine; you are the branches. One who remains in me, in him I shall remain also, he will yield much fruit; but without me you are able to do nothing at all."

Acts 17:28, "In him we live, in him we are moved, in him we have being." Note, one who thinks himself capable of doing or finding anything good, of setting up or founding anything which does not come from Christ, must needs find his beginning and work to be dead, without fruit, a nothing, blasphemy, selfwill, sin. "For it is God, (says Paul in Phil. 2:13), who accomplishes in you the will and the perfecting according to his good pleasure." Note the Spirit of God to be captain of our will and the perfecter of our works. Therefore Article 10 must logically follow now.

THE TENTH ARTICLE

As a person is demented when the members of his body effect something without the head, tearing, wounding and damaging themselves, so are the members of Christ demented, [66] beating and burdening themselves with unwise laws, whenever they undertake something without Christ, their head.

Everything to the very last word is self-evident here except for the last phrase, namely that those are demented who burden themselves with unwise laws. We will have to state then which are unwise laws. Unwise laws are those which arise out of a person's opinion who vaunts himself of being able to find something good within himself but who never gives attention to what God says to him. For every good has to come from God, James. 1:17 and Hos. 14:8, "His fruit (i.e. Ephraim's) has been found in me." And again, "Whatever we invent is foolish and vain," Eccl. 1 and Jer. 10. Is it not utter foolishness when Christ says, "Come unto me all you who labor and are burdened and I will give you rest," Mt. 11:28 and when we respond, "run here, drive there, buy indulgences, paint the walls (with images of saints), give to the monk, offer up to the priest, fatten the nuns, then I--one person to another--will absolve you, etc"? Examples of this sort are all too numerous.

Now, these things have been imposed upon the simple Christians while the work of God has been left undone, even though Christ has explicitly forbidden such burdens. Mt. 24:48-51, "If then the evil servant should say to himself, my master will not return soon and thereupon should start beating his fellow servant, drinking and carousing among the drunkards, and his master should return on a day and at an hour when he least expects him, he would break him in two and relegate his position to the dissemblers." What might those wanton bishops, indeed, the entire lazy horde of spirituals think, when they read this saying of Christ and recognize themselves to be a burden upon common christendom, yet continue to pursue their willful game! But hear this, God shall punish them like hypocrites and cut them to shreds as one quarters spies, because they have given a twofold meaning to the teaching of the one unified Spirit of God. It is certain, indeed, that they are godless and unbelieving if they do not repent and change instantly. For had they believed the word of God, they would have become softened and anxious to avoid heavy penalties. [67] But since they fail to do it, one would have to conclude that they are not in their right minds.

Christ also reprimanded the Jewish scribes and pharisees on account of such burdens, Mt. 23:4 and because they were placing overly heavy burdens upon people's shoulders yet did not move a single finger themselves, etc. You say, "How does what he said to the Jews affect me?" I answer: It is to be used even less in the new covenant than in the old--if there even it was objected to, though there still were numerous external works, burdens and ceremonies. For if we sin against the little flock of God in the same manner in which the Jews did, our punishment also shall be like theirs, as pointed out above. Peter also rejected such burdens, stressing that they should not be imposed on the disciples which neither we nor our fathers were able to carry?" Note, what it is to tempt God. It is nothing less than to dare place something upon the little flock of Christ according to human wisdom and to see how God accepts this and whether our deeds might please him. This is truly anti-Christian; for thus one rises against God. And when I speak here of statutes, I speak solely of those which clerics thought to be good, as if one could gain salvation thereby or suffer damnation by not honoring them as ordered, such as fasts, processions, the singing of litanies, burning of incense, sprinkling, cowls, tonsure, the wearing of Iipus, pretense of continence, simony, the buying of indulgences, the decorating and building of churches and such things; some of these are very much against God while others might be tolerated, as long as they are used sparingly.

In sum: When will you recognize the utter folly of imposing upon Christian people such statutes in which God has no pleasure and which contribute nothing at all to salvation, but rather detract from it? For a simple person leans on these and then departs from the will of the word of God. [68]

THE ELEVENTH ARTICLE

From this we see the statutes of the so-called clerics with all their pomp, riches, status, titles and laws to be the cause of every folly; for they do not in any way correspond to the head.

That the statutes of the clerics are a cause of dissension, everyone, I trust, who has eyes, may clearly see; for they shout nothing other than Fathers, statutes, and not to consider the Fathers fools. These they protect, regardless of how Christ fares in the process. For this reason I have written the part of this Article which immediately follows, namely that their statutes do not correspond to Christ, their head. At this point they clamor, "Show us how the statutes of the Fathers or of the church are against Christ? If they were contrary to him, we would not follow them." Yet, when one points these out, they minimize everything which contains the word of God and explain their teaching so clearly that they almost convince the world that their own devices are better than what the word of God demands. But in order that everyone may determine by himself how human statutes are at odds with the word of God, give heed briefly to several examples.

1. Christ is the one, eternal head of the church. Now one might say, "The pope is the head of the church. Comment: Indeed, we know well that he is merely a deputy of Christ." I object: Where is the deputy instituted? Or why should one be in need of him, if Christ is to be with us to the end of the world? Christ is God. He illumines everyone who enters this world. Whom does the pope illumine? Or has the hand of Christ become too short so that it can no longer reach every place unless a sinful person be administrator in his place?"

2. Christ admonishes his disciples not to rule like the princes of earthly kingdoms. Human teaching says, "The pope is a sure lord over kings, princes and lords. Bishops are princes and everything ought to be in their hands. [69]

52

3. Christ says that all who believe, shall be taught by God. Human teaching says: The teaching of God must first of all be approved by the gathered bishops.

4. Christ says, [Jn. 6:47], that he who believes in him shall have eternal life. Human wisdom does not allow for this and speaks as follows: "Thus all good works would be left undone." It wants to be wiser than God as if God had been somewhat too hasty in showing such grace.

5. Christ says: If one honors God with human teachings and statutes, it is for nothing. Human wisdom [on the other hand], trusts in nothing but cowls, clamor, [1] signs and foolishness, invented by humans.

6. Christ bids his disciples go about without bags and purse to preach the gospel [Mt. 10:9]. People do not allow it to be preached unless it has first been purchased; and nothing is given free of charge--not even that which God alone can give. There has been no religion or order which has gathered up so many riches and has kept them more shamefully than said clerics have.

7. Christ says: You should not set up for yourself a father upon earth. Humans have set up for themselves countless sects, corporations and Fathers, applying greater diligence to their protection than is used to safeguard the honor and name of God. Indeed, the name of God is often neglected and disregarded.

I have selected these seven testimonies from the many so that they may not forever claim before simple folk that their own teaching and statutes are in keeping with the gospel. One has to have seven witnesses to convince a priest of a lie (as their law suggests); for this reason I could not muster fewer [witnesses] here. [2] Thus, I trust, [70] it to be quite clear that the cause of current dissentions are those nonsensical human statutes. They cannot tolerate giving them up, therefore they rebel, as is actually shown in Is. 9:5, "No great robbery is without violence." The hypocrites have robbed christendom. But where Christ is preached the hope of the hypocrites vanishes as Job says [8:13]; then loud lamenting starts, for Christ cannot deny his nature. And though he is born small and impoverished for us, he is, nonetheless, Son of God and a wonderful counsellor, a strong God, and in these last times, a Father, a prince of peace whose kingdom shall grow and whose peace shall know no end. Thus he overcomes the yoke of its (i.e. his people's) burden and the rod of its shoulder and the sceptor of its oppressor, Is. 9:4. The hypocrites, too, cannot change their nature. If they have ever opposed God they shall do so again. Christ is not too big for them. Not only dare they persecute him but with the aid of Caiaphas and other Jews they even kill him. But in the end, Christ has the upper hand; together with miserable Jerusalem they shall be thrown to the ground pitifully and destroyed.

NOTES

1. Cf. Zwingli, **The Labyrinth,** Z.1 55, lines 59/60: "Das nun ein grusam gmuemmel macht, als het der ochs ein luoy verbracht (as much as "an unseemly roar").

2. According to Finsler/Egli (Z.11 69, n. 17) Zwingli may have confused the Canon which regulates disciplinary action, the so-called purgatio canonica, with the simpler form of legal action against a priest. A judge was fairly free to decide whether the two traditional witnesses were sufficient or not. In practice, therefore, he could have required seven witnesses, thus giving a priest preferred treatment before the law. Cf. Canon 12, causa 11, quest 5 and can 19, causa II, quest 5.

THE TWELFTH ARTICLE

Thus they still rave, not on account of the head, (for the latter--by God's grace--one eagerly tries to uphold in our age), but because they are not allowed to rage any more but are forced, rather, to heed the head alone.

This Article is the finger or little rod with which I shall point to the reason for their raving. It is not on account of Christ the head, even though they fittingly shout out the phrase, "God must take pity [71] if this is the way things go in the Christian church." But if one looks closely, one notes that they are concerned with the money box and not with the Christian church. [1] The Christian church to them means their power, riches, pomp and self will; these they bemoan so deeply. For if they were concerned with the sweet Lord Christ they would wail thus, "Oh, oh God has shown overflowing grace toward us poor sinners, having given his own Son for us, yet we recognize it not and are not grateful. Yet he wanted to draw us forcefully in his love with such great grace shown to us, so that all good works might appear easy to us if we would only do them in love. Unfortunately, it has come to this that his wholesome word has not been believed by us; it is not worth anything to us for the simple reason that we do not know him and his grace. In short, we are not of God or anything like it." Thus they bemoan not the loss of the head but the loss of the mug, like drunken old hags. [2]

But that the gospel is to be brought out in our time we learn first of all from the sign which 1 Jn. 4:2 gives, "Every spirit which confesses that Jesus Christ has come in human weakness, is of God." And a bit later [1 Jn. 4:5], "The Antichrist, i.e. the enemies of Christ, are of the world, therefore they speak of the world and the world heeds them." If, however, in this our time one seriously seeks to emphasize the honor and grace of Jesus Christ, one ought not speak of the world, i.e. of human glory, as do the Antichrists. Therefore the teaching which speaks of God must be of God; for whatever teaches earthly things, is of the earth.

We learn it secondly from the fact that we are so splendidly taught humility, rejection and subordination of ourselves and the exaltation of God. [3]

Thirdly, we are taught to have sure confidence in God alone, for he does not deceive.

Fourthly, by the eagerness of the listeners who come in droves and want to hear it by force, even though they are severely admonished [72] in this by the godless. You may see from this that the kingdom or the word of God is drawn away by force, for though it is bitter in its punishment, it is sweet and beautiful in its comfort, which is surely to be found in it; for it brings with it the life giving power of a heavenly spirit, [4] as Is. 55:2ff shows in pointing to the person of God. "Hear me, hear me and eat what is good and your soul shall be enriched with fatness. Incline your ear and come to me. Listen and your soul shall live and I shall make with you an eternal covenant, the sure compassion of David." If then one is diligent in adhering to the pure word of God, those will lament who no longer gain anything from their own teaching.

This is a short exposition. Everyone may discover from it how the teaching which is proclaimed tastes.

NOTES

1. Zwingli engages in a play on words: "So ist es um die kistenlichen, nit christenlichen Kilchen zu tun."

2. Another word play on the term "houpt"-kopf; an alternate meaning of the term is "mug" (drinking cup).

3. The Egli/Finsler text in Z.11 71.28,29 requires a comma after "demuetigkeit" to give a meaningful reading of the sentence.

4. Zwingli writes, "die säfte des heiligen geistes."

THE THIRTEENTH ARTICLE

Whenever we give heed to the word, we acquire pure and clear knowledge of the will of God and are drawn to him by his Spirit and transformed into his likeness.

The first part of this Article is clear; for where else but in his word can one learn to know God's will more fully?

The second part, namely that a person is drawn to God by God's Spirit and deified, [1] becomes quite clear from scripture. "No one comes to Christ unless the heavenly Father draw him," Jn. 6:44. "And when the Spirit of truth comes, he shall teach all truth," Jn. 16.13. Even the carnal nature into which we are born, shall be transformed into God, if we can speak with Paul, "I do no longer live, but Christ lives in me," Gal. 2:20. For although we sin no less for being in Christ as long as we walk in the flesh, the unquestioning faith which we place in Christ our salvation brings about that Christ lives in us; for whoever has the spirit of Christ, is Christ's, Rom. 8:9f. You ought not [73] object at this point, as do those who are inexperienced in faith, "Thus no one is capable of doing good." For wherever the Spirit of Christ is, there you need not worry how the good is to be done. Here you recognize the smallness and weakness of your faith in that you do not let go of the bench [i.e. your reason] and give your hand confidently to God, allowing him to lead you. [2] For you cling to the elements of this world which is human reason. But if you desire to be God's, you must submit freely to him; let him govern and direct your life, food, counsel and all things; then God lives in you. And though you might fall into sin because of your weakness, God allows it so that your faith and confidence in him may be renewed and strengthened. For absolutely everything, even sin, helps a Christian to achieve the good. Thus one must be drawn to God and deified so that we might be fully emptied, cleaned and able to deny ourselves, no longer trusting in our own mind, heart and works but putting all our confidence in God our sole hope to which we cling. For thus we are being transformed into God. This is not a work of the flesh but of the Spirit of God.

57

NOTES

1. Zwingli says, "und in got verwandlet." The term implies deification.

2. "Vom banck lassen" and related proverbial sayings suggest the significance of the bench—later the chair—for recognizing status. Zwingli suggests that inflexibility in matters of faith might jeopardize one's salvation through Christ. Cf. **Idiotikon** IV for other sayings related to "banck."

THE FOURTEENTH ARTICLE

Hence all Christians should do their utmost so that everywhere only the gospel of Christ be preached.

Since through the gospel a person is clearly taught that he is nothing and not capable of anything apart from God and that God is so gracious as to have given us his own Son for our sure salvation that through him we may dare come to God, it follows that nothing should be preached to humankind except that in which their sure salvation is found, which is none other than the gospel. Christ has commanded this one thing to be preached and that it be preached to all creatures. Mk. 16:15; Mt. 24:14, "This gospel of the word of God or this sure proclamation of the kingdom of God is preached in all the world as a testimony and for the knowledge of all nations." The heavenly Father spoke thus in the baptism of Christ and on the Mount [74] of Transfiguration [Mt. 3:17; 17:5], "This is my beloved Son in whom I am well pleased or in whom I shall be reconciled; hear him." He does not say, listen to another one, hear the Fathers, hear the philosophers, but "hear him". Therefore the gospel alone must be preached.

THE FIFTEENTH ARTICLE

For belief in the gospel constitutes our salvation, and unbelief, our damnation; for all truth is clear in it. [1]

In this Article I wanted to point out two benefits for whose sake one should really hold the gospel in highest honor.

The first is, that if we believe in it, we shall be saved, Mk. 16:16, "Whoever believes and is baptized, shall be made whole or saved." Whoever believes and surely trusts in the good which God has graciously given us to be our salvation, named the Son of God, will be saved. But at the same time, whoever does not have Christ as his salvation and sole comfort, will be damned. This is beneficial for a person to know so that one may guard against damnation.

The second benefit is, that all truth is clearly in it. If we desire to know the truth, we will not be able to learn it anywhere else but in Christ who is the truth, the way and the life, Jn. 14:6. One cannot find truth with people (except God give it), however highly they may esteem themselves; for everyone is prone to lie, Ps. 116:11; Rom. 3:4. If then everyone is prone to lie, how shall we believe them? For this reason I do not like to let just anyone judge scripture, which my opponents think strange. Yet if they should ever show me a person who is not vain or full of lies, I will gladly believe that one; but if they cannot do that, how can I be expected to turn to them to judge scripture aright when I can see them forcing scripture according to their own wantonness? But when I know, on the other hand, that God alone is true (Rom. 3:4), I will cling to his word alone and learn it from him alone; [75] he is truthful and has promised to give whenever we shall ask him. Thus I shall ask him, the fount of all wisdom; and he shall teach me aright. And James says [James 1:5], "If someone desires wisdom, let him ask it of God, who gives to everyone abundantly without any bickering and grudging." And 1 Jn. chapter 2:27, "We are not in need of anyone teaching us, for what you have learned through the anointing by him, that is the truth, etc." With these words, I hope to have clearly shown the reason for my view that I do not tolerate a judge over me when it comes to scripture. On the other hand, I gladly let scripture judge me. When it judges me, I shall accept its judgment, for scripture alone is truthful. Further, those only shall know the truth who cling to the word of Christ alone. Jn. 8:31, "If you remain in my word, you shall be truly my disciples and you shall know the truth and the truth shall make you free." I have amply shown earlier that one cannot learn the word and mind of God from any person except through the one Spirit of God; in him alone a person is assured, firm and certain, Jn. 3:33, "Whoever accepts his testimony has attested that God is truthful (i.e. he has confirmed it, as if by letter and seal). Note, beloved brothers, certainty of the word of God does not come from human judgments but rather from God, so that when a person has such a clear faith that he trusts God in all things, indeed, gives full credence to him alone, he fully knows that God is truthful. He knows the mind and purpose of God and is as sure and firm in this as if he had letter and seal. He also examines everything which people consider to be truthful. Should he find it in his gospel, i.e. in the teaching which flows from God's Spirit and grace, he does not just accept it at that point, but he is so clearly informed and illumined beforehand that he accepts nothing except that in which God has guided him through Christ. And when someone speaks what is God's, he does not need to confirm that person's word, but says rather, "This is to be believed, since it is of God." And everything will be clear to him through his faith in the gospel, provided he clings to Christ. For God's Spirit informs our spirit that we are sons of God, Rom. 8:16. How are we to know that we are sons of God except God assure us in our hearts through the spirit of his grace? [76] Or how are we, who are full of lies, to know the truth, except it be by the breath of his Spirit? In short, nothing is true except that which God shows us. Everything that is not grounded in God's word cannot be found to be truthful, for human beings are prone to lie.

NOTE

1. The pronoun "im" is dative masculine or neuter. Although Zwingli obviously refers back to "the gospel" of the previous Article, it becomes apparent from the context that "im" may also refer to Christ--the true gospel.

THE SIXTEENTH ARTICLE

In the gospel we learn that human teaching and statutes are of no use to salvation.

Here I have set out to enumerate several main points [of doctrine] which I have preached from the word of God. Unfortunately, these have been passed over in silence by some, though they ought to have been preached above all else, so that the grace and kindness of God might have appeared all the sweeter to people. I understand that gospel here means everything which God has made known to us through his Son; indeed, it is gospel, too, when he says, "You shall not be angry with one another" [Mt. 5:22], or again, when he says that one commits adultery even in one's desire [Mt. 5:28], or when he says that one must not resist the evil one [Mt. 5:39], and many other such laws which, undoubtedly, will appear distasteful to many people. I understand this as follows: The true believer rejoices and is nourished by every word of God, whether the same goes against the desires of the flesh or not. The unbeliever, however, takes every word wrongly and without trust. If you say to him that Christ not only forbids killing and blasphemy, but that he forbids even becoming angry, he will say to himself: "This is tomfoolery; who is to abide by it?" Thus he rejects God's word. If you say to him on the contrary that Christ has borne all our sin and weakness on the cross and has sought to draw us into the love of God with such overflowing grace, he considers it to be a lie and impossible. But if you say that to a believer, he does not take offence at the word of the commandment, "You shall not even get angry." Rather, he will reply (or better, the Spirit of God will teach him inwardly), as follows, "note, God is so good that everyone who desires to live in his will, must be free from animal and carnal weaknesses and temptations; he must [77] not allow anger to enslave him. He must forgive again and again, as does the heavenly Father whose sun shines upon the good and evil, etc. He has to be satisfied with his own wife and not only should he not commit adultery with another's wife, but he must not even desire her. Not only must he not harm his neighbor, but when he has suffered loss at his hand, he should not seek revenge, but forgive again and again and do good to him." Indeed, in this fashion a believer accepts the word of God, for he sees in these and all other things which God demands, how God acts in all of them. And when he observes that the Son of God lived according to his word and now is seated at the right hand of God the Father, he realizes at once that no one shall dwell in the house of God unless he be guiltless, upright and pure, as God demands. This is just like those who do not tolerate among their servants any who do not conform to their custom, traditions and life. David indicated this also in Ps. 8 and Is. 33:14-16, "Who among you is willing to live amidst the consuming fire? Or who among you will dwell in the eternal furnace?" Answer: Whoever walks in righteousness and speaks the truth, who puts away envy and evil thoughts and keeps his hand free from bribes; whoever plugs his ear so that he does not hear of blood guilt and closes his eyes that he might not see evil; such a one shall dwell in the heights, etc." Here a believer learns, first of all, of the consuming fire which is God. He then discovers that no one who is afflicted with vices is able to live with such fire and heat for these are consumed by the fire. Yet this does not lead him to despair or unbelief. On the contrary, he catches a glimpse of how upright and pure God is and learns how good he is and how good everyone should be who desires to dwell with him. But he finds also in all of this that he is unable to attain guiltlessness and purity on his own. And since he cannot find any comfort in himself, he discovers right alongside the commandments the gracious promise of the grace of God, "Come unto me all you who labor and are burdened, and I shall give you rest," Mt. 11:28. And again, "Everyone who puts his trust in me, has eternal life," Jn 6:40. Such promises bring joy and comfort to a believer, but are a laughing matter to the godless person. Now the godless person is at a disadvantage even where he cannot [78] and will not do the will of God and despises his grace. Now take heed, whatever is teaching and direction from God to a believer, is oppression to the godless; it pinches and burdens him, for he does not want to learn how to know God by his word and commandment. Rather, he follows the evil knave, the flesh, which neither knows nor does any good and falls under God's wrath, since his will and our desire are totally opposed to each other. But the believer is drawn by the love of God, for when he sees God to be such an upright, pure being, he is driven to love and acquire such goodness. And for that which appears to be impossible in himself, he is consoled and reproved by the word of the grace of God. He is not driven to despair by it as is a carnal sinner when he discovers God's beauty and sees at the same time that he cannot attain to the same. Rather, when he discovers that God offers his hand in grace and support, he is fittingly kindled in the love of God. Thus, a thing may be salvation and wholesome teaching to the believer, but to the unbeliever it is despair or folly.

Note then, that everything which God has made known to us is either command, prohibition or promise. A commandment teaches the believer, but the unbeliever despairs of it. Prohibition protects the believer, but the godless is further tempted by it. Promise assures and comforts the believer, but to the unbeliever it is folly.

This will become clear through examples.

The first example: You shall love your neighbor as yourself. This instructs the believer as follows: "Note that the Son of God was not proud because of his great power and honor, but he became human for us and took on our work, misery and sorrow. He wants us to do likewise and to take upon ourselves the concerns of our neighbors. But the godless person reacts against this: "Who is able to keep that?" And that is a command.

The second example concerns the prohibition, "You shall not covet."--Understood is carnal or human temptation.--This prohibition warns the believer who lives in the Spirit of God that God is such a pure, beautiful good that no one is capable of realizing his will unless he were capable of not doing anything which is motivated by the desire of the flesh. But the godless person despairs in this law and in himself. He seeks to do evil even more and does not seek his comfort with God.

The third example looks to the promises of God and how in Is. 55:1 the grace of God calls us to Christ, "All you who thirst, come [79] to the water. And if you have no money, hurry, buy and eat. Come take away without money and price wine and milk, etc." This word encourages the believer. He rejoices. And when he finds something to be impossible--and all the good is impossible--he draws from God. But the godless and unbelieving person does not believe this word; his hurt conscience is like Cain's and he says, "My evil deed is exceedingly difficult to forgive; it cannot happen that easily" [cf. Gen. 4:13]. He is, in fact, so godless that he trusts in his own reckoning more than in the gracious assurances of God. He rejects as folly what might be his full salvation. Here then they find their weaknesses.

Now to draw things together, I call everything "gospel" which God opens to human beings and demands of them, as shown above. For whenever God shows his will to people, it delights those who love God and thus it is to them certain and good news. For this reason I call it "gospel", preferring that term to the term "law"; for it is more fittingly named to suit the understanding of believers and not of unbelievers; and at the same time we overcome the tension between law and gospel. Besides I know well that Christ is the sum and perfection; he is the certain manifestation of salvation, for he is salvation.

The gospel thus understood--namely as God's will made known to human beings and required of them--contains in it (as earlier stated), command, prohibition, promise and fulfillment in such a way that all commandments and prohibitions of God shall be unheld to all eternity. For heaven and earth shall pass away before God's word will, unless of course, they are laws which he has given for a time with the intention of doing away with them later. In this sense one must understand what Christ says in Luke 16:16, "The law and the prophets lasted up to the time of John." In other words, all commandments which God gave, humankind was responsible to keep without any exception, even though it might not have been possible to keep them all, up to the time of John. At that point the law began to cease and in me it has fully ceased. This is not to say that we are no longer required to do right; but it has ceased in this that earlier the law condemned everyone who transgressed it. Those who sinned against [80] the law were condemned by the law; no one was able to fulfill the law. For who is there that has been capable of carrying out the law, "You shall love the neighbor as yourself" in its entirety without becoming guilty of transgression? I shall not even mention the first commandment. But I, Christ, am the life, I am the lamb which takes away the sins of humankind; and since no one was able to satisfy the law and thus come to God, I have taken away the power of sin by fulfilling the law and satisfying the righteousness of God on behalf of the guilty through my guiltlessness. For this reason then, the law can no longer condemn anyone, for it has been cancelled. Whoever believes in me, has the Spirit of God now which shall always cleanse him and redeem him from sin in that he teaches him to find grace with God through me. Whoever finds it, does so not without my Spirit who also will instruct him concerning what else he ought to do. Thus for the believer the law has been lifted through Christ; for wherever the Spirit of God is, there is freedom, 2 Cor. 3:17. And where there is true faith, there the Spirit of God is also, Jn. 6:63. Thus it follows that where faith is, there freedom is. All this becomes clear in Paul's words, Rom. 8:1-11, "Therefore there is nothing else which may condemn those who are in Christ Jesus, who do not walk according to the flesh but according to the Spirit. For the law of the Spirit of life has in Christ Jesus set me free from the law of sin and death. For what was impossible for the law to accomplish because it was weak on account of the flesh, God has replaced in sending his Son in the form of sinful flesh. And because of sin he condemned or mortified sin in the flesh so that the keeping of the law may be accomplished in us who do not walk according to the flesh, but according to the Spirit. Those who walk in the flesh do carnal things of themselves, those, however, who walk by the Spirit, do those things which are of the Spirit. In these words you find, first of all, that nothing can condemn or kill those who are in Christ Jesus, provided they do not walk according to the flesh, but according to the Spirit. But to walk according to the flesh is not to be understood as if one may do nothing [81] of that which the flesh demands; for then no one would be able to live according to the Spirit since one would have to disregard physical necessity even. To live according to the flesh is understood to mean living according to human reason and strength. To live according to the Spirit means to extricate oneself from the reason and power of the flesh, i.e. human nature, and to trust in the Spirit of God alone. Those who trust in the Lord Jesus Christ with all confidence will no longer be damned by any law. The proof follows shortly. For the law of the Spirit which gives life, namely the teaching and directions of the divine Spirit who quickens all living things, has set me free in Christ Jesus. This means that from the moment I trusted in Christ Jesus in all confidence, knowing him to be my salvation, Father, provider, through whom I have been set free and made a child of God, all fear of the law and of death was dispelled.

Of the law: In that it was no longer able to condemn me, for I no longer lived under the power and guardianship of the law, but under the guardianship of the Spirit of God; of this the latter instructed me. "And where the Spirit of God is, there is freedom," 2 Cor. 3:17. For the Spirit is above the law and where he is there is no longer any need of the law. Now where there is faith, there the Spirit of God is also.

Of death: Since death is punishment of sin, and since sin has been mortified, I rise again in Christ and live, not by my own breath or spirit, but in the Spirit of God in whom I understand and believe this. Death here means lack of God's grace and that is condemnation.

It now follows: While this was impossible for the law to do in that it was weak on account of the flesh, (i.e. that it was impossible for the person who trusted the law to save himself, because the infirmity of the flesh cannot fulfill the law), God fulfilled and replaced the impossible and weak by giving us his Son in the form and manner of sinful human nature so that he who was without sin may condemn sin in the flesh, in other words, that he may mortify it. On account of sin: The fact that Christ, who was without sin has been murdered like a sinner, atoned for our sin. Yet sin or the devil, a cause of sin, has been overcome and deprived of the dominion which he had over humankind on account of the flesh, because he falsely attacked and killed Christ. Because of the sin, committed against Christ, the sting and damage of sin [82] living within us, has been removed, Hos. 13:14. Hence, righteousness or guiltlessness according to the law is not because of any human deed, but through Christ alone whose own sinlessness purged our guilt before God so that if we cling to him, as stated above, he shall be our innocence and righteousness before God to all eternity. To have such confidence in Christ is to walk spiritually.

Thus a person is redeemed from the law through Christ. If he lives by faith in Christ, then Christ becomes his reason, counsel, righteousness and innocence. To sum up: Christ becomes his full salvation and lives in him. Therefore he is in need of no law, for Christ is his law. Upon him alone does he look. Indeed, Christ alone guides and leads him; he no longer needs any other guide. For Christ is the end of the law, Rom. 10:3. At this point faith is generally lacking, for few, indeed, are found who trust so completely in Christ. Therefore they are so ignorant and not sure enough of the pledge of the divine Spirit to know that they in themselves are nothing and that God is everything. They are almost like the Jews of whom Paul speaks, Rom. 10:3, "For they do not know the righteousness of God and that no one can make himself in its likeness nor become worthy of it, unless the Spirit of God accomplishes it. They undertake to become righteous by their own piety which means to walk in the flesh. Thus it happens that they are not submissive to the righteousness of God which is nothing other than to lean upon God and trust him. Since they have their own minds and follow the flesh, it appears well and good to them to desire the elements of the world and they gauge their righteousness and innocence by their own deeds. Note the sheer folly of this. If one were to reward a person's deeds on the basis of his own estimate, no one would be able to pay up fully. Thus it is godlessness when some people seek to measure their righteousness by their own estimate and not by the grace and Spirit of God.

Now someone might object at this point: What if someone should hear then--especially a most carnally minded person--that the law has been removed through Christ! He would have to conclude: "Now it is fitting for you to live without any law, discipline and righteousness." Answer: Anyone who speaks thus [83] is not a believer, though he may say, "Thus I am free." He is not free at all. His conscience is made uneasy by the Spirit of God so that it accuses him inwardly, though it may appear clever and aloof outwardly. The law has been cancelled only for the one who has totally surrendered to Christ. The same is led by God so that everything that God wills, pleases and does not burden him. Again, every godless person is under the law and the law condemns him, for he lives according to the flesh, which is, according to human wisdom and knowledge. In such life there is no peace or freedom but fear upon fear, condemnation upon condemnation. Though the flesh may put up an outward show of boldness, it nonetheless knows its present death and is condemned by itself. And when it says: I am free also, it is already dead in its own being, for there are no more than two parties: grace and the law.

If you do not put your trust in God's grace, the Spirit of God does not lead you, and you are under the law though you may say, you are not. You are now no longer free, for you do not have Christ who is freedom. Yet if you have him, you are no longer under the law, but under grace, Rom. 6:14. But if you live according to the flesh or human righteousness, you shall die, Rom 8:13. For the prospect of the flesh is death, the prospect of the Spirit is life and peace. Again an example: If a state should forbid any of its citizens to accept rent, gifts or money from a foreigner on penalty of torture or spiking, such a law would be accepted in different ways. Those who do not want to transgress it from love of justice and of their nation, will not be burdened by the law. For even though there may be no law imposed at all, they would still not accept any gifts. But those who are out for themselves, are oppressed by the law. Therefore they express objections. Now the righteous person is not under the law, but those who seek their own interests, are. For the righteous person lives by love of righteousness, joyfully and free; the selfish one lives only under the pressure of the law, which causes him to have no love of righteousness at all. Thus one who is freed by the gospel is under no law at all; rather, the Spirit of God [84] who led him to the knowledge of evangelical freedom, is his plumbline. He spurs him on to do whatever God wills. Whatever is commanded or forbidden does not offend him; for the Spirit of God which has already breathed on him, shows him what God's will is. And as soon as he sees what God desires, he rejoices in it, though it may be against the flesh, for he is aware in the surety which is God's Spirit that nothing but pure grace can save him. But the one who is not free through the gospel, is oppressed by everything which is commanded. He is under the law, bound and sold under sin. (When I speak always of laws in this context, it is to be understood first of all with reference to the laws which God has given, but, secondly, also of human laws which are given as if they had come from God to save us. On temporal laws I shall have a separate chapter, but we do not speak of them here.)

For the flesh is always against God and everything which is against him, knows of no rest or comfort, as one may readily observe in the case of the devil. Where the Spirit of God is not, there we have no freedom. And where there is no freedom there the law has to be. Where the law is, there is no grace (understood is the law as it pertains to the person who does not have the Spirit of God). Where grace is not, it is impossible to attain salvation. From this follows that one who wants to be saved must depend solely on the grace of God which is Christ. All this could have been verified by a great deal of scripture from the Gospel of John, from Paul, Romans and the first Epistle of John. These are the sources of my thought from which I have learned.

Having established our foundation, let us now focus on the words of this Article, namely that we learn in the gospel that human teaching and statutes do not contribute anything toward salvation. That has to follow first of all. If salvation derives from the grace of God alone, it cannot possibly come from human teaching and commandments, even though one might keep these. The reason is, such things are nothing but hypocrisy and outward appearance. Now all hypocrisy is basically opposed to God. Therefore Christ warns us to guard against the sour dough of the pharisees which is only hypocrisy. That humanly ordered works are nothing but hypocrisy I prove as follows: "Whatever comes from the flesh is carnal" Jn. 3:6. Whenever human beings command anything on the basis of reason, it is [85] carnal, Gen. 6:3. It follows from this that all commandments which originate with human reason are merely of the flesh. Further: Where the flesh rules, there God is not. Where God is not, there no good can be found. From this it follows that where the flesh is, there nothing good can come. From these two expositions we conclude, that humanly invented commandments and works are carnal, and since they are carnal they cannot be good. Since it is now certain that they are no good but merely pretend to be, they are nothing other than hypocrisy. For that which makes a pretense of what it is not, is false and full of lies. And whenever that which is first among evils, passes itself off as divine, true and good it is blasphemy of God, an abomination, and despicable folly. Yet another instance: Those who seek to please God are eager to do only the works which are within God's will, Jn. 8:38 and 13:34. But those who seek to please people, cannot please God, Rom. 8:8; Gal. 1:10. Thus it follows: Everyone who seeks to please people does not apply himself to doing the will of God. Further, those who do not endeavor to do God's will, look to desire, advantage or excessive honor only. All who do the works ordered by human beings, do not apply themselves to God's will. From this follows that those who do the works imposed by human statutes look to desire, advantage or honor. Proof of the central clause, namely, that those who do humanly ordered works, do not apply themselves to doing God's will, is found in the fact that they look upon the person who orders or commands them to do this. They certainly do not look upon God, or else they would have to heed his word alone and give no attention at all to human directions.

From these two proofs we deduce clearly that those who fulfill human teachings and commandments (I speak here solely of the works which the false prophets have taught as justifying), do so only for the sake of gratifying their desires and to gain advantage and honor. In sum: Any work which is good, God accomplishes in us; nothing is good unless it comes from God. But God does not effect the works which we do because of human teaching or law. Rather, these are utter hypocrisy, farce and mockery. God effects in us only that which is good; but everything in us which we ourselves may accomplish or which is of other creatures, is useless, vain, deceit and sin. Nor does it help if you retort: Is it not good [86] for me to be a pauper that a rich person may give gifts to me? Or to be a sinner, that the learned person may admonish me? Answer: Indeed, it is not good if what we are now discussing is done by humans and not by God; but whatever comes from God, is good. Why then do you want to ascribe to humans what is God's alone?

Now let us be done with these arguments which we have brought out only so that those who desire to pick a fight might have something to chew on (for otherwise they read little of God's scripture), and that they may have some logical deductions to pick on. Now look what opinion God's clear word has concerning human machinations [Menschentand]. In Is. 29:13f hypocrites are well exposed, as follows, "Because this people approach me with their mouths and honor me with their lips, while their heart is far from me, and have held me before their eyes through human laws and teaching only, therefore I shall from now on do a terrible and strange thing to them. Their wise men shall lose their wisdom and the understanding of those who know shall be lost, etc."

Note how beautifully the Spirit of God has delineated our hypocrisy. We act that way to this very day. We honor God with our thoughtless prayers, with "stuffed fasting", with outward pretense of bleached cowls and carefully shaved heads, with starched long coats, carefully pressed, with well guilded donkeys, [2] and with numerous vigils and psalms; now we mumble, then we cry; now we don't eat eggs--then we stuff ourselves again; we are so pleased with ourselves in this tomfoolery that we actually think ourselves to be pious even though God denounces it all. But the heart is far from God. If it were near God, it could not tolerate to have anything clinging to it which might displease God but would rather, learn the things which please God, such as righteousness, hope, faith, mercy. It would not desire either goods or honor, ease of living, or oppression of the neighbor. It would help the needy, comfort the distressed, tame the intemperate and do good toward everyone. But as long as we ourselves desire to bring forth something good and work to the point of thinking that we may honor God through human teaching and commandments, [87] we forsake the righteousness of God and set up our own; we may believe thus to atone for our sin, but it proves to be nothing but outward appearance and hypocrisy. Go up once again and look at it; what a nice mess it turned out to be. From thence we have contracted the plague which is that those who ought to have been wise, who were to shepherd the church of God, have become fools. Indeed, they are not accepted for ministry unless one knows well beforehand that they are neither wise nor learned in God's teaching. They have to be fools and uncouth in it; they must also not be without the great evil which is avarice; for if one is not full of avarice he cannot be bishop, provost, abbot, etc. See what evil plague all this is. Note also the sins which cause this plague to be spread. It is because they vaunt themselves in thinking to honor God with their foolish deeds, i.e. with their teaching and commandments. Go forth then and shout, "the holy orders, the worthy priesthood, the honorable traditions of our forebears, the teaching of the pious Fathers; should our fasting, our holy days, our seasons, the burning of heretics, the burning of incense, the blessing of holy bread, the pouring out of holy water and such things be done away with if we hear that these offend God?" He knows well what arises out of these things. Therefore he does not want to be honored by them. For one tends to rely on these foolish things and disregard the things that please God. For this reason Adam fell, since he wanted to know something other than what God had commanded him; that, it seems to me, is the tree of the knowledge of good and evil.

These words of Isaiah, Christ also used in Mt. 15:9, bringing them out more clearly when he said, "They honor me in vain when they teach human doctrine· and commandments." These words of Christ are so clear that no others are needed to overcome every doctrine and commandment, thought up by people. Bring out whatever you like. Throw, shoot, beat as much as you like with your shouting of "Fathers, good things, only wise; should these have erred?" I will not be distracted. Christ says, they honor me in vain, for nothing, foolishly ("maten" in Greek). Indeed, they are childish and vain if they honor me through human teaching and commandments. Cover up your dirt through learned words as much as you like; it will be in vain, a flagrant under-[88] taking; for the true believer listens solely to what his Lord God says and when he looks at himself he finds that he has never done the will of God. How then is he to think up something new if he has not even done the things he ought to have done? How is he to wear something new, if he has not yet worn out the old frock? Therefore it is blasphemy to make changes and to sell something as good when one departs from the word of God. Truly, human folly and its works take this form. If a master in his household orders each servant to do as he pleases and a bold servant undertakes something which pleases him well and if, when he is bid to fence the wheatfield or the vineyard against thieves, he sits down with the children to weave tumblers for them out of reeds, he will not only displease the landlord but will actually be dismissed. Thus it is in the kingdom or community of Christ. God demands of us some very daring, bold things, that we cling to him alone, put our confidence in him, listen to his will only as we bear all burden and discomfort for his sake, never coveting someone else's goods, neither being proud; in short, never to walk according to the flesh. Yet, we act like children and build little houses from reeds i.e. we think up these outward works, the burning of candles, the sprinkling of holy water, nun's prayers, monkish chatter, priest's chanting and such junk which we are well able to achieve through other people, without overcoming evil temptations, but we leave the work of God undone. Now I know well that I speak in rather simple, childlike language concerning good works. I do it for the sake of those who bemoan the disappearing of good works. But if they are so eager to do good works, I shall speak in Micah's words who says in the sixth chapter [Micah 6:8], "I shall show you, O man, what is good and what God demands of you, namely, to act justly, to be merciful and to walk faithfully before your God." But what does "to dwell with care before God" mean other than to look carefully upon the things God [89] wills? If then you desire to do such works, forgive your enemy, avoid any divisions, share food, drink and clothing with the poor, stop talking which is good for nothing, draw in the finger with which you point at people, stop blaspheming God, filling yourself with wine, engaging in warfare, gambling, exacting money from others, committing adultery, being unchaste, robbing and cheating. Pray for your enemies, give away the jacket as well as the cloak, turn the other cheek also when struck, do good to those who hate you and do such things as God bids you do.

However, you come along now after having gained 5000 guilders through usury to set up an endowment, and to buy indulgences with the hundredth portion of your theft. (Even that you do merely to impress people. This is apparent from the spotted wild cats which decorate the paraments). [3] And though your own conscience shouts, "It is not right" and "God hates robbery even though one may sacrifice it to him", Is. 61:8, you nonetheless do not leave the property of your neighbor alone nor do you distribute your possessions. Yet you stand there, cleverly bemoaning the demise of good works. Go, do the works which we first mentioned. But you prefer to give the penny for which you have no regret so that you will not have to do anything about the lusting of your heart and mend your ways. Do you see now where the knave sits? But lest all my reproaches be in vain, I shall show you why it is that there is no love toward God's work, though there is a great deal of eagerness to do something. Grant understanding, O Lord God! Note, you simple fellow, that the doing of good works is not ours, but alone God's, Jer. 10:23. "Lord, I know that a person's way is not his own nor is it within the strength of a person to direct his own path." You should easily see by the fact that God's works do not in any way please you, that it is not within a person's power to like the good or to be able to do it. Whose then is it? It is solely within the power of the Spirit of God. But how can I receive this Spirit? Call on God to give you understanding. As soon as you call, he says, "I am here." Indeed, he even causes you to call. As soon as he is present you will believe his word. As soon as you believe his word, you are assured of his grace and certain of salvation. From then on the Spirit of God which [90] has effected this in you will never again let you go idly and he will cause you to love the works which please God and you shall not again ascribe such works to yourself; for you have seen quite well that you were unable to do them before. You will ascribe them to God alone and dismiss your own works as stench and dirt. You will finally learn on your own that the good is not yours and that the things which you upheld as good are utter deceit and hypocrisy. At this point you may make a flimsy retort: "Yes, indeed, I share your opinion. It is for this reason that I desire priests, monks and nuns to pray for me since I well know myself to be a sinner and unable to do anything." Answer: See now, how you twist out of this in vain. First of all, do away with all hypocrisy and then see how much you should actually give them, for God's sake. Secondly, do you not know that just as I have taught you to be, they too should be? If they were like that, they would not sell their vigils, masses and matins, but they would only teach that everyone is to strengthen himself in the grace of God, Heb. 13:9. But as long as they take money for their worship, they are as evil as you are; in fact, more so. For they honor God in vain in that they honor him through works, invented by people. But if it is in vain how greatly, would you think, do they sin by taking money for it? It is just like placing iceblocks upon iceblocks. [4]

Christ says further in Mt. 9:16f, "No one puts a patch of new or rough cloth on an old dress, for the improving or mending harms the dress, making the hole even worse. Neither does one put new wine or cider into old containers. Where that is done, the containers will burst and the wine will be spilled, thus spoiling the containers. Rather, one puts new wine into new wineskins thus preserving both." These parables Jesus told to John's disciples and to the Pharisees in response to their complaint which they had made concerning the reason for their own observance of fasts, while his disciples fasted little. Upon this, he answered them, just before this one, by yet another parable saying that as long as the bridegroom is with his friends, they do not have any sorrow, but when the [91] bridegroom is taken from them, they shall fast and be sorrowful knowing that where Christ is, no one needs to be concerned about how to please God. Rather, where he is, there God is pleased by everything; there is no need for sorrow but there is rejoicing as at a wedding feast. But if he should depart from them it is solely because they have become carnal. Therefore one would have to subordinate everything once more to the Spirit through fasting and sorrow.

Soon after this he then cites the passage, mentioned earlier, in which he relates that in the same way in which one who seeks to mend a dress, should not take strong, new or unpressed cloth--since the new is too strong for the old and would tear it--so also does the person err who seeks to mix the gospel--the word of the grace of God--with the law of works, thus causing both to become useless. The new patch falls off and the old dress will be torn; now the new patch falls off because the old dress is too weak to hold it in place. This is nothing other than, "Whoever is not born anew, leaving the old pieces and rags of outward works, dropping any hope in his own work and clinging freely to the grace of God--just like a child who gives up walking along benches--will become worse." For it would be better had such a one never known divine righteousness (i.e. his grace which alone justifies), 2 Pet. 2:20, than for him to turn again to the weak elements of this world, after having received the knowledge of the gospel which is to turn again to oneself, one's wisdom, and advice which places so much value upon itself that it intends to attain salvation by itself. This new cloth and dress cannot bear to be sewn together with an old patch, but desires to remain pure and unmixed; this causes us to love God as he loves us. A similar meaning is intended by the other part of the parable concerning the wine containers, which also does not say anything other than that the word of the grace of God is to be preserved in new dishes which do not have the sour dough or taste of the old ones. In other words, we are not to bank on the elements of our old foolish nature which likes so much to be something; rather, we are to trust in the grace of God alone, letting him care and govern.

If then it is understood of all works that they are nothing inasmuch as they come from people, how much more is it so for the outward works which we ourselves have invented, in which the Spirit [92] of God is not found. For if he were there he would not have said, "They honor me in vain"--not at all, vainly and for nothing. Indeed, worse than child's play and mockery for no one at all gives a hoot for such. If one depends on these works out of simplicity and because of the confidence one places in them, one then leaves the works of the grace of God and no longer recognizes them at all. To prevent such from happening, Peter says therefore in Acts 15:10, when some who had been converted to Christ from the Jewish faith, undertook to impose upon Christians outward works or the law of works, "Why do you tempt God in daring to place upon the neck of the younger ones this yoke which neither we nor our forebears were able to endure? For we retain the faith and are saved through the grace of our Lord Jesus Christ, just as they." Note, St. Peter warns the entire community of Christians not to burden themselves with the laws of works but to cling, instead, to the grace of our dear Lord Jesus Christ alone.

At this point the lazy lot of work-righteous people invariably cry (for no one does fewer good Christian works than those who cry most for works), "Should one not have laws to do good? Why then does Christ say, "If you want to enter life, keep the commandments,'" Mt. 19:17? Answer: The commandments of God cannot be kept by anyone, except the spirit of divine grace works in him so that that which God commands, is pleasing to him and initiates such work. Reason: Without him we are not able to do anything, Jn. 15:5. If then without him we are unable to do anything, we have to live entirely by his grace. If this is so, it follows that once a person has resigned himself to the grace of God, he ought to let God lead and direct him for he will not let him go idle but give him plenty to do. Observe how.

Did Peter, Paul and Andrew cease doing good works just because they preached the grace of God alone? Not at all. Who planted the word of God more anxiously than they? Who has had more to do and care than they? Look at the life of Christians from the beginning and see whether they have ever been as righteous as at the beginning on account of good works and you will find the contrary. What then made the early [Christians] so godly? Nothing other than that they trusted entirely in the grace of our beloved Lord Jesus Christ, not only in matters pertaining to salvation but also in things pertaining to physical [93] necessity. For they sold all their possessions and brought the proceeds for the common use of the brothers. But when Ananias pretended to depend entirely on the grace of God, which was not really the case, (for he, together with his wife, kept a portion to himself secretly), Peter said to him, Acts 5:3, "Ananias; why has Satan filled your heart so that you cheat the Spirit of God, etc?" And shortly after, both of them fell down and died on the spot. This seemed a bit harsh to me since I thought I knew something too and that God should give me an account of why he would do such a thing. But when I see the strong excellent faith of simple Christians at that time, and the great faithfulness and diligence which sprang from it and when I see alongside it how Ananias allowed the devil to tempt him so that he dared be unfaithful in this holy company and, as if God were blind, pretended to stand in the same grace and faith in which the others were found, I understand the matter readily. For I see that God actually set him to be an example and a warning that we should not undertake such patchwork, but should rely wholly on God's grace and not keep a portion unto ourselves, saying: "Lo, I have to do something, too, God can't do it all. Thus I can't leave everything to God. I must see that I too have something in my hands as if God is so slothful and untrustworthy that he should not admonish and teach, and point to the food and nourishment of one who trusts in him."

If God were still to throw down suddenly all who are half believers, how many young men would have to be carried out and buried? Now God is not about to diminish his righteousness. If they do not submit to God's grace, they shall receive full justice; and what he does not punish with awful measures in this life, he shall even out with fearful pain in the life to come. For this reason I dare promise in the name of the Lord Jesus to all those who fear that good works might diminish, that every good work shall grow all the more, the more one trusts in God. [94] And let them not forget the answer, earlier touched on, for I do not want to repeat a thing ten times. But the entire array of humanly taught works comes to nought at this point; for one may clearly see that only those works are good which God orders and effects and further, that it is a grave matter and eternally damnable to leave God and not to trust him, but instead to trust in oneself. For this is blasphemy of God and sheer idolatry; for all trust in creatures is idolatry; thus Paul rightly considers avarice to be idolatry also; for the avaricious person places his hope in material goods.

Now of course, these lazy bitches [5] and patchworkers [6] object: "The apostles too ordered ceremonies; for not to eat the food, offered to idols or that which is strangled or blood, are ceremonial acts." I shall retort to this objection in the 64th Article. Until then you must have patience and be content with the words which are found in the epistle to the Christians of Jerusalem, Acts 15:28ff. "It has pleased the Holy Spirit and us to place no other burden on you than these necessary things, namely, that you do not eat of the sacrifice offered to idols, etc," as above. To sum up: The Christian church at Jerusalem saw with the aid of the Spirit of God that nothing was to be placed upon a Christian; however, the hypocrites who came after them invented something.

Paul says in Col. 2:8, "Take heed that no one rob you through philosophy and useless or idle temptation, which follows human statutes and teachings and the elements of the world rather than Christ." Here Paul clearly teaches to beware of human trifles, that no one allow these to rob us of the grace of God which has redeemed us. Everyone who knows himself firm in the grace of God and trusts him, must watch human philosophy, i.e. he must guard against the wisdom, invented by humans. But for some time now those who should present the word of God only, have worked on nothing else but on how to press human trifles and philosophy, which is merely a foolish, unreliable delusion, upon those who should be fed through God's word alone. He also warns of unnecessary and idle temptation which he calls thus [95] because humanly invented statutes and commandments appear to be beautiful to human eyes, but inwardly they are empty, vain, barren and useless; for where the Spirit of God is not, there nothing other than falseness, hypocrisy, despair and a condemned and terrible conscience are to be found. And God is not present where the flesh is (which is, as we touched on above, nothing other than our knowledge and reason). Therefore Paul has rightly called this appearance of human hypocrisy a barren or loose, vain temptation; for everything which is of the flesh is carnal.

From this it follows that all human statutes which are called good works, and which we pass off as good, are a sign of true hypocrisy; and all who cling to these are hypocrites. Indeed, they are unbelievers, without soul and in despair. Reason: If they were true believers whose confidence is in God alone, the Spirit of God would be with them. For exclusive dependence on the grace of God, is wrought solely by the Holy Spirit. If he were with them, he would urge them only to do his works and will. But since they put too much trust in human trifles, it is certain that God is not with them, for he curses everyone who turns from God to creatures and the flesh, Jer. 17:5. Now let them prattle as much as they like and you may be sure from this one sign, which is that they do not set forth God's teaching alone and that they do not teach his grace to be our only salvation, that God is not with them. Therefore nothing other than hypocrisy and despair is to be found with them. Let their works shine as much as they may, they are nonetheless an abomination before God, as Christ himself has taught, Lk. 16:15, saying to the Pharisees, "You are the ones who appear beautiful and righteous before the people, but God knows your hearts; for whatever seems exalted in human eyes is an abomination before God." Oh God, Lord! What besides this single word of Christ do all these defenders of human trifles want? Is it not in itself clear and strong enough to inform them that everything which appears to them to be wise, beautiful, high and good is an abomination before God?

He further warns not to let human statutes and teachings rob one of the grace of God. Paul actually knew that carnal beings will not leave their nature and wiles since even in the Garden of Eden man was so pleased with himself that he wanted to be wise too and was not [96] satisfied with the grace of God which would have led and directed him graciously, as a father leads his child. Therefore he sought to prevent everyone through those words [from] ever relying on human teachings and statutes; for as soon as that happens, the word of God has no longer any value with us. Reason: That which we should find according to the elements of this world, i.e. according to human boasting, wisdom and commandments, would please us so very much that we--giving attention to the flesh--would forsake God altogether. Here let him look out who on the day of the dispute is about to prove on the basis of St. Paul's word in 2 Thess. 2:15 that Paul, in his estimation, also issued statutes, ordinances and teachings of his own because he used the term "traditiones", [7] which Paul uses there to indicate the order and directive of the gospel. In the same sense he also uses the term in 1 Cor. 11:2. But there it is taken to mean human order, direction and teaching. For the term traditio--paradosis in Greek--translated means "direction". [8]

Yet another objection. Those who bank on human prattle are accustomed to object as follows, "Christ says, 'They honor me in vain', but you say that even human teaching and statutes are of no use to salvation; it still remains that they are useful in the good ordering of the common weal and in good behavior." Answer: Like Christ in Lk. 9:41, I must first of all scold you,

"O you unbelieving and perverse generation. How long shall I be with you? How long shall I suffer you?" Can a state not be good without being mixed up in spiritual pomp and wantonness? How did people rule ere such pomp was generated? Where does that originate which is good for decent government and behavior? Does not every good thing come from above, from the father of lights, James 1:17? Or is there anything good that may come from humankind even though all flesh is nothing other than a brilliant flower which wilts instantly; and aren't all persons liars? Therefore learn to know your weaknesses. If there are any decent laws and teachings on earth, you should know that these are of God and not of men. For God in his providence administers all that is good and turns all that is evil into a good. If then you [97] see good government, take care not to think that this is because of wise persons. If it were human, it would not be good but merely a false appearance. Yet, if it is good, it is also of God who ordains and instructs governments Rom. 13:1. At this point, however, your faith is weak, for you do not yet rightly know that God in his providence surely governs all things; but that which in your folly you ascribe to persons, is really God's. Now of those laws which enable governments to maintain justice, we shall speak later on. At this point we speak only of those statutes, as mentioned above, which are prescribed for people as if those who live by them could thus please God or be saved. This, however, is mere childish folly, for by the grace of God alone may we be saved and through no other thing, as has been pointed out before. From this we deduce that the behavior of only those persons is good who have placed their sole trust in the grace of God, for these are led by the Spirit of God; but whatever is not of the Spirit of God, is nothing other than deceit. But if there are ordinances which are fitting or needful for us, God will teach us those through his word that we may follow and institute them; but in that case they are God's, not ours.

What value then to human governments is the multiplicity of human pretense? Surely none other than great calamity and dissension; for no greater calamity has come upon humankind since the world began than the great rotten number of hypocritical priests, ministers, monks and nuns. These come from nowhere else but from the flesh which is human vainglory; Christ knows no other spirituals than his sheep. Those who have his Spirit are his, Rom. 8:6-8; they are spiritual, Jn. 3:6. Those who appropriate to themselves the term "spiritual" are indeed spiritual--they are of the evil spirit, devilish. Of what were the sheep of God found guilty to have been burdened with those fat oxen, entwined with the ropes of unnecessary statutes, though God states clearly in Deut. 4:2 and 12:32 that nothing is to be added to his law, nor is anything to be taken away though the Spirit of God taught the Apostles all truth and though Paul [98] stated so well in Galatians and in other places that one ought not accept such carnal inventions and burdens. Indeed, he makes such a good case in one place alone that it would be sufficient in itself to reject all human statutes, yes, to forbid them altogether and cast them aside as sinful and anti-Christian, Gal. 3:15, "Thus my brothers, I shall speak plainly with you as everyone may readily perceive. No one adds to or takes away from a human last will and testament which has been probated." Upon this I argue as follows: It is not fitting for anyone to put aside or to add to someone's last will and testament once it is probated. Much less fitting is it to add or subtract anything from God's testament. His testament which he has made through Christ is prophesied in Jer. 31:31 and Is. 55:3 to be nothing other than grace; whoever depends on it shall be made whole; few laws and even fewer artful devices are needed. It is so short and simple that one does not have to learn it from one's neighbor. Rather, as God was faithful toward David, so he shall be faithful toward all those who are persons after the heart of God. Toward them he shall be as merciful as he was toward David. He shall direct them whereto and how they should walk so that they will not need anyone's teaching or law. For everyone shall know God from the smallest to the greatest. In other words, no one shall find it difficult on account of his smallness or weakness; it is not human work or doing, but God's. How did anyone dare chain the mercy and grace of God to their laws and imprison them in such a way that they would open them only to those who listen to their trifling? Why have they added their own works to justification through Christ alone? Why have they caused the word of God to be disbelieved by forcing their words to be believed as much as God's word? Note, what state our flesh, i.e. human or natural reason and wisdom, is in.

From it nothing good can come forth, for it is evil in origin and nature, as God himself said in Gen. 8:21, "The intentions and thoughts [99] or designs of the human heart are evil from infancy." In Latin this reads as follows, [9] "Sensus et cogitatio humani cordis in malum prona sunt ab adolescentia sua; the mind [the senses] and thought of the human heart tend to or are prone to evil from youth." The meaning of this has caused theologians to err a great deal, for which the translator should perhaps be blamed; they have been misled by him when he says, "The senses and thoughts of the human heart tend toward evil." However, he should have said, "The designs, senses or thoughts of the human heart are evil," and not just "tend toward evil". They are evil without any qualification or excuse. The mouth of God expresses these words as follows, "Jezer lib haadam re mimeurau". Those words are so straightforward and clear that neither doubt nor ambiguity may be found therein: "The intention or thought or counsel of the human heart is evil from infancy."

Yet, theologians have tried to deduce from the term "tend toward" the fact that there is merely an inclination toward evil in us and not that we are evil, vain and useless by nature--which has been broken in Adam. [10] From this have sprung the bold opinions about free will, our own abilities, the light of our understanding, which were then followed by human teaching, statutes, the sale of good works and every other hypocrisy. For everyone was able to fool himself in the phrase "tend toward" as if he himself has overcome the tendency; yet knowing full well how it really was at homebase, i.e. in the inner being. But had this word, "human feeling and counsel is evil" been spoken without any equivocation and clearly taught, no one would have dared pride himself with such obvious hypocrisy; for everyone would have know that all our intentions are evil; and however much good might have been drawn out of human wisdom, everyone would have suspected right away that it originated with human wisdom; and since the source is evil, the rivulet itself cannot be good; thus neither human teaching, nor law nor work would have been believed.

To sum up: We learn with certainty from God's word that all our ideas, intentions, thoughts, counsel and insight and our feelings are thoroughly evil. Therefore it follows that everything arising therefrom is evil also, for "no evil tree is capable of bringing forth good fruit," says God in Mt. 7:17. Therefore everything which is not of God is evil. How [100] then can those who claim to be wise and who boast to be able to perfect what Christ himself did not perfect, bring forth any good from themselves if they hear that the trunk is evil? When will they stop their folly? When will they cease to ridicule God? For is not this vile blasphemy of God and a rejection of Jesus Christ when they say they have made whole and perfect what Christ himself has left in an imperfect state? Was he that ignorant that he could not do it? Or was he that weak that he could not carry it through, or so ill-willed that he did not want to do it? He is the divine wisdom and in him all treasures of wisdom are contained. All things have been given him by the Father so that he raised the dead, and led unbelievers to the light of truth. He has come into our time to redeem us and proclaim his grace. How could he be unfavorable toward us?

Look at the end of human audacity when it sets out to defend itself in its own intentions. It leads to a person seeking to justify his folly by God's own ignominy and by claiming to be wiser than God who said to his disciples, however, "When the spirit of truth comes, he shall teach them all truth." Now God does not lie. The spirit has come; and the apostles and all believers have learned truth from him. And God did not, as they say, keep a part of his purposes to himself which he has revealed only now during the subsequent thousand years. This they want to prove from the word which Christ speaks in Jn. 16:12, "I still have to say a great deal to you, but you cannot now bear it. But when the spirit of truth comes, he shall teach you all truth."

Yes, they say, do you not perceive that he did not tell them everything? Therefore he revealed it afterwards to the Holy Fathers because the disciples could not bear it in their own time. Note, how once again they seek to tear God's own word out of his hand to falsify it--in his name. The disciples were of simple understanding before they received the Spirit of God; they understood less still when Christ after Supper spoke to them of his betrayer and of other difficult future things, and cast them into a state of great fear. Now when they were unhappy and sorrowful, he says: "You cannot now [101] grasp the things which I make known to you, but when the spirit of truth shall come, he will teach you all things." He says, "You apostles, he will teach all truth." He does not say, "I shall after this time reveal much more which I did not reveal to you, but I shall reveal it to these or those. Rather he says, "The spirit of truth shall teach all truth to you"--the apostles with whom he speaks. God does not lie. Thus it follows, as reported earlier, that they are instructed in all truth by the Spirit of God. How else could Christ have said on the cross, "It is accomplished," if one were to receive righteousness only through human understanding, flesh or counsel? These are fables.

But how little God is pleased by our intentions, though we think them to be good and just, may be learned from 1 Sam. 15:1f, "Then God ordered King Saul to fight against the Amalekites and to kill every living being among them: women, men, children and old people, also all cattle, horses, cows, donkeys, camels, and to desire nothing for himself from among these. Saul defeated them all, from Havilah to Shur. He took King Agag prisoner, but killed all the people; he kept, however, the best of their belongings of clothes, jewelry and cattle. Therefore God sent the prophet Samuel to him who was greeted by Saul, "You chosen friend of God, I have fulfilled the ordinance of God." Then Samuel said, "What then is all the noise of cattle which I can hear?" And Saul replied, "The people have kept the best cattle for a sacrifice to the Lord." Said Samuel, "God ordered you to fight the Amalekites and to extinguish them totally. Why are you not obedient to the word of God, turning instead a blind eye to the plundering and thus committing evil in the sight of God?" Then Saul answered, "I have been obedient and walked in the way which God showed me. I have taken King Agag prisoner and killed all Amalekites, but the people kept the best specimen of cows and sheep to offer them up to God at Gilgal." Then Samuel said, "Does God desire sacrifice? Does he not prefer obedience to his word? For obedience is better than sacrifice and to listen to God better than kidneys and the fat of rams. For defiance of him is no less a sin than witchcraft and soothsaying. Also, it is equally as evil [102] as idolatry not to trust in him." And thereafter he denied him the kingdom and cut King Agag in pieces.

Note at this point: Saul also thought that he had well weighed the entire matter by ordering the sacrifice of that which God had bidden him to destroy. He sought to improve what he disliked in God's commandments. You hear, however, how God states through Samuel that such arrogance is held to be idolatry in God's sight. For one ought simply to listen to his word and to be content therewith alone. Thus one honors God when through obedience toward his word one recognizes him to be the wisest and most faithful, sure that he orders and governs everything for the best. Whoever is subject to God in this fashion does far better than if he were to make living sacrifices. At this point the false ministers misuse the word concerning obedience, saying, "Note, how good it is to be obedient." But by obedient they understand submission to persons. Yet the intent of the word is to be obedient to God alone.

Since God did not bid these spirituals to be obedient, they act like Saul. Since they seek to improve on God's commandments by their own wisdom (although orders and sects do not come from this understanding, but through human hypocrisy), they make it worse and are rejected like Saul. Then they will shout, "Is one not to be obedient any more?" "Who teaches you that, you rotten tree? Of course, you are taught to be obedient to him who is lord over all things. Do that and you will be obedient in your work to everyone whom you ought, for he bids you be obedient to those who are above you. But orders and sects are not your superiors; regarding them, Christ commands nothing. Rather, he rejects them." More is to follow later concerning the superiors whom we ought to obey. Suffice it to say at this point that the term "obedience is better than sacrifice" should not be applied to human obedience, but rather to divine obedience. From this beautiful story of Saul and Samuel I hope everyone can see how good and well-pleasing to God all that is which comes from human boldness and thought.

Now I should like to bring many more proofs from scripture to sustain this 16th Article; however, on account of brevity, I shall leave it as is. I shall marshal them when my enemies remonstrate. [103]

NOTES

1. See below, Articles 23 and 28.

2. Zwingli may have in mind the donkeys in Palm Sunday processions which were decked out ornately for the occasion.

3. Both A and B have the marginal gloss: "Coat of arms in temple ornamentation". Wealthy donors of liturgical furnishings had their coat of arms engraved to indicate the sources of the donation.

4. An hoc est glaciem super glaciem aedificare.

5. Cf. **Idiotikon** III 1533ff. The term "fule leutschen" refers to a dog in heat who roams the streets; metaphorically, any lazy person with evil intent is meant.

6. Cf. **Idiotikon** IV 2034. An "altbutzer" occasionally describes a teacher of religion who concocts teachings from fragments of orthodox doctrine.

7. This is likely a reference to John Faber's line of argument during the First Zurich Disputation. Cf. Z.1 553.

8. The German term would be "angeben, anzeygen".

9. The reference is to the text in the Vulgate.

10. Recent Zwingli research has stressed the fact that "praesten" is to be understood not only as weakness but as total irreparable break. Cf. G. Locher, **Huldreych Zwingli in Neuer Sicht**, Zwingli Verlag, Stuttgart, 1969, 240. Cf. also Article 2 above.

THE SEVENTEENTH ARTICLE

"That Christ is the one eternal high priest; from this we deduce that all those who pretend to be high priests, oppose the honor and power of Christ; indeed, they reject it."

That Christ is the true high priest is grounded firstly in that he is the highest because he is the only head of all Christians. Of this we have amply spoken in Article 7; for to be head is the same as being the highest. Further, we find that he is high priest in the very sacrifice which he himself has made; for no other priest has ever made such a sacrifice. For even though many good people have died for God's sake they were unable to be a sacrifice for others, much less such a costly eternally valid one. Thus we may well say with David, "Lord who is like you?" Ps. 34, 35:10. This David, speaking in the Spirit of God, has also said that Christ is an eternal priest after the order of Melchizedek. Ps. 109. 110:4, "The Lord has sworn and he shall not regret it. You are an eternal priest, after the order, i.e. in the form of Melchizedek." That this Psalm is to be understood as referring to Christ, he himself attests to in Mt. 22:45 when he quotes it to the Jews, drawing attention to himself from it. Paul also uses it in Heb. 7:21, "The others (i.e. the high priests in the Old Testament), have become priests without an oath; this one, Christ, however, did so by the oath of him who said, "The Lord has sworn an oath which he shall not regret. And this is the oath, "you shall be a priest in all eternity." Thus Jesus has become a sponsor of a better testament. Of the others who have become priests, there were many, because death did not spare them. But this one--Christ--has an eternal priesthood that he may remain a priest for all eternity. Therefore he shall keep it unto all eternity in that he himself has gone to God, alive forever to do satisfaction and to intercede for us. [104] In Paul's words we hear first of all that God, to assure us, has sworn an oath to give humankind a high priest who would be eternal, whose office would not be cancelled, as the priestly office of the Old Testament was cancelled. The reason that his priesthood shall not be cancelled is to be found in God's oath according to which Christ would be an eternal

84

high priest. The reason for cancelling the old priesthood is found in the fact that they had high priests concerning whom God did not swear and oath that they would be eternal.

Secondly, we hear that the excellence of the New Testament is measured by the high priest. For the sponsor and high priest is the one Christ who shall remain high priest forever. From this it follows then that his (i.e. the New) Testament is imperishable and that it is far better than the Old; for that one has been superseded; but had it not been imperfect, it would not have been done away with, Heb. 8:7.

Thirdly, we hear that the difference between the high priesthood of Christ and that of the Old Testament lies in the fact that there have been many of the Old--one after another. For since they were mortal, and priest of a mortal, perishable testament they could not be lasting and eternal. But Christ, who is eternal God with the heavenly Father and the Holy Spirit and who is life, lasts eternally and is imperishable. Therefore his high priesthood also is eternal and will not suffer any successors. Or else, he would not be eternal which, in turn, would mean that God's oath is ineffective; yet he has sworn that he would be high priest forever.

From these words follow the words of the second part of this Article which are as follows: "Those who pretend to be high priests, oppose the honor and power of Christ; indeed, they reject it."

For if power and dignity are Christ's alone, how then does a person dare usurp them? How dare he claim that to be his own which by an oath God has so clearly ordered for his own Son? Is not this to take Christ's honor away? And to fight against God's oath, is that not as much as to make him guilty of a false oath? Is it not to reject God, to despise and ridicule him? Is not this the work of anti-Christ who places himself in God's temple and sets himself above everything which is God's and above all worship of God so that he allows himself to be worshiped [105] as if he were God? 2 Thess. 2:4. Indeed, he allows himself to be called God on earth and desires to be God. Yes, he allows the flatterers to tell him that as soon as he has been elected by humankind he would immediately be full of the Spirit of God and no less powerful than Christ himself. Is not this the abomination of which Christ speaks in Mt. 24:15f in whose spirit Paul undoubtedly expresses the above stated opinion in 2 Thess. 2:4, "When you shall see the abomination of destruction, which has been indicated by the prophet Daniel, standing in the holy place, (let this be read with understanding!), then take flight, etc." Christ has foreseen all these things and therefore expressed a warning. He forbade that we should elevate anyone on earth to be father,

Mt. 23:9, "And there shall be those who lust after honor and riches, who seek to force humankind into taking them to be gods, to worship them and to leave all things in their power and lust, [claiming] that everything is theirs even the soul, not just material goods; and though they pull down unto damnation a multitude of souls, no one should or could object. Is not this the most miserable thing which ever a person has heard? Who does not see that God has afflicted the human race with blindness? For whoever could have been so utterly senseless as not to think to himself: "For heaven's sake, it is without doubt wrong for a person to elevate himself so highly, it is without doubt idolatry and deceit." From this one may clearly deduce that Almighty God in his wonderful judgment has closed our eyes for a while to punish us so that we were not able to see anything, Is. 6:9, Mt. 13:14, in the same way in which at this time he opens the eyes of the simple that they may see, illuminates their minds that they may understand; for it is ever the counsel of God to make his wisdom known to the insignificant and to reveal it through them, Mt. 11:25.

Since then Christ quotes Daniel, I deem it necessary, to clarify what he means, so that everyone may see what human folly leads to, if one puts too much store in it; besides this to show what genuine true believers must suffer when they turn to creatures and away from the creator. Daniel's meaning [106] is as follows (Dan. 6:3ff), "When Daniel was esteemed more highly than the others by King Darius, the rest of the powerful people began to hate him and plotted how they might once again humiliate him or kill him; they agreed in the end that no other God should be called on or worshiped for thirty days but King Darius: he confirmed the law and let it go out." (Note here the folly of these most excellent lords. Where does their folly lead them? It gets them to the point of thinking themselves to be gods). But Daniel was observed turning to Jerusalem and boldly worshiping his Lord God three times daily. For this the king ordered him to be punished and he was condemned to be thrown to the hungry lions; but God guarded him so that he remained unharmed. By this the king saw the power of the God whom Daniel worshiped and he ordered all people to honor Him as a mighty and true God. Moreover, the enemies of Daniel were punished by the same penalty that had been imposed on Daniel. But the lions did not overlook them, they tore them to pieces instantly.

The other place concerning the abomination of destruction i.e. the gruesome folly by which humans dare pretend to be God and put themselves in God's place, turning God out and isolating him, you may find in the 11th chapter of Daniel where you will actually find portrayed an image and prototype of the present age. But now the papists come with this excuse: "No one is so foolish as to take the pope for God; he is taken to be a deputy and ambassador of God; for we poor people who are weak in knowledge and faith, we need a visible person who is above all other teachers and through whom alone faith may be strengthened and made safe, and in whom all differences of opinion concerning scripture may be taken up and resolved."

I answer: Show me first of all where God has ordered him to be his ambassador. You say, Mt. 16:19, "And to you I shall give the keys of the kingdom of heaven, etc." I answer again: You know well that "to give the keys of the kingdom of heaven" does not mean "be my ambassador--take as great a power as I have." Then, too, you know well [107] that those very same keys are not exclusively the pope's or Peter's but they are keys of all those who by the word of God loose and bind; they are common to all those who belong to the common group of disciples, Jn. 20:23.

You may say secondly, [quoting] Mk. 16:17, "In my name they shall drive out devils, speak new or strange tongues, swallow poisons without danger to themselves, etc." Do you not see that the pope and the worthy priesthood has been given power in the name, i.e. in place of Christ, to do these things with the aid of divine power? Answer: First of all, Christ does not promise such to Peter and the apostles alone, but to all believers by saying: "And these signs shall follow after everyone who believes, etc." Secondly he says, "in my name" not "in their name". If then all things take place in the name, i.e. in the power and strength of Christ, how then dare a person appropriate these to himself?

You may say thirdly, Christ asked Peter after the resurrection whether he loved him more than all the others and after he said, "Yes Lord, you know I love you", Christ commanded him, "Feed my lambs" and that for a second and third time, until Peter replied vehemently, "Lord you know everything, you know that I love you." Then Christ said for the third time, "Herd or feed my sheep". Here one hears without a doubt how Peter loved Christ more than the other disciples did and consequently he was also given power over the sheepfold of God. My answer to the first: Show me where Peter claimed to have more love for God than did the other disciples, since you think that Christ's commandment depended on his loving Christ more than did the others. Yes, I say, had Peter claimed that he loved him more than the others, it could not have happened without presumption. Therefore Peter banks entirely on God's knowledge, "Lord you know that I love you; you know also how dearly I love you; how much the others love you, you also know well; how can I claim of myself to surpass them? You know how I love you; you know also how they love you."

Secondly, why do you quarrelsome papists not cling equally much to the Fathers on whose behalf you shout so miserably? Ah, the holy Fathers; shall one not believe them? Why do you yourself not believe them? They all interpret Christ's question [to Peter] and the reason for his asking it three times with reference to his denying him three times so that his threefold denial might thus be amended and that all shame which might have attached to Peter in the minds of the disciples and the believers on account of his denial should be taken from him and diverted.

Thirdly, I ask, does "herd or feed my sheep" mean "be pope in Rome" or "be above all believers?" Did not the other messengers, too, feed the flock of God? Did Paul not work more than any of the others? Note on what solid ground the glory of the pastor of Rome is built. And this I do not say because I envy him the first place. Where there are many, someone has to be first. For in this sense Paul also says that one ought to value another more highly than oneself, Rom 2:3. I say it, rather, so that (since the pope has no confirmation of his pomp and supremacy in God's word), everyone may see how deceitfully they dare bend scripture to suit human wantonness; and further, that everyone, may see that such defence of [his] power is not of God. For wherever one protects the sovereignty of God. there one does not elevate a person's name and no one desires to be the highest or foremost among other believers. Rather, as has been pointed out earlier from Paul's writings, he desires others to increase and to advance before him.

Furthermore, that one may see that the papacy has come from humans; and since it does come from humans, it may also be recalled by them with as much ease as in any given city the mayor or city councillor may be changed if one is burdened with an unskilled one. [1] This I say only with reference to the primacy, for sovereignty is Christ's alone; but the one who assumes the same for himself is an anti-Christ, even though I do not want to appear anxious about primacy, as some of the ancient Fathers [109] were who thought it good if there were a supreme bishop--for there was no primate in those days; God grant what they say about the Chair of Peter. For this reason I did not really concern myself greatly with the meaning of "first" in what Christ says in Lk. 22:26, "Whoever among you seeks to be the greater, let him be the least and whoever seeks to be a leader, let him be as a servant." Since the word of God can neither mislead nor deceive, I would that all power which is used in protecting the authorities or those who are first, were used for the advancement of greater humility; and if one were to let God arrange the spreading of his teaching instead of letting us set up unity out of our own heads, he would see to it that greater unity among Christians would come about, as it was in the beginning at Jerusalem.

I dare say also that since there has been among the scribes a growing reluctance to work, in the word of God, God's word has been forsaken. Otherwise they would practically have to lie down on it, if they hope to guard truth. In short, let everyone see to it, when he is about to be elevated onto the highest pedestal, that he flee, as did Christ when the people wanted to make him king, allowing divine providence to take care of order among the faithful. But here, faith is lacking, for we do not surrender to the word of God. Therefore any human scheming is mere desperation, self-aggrandizement and waggish boldness. That's all on the deputy.

The other part of the objection was that one needs an arbitrator if there is disagreement in the understanding of scripture and a visible representative to assure the simple-minded.

I answer: Who is better able to judge a person's word and how the speaker intended. it than the one who spoke it? Is it not possible that the speaker may have intended a meaning, not understood by anyone else on earth? Note, how in so many ways [110] the **Paradoxa Stoicorum** and the hidden sayings of the Pythagoreans, the questionable answers of false gods and other dark sayings, have been interpreted without being understood by people. [2] How then does any person dare set himself up as judge over the holy word of God by judging out of his own head that this or that is to be the meaning of scripture? But whenever the one who speaks the hidden word himself decides the meaning of that which is doubtful his intention will then be understood. Thus it is nothing but arrogance to look for the meaning of God's word somewhere other than with God alone. Christ teaches this with his own mouth, Jn. 6:45, "They shall all be taught by God" and in Jer. 31:33, "I shall write my law upon the heart of believers." He does not say, "I will place it in the pope's mouth." But in Jn. 16:13, he says, "When the spirit of truth comes, he will lead you into all truth." The Spirit of God teaches God's intention in human hearts not by the pope's mouth nor by that of anyone else. But even if a person were to expound the word, he will, nonetheless, not be able to convert human hearts. In this vein it is written in 1 Jn. 2:20, "You need no one to teach you, but as the anointing--i.e. the invocation of the Holy Spirit--teaches you concerning all things so it is true and there is no deceit in it." Note, who else could teach God's will but God himself, since another cannot know the inner hidden being? How then is he to know the mind and intention of God? The things which are God's, no one knows but the Spirit of God, 1 Cor. 2:11. Nor does it help to say: "If then the Spirit of God teaches everyone whom he wills, he may well teach the pope also." I'll gladly concede that. But I do not want to tie the free will of the Spirit of God so that everyone would have to believe that if someone is pope he may no longer err and that he is set as an overseer of God's word, alone capable of understanding it, so that all persons would have to rely on his understanding. For God reveals it to whom he wills, Jn. 3:8, "The wind blows where it wills. Thus is everyone who is born of the Spirit." In other words, he is touched by God's Spirit, as it pleases the Spirit. How many popes have erred miserably. What was the view Anastasius had of Christ in the Arian controversy? [3] What of Liberius and others with regard to whom you could not boast, [4] "Indeed, they cannot err in the things pertaining to [111] the faith, etc." In short: Of that erroneous controversy I have amply spoken in the booklet concerning the power and certainty of the word of God. [5] Is Christ not with us to the end of the earth? Has his hand or power been shortened or cut off so that he is no longer capable of drawing human hearts to the pure and simple understanding of his word? Enough.

The other part of the controversy: One need not have a visible person in order to believe; for one person never converts another unless the Spirit who draws heart and mind, does so. Though one may need a preacher, he still does not cause the heart to believe; the Spirit and word of God do that. Whoever claims that he assures or decides, is a deceiver and an anti-Christ, for he attributes to himself what is exclusively God's: "The Spirit of God brings about all things in every one," 1 Cor. 12:11. People are no more than stewards and guardians of the word, as Paul teaches in 1 Cor. 4:1. And this, by God, is as true of every person as it is of the pope. For who would want to force or hold back or imprison the Spirit of God, Acts 10:47?

With this, enough is said about the detractors of Jesus Christ who make something of themselves to which no creature is entitled, for they make themselves into God. But whoever wants more understanding of these things, should read Eph. 1; Heb. 5, 6, 7, 8, 9, indeed, the entire epistle and the Book of Revelation regarding the Lamb who alone has power to open the book with the seven seals, etc.

NOTES

1. See Article 61 for a related argument.

2. Does Zwingli intend to suggest that recent interest in the Greek classics, notably among humanist scholars is misplaced? Sebastian Franck was to make a significant attempt to accommodate Greek philosophy to the philosophia

Christi in his publication in 1534 of the **Paradoxa.** Zwingli seems to anticipate Franck and counters his argument on the basis that each text must be its own interpreter.

3. Anastasius II, (AD 496-498, Bishop of Rome), sought to bring about a reconciliation with Constantinople. Because he was condemned in the Gratian Decretals he was considered a heretic up to the 16th century. Cf. J. Doellinger, **Die Papsttafeln des Mittelalters,** 1863, 124. Zwingli quotes both ancient authors in his **Archeteles;** cf. Z.1 292.

4. Liberius, (AD 352-366, Bishop of Rome). Because Liberius took the side of Athanasius in the Arian Controversy he was exiled in AD 355, but re-instated three years later when he condemned Athanasius. Cf. Doellinger, op.cit., 106ff.

5. Cf. **Von Klarheit und Gewissheit des Wortes Gottes** (Sept. 6, 1522) in Z.I 338ff.

THE EIGHTEENTH ARTICLE

"That Christ who offered himself up once as a sacrifice, is a perpetual and valid payment for the sin of all believers; from this it follows that the mass is not a sacrifice, but a memorial of the sacrifice and a seal of the redemption which Christ has manifested to us." [112]

This Article is grounded, first, in the office of Christ. For if Christ is a unique high priest to all eternity who sacrifices nothing but himself, it is impossible for him to be frequently offered up for us. Now he is a unique, eternal high priest, as has been amply shown in the preceding Article; it follows therefore that he cannot be sacrificed more than once. For were the sacrifice to take place more than once, he would not be eternal, but would be like the priests and offerings in the Old Testament which had to be used and taken frequently because of their imperfection. Should, however, Christ, too, have to be repeated, it would be because of imperfection and weakness, as might be clearly discerned from several places in the Epistle to the Hebrews.

Secondly, this Article is grounded in Paul's words, Hebrews 7:26f, "It was fitting that we should have such a high priest, holy, blameless, unstained, separated from sinners, exalted above the heavens, who had no need to offer daily sacrifices for his own and then for the sins of his people; for he, Christ, did this once by offering up himself." Note how Paul shows, firstly, the clean, spotless host, Christ, so that the power of his death and sacrifice be understood the better; then, how he distinguishes the perfection of Christ from that of the priests in the Old Testament [by pointing out] that he had no need to sacrifice for himself.

Thirdly, [the Article affirms] that his death is a perfect sacrifice; that he, having been sacrificed once, cleanses all sins for all eternity and that it need not be repeated like the sacrifice of the priests who preceded him.

Hebrews 9:11f, "But when Christ appeared, a high priest of the good things that before were still to come, eternal salvation came and was born through a greater and more perfect tabernacle, (not made with hands, i.e. not built by us, nor by the blood of goats and calves but by his own blood which once only entered into the holy place, i.e. heaven). The meaning of these words is, in short, that Christ is by far a stronger high priest than were the ancient ones in the Old Testament. These went into a temple or tabernacle which was temporal; for it was made by human hands and they [113] sacrificed, in the same temple, the blood of animals. But Christ did not enter such a temple, but heaven which cannot be destroyed since it is not made by human hands. Neither did he offer the blood of goats or calves but his own blood. Nor did he offer this sacrifice of his death often. Otherwise there would be no distinction between him and the sacrifice of the ancient priests. He has been offered only once. Nor has he cleansed for a short time only, as did the sacrifice of the ancient priests. But by his one unique sacrifice he has gained salvation unto eternity.

Shortly thereafter, however, he says in the above mentioned chapter [Heb. 9:24-28], "Christ has not entered a holy place which is made by human hands, nor was it to be understood as a parable (understand: like the material [physical] temple which has only given us an image of the heavenly temple and dwelling). Rather, he entered heaven itself so that henceforth he may appear in the presence of God on our behalf. Neither has he gone there to offer himself repeatedly like the high priest of the Old Testament who went each year to the holiest place in the temple with strange blood (frombden) i.e. with the blood of animals. Otherwise he would have had to suffer often from the beginning of the world. Instead, he has now appeared at the end of time that he may destroy all sin by offering himself once. As all persons are destined to die once and thereafter the judgment; so Christ, too, is offered up once to take away the sin of the multitude, etc. These words of Paul are in themselves clear enough, viz. that Christ did not go into the temple, but into heaven; that he has not offered the blood of others but his own, and that he has not done this repeatedly. Otherwise his offering would also be insufficient like the sacrifices in the Old Testament. Rather, he sacrificed once only and that in these last days. For just as all persons die only once, and immediately after their death follows the judgment of God, so Christ has offered himself only once through the death he suffered. And after his death follows the taking away of the sin of all, [114] i.e. of all who believe. Likewise, Paul says later in Heb. 10:10, "By that will or submission (understood is: Christ's) we have been sanctified through the sacrifice of Christ, which happened once."

In the same place Paul says further, (Heb. 10:12-14), "Christ, after he offered a single sacrifice for sin, sits in eternity at the right hand of God there to wait until his enemies should be made his footstool. For by a single offering he has perfected and established all who shall ever attain salvation or be sanctified." Here we find the other part of the offering which the simple-minded lack and by which they have been led astray. For it was said, "If we sin daily we must also offer up the sacrifice of the altar daily." But that is a belittling and degrading of the offering. For Christ is such a perfect sacrifice that he--offered but once--fulfills for all eternity or perfects all those who believe in him--who are called saints.

But if he were to be offered up again and again, he would be much like the sacrifices in the Old Testament which had to be offered up repeatedly because of their imperfection. This would mean a belittling and degrading of the perfection of the sacrifice which is Christ who through his death has offered himself up to God for the sins of all who have ever been and ever shall be. For what would it be, had Christ earned salvation for all the Fathers by his death, suffered once, if the same death, offered once only, should not be eternally fruitful on behalf of all who have come after them and satisfy the righteousness of God for all our sins. There would then have to be two Christs, one who perfectly saved the ancient fathers, the other, who less perfectly than the former, suffered death for us. Or else the suffering of the one Christ, might not be deemed as fruitful and good for those believing in Christ in the New Testament as it was deemed for the Fathers, should we have to offer him up frequently. For the ancients never offered him up, but came to God because Christ had first suffered. In the same way also our sins are forgiven and we may come to God on the strength and efficacy of the suffering which Christ endured once, for us and all persons. So costly and precious it is before God that [115] it has become for all eternity the pledge and price for all humankind by which alone they may come to God.

This becomes clearer still in the following form: Christ who is the truth speaks thus in Lk. 22:19, "This is my body, which is given for you." Here "for you" means as much as "for all human-kind". For in the persons of those present then, Christ addressed all believers, as the words of institution indicate clearly, Mt. 26:27f, "Drink all of it, for this is my blood, the blood of the New Testament which was poured out for the remission of sins." In his salvation Christ has observed a tradition which is common also in human tradition. Whoever redeems a prisoner, first offers the ransom money for him. Thereafter, if he is still unclean or disheveled, he washes and cleans him. This form Christ, too, observed, as Luke points out [Lk. 22:19], "He has given his body for our redemption saying, 'This is my body which is given for you'." Note the ransom money is meant to be the "body". Thereafter he cleaned the prisoner by washing him through his own blood, saying in Mt. 26:27, "Drink all of it," etc, as was said above.

This I point out not because I think he accomplished one thing with his death and another by the shedding of his blood, but rather because he himself demonstrated the efficacy of his suffering in two forms of the sacrament so that the simple person may learn, in passing, the efficacy of both kinds. I did not get this out of my own head but from Christ's very own words. From all this we must be rather perplexed by the fact that throughout the church of Rome, the form of the blood has been withheld from the common person even though Christ always expresses it, to be sure, whenever he speaks of the sacrament. Indeed by the "shedding of blood" the full efficacy of his suffering is expressed, frequently in the Epistle to the Hebrews, as you may readily see in the former expositions, and in Eph. 1:7 [116], and Rom. 3:25. Now these words of Christ refer so clearly to his suffering that they become, as we tried to show, a surety, price and payment for our sin, sufficient and inexhaustible for all eternity, as is written in the first chapter of John [Jn. 1:12f]. Thus, as often as we want to go to God we ought to remind him that Christ has suffered for us. His blood is the blood of the eternal testament, i.e. his suffering and sacrifice have paid eternally for human sin, "May the God of peace, who has brought back from the dead the great, and excellent shepherd of the sheep, the Lord Christ Jesus, by the blood of the eternal testament, equip and protect you . . . etc."[Heb. 13:20f].

At this point the papist disagree (I call all those "papists" who respect all human teaching, statutes and vain behavior, along with the word of God; indeed, they esteem these higher. For the word of God may say whatever it will, they will nevertheless defend the opinion of the Romish popes and reject the word of God). Indeed, the papists fight as did Dr. Martin Blansch of Tübingen on the day of the Zurich Disputation. [1] "Yes", he said, [2] "the term 'semel'--'once', in the Epistle to the Hebrews, I understand in this way, 'Christ has been sacrificed once only, i.e. he has been killed or he died,' as it is written in Rom. 6:9, 'mors illi ultra non dominabitur,' [3] 'death no longer has dominion over him', 'but you may sacrifice him up daily without him therefore dying again'." I gave him this answer, [4] "Dear sir, these two opinions are found in the Epistle to the Hebrews. The first, in the tenth chapter [14], 'Christ has perfected by one offering all who are thus sanctified for all time.' Here you have an offering which is so precious that it perfects all believers (called 'saints'), to all eternity. But in order that you may not say now that it is one offering, indeed, which may be offered up frequently, listen, therefore, to the second opinion which is found in Heb. 9:28, 'Christ has been sacrificed once to cancel the sin of many'."

Note first then, "only one sacrifice", and secondly, "offered up once only." Only one and sacrificed only once. How then do you intend to prove to me in light of these words that he may be offered up frequently, when Paul repeatedly says once?

After this he gave me no further reply to my stated opinion, for other speeches broke in. I need not belabor this point any longer to prove that Christ cannot be offered up any more, since the words of Paul, which I cited now and earlier, have shown this clearly, were it not for the slaves of the mass who make a distinction between "offering up" and "death" (which in Christ are the same thing), so that they might keep up their profit. Thus when it is written in scripture, "Christ has been sacrificed for us". It means as much as, "Christ has died for us and for our sin." And again, when it is written, "Christ has died for our sin." It means as much as, "Christ has been sacrificed for our sin." I substantiate this from scripture thus, Heb. 9, (I earlier referred to these words), "Jesus did not enter a holy temple made by human hands which, furthermore, is merely a model of the true temple, i.e. heaven. Rather, he entered heaven so that henceforth he may appear before God on our behalf. Nor did he enter to offer himself up repeatedly like the high priest (read, in the Old Testament), who yearly entered the innermost part of the temple with foreign blood; otherwise, Christ would have had to suffer often since the beginning of the world. Do you see how the two words, "offering up" and "suffering" are interchangeable and have the same meaning? For one, he does not say that he shall sacrifice himself repeatedly [Heb. 9:25]. And immediately following [Heb. 9:26], "or else he would have had to suffer often," i.e. he would have had to offer himself up frequently. For Paul began the above passage with the term "sacrifice" and concluded it with the term, "suffering", without changing the meaning. The same meaning also is found in Christ's words, Lk. 22:19, "This is my body, given for you." "Given for you" means as much as "offered up for you". But when was Christ offered up except when he died on the cross? There our salvation and his testament were fully perfected, as he himself said before he commended his soul to the Father, "It is [118] finished or completed or perfected or accomplished (consumatum est). Only when he suffered death was the work of Christ complete.

The word "offering up" in the form in which we use it here of Christ is "zaba" in Hebrew. [5] This means as much as "to be killed" because the hostages were killed for sin which could not be forgiven without blood, Heb. 9:22. Therefore the Hebrews call the altar "mizbach", for the killed victim was placed on it and burned. The Greeks call what we mean by "offering up" "thyein" which also means "to kill, beat to death or butcher". The Latin terms "sacrificare", "mactare" mean the same, but our word "to offer up" [opfren] does not mean "to kill", but rather "to donate, honor, lend [meiten]. But when we speak of Christ, we must understand "offering" to mean "suffering and dying". For thus it is understood in the language from which we got the German word "to offer up". And as Christ suffered and died only once, he has also been offered up only once. For no one can make the offering but Christ alone who offers himself. See also Isa. 53:4-7; Ps. 39 [40:7]; Heb. 10:10-18, "Now then Christ has offered himself no more than once." Therefore it is blasphemy to say, "We offer him up to whom alone is given to lay down his soul and to take it up again unto himself." Now we want to bring out the meaning of scripture whereby one may learn that "offering" and "dying" or the suffering of Christ are one deed. When we say then that Christ has been offered up for us, we mean that he has redeemed us, and when we say, "Christ has died for us" we understand again that he has redeemed us. If then the deed of voluntary suffering has wrought this and he has suffered once, [it follows] that he has been offered up but once. For his offering, made once, has paid once for all sins, Rom. 6:9f.

Now let us turn to the words, "Christ, risen from the dead, dies no more; death shall no more have dominion over him. For that he died was on account of sin; and that only once." You note in this context that he has suffered death for the sake of sin. Should I ask you then what Christ meant by offering himself for us, you would undoubtedly reply, "He offered himself for our sin." I then go on to say, "If then to be offered up and to have died or been killed have one reason or purpose, namely the taking away of sin, then "to be offered up" and "to be killed" must be one and the same thing. Thus it follows, "if [119] he has been killed once, he has been offered up but once. For this is the perfection of his suffering and death that it is a surety and price for our sins unto eternity, offered to God once on behalf of us poor sinners. Peter says in 1 Pet. 2:24, "Christ himself has borne our sin in his body on the tree, etc." Peter says here that he already has carried our sin; he does not say that he shall carry it, Eph. 1:7, "In Christ we have redemption of sin through his own blood," Col. 1:20, "God has reconciled all things--be they in heaven or on earth--through the blood of his [Christ's] cross." If then Christ by his death has reconciled all people who are on earth when he poured out his blood on the cross and if we are on earth, then our sins, too, and those of everyone who has ever lived, have been recompensed by the one death and offering. All scripture is full of this fact. I think this is sufficient proof to show that the death and offering of Christ is a matter or a thing to which those who are slaves to the mass can no longer bring the counter argument, "He has indeed died once, but he may be offered up frequently." Who has ever offered up Christ? When Christ was offered up on the cross and died, no one offered him up but he himself. Consequently, if you want to offer anything to God, offer up yourself to him, just as he has done for you. How can you say that a person offers up God if this did not take place even when Christ suffered death?

Now follows the second part of the Article which will clearly teach the simple folk everything that is not plain to them as yet.

"THEREFORE IT BECOMES PLAIN THAT THE MASS IS NOT A SACRIFICE BUT A MEMORIAL OF THE SACRIFICE AND A SEAL OF THE REDEMPTION WHICH CHRIST HAS MANIFESTED TO US."

In the earlier part of this Article we mustered strong enough proof that Christ, having died once and having been offered up, is such a precious offering that he saves eternally and redeems all who believe. In order that the papists may have no cause to shout (as is their habit), "O pious Christians, look what these people intend to do; they want to present the body of Christ, our beloved Lord, as being nothing at all [120] and rob us poor people of the celestial food." I intend to show briefly in these words, God willing, how it is with the sacrament. First of all, however, I wish to expose the unworthy clamor of the abovementioned. Tell me, "Who dares rob christendom of the body of Christ?" When I say, "Christ can be offered up only once" and prove it by scripture so many times over that you cannot touch even a single point, have I said then that "Christ is nothing at all" or that "the sacrament of the altar is nothing at all?" Just look how you cloak your greed in another garment so that you may turn the simple folk from the truth in a shameful manner. These people who do not use these elements as Christ has set them up and ordered them, degrade and profane the body and blood of Christ. Rather, they changed the name of the body and blood of Christ and have reduced the receiving of both kinds to one. For that which is a testament, legacy or covenant and memorial, they have called a sacrament or offering. But these names contradict one another. For if a sacrament is an offering why then is marriage or the last unction not an offering, too? If then this body is an offering, as you say, why then do you designate it by the name sacrament? Therefore, listen for the sake of God and truth to the view which I am not drawing out of my own head, but which I shall endeavor to prove from the very words of Christ and Paul.

Firstly, you know the term "sacrament" is an ancient Latin word which did not have the same meaning then as it does now. Rather, "sacramentum" actually meant "oath". If then you wish to call those things "sacramenta" which God has set up by his own word which is so firm and certain as if he had sworn an oath, then many things are not sacraments which we consider to be sacraments--for God has not spoken of them--such as confirmation, ordination, [i.e. the consecration of a priest], extreme unction, in the manner in which we use them. On the other hand, some would be sacraments which we don't look upon as such, e.g. almsgiving--for of it God has spoken, "What one does to the least in his name, he intends to honor as if it had been done to him"--without fail. The ban, too, would be a sacrament. For Christ said, "What the church binds is [121] to be bound in heaven also;" absolutely. Thus it ought to have the form of a sacrament.

But the theologians do not interpret sacrament in this way. Rather, they say, "sacramentum est sacre rei signum--sacrament is a sign of a holy thing." If then the body and blood of Christ is a sign of a holy thing, I should really like to know what it signifies, and if it only signifies, how can it be a sacrifice? How do you theologians tolerate that the body and blood of Christ are subsumed under the term sacrament, when sacrament is merely a sign of a holy thing? Yet you have carefully investigated how the substance of bread may be transformed into the substance of the body, etc. Even a child can tell you that you have not properly explained the word "sacrament" when you say, "yes, it is a sign of a holy thing." For the body and blood of Christ are not a sign, according to your teaching, but a sacrifice. If a sacrifice, how then can it be a sign, even before the New Testament? But take note that "sacramentum", which you have used according to your whim, now means as much as "sacred mystery" or "a sacred, hidden thing". But why do you want to give such a name to the wholesome body and blood of Christ, since thereby the simple person is only made more ignorant? Why did you not leave its original name, calling it the body and blood of Christ, as Christ himself and Paul have called it? You say, "We do call it thus." Why then do you call it a sacrament, using an unknown name--just as the last unction is so called--instead of "body and blood of Christ"?

You say, "What is this crafty differentiation of 'sacrament' good for?" My answer, "Good for nothing, to be sure, except to show that you handle the sacraments imprudently and that you have forced the body and blood of Christ under the term 'sacrament', even though your definition does not fit it, since you consider these to be a sacrifice." Yet, the body and blood of Christ is more sacred than to be contained by the term "sacrament" (by which you mean a sign of a sacred thing). But you have found a benefit in your error in that you now overpower the simple [122] who are unwilling to place any confidence in your consecration as you shout, "No one places any value on the sacraments any more." As a result they become uncertain and think that one rejects the body and blood of Christ, baptism, marriage and the forgiveness of sins; for they do not know the meaning of sacrament. If, however, you are willing to call "sacramentum" a sure sign or seal, I can well accept your calling it a sacrament; but your definition or exposition does not allow for this meaning. For in the form in which you use them, you will have to discard your consecration and last unctions, for you cannot justify them on the basis of the word of God. I allow that extreme unction is a kindly visitation of the sick person. But one cannot say that it has an express word of God in which one may firmly believe. I allow that confirmation is a sign somewhat like a white garment. [6] But to consider it a sacrament on which God has spoken an express word and made a promise in his word, cannot be allowed. Since we have come to talk about confirmation, I shall now state my opinion concerning it.

CONCERNING CONFIRMATION

I believe that confirmation has arisen (since neither holy scripture nor the Fathers make any mention of it, I have to content myself with guess work), because it was realized that children who confessed their faith through father, mother or god parents and not with their own lips, ought to confess it in their own hearts and with their mouths when they reach the age of understanding. They were thus led to the priest to be well instructed in the faith and after due instruction to confess it publicly before everyone. [7] This is supported by the fact that even in our day, when done rightly, one preaches the faith before one confirms. Nonetheless, there are some consecrating bishops now who commonly proclaim that confirmation is of sacred character and that one ought to bring recently baptized and immature [123] children so that the sacrifice be the greater for it. But I have learned from the Fathers that one used to ask the person about to be confirmed for his name. After that he was asked whether he is able to repeat the Confession of Faith and the Lord's Prayer; only then was he anointed with consecrated oil or chrism.

From these customs and from the fact that one still asks the name, I am led to think that confirmation came into use at the time when children were generally baptized in infancy and subsequently right after birth, so that the faith which father, mother and god parents affirmed for them did not remain unknown to them. Yet, although I know, as the Fathers indicate, that children were baptized from early times, I also know that the practice was not as common as it is in our day and age. Rather, together they were instructed publicly when they reached full understanding. For this reason they were called "catechumeni" i.e. those that testify to the word of salvation. And when they had faith firmly established in their hearts and were able to affirm it with their lips, they were baptized.

This manner of instruction I should like to see adopted

again in our own day, namely that inasmuch as children are baptized so early, we undertake to instruct them when they reach that degree of understanding at which they are capable of hearing the word of God. Otherwise they might be at great disadvantage which could be harmful to them, should they not be well instructed in the word of God right after baptism, as the young were instructed in times past, before baptism. Several sermons of the Fathers addressed to catechumens (i.e. those who were instructed in the faith and in the teaching of God) still point this out to this day.

For this reason we started about a year ago right here in Zurich to call together all youths twice a year, [8] to teach them all together to know God and then to make known to them his word and how they are to conduct themselves toward him and toward their neighbor; further, how they are to relate to him as to a sincere, dear father and run to him in all distress of body and soul. We do this during the Easter season and a second time in late fall or at Christmas on Innocent's Day [December 28]. I believe, confirmation ·should be handled thus, so that those who were earlier baptized without their knowledge might then themselves confess their faith, knowingly [124] but only after they have been well informed in the matter of salvation. This is indicated also by the term "confirmatio" which means an affirmation. However, if confirmation were to be a memorial of the coming or receiving of the Holy Spirit, it should go by another name. I know well what the Master of the **Sentences** writes on this matter; [9] it does not bother me at all. To stress its seriousness, the act of anointing was added; this the theologians have turned into a sacrament, but the consecrating bishops have left out the most important feature, viz. instruction in the word of God.

I want to say by this, that I am not greatly concerned whether they call holy water, incense and such things **sacramenta** if they had only not obscured the meaning of baptism, and of the body and blood of Christ by using the term "sacrament". For there must ever be a distinction between the things God has instituted and those which humans have set up. If you are going to call baptism and the blood of Christ sacraments you should not use the term sacrament in common with things which have been thought up by human brains. Otherwise you elevate human reason and elementa to a place next to God. But if you insist on dressing up with the name "sacrament" a thing which has been thought up by human minds, you should not subsume under that same name the things which come from God. I say this regarding the meaning of the term sacrament, as the theologians have used it up to now. But if you apply the term "sacrament" to anything which is blessed or consecrated then not only [125] confirmation, chrism and blessing but also holy water, incense, cakes and the consecrated St. John's drink, become sacraments. [10] Therefore those who oppose the teaching of Christ, rant without cause when they shout that one does not make anything of the sacraments. For if you understand **sacramentum** to be a sign, blessed or consecrated by the word of God or of persons, then there are even more than seven sacraments.

If, however, you mean by **sacramenta** those signs or seals which God has given, sanctified and established in his own word, those which are derived from the prestige and word of persons must not be called sacraments. Therefore, when I call the body and blood of Christ or baptism a sacrament, I mean by sacrament what was first said of it, namely that which has been instituted by the unerring sure word of God. When I call the other consecrated things sacraments, I understand by sacraments, a sign which is blessed by the word of God or by human word. But in the way which the theologians define sacrament, it cannot in that meaning have anything in common with the sacrament of the altar. But it is utterly foolish to quarrel so unpeaceably on these matters, as some do; for what does it matter to me what term the Romans gave to holy things? "Sacramentum" is a Latin term; the Greeks did not use it. They used "musterion", but not with the same meaning as the Latin **sacramentum**. We Germans do not need the term sacrament. The things that are holy to us are: baptism, the body and blood [of Christ], marriage, grace of God or forgiveness of sins, chrism, confirmation, dedication [consecration] or intercession or benediction. Thus each is known by its name.

Since I have spoken of confirmation, it is not inappropriate that I also speak of chrism. Of it James 5:14f. writes, "Is someone among you sick, let him call the elders of the parish [126] or congregation [11] and the same shall pray over him, anointing him with oil in the name of the Lord. And the prayer of faith will restore the health of the sick person or save him and the Lord will raise him up; and if he has committed sins, he will be forgiven." By these words of James, the papists prove that the anointing is a sacrament. Yet James here has taught nothing other than sincere sympathy for and visitation of the sick; one ought to heal them with anointing by oil; he says nothing of consecrated oil, but only of oil as such. Neither does he ascribe the forgiveness of sin and salvation to the oil, but rather to prayer for the sick which is made in faith by the leaders of the church. This anointing is not supported by any word of God which states firmly that sin is forgiven in the sign of the anointing; rather it is ascribed to prayer. According to their opinion, prayer, then, would be a sacrament. But let no one be troubled by the term sacrament, as stated above. Of what concern is a Latin term to us which was poorly understood even by the Romans? We know that baptism, the body and blood of Christ and marriage have been instituted by God, that the forgiveness of sins is grounded in the word of God, that anointing and confirmation are sincere endeavors, [opus charitatis], used by us, but only after the right and essential work. Anointing is inferior to prayer; confirmation or chrism is inferior to the word of faith; we shall deal with that there, [i.e. when the topic is being discussed]. The same might be said of consecration. I might easily tolerate those to be anointed with oil or butter to whom the word of God has been entrusted; if certain blockheads were not so foolish as to regard these as sacred from then on and to behave in such a silly fashion that it were better by far to cease the anointing altogether.

Pardon me, dear brother in Christ, for not having immediately completed the matter of the body and blood of Christ, as I had promised. It so happened that I had to stray off the subject at this point and speak of the term sacrament on which some people have so foolishly ventured, going on a wild goose chase. [12] Yet in German we do not need the term, [127] for even though we have it, we do not know its meaning. Let everyone call a thing by the name he fully understands; let him not burden himself with foreign words. Christ did not ever use the term sacrament; yet he is the source of the wholesome things which we call **sacramenta**. Nonetheless, we wage such a battle on how stones, earth and lowly persons [13] may become holy because of the anointing of bishops engaged in simony. Let the anointing be a pleasant custom; for it is not at all grounded in the word of God. Nor is it sufficient to call it a sacrament; give it a more clever name. But if you insist on calling these things sacraments I do not want you to uphold them alongside the sacred signs which Christ has instituted. Nor do I want you to call the divine signs "sacraments" if you use the term to indicate the act of anointing by masquerading bishops; [14] for sacraments are more worthy than to be placed alongside signs, invented by people.

I have clearly and sufficiently shown (as stated above), that Christ should and could have been sacrificed once only. It is appropriate to him alone, who offered himself up to God, to be sufficient ransom for the sins of everyone unto all eternity. Consequently the mass is not a sacrifice, (such could have been offered once only), but a memorial of a sacrifice. It is a warranty of salvation through Christ to the weak by which they may recognize the merits they have received. But they must believe with understanding that Christ has paid for their sin on the cross, and that they eat and drink his flesh and blood in this faith, knowing that it has been given them as a seal of the fact that their sins are forgiven, as if Christ had only now died on the cross. So powerful is Christ and present at all times; for he is an eternal God. Therefore his suffering, too is eternally effective, as Paul says in Heb. 9:14, "How much more shall the blood of Christ--who has offered himself up to God, spotless, through the eternal Spirit-- [128] cleanse our conscience, etc."

Paul here does not speak for nothing of Christ having offered up himself to God through the eternal Spirit, for in the Latin version [i.e. the Vulgate], we read, "per spiritum sanctum"-- through the Holy Spirit. For Paul explains in the same context how Christ, though offered up once only, has become forever a gate and a valid offering for the sins of everyone. And since he is eternal Spirit and God, his suffering, too, is effective for ever. Simple folk should learn at this point not to quarrel about whether or not the body and blood of Christ is to be eaten or drunk (no Christian doubts this), but whether it is a sacrifice or merely a memorial. This comes about because the erring priest- lings teach two contradictory things. The first thing they teach is that the mass is a sacrifice. They have taken in more from this teaching than the cash of all lords and princes down to our own day put together. The other thing is that they themselves use a large portion of the bread while they give only a small bit to the common people. And should one ask them about the form of the blood, and why they do not give it to the common Christians, they reply that one should pay no attention to the matter, for there is no distinction. One who eats Christ in small portions, eats no less than the priests; in themselves both are the same. But if you say: If it is the same, why then do you call your portion a sacrifice? And how is it that mine is not a sacrifice? If mine is not a sacrifice, yet both are the same, yours cannot be a sacrifice either. At this point they begin to draw distinctions. They apply the words of Christ to themselves only. If that were really true--as it is not, of course--the body and blood of Christ would belong to priestlings only. Far be it from us to think that. Let the simple person remember this objection. The moment you stuff it down their throats, they choke on it, unable to swallow it. If it is a sacrament, how then can yours be a sacrifice, yet mine not? Are offering and sacrament one and the same thing? In order that the deception may be uncovered, when they say that theirs is a sacrifice, let us look at the matter more closely.

Whatever a person sacrifices, be it ever so dear, is less precious than if he offered up himself. Therefore Christ [129] offered up himself so that as mediator he may offer to God the highest that he had. But how can a person offer up God? If he wishes to offer up to God the greatest possible sacrifice, he must do like Christ, he must offer up himself, for Christ did not offer up another, but himself. Even if a person were to offer up Christ, it would really not touch him, but Christ. And if the offering of Christ is nothing other than to suffer death for us wretched sinners, as has been shown above, it would have to follow that anyone who offers up Christ now, crucifies him. But no one can make the supreme sacrifice except he were to offer up himself. Who dares to offer up Christ when no one can do so except he himself? Is a human being higher than Christ to be able to offer up Christ yet preserve and save himself? "Go, offer up yourself to God, if you ever wish to make a sacrifice." You say, "How"? "Go on, deny yourself and carry your cross after Christ," Lk. 9:23f, "Whoever wants to follow me, must deny himself and take up his cross daily and follow me. For whoever desires to keep his soul (i.e. to preserve himself), shall lose himself; whoever loses his soul for my sake, shall preserve it, etc."

To deny oneself is a great sacrifice; for a person is always great in his own eyes. He says to himself, "You are deserving of so many riches and honors; you are wise and beautiful and clever." If he then denies this opinion of himself so that he has no worth even in his own eyes (that's what makes him poor in spirit), he has, indeed, denied himself. It follows then that he will take up his cross. As long as a person lives in this world, he is never without a cross. If he is not poor in spirit, as stated above, and if he has not denied himself, he carries his cross; but he is carrying it after the devil. But even though he denies himself, he is not free of the cross. Rather, he will have to take up his cross, i.e. he will bear everything with patience whether it be something that is opposed to God and himself or whether it be pleasing to God, but not to himself. He must patiently endure all sickness, pain, and the loss of goods and consider as worthless any honors. He must chase off the devil who attacks us most effectively by bestowing lavish honors and glory upon us. He must follow the Lord through unceasing suffering and with great sweat and labor. In other words, as he has given himself [130] to suffer for our sakes, we too should likewise give ourselves for his sake and bear all suffering. We call that "following him", if we do as he has done. Indeed, if you intend to offer up anything to God, why not offer up your arrogance? Deny yourself, your possessions, your soul, i.e. yourself, or your soul, i.e. the mind and will of your spirit; for the human will and spirit are proud. This I have said by way of introduction so that everyone might understand what the term "sacrifice" actually means and that the highest sacrifice is to offer up oneself. On the other hand, no one can offer up a person except for that person himself. Likewise, no one may offer up Christ, except he himself; and he has done that once only. Thus the act in which we engage daily must needs be a memorial of the sacrifice of Christ, accomplished once and for all. It cannot be a sacrifice.

Let us now cite the words of Christ and Paul by which we may understand the entire matter more clearly.

Mt. 26:26-28 states it as follows, "When they were eating supper, Jesus broke the bread which he had taken and blessed. He gave it to the disciples, saying, 'Take, eat; this is my body'. And when he took the cup for which he gave thanks also, he gave it to them saying, 'Drink of it; all of you; for this is my blood;

the blood of the new covenant which is poured out for the many for the forgiveness of sin'." These words are clear and familiar to everyone. You do not have here, however, a reference that implies that he ordered his body and blood to be sacrificed. He says, indeed, "This is my blood, the blood of the New Testament which is poured out for the many for the forgiveness of sin." From these words you may actually note that the pouring out of his blood has taken away the sin of the many, i.e. of the believing world. It follows then that the pouring out of the blood and the death are the sacrifice by which our sin has been paid up. For if his sacrifice has paid for our sin and if the shedding of his blood has paid for our sin and if his death has paid for our sin, it follows that "sacrifice", "the shedding of blood" and "his death", are one and the same thing. It follows further, when Christ dies and sheds his blood, he offers up himself. Now he does not die any more, Rom. 6:9, therefore he [131] is not offered up any more; but rather, in keeping with his own words, stated here, when his blood was shed, sin was remitted and forgiven. Since we have in these words of Christ the term, "blood of the New Testament", it seems necessary for me to give my understanding of the term "testament".

Testamentum, pactum and **foedus** are often used interchangeably in scripture. But testamentum is used most often. We therefore refer to it here. It means "legacy", but it also used to mean "agreement" or "covenant", the latter of which one usually makes between two people for the sake of peace. In this sense one speaks of the Old or the New Testament, i.e. the covenant, agreement and commitment which God has entered in with the patriarchs and which in Christ he entered in with the whole world. But as often as an agreement was reached in the Old Testament between God and the friends of God, it was customary to strengthen the same through blood and sacrifice. Read of Noah and Abraham and you will see. Better still, read Exod. 24:3-8, "When Moses had read all the ordinances of God to the people of Israel and when they had submitted themselves to these, he ordered twelve calves killed according to the twelve tribes and had them offered up to God. Then he took the blood and sprinkled it on the book of the law, Heb. 9:20, and upon all the people, saying, 'This is the blood of the covenant, which God has made with you in accordance with his words and ordinances, etc'." We note the likeness of the words of Moses (by which he affirmed the testament), to the words of Christ, concerning his blood. Everyone can see. thereby that Moses' act was a sign of that which Christ has done. For when God made a covenant and legacy with the people of Israel and their descendants (i.e. a testament), death and bloodshed were involved--but of dumb animals only, as stated earlier. But when Christ made his testament with humankind, a covenant and legacy which would last unto all eternity, he did not sacrifice by killing animals but by offering himself. He did not sprinkle us with the blood of animals but with his own blood which he bid us drink for a sign of an eternal testament--since it flowed from him [132] who is eternal God--we were not to paint the doorpost with it nor sprinkle our skin, but our inner soul was cleansed thereby.

Now then, where there is a testament it can be executed only after the death of him who has made it, Heb. 9:15-17. Hence, when Christ left us an inheritance by grace that through him we may become sons and heirs of God, he died, thus to strengthen his legacy with us. He has given us his flesh as food and his blood as a drink unto our souls, so that our hope might have a seal and sign and that we, too, when we die, might receive the inheritance of which he has made us heirs. Therefore Luke calls the blood of Christ not only "the blood of the covenant" but rather "testament" in the following words, "This drink (I thus translate the term 'poterion'), is the new testament or covenant in my blood which is poured out for you." These words bring to our attention that the New Testament is confirmed by the blood of Christ. Indeed, that it is the very testament itself so that all of us are saved by virtue of the shed blood (that is as much as to say the suffering and sacrifice of Christ); for salvation is often credited to the blood of Christ which derives from the death of Christ, as shown above. And this takes place in order that the blood may be credited with affirming the testament. It is further given us, as a seal of that which has been agreed on once, yet is effective for all eternity and serves as food and drink.

Before we turn away from the words of Matthew we wish to point out that Christ has bid everyone in unmistakably clear words to drink from his cup, i.e. his blood, when he said, "Drink ye all of it." The fact that the term "all" has not been added when speaking of the bread, does not mean that bread is to be withheld from anybody. Rather, the words have the same meaning in Greek and Latin, viz. that all of us are to eat his body. I put my full confidence in God's providence by which this word "all" has been added to the figure of the blood, because [133] it anticipated some bold people who would dare withhold the element of the blood from some persons. But in order that this may not happen, he has given the express directive which could not possibly be any clearer: "Drink ye all of it". He who says "all" does not exclude anything. How then did these foolish persons presume to change or to shorten the order and institution of this holy good, particularly since God's word is so clear? And especially since the two kinds are publicly used in German lands, and in Switzerland if not elsewhere, and are given to women and men, to young and old. I am able to demonstrate this from certain knowledge. When I was pastor of the honorable citizens of the country of Glarus, I discovered a church register [obsequial] at Mollis which is a book used for entering baptisms, marriages and deaths. Though it was old, it was still in one piece and unchanged. I found there a Latin entry, made immediately after the baptism of a child. It said, "Thereafter one ought to give the child the sacrament of the Eucharist and likewise the cup of the blood." I do not want to make too much of the fact that the sacrament was given to children. [15] Rather, I want to prove by these words that the celestial food was distributed in both kinds in our country. Among them were the honorable gentlemen, Mr. Adam, then pastor at Mollis; Gregory Buentzli, pastor at Weesen and John Varschon, pastor at Kerenzen. In this year the learned Valentine Tschudi, my successor at Glarus and John Heer [16] have come to me, pointing out that they had found similar church registers in their own parishes. These were so much like the one at Mollis that they thought one had been copied from the other because the above mentioned opinion was expressed in the same manner. [17] How long this custom existed in the area of Glarus, [134] I was unable to determine. It is, however, not more than two hundred years that such a book has been used in Mollis, for I found old church letters concerning their separation from Glarus. These are about two hundred years old. Before this separation, as anyone knows, they did not have a church register in the church for they did not administer sacraments in that church. One must assume therefore that said church register was a copy of the Glarus register and used in the new parish. I point this out in such detail and with reference to witnesses who are still alive and very much my brothers in Christ Jesus in order that one may see that it is not heresy to eat the food of the soul, Christ, in both kinds. Rather, it is proper and more like the institution of Christ than if we partook of it in one kind only. I want to have it said at this point that I do no wish to deny that those also fed on Christ who, either from ignorance or by force had to be content with the bread only; for if they believed Jesus Christ to be their salvation, they found their salvation in faith though they had been denied both kinds. Yet, I cannot excuse from having sinned and done evil those who have withheld the cup from common persons. They have been too shameless in withholding the cup, for as we pointed out earlier, nothing should be added to or taken away from the word of God. However, I am not quite sure when the modifications were made. First of all, I think that when Rome set out to have all christendom take its laws, orders and directions from her, she made sure with great care to draw attention to every tradition, practiced there. This is still apparent in all rescripts or replies. Here, too, as soon as the custom of nourishing the common person with one kind only was begun in Rome, she drew [135] other nations into the same habit or misuse. This enabled her to overcome and rule in those matters also, which she had initiated against the word of God from ignorance or because of sheer malice.

Secondly, I guess that the false priests attempted to

stress the fact that the mass is a sacrifice, in the hope that simple persons when seeing the so-called spiritual ones drinking the blood which they themselves did not drink might thus believe more readily that the mass is a sacrifice. Their usual reason for withholding the blood namely, that it is not too easily handled and much more readily spilled than the body, is a rather lame excuse. For if the "accidents"--as they call them--are "sine subjecto", it is quite impossible for the body or the blood of Christ to drop to the ground. Only the accidents would fall down, anyway. Observe, how well-founded their teaching is. Moreover, one could handle the blood with such suitable vessels that nothing at all would be dishonored.

Mark relates this matter as follows in chapter 14 [Mk. 14:22-24], "As they ate, Jesus took bread, gave thanks to God, broke it, i.e. distributed it and gave it to them saying, 'Take, eat, this is my body'. And when he had taken the cup and given thanks, he gave it to them and they all drank of it"--take note, he said "all"--and he said to them, "This is my blood, the blood of the new covenant or of the New Testament which is shed for everyone." These words need no further discussion.

Likewise, we read in Luke 22:19f, "And when he had taken bread and given thanks, he broke it and gave it to them, saying, 'This is my body, given for you; this do in remembrance of me'. In the same manner also the cup, after supper, saying, 'This cup is the new testament in my blood, which has been shed for you'."

Weigh firstly the words concerning the blood. He says, the cup--meant is the drink, found in it--is the New Testament in my blood. It is customary for the Hebrew to use "in" when we use "with" or "of"; e.g. when they say, "in a strong hand" we say "with a strong hand" or "through a strong hand" or "by the strength of the hand". [136] So also here, when Luke records the words of Jesus, he uses them according to Hebrew usage. They mean: "The drink is the new testament or covenant which has been established through the blood which I have shed for you or which has power and a firm base in my blood which was shed for you. You note, first of all, that redemption is ascribed to the blood which is of the death and suffering of Christ; this is all the more reason not to withhold the cup. Secondly, the redemption which has been wrought in the suffering and the shedding of blood, is perfected through his statement that a testament has been made by the blood which was shed for us. We hear rightly that at the very moment it was shed, the testament was brought into effect. Yet, since it has not been shed in our age, it is therefore not a sacrifice but a memorial and renewal of that which Christ has once poured out and which has made us whole for all eternity.

Having mustered such strong proofs from scripture, it is apparent then that the holy nourishment [18] of the soul is not a sacrifice, but rather a memorial and renewal of that which took place once and is strong and precious enough unto all eternity and satisfies God's righteousness on behalf of our sin. Proof of this is found in the very words of Christ which we just heard in Lk. 22:19f, "This do in remembrance of me." Had Christ intended the food of his body and blood to be a sacrifice, he could easily have said, "This offer up unto me." But he says instead, "This do in remembrance of me." It means, "Practice it among you so that you may eat my body and drink my blood in remembrance of me, which is to renew through recollection the good deed which I have shown to you." This interpretation becomes clearer still when we listen to Paul's words.

He says in 1 Cor. 11:23-26, "That which I have given you, I received or learned from the Lord, namely, that the Lord Jesus in the night in which he was betrayed took bread and broke it and after having given thanks, he said, 'Take, eat, this is my body which is broken for you, this do in remembrance of me.' In the same manner also the cup (read, he took the cup), after supper, saying, 'This cup--meaning the drink--is [137] the New Testament in my blood. This do as often as you drink it in remembrance of me. For as often as you eat the bread and drink the cup, you proclaim the Lord's death until he comes'." Above all, I say that everyone who considers these words of Paul must, surely discover how wickedly christendom is treated by those who have withheld from it the mode of the blood, since he says, "As often as you shall eat the bread and drink the cup, etc." For Paul has conjoined both of them, as Christ has done who taught him. Thereafter he makes clear the meaning of remembrance by reference to the cup. "For as often as you shall eat the bread and drink the cup," he says, "you proclaim the death of the Lord until he comes again." With these words he intends to say no less than this: that as often as we shall partake of his flesh and blood, we should recall thereby the great peace and tranquility which Christ has secured for our poor soul by his death, and thus proclaim this great deed, i.e. praise, rejoice, and testify among men until the last day. Note, Paul actually underscores the word remembrance and what it actually is. For it is nothing other than a sincere thanksgiving for the great deed and a memorial of his humble suffering by which he has united us with God. This undoubtedly has made the believing person so happy that he cannot sufficiently proclaim and praise the great work of God. This is to continue until he shall come again on the last day. It shall not ever be anything other than a memorial of that which took place once and is to continue as a remembrance of the suffering of Christ and of how wholesome it was and ever shall be. Now then, if it is a memorial it cannot be a sacrifice, for a sacrifice is not a memorial. Christ does not annul his words; neither does Paul. Hence the eating of this food is a memorial and not a sacrifice.

Therefore I called several years ago, the eating of this food a memorial of the suffering of Christ and not a sacrifice. But after some time, Martin Luther called this food a testament. I gladly concede his point; for he named it [138] after its nature and characteristics. I have named it according to custom and the manner of eating the food. There is no real difference in the two names. For Christ used both terms and so did Paul. The meaning is as follows: The blood and death of Christ are the things in which the new and eternal testament is grounded. Thus all who desire to be friends and children of God, cannot come to it, except through the blood of Christ. As soon as they believe that Christ has redeemed and cleansed us by his suffering and blood, they have. become children of God for this is the testament which Christ has established with his very own blood. Thus the term "testament" points to the nature, quality and essence of the body and blood of Christ; therefore, I gladly withdraw my own term. But the term "memorial" has its name from the custom we have, namely, that whenever we eat and drink the body and blood of Christ--which are a testament of Christ--we do so in remembrance of that which has been transacted once only.

In keeping with God's word I called this a memorial in order to put down the opinion of those who made it a sacrifice. Take an example. That which we are accustomed to inherit from another person is called property or possessions. But in order for someone to inherit it, it has to be ordered and confirmed through a last will or legacy. The inheriting afterwards is no more than a receiving and enjoying of that which was once actually transacted and willed. Thus, in this case, the property which has made us, who were at one time evil, good and children of God, is the body and blood of Christ. To make sure of this, he himself said through his word that such will and testament is set up through his blood. To document his intention he has given us this testament for food and drink and has bid us do this in remembrance, whenever one takes and eats.

Lastly then, the taking and eating of this testament is none other than a memorial of that which was transacted once so that when we take and enjoy the property of this testament, we do no more than fully believe that Jesus Christ, the guiltless one who was sacrificed and killed just once for us poor sinners--has made amends for our sins before God and paid the ransom for all eternity. As a surety he has given his own flesh and blood for our nourishment so that we, as often as we enjoy this food, proclaim the death, i.e. the redemption and sacrifice of Christ, giving thanks that he our salvation [139] has so generously affected and strengthened our salvation by his dying once and for all.

Therefore all those who believe that Jesus Christ is our "pledge" and recompense, should approach the table, even though they may be the greatest of sinners. For if they have such faith as we have delineated here and elsewhere, they are never again to be called sinners, but sons of God. For in everyone who confesses that Jesus is the Christ, i.e. everyone who knows that Jesus is the anointed savior of God, God is and shall remain; he is born of God, i.e. the Spirit of God has taught him this, 1 Jn. 5:1. This food has been given to poor sinners unto salvation and not unto damnation.

At this point the papists object and misquote the words of Paul in 1 Cor. 11:27 when he says, "Everyone who eats the bread and drinks the cup unworthily is guilty of the body and blood of the Lord." They say, "See, no one is to go to the table unless he be worthy, as Paul himself says." And should you retort, "And how is one to be worthy?" they reply, "One must have done penance, one must have gone to confession and be without any mortal sin." See, what confused people they are who do not believe the word of God and who do not understand scripture. If it were true that no one should approach the table, except he be without sin, not a single person would be alive who could approach the table, for no one is without sin. And if we were to say that we are without sin, we would deceive ourselves and the truth would not be in us. 1 Jn. 1:8.

If then no one is without sin, how then is one to approach the table worthily, since "worthily" is taken to mean "without sin"? Therefore, "unworthily" here does not mean "with sins", as you would have it. Rather, it means as much as "not in the right attitude" in the Lord's eyes; i.e. someone approaching in a manner other than that which the Lord approves. Therefore the Fathers read, "the one who eats or drinks unworthily in God's sight, i.e. one who eats and drinks other than in the way which God has established, is guilty of the body and blood of Christ."

And Paul uses these words in the conviction that there were some, to which he also refers earlier in chapter 10 [1 Cor. 10:14-22], and now in this eleventh chapter, who thought that it behooved them to partake and eat of the sacrifice, offered to idols. However, Paul does not grant them this at all, saying, 1 Cor. 10:21, "You cannot drink both [140] the cup of God and that of Satan. You cannot share the meal or table fellowship of the Lord and the meal of the devil." According to this, they indulged excessively when going to the table of the Lord, as if they were at a festival for idols which Paul also forbade them to indulge in, in the course of chapter eleven. Even one who is half blind can easily see from these two abuses that Paul's term "unworthily" is to be taken to mean "inappropriate" or disorderly and not, as we have heard its meaning to be, viz. "Whoever eats this bread and drinks this cup unworthily, i.e. the one who does not honor the food and its value any more than if it were only debauched food, sacrificed to idols, or the one who in addition also wishes to eat and drink of the sacrifice, offered to idols, is guilty of the flesh and blood of our Lord."

Undoubtedly, because this is so, such a person fails to distinguish and differentiate between food offered to idols and body and blood of Christ. Therefore Paul goes on to say in the same passage [1 Cor. 11:28f], "Let a person examine himself, i.e. before he takes this food, he ought to recall how he esteems this food and whether he has the right faith which it requires. Only then should he eat and drink. For whoever eats unworthily, i.e. without the right faith and proper instruction, eats and drinks unto his own judgment, because he does not discern the body of Christ." Note how this one word, "discern" indicates that worthiness depends on whether or not the food of Christ is properly distinguished from other types of food and is not considered too lightly. Thus we become skilled in the Lord's will when we learn to discern and know the basis, essence, power and right use of this food, in keeping with the intention [meinung] of the Lord.

What follows now should be simple for everyone, from the above context. Since, however, those who are remiss in unceasingly reading scripture, have interpreted these words of Paul to their own advantage, they have so pitifully tortured the pious consciences who are in need of comfort that they have turned this wholesome food into a horror, just as though they were to eat thereof unto their own death. I only wonder how those who taught thus, approached the food. If they considered themselves righteous and blameless, [141] they deceived themselves, as is indicated in 1 Jn. 1:8. They are mere hypocrites who in the sight of God are the most despicable kind of persons. If, on the other hand, they considered themselves sinners, yet knew the food to be comfort to the soul although they were in sin, and if they themselves often partook of it joyfully, what monstrous murderers of souls they were in not pointing out such comfort to everyone. But if they themselves truly believed what they taught and knew that they themselves were sinners, never without sin, yet went, nonetheless, to the sacrament, what utter evildoers they were. I sound harsh, I must admit. But how can I let those godless papists get away with it? They fight truth vehemently. Though they are unable to escape from the three prisons, they nonetheless snort about wildly, like an unreliable horse.

I now wish to indicate briefly and clearly how the content of this holy food is to be understood. Christ Jesus taught in Jn. 6:33 in several beautiful parables and words how his word is nourishment for the soul, saying that his word has come down from heaven to give life to the world in the same manner in which bread strengthens the body. Therefore he has called it a bread. For what else is able to restore a hopeless person as surely as the word of his creator? What better thing is there that could preserve him in health of spirit and divine goodness than the word of God of which he himself says that a person lives thereby? But which of the many words that God has spoken through Christ is the one sure and actual word in which we may find comfort and strength? I say the one which states that Jesus Christ has given his body for our redemption and his blood for the washing and cleanness of the soul. There is nothing that can revive, strengthen and preserve the burdened soul more than when it believes with certainty that Christ has suffered death on its behalf. Neither, is there anything that could make [the soul] more joyful than the faith that he has washed and cleansed us with his blood and thereby, through a pleasing sacrifice, united and reconciled us to God once again. Look now, what else is the food of the soul [142] than certainty of the fact that Jesus Christ is its salvation before God. Therefore Christ says rightly in Jn. 6:51, "The bread which I shall give you, is my body." This means, "That which strengthens and revives the soul is the one word which it believes, viz, that I am its salvation and the ransoming sacrifice before God. For my body is given for the life of humankind." His suffering and death are bread and nourishment.

This opinion he expresses a bit later [Jn. 6:53-56] when he says, "Truly, truly I say to you, if you do not eat the body of the Son of Man, nor drink his blood, you will have no life in you. Whoever eats my body and drinks my blood has eternal life." This means, should you not put your trust in the body and blood of Christ, in other words, should you not count on his death which is your life, you have no life in you. But if you believe without doubting that my flesh and blood, killed and shed for you, has redeemed and cleansed you from all sin, you shall live eternally. For my body or flesh is truly food and my blood is truly drink. Everyone who eats my flesh or body and drinks my blood, remains in me and I in him. If then his flesh or body has suffered death for us and his blood, which was shed for us, has redeemed us poor sinners, no stronger food of the soul can be offered to us than to believe this with all certainty; thus his death and the shedding of his blood become life and joy to the soul. That these words of Christ are to be understood in such a way as to signify the word of faith by the term "flesh and blood", he himself teaches in the same context [Jn. 6:60-63]. When several of the disciples said, "This is a hard saying (for they lost their appetite when they visualized the eating of his body which they saw before their eyes), who is to discern it?" Jesus said to them, "This gives you a fright; what then, when you will see the Son of Man ascending to where he was beforehand? The Spirit makes alive; the flesh is of no use. The words which I tell you are spirit and life." Christ implied by these words that they did not yet believe and he went on as follows, "There are some among you who do not believe." But when these would see him with their very eyes, ascend to heaven, they would know that nothing is impossible for him. What he talked to them about they took to [143] refer to the physical eating and drinking of his flesh and blood. This was not his intention, however. Rather, his flesh and blood means that the soul which believes would have these for its salvation, surety, treasure and ransom before God. This happens through the Spirit of God. He makes a person's heart a believing one; and thus a person is made alive; for the flesh (as the erring disciples knew full well), is of no use at all. The words which he spoke to them are the promises of life and spirit viz. that his body or flesh and blood are as certainly our life, as physical bread or nourishment sustain a person. Indeed, if we surely believe, as has often been said, his death is a ransom for us.

Take note then, good Christians, for the body and blood of Christ are none other than the word of faith which is that his body, given for us and the blood which was shed for us, have redeemed and reconciled us to God. If we believe that confidently, our soul has its food and drink in the flesh and blood of Christ. For Christ has given an edible form of his body, namely bread and a cup of his blood to make more concrete to the simple of heart the essential nature of the testament. Thus they are strengthened in their faith through a visible act, just as in baptism, sin is not cleansed by the act of immersion, except the one who is being baptized believes in the saving power of the gospel, i.e. in the gracious redemption through Christ. Thus I speak here in the words of Christ, "To him who does not first believe in his word before he approaches the altar (i.e. that we believe in him and trust him fully to be our salvation), the body of Christ will be of no use." Indeed, I say with Paul [1 Cor. 11:29], that he will eat and drink unto his own condemnation. But if he goes to the table in the manner and meaning which Christ here [Jn. 6] speaks of and teaches, he shall live. If he is alive in faith, the food shall strengthen him. Therefore no single sinner has to stay away from this meal because of the greatness of his sins; for even if he had committed all the sins of the world, the grace of God is, nonetheless, richer and [144] larger. Its nature is to make itself desired by us in its greatness. See Luke 7:47, "The one whom much is forgiven, shall love all the more." Rather, he would pray God that he may give full confidence to the word of faith, to rely on it (viz. that Christ is our salvation before God, etc), and then approach [the table] in such faith and partake also in a visible act of the body and blood of Christ. In this way he approaches worthily, i.e. in the spirit of Christ. Nor will he allow anyone to divert him through some other teaching such as to avoid this precious food because of sins, unless he should feel within himself the absence of a true, genuine and firm faith in the Lord Jesus Christ. In that case he should not go to the table of the Lord, for he lacks faith. I am not concerned with what the theologians invented concerning the transformation of wine and bread. I am fully satisfied to know clearly through faith that he is my salvation and the food and comfort of my soul.

Whereas I recalled earlier the able servant of God, Martin Luther, when I showed how he calls the body and blood of Christ a testament (not in his own words, to be sure, but in the words of Christ), and whereas I call the Supper a memorial, there is nonetheless no contradiction here, for in itself it is a testament while the term "memorial" is a name used for the custom itself. In doing it, we think anew of, praise and proclaim that which Christ has accomplished once and believe firmly that this very work of Christ is our salvation. I reserved opinion on him until now. The great and mighty in this world have begun to persecute this teaching of Christ as it appeared in Luther's name. They have caused it to be hated so that all teaching of Christ, regardless of who on earth proclaims it, is called Lutheran. Though a person may not even have read Luther's teachings and kept himself strictly to the word of God, they dare, nonetheless, to denounce him as Lutheran. This has happened to me.

Before anyone in this area had even heard of Luther, I began [145] to preach the gospel of Christ in 1516 [19] so that I never entered the pulpit without looking up the words which were to be read in the mass that day and expounding them on the basis of scripture. Although in those days I tended initially to cling to the ancient teachers as the purer and clearer, though at times I objected to them, too, as mylord the Rev. Diebold of Geroldsegg, [20] Provost at Einsiedeln, will remember well. I had suggested to him at the time that he should read Jerome with all diligence, but I said to him at the same time that there will be a day when neither Jerome nor any other will mean much among Christians except scripture alone. [21] It struck him as rather peculiar that I should recommend Jerome, yet suggest at the same time that he might soon mean very little, indeed. This then was the opinion I began to have at the time, that Jerome and others were doing violence to the meaning of scripture, though they treated scripture much better than the sophists. [22] Thus when I had to leave him in 1518 to go to Zurich and could not always be with him, the above-mentioned gentleman was to read Jerome so that he might not stray from scripture, for at that time he was still greatly taken by learned Latin.

When I began to preach in Zurich in 1519 [23] I indicated to the honorable gentlemen of the Chapter how I intended to preach on the gospel of Matthew, God willing, without any human addenda and without any hesitancy or wavering because of counter arguments. [24] At the beginning of that same year (for I reached Zurich on St. John the Evangelist day), no one in our midst knew anything of Luther, except that he had said something concerning indulgences, which did not teach me anything new since I [146] had been informed earlier that indulgences were a fraud and false appearance. [25] I had learned this from a disputation with Dr. Thomas Wyttenbach of Biel, mylord and faithful teacher had engaged in at Basel some time ago, though I was not present at the time. [26] Consequently Luther's writing at the time did little to help me in my preaching on Matthew. Nonetheless, everyone eager to hear the word of God came hurrying to my expositions so that I was quite surprised myself.

Now I want to ask the enemies of the teachings of Christ, "Who then accuses me of being Lutheran?" However, when Luther's booklet on the **Our Father** appeared, after I had expounded on the same thing a short while before that, I remember well how some people came to me who straightway suspected me of having written it and published it in Luther's name. [27] Who could call me Lutheran? How is it, that the cardinals and legates of Rome who lived in Zurich at the time did not call me Lutheran until they recognized Luther to be a heretic though they had begun to hate me and bribe me with money. When they could not turn him into a heretic they then clamored that I was a Lutheran, etc. This, my dear and good Christians, I point out to you in some detail so that you may learn from it what kind of shameless mischief some nobles or ennobled beggars use in that they undertake to turn aside everyone who preaches the gospel by calling them Lutherans. They call the entire teaching of Christ, be it preached in whatever way it will, "Lutheran" thus making it displeasing to people by giving it the name of a person.

This, indeed, is nothing less than grave blasphemy and a sure sign of a desperate godless conscience. For who has equipped me to preach the gospel and to preach from the writing of one evangelist from beginning to end? Did [147] Luther? I started preaching the gospel before I had ever heard Luther's name mentioned and in order to prepare for the same I started to learn Greek some ten years ago [28] so that I might learn the teaching of Christ from its original sources. How well I have mastered Greek, I let others judge. However, Luther, whose name I did not know for at least another two years, had definitely not instructed me. I followed holy scripture alone. But the papists burden me and others with such names from sheer malice, as I have stated earlier, saying, "You must be Lutheran for you preach just as Luther writes." My answer is, "I preach the word of Christ; why do you not take me to be a Christian as well?" They practice sheer malice.

Luther, in my opinion, is a good warrior of God, the like of which we have not had on earth in a thousand years (I ignore at this point that the papists will call me along with him, a heretic for this). No one in all the history of the papacy has equalled him in the bold equanimity with which he attacked the pope at Rome; and with no offence to anyone. Whose then is such deed? Is it God's or Luther's? Ask Luther himself. I know full well what he will say. He'll say, it is God's. Why then do you ascribe the teaching of other persons to Luther when he himself does not do so and when he does not promote anything new except what is contained in the eternal, unchanging word of God. This he brings out richly, showing the heavenly treasure to poor misled Christians without regard to what the enemies of God undertake against him. He does not heed their sour looks and threats either. So far I should not want to bear the name of Luther; for I have read very little of his teaching and have often intentionally refrained from reading his books just so that I might please the papists.

But from what I have read of his writings (pertains to dogmatics, teaching, meaning and intention of scripture [148] only; for I have no concern for his quarrels), I have generally found so well grounded in the word of God that it would be impossible for any creature to twist it. I also know that he concedes a great deal to those who are weak in the faith and that he would act differently than I would in things in which I am not of his opinion; not that he says too much but rather not enough; an example would be the booklet on the ten lepers [29] (this I have been told, for I have not personally read it), where he makes some concession to the practice of confessions, that one ought to show oneself to the priest, which can certainly not be taken from that very deed of Christ. For Luke 17:14ff states it as follows, " 'Go then and show yourselves to the priests.' And as they went they were cleansed. One of them, however, when he saw that he was made well, returned to praise God with a loud voice." When I read this story it tells me that the tenth returned immediately upon seeing his health restored. He did not go to the priests in order to show himself, for he was a Samaritan who had no great respect for Jewish priests and did not need their approval but rather the approval of him who had given him his health.

If you wish to apply this to the penitent, it follows that the true believer, from the moment he learns by faith that God has forgiven his sin through the Lord Jesus Christ, who is the sacrifice for our sin, will say thanks to him alone for his forgiveness. He will not tolerate that such a deed be credited to a creature, since it is God's deed alone. But the weak ones ought to go to the priest that they may be the better informed of this and confirmed in their faith. In this one thing I am willing to recognize that access to the priest is at best tolerated by God; for there are still a number of people who place great value on confessions and who would be greatly angered if they were to be done away with suddenly. Otherwise this deed of Christ is directed more against auricular confession than in its favor. Similarly with regard to the term "sacrament", [149] he [i.e. Luther] concedes too much to the Romans. For what do we Germans care what the Southern death pipers [30] call the holy signs which God has given us or under which word they subsume them? There is baptism, the body and blood of Christ, penance, marriage. Each of these is well known among us by its name; what do I care whether the Romans call them all by one name? One thing is sure, the Greeks do not call them sacraments.

The same may be said regarding intercessions for the departed and other things in which, as I understand it, he makes several concessions for the sake of the weak. But to those who are wantonly unwilling to understand such meaning of scripture as he and others are now bringing out, he concedes nothing at all; for they are in despair, unbelieving and condemned in their own conscience, Titus˙ 3:11. Though they themselves dare not be judged by scripture, they, in turn, dare to weaken the teaching of Christ with falsehood. They first of all condemned the bold, fearless warrior and servant of Christ, Martin Luther and subsequently they gave his name to the unworthy so that they may turn the teachings of Christ into sectarianism and heresy. But let no one impose on you the name of another person, my dear good Christian, and do not in turn impose such on anyone else. Do not say to your neighbor, "Are you Lutheran, too?" Rather, ask him what he thinks of the teaching of Christ, how the word of God pleases him and whether he is a Christian, i.e. an untiring worker of good toward God and people. And should the papists also claim to be Christians, say to them, "Let everyone bear the name of him for whom he fights, whose servant he is." If you are servants of Christ and guard his honor alone and his word, you are Christians indeed. If you fight for the pope, and guard his honor and his word, then you are the pope's. Therefore, my good Christians, let not the genuine name of Christ be changed into the name of Luther; for Luther did not die for us; rather he teaches us to know him from whom alone we have our salvation. Nor must you accept the papists by this glorious wholesome name until they are prepared to confess Christ rather than the pope; then, however, they must be to us dear brothers and children of God. By the same token, I do not want the papists to call me Lutheran; for I did not learn the teachings of Christ from Luther but from the very word of God. If Luther preaches Christ he does the same thing I do, though, [150] God be praised, through him a far greater number of people are led to God than through me and others (whose measure God increases and diminishes as he pleases). So far I wish to bear no other name than that of my captain Christ; whose foot soldier I am. He shall give me orders and pay, as he sees fit. I hope that some will understand by now why I do not wish to be called Lutheran even though I esteem Luther as highly as any other person. Accordingly I testify before God and all people that all my life I have not written a single word to him nor has he written to me. Neither have I caused a letter to be written as some pious fellows have accused me of doing. I have refrained from doing so, not because I feared anyone on account of it, but rather to show everyone by this how singular the Spirit of God really is in that we, though separated by such a distance, have, nonetheless, been of one voice in teaching the doctrines of Christ without any prior consultation. Granted I am not to be compared to him but everyone does what God directs him to do. However, to return to my original intention, I called the eating and drinking of the body and blood of Christ a memorial of the suffering of Christ before I heard of Luther at all. And Luther called the body and blood of Christ a testament. Both are correct and have come from the mouth of Christ. The one is an essential term; the other the name of a custom and practice. The body and blood of Christ are an eternal legacy, inheritance or testament; in eating and drinking thereof one does not sacrifice. Rather, one remembers and renews that which Christ has done, once and for all.

At this point the papists drop a red herring [provide a feeble block] [31] by saying, "The mass has the name missa not in vain, for it is a Hebrew term missah which means a gift or a sacrifice. Hence the mass is said to be a sacrifice." [32] My response, You wicked devil of mammon. How hard it is to get you to yield. Tell me has this term missah become Hebrew after the suffering of Christ or [151] has it been Hebrew from the very foundation of the world? You will have to concede that it has been a Hebrew word from the very beginning, for you often find it in the Old Testament. But at that time the term missah could not have meant the body and blood of Christ, since it was not instituted as yet. Since Christ is the author and originator of this holy thing you will have to show me where he has called it missah; you will not find it anywhere. Thus it follows that you and not Christ have given the name. I don't find that the Fathers called it missah either. Thus I have to conclude that you papists, have called it missah after you started to sell out Christ and to offer him up for money. Indeed, as much as you and your clearly limited understanding are concerned you killed and butchered him and then only called it missah. What do I really care what you call it. You call it a sacrament, yet have never been able to show why it is called a sacrament or what a sacrament really is. Then again you call it a mass (missah). But the right name which Christ has given when he called it his body and blood, a foundation and marriage of the new covenant which he entered with us and that he has called that very thing a memorial, you will not understand. You do not want to accept those very names, for they are not as profitable as sacrifice is.

The papists bring yet another retort, "The Fathers,"

they say, "have held it to be a sacrifice, calling it sacrificium."
I answer: What the Fathers have said about it would take too
much space to write about here. However, that they so named
it, does not prove it to be a sacrifice, unless they prove by the
word of God that it is a sacrifice indeed. It seems to me, however,
that several of them used the term sacrificium or oblationem,
i.e. sacrifice of honor or sacrifice in keeping with the understanding
of the times, meaning not that it should be a sacrifice made at
the time, but that, because it had been made once and for all,
it would be eternally effectual to atone before God for human
sins. Thus they called it a sacrifice in their own day not because
they were making the sacrifice but rather because Christ had
made it. Take an example: We say at Easter, "Today Christ our
Lord is risen from the dead" or again, "This is the day on which
our Lord Jesus Christ rose." We mean thereby not that Christ
arose in our own home on this very day but rather that the day
on which he once rose has received the name by which it is forever
referred to as the day of resurrection. [152] Thus it seems to
me that several of the early Fathers termed the body and blood
a sacrifice, not as if it were their sacrifice or offered up by them
but because Christ offered himself; thus it is nothing other than
a memorial of that which once took place in the same way in
which Easter, which likewise took place only once, is called the
day of resurrection.

Read what St. Chrysostom says about the Epistle to
the Hebrews in Homily No. 17. Since he deals with this term "semel",
meaning once, you may note how he wends his way through the
terms "a host" and "sacrificed once and for all". As a result,
he says quite often that we sacrifice a host or sacrifice, the very
one which Christ has sacrificed, which cannot be consumed. And
when he sees right beside it this term "semel" he is hard pressed
and is almost forced to change his opinion; for since it has been
sacrificed once and for all we cannot offer it up any more. Thus
in the end he reaches the point where he has to say that it is
more of a memorial of that which Christ has done. Similarly,
Nicholas of Lyra [1270-1340] says about Luke 22:19, "That do
in remembrance of me," that the sacrament is a memorial of
the suffering of our Lord Jesus Christ. Now I do not esteem this
opinion so highly as to build upon it, but I wish to draw out from
among the ranks of the papists one who shares my opinion. I know
full well that some of the Fathers have called the meal a sacrifice;
but they cannot [153] prove it with the word of God nor have
they made quite as much trade of it as has unfortunately been
done by those who came after them and were not satisfied with
what they took in from the living for the saying of mass. They
also brought the dead into their calculations although they could
see that while it was considered a sacrifice (as they fancied)
it is truly sacrificed only when it is eaten and drunk and that
it nourishes only the person who eats and drinks it. For if by

my eating anyone else could be fed, why then does anyone have to be forced to approach the meal since it would have sufficed had I gone there to eat and sacrifice on behalf of another. Thus if the dead really eat and drink the body and blood of Christ they also recall the suffering of Christ. If they do not do it, this testament does not touch them in any way at all. What I mean here becomes still clearer by reference to purgatory. Further, they themselves call this sacrament a viaticum which means food supply or nourishment for the road. Thus it can be of use only to those who are on the way. But the dead are really off the road; for their journey is accomplished. Therefore the food is no longer for them. For either they no longer need it, since they are with God (for they see him and take unto themselves or possess what here they ate in a hidden manner by faith), or else, the food is of no use to them if they are under eternal damnation.

Here I have to give satisfaction to an impudent preacher monk whose name, for the time being, I shall leave unmentioned in the hope that he will mend his ways. However, should he not, his name together with his evil deed shall be clearly spelled out, God willing. This man dared say in the hearing of honorable people, that the term "consecration", meaning sanctification of this food, is patchwork like the cloak of a beggar, since we have allegedly no genuine word of sanctification. Answer: Dear brother, I praise God that your awkward and blasphemous words have first revealed your own inept nonsense and have further shown what kind of person he is whose vicar you claim to be, [154] if he allows you, as ignorant of scripture as you are, to lie so shamelessly in the presence of God-fearing people without punishing you for it but allowing you again and again to babble out your devilish endeavors. Note then where the words of sanctification are to be found. In Mt. 26:26 it is written, "This is my body." Is not this a clear, succinct and certain word of God? How more succinctly and to the point could God have spoken? Turn to your Peter of Spain and find out what kind of a statement this is. [33] He calls it a "propositio singularis per rotam demonstrationis, hoc, de est tercio adiacente." [34] There is nothing shorter, clearer and more precise. Therefore if you say the words of blessing or sanctification have not been stated appropriately and clearly, you lie against God and his holy word. This in itself would not be so unfortunate were it not for the fact that you make these statements before common people who think thereafter everything is exactly as you dared babble it. They then suspect all that God has given for their salvation. If you do this from ignorance, it is disgraceful that you are permitted to mount a pulpit because you are so little familiar with scripture. If you do it from sheer malice no one can condemn your frivolity harshly enough or sufficiently fathom how much damage you do if you deny that to be in the words of Christ, which is so clearly written there. For what can be said more clearly than, "This is my body"? Take if you will, the words of the other gospel writers as they have been cited earlier, and you will find them to be as clear about bread and wine as these are; in other words, they are essentially expressed to show what Christ has done, what words he used and why he has bid us do likewise. For you to say that the words of the saints are patched together like a beggar's cloak, shows up even more clearly you gross wantonness. The papists, whom you treat like idols, have done it. You should therefore not disparage their deeds, though they deserve criticism; [155] yet I do not think the putting together of the words of Paul and Christ a bad combination at all. But it would have been enough if one had used only the words of one of the gospels or of Paul, for they are really not the words of the gospel writer but of Christ. But since the words of this food are put together from the writings of the gospels so that no one might miss anything, you compare these wholesome heavenly strong words of Christ to a beggar's cloak. Where are your bishops and your abbots who protest loudly if one calls you beggars, whore-mongers, usurers, money changers, blessers of cakes, abusers of peasants? Who can tolerate such blasphemy? The scoundrels should be killed and burned, etc. Note, first they say that no one knows the words with which Christ has instituted this food; yet then, they are likened to a beggar's cloak. How can you tolerate that? If one were to ridicule your costly cloaks [35] or your precious coats, you would call for revenge. But if one speaks of God's word in such dishonest or derogatory fashion, you are even pleased. I do not speak in order to bring revenge upon this bungling fool, but simply that you might know what people think of you when you can swallow blasphemy so easily, yet cannot tolerate to be touched yourselves. You foolish brother (for you cannot be let off more leniently than to have this blasphemy of yours treated as folly), you ought to be admonished by the grace of Jesus Christ and by the prospect of the last judgment to desist from persecuting the teaching of God; should you do so, I make bold to promise that God will forgive you all such lies and wantonness. But if you do not desist, you will suffer the same fate as Thersites; [36] you will be treated badly, yet not accomplish anything except to suffer eternal punishment from this time on. It is a difficult thing, indeed, to fight against or kick the goads. Furthermore, the rock upon which the ever growing teaching is founded is too hard; it cannot be routed out with monk's [156] cowls or cassocks; it will not and cannot tolerate to be broken in pieces; it is destined [verordnet] to be built on exclusively. The house of one who does not build upon it, will topple when the floods of the river shall knock against it. Therefore seek to build upon it also. Should you have ever intended to use this rock to acquire riches, honor, or the favor of the mighty, forget it; it cannot be abused thus. One cannot expect anything else of it than what it is willing to do. Try to understand all these things in the best spirit, dear brother. I handled you a bit harshly, perhaps; but I have done so merely to draw you toward salvation. Should you not heed me, your head will be tousled even more roughly (not by me, but by others), not by a beating which would be a mild treatment, but by the sword of the divine word. God be with you; fear him.

I hear, too, that a certain nobly born chap has stuck out his ears like the lion of Cuma [37] by saying that nowhere in scripture can the word of the eternal testament be found as it is used in the usual words of consecration. I would ask that same fellow to put his spectacles on his nose and then check out Isaiah 55:3. He will find there that God promises to enter an eternal covenant with us, the sure and faithful heirs of David. Earlier everyone understood this covenant to have been made and grounded in the blood of Christ who is an eternal God; hence, the covenant, too, is eternal, Heb. 9:15. But I am sure this does not satisfy him; I hear he is very argumentative. Let him take the words of Paul then, Heb. 13:20, "The God of peace who has brought again from the dead the great shepherd of the sheep, the Lord Jesus Christ, by the blood of the eternal [157] covenant, etc." Do you note in this text the term, "eternal testament"? I do not point this out to you because I am concerned about the humbug with which, as I hear, you treat the words of consecration, but rather, that you may learn to recognize your blind spot which hinders you from seeing the words of Paul. For I am little concerned about what names you give the words of Christ, whether "consecrationis," "benedictionis," or "transubstantionis"--I do not really need the names at all. I know that when I act and talk what Christ has ordered so that I do right by him and that when I rely on his word, I am free from all sin; call that what you will.

They string together many other objections, which are all trifles [and]; anyone should be able to resist these readily on the basis of the opinion I have just expounded. That's all for this Article.

NOTES

1. Meant is the First Zurich Disputation, Jan. 1523. Blansch or Plank was present as representative of Constance. His contribution is recorded in **Handlung der Versammlung in Zurich, 29, January 1523.** Cf. Z.I 534ff and 559.

2. It is apparent from the **Handlung** that this point was made by J. Faber, not by Blansch.

3. The quotation is from the Vulgate.

4. Cf. Z.I 555-556. Zwingli does not recall the statement verbatim.

5. A marginal note suggests that Zwingli was struggling for the most suitable term to express what he found in the Hebrew text. He concludes that the term in German is too limited: "Opfren ist im tuetsch ze eng".

6. The chrism shirt is a white shirt worn by infants for baptism.

7. The meaning attached to this ordering of events was simply to urge catechetical instruction. Anabaptists like Hubmaier read it as supportive of the injunction to "preach, teach and baptize" in that precise order. Zwingli seeks to clarify what he meant and to correct any misinterpretation in his **Antwort über B. Hubmaiers Taufbuechlein** (Nov. 5, 1525). Cf. Z.IV 577-647.

8. Zwingli states that "confirmation classes" were begun in Zurich about the middle of 1522. I have not been able to find documentation to corroborate this claim. Instruction of young people in the so-called Prophezei was not begun until 1523-24. A clear pattern for catechetical instruction did not get established until 1628 in the so-called "Predikantenordnung". Cf. G. Schmid, **Die evangelisch-reformierte Landeskirche des Kantons Zurich**. Zurich, Schulthess, 1954, 1331.

9. Peter Lombard, magister sententiarum, writes regarding confirmation in Book IV.VII.I of his **Sentences**.

10. Catholic rites in Switzerland include to this day the blessing of wine on St. John's Day. Cf. **Idiotikon** III.31. Similarly, the blessing of palm branches has roots firmly embedded in tradition. The editors of Z.II suggest a date as early as the 8-9th centuries. Cf. Z.II 125, n 2. See also, **Idiotikon** IV 1217.

11. Kilchoere oder gmeind. The English has no adequate term to encompass the many shades of meaning of the German terms.

12. "Und kempffend umb geisswullen". Cf. Wander, I 1449 and Grimm, **Deutsches Wörterbuch** IV/I - 2 Teil, 2807-2808.

13. Zwingli uses "scheissenden menschen" which suggests by reference to the natural process of excretion that they are of low, unworthy estate. A vulgarism is not implied or intended.

14. Böggenbischoff - disguised, dressed up. Zwingli suggests their pompous appearance in the act of worship.

15. According to J. J. Hottinger, **Helvetische Kirchen-Geschichten**, II.642f. The cup for the laity was given to children who had been baptized on Wednesday after Palm Sunday, on Saturday before Easter and on Pentecost Sunday. The practice followed the Zurich Breviary of 1260. In some communities of St. Gall the practice seems to have survived into the 16th century.

16. Cf. Zwingli's **Correspondence.**

17. In his **Amica Exegesis,** Zwingli states the same about Zug.

18. The term used here and elsewhere is "mass". Cf. Z.II 140.16, 31; 141.15; 143.31. According to usage listed in **Idiotikon** IV 444 it is an alternate expression for "mal" - cibus - food.

19. Cf. Z.I 256.13ff, especially note 4 and I 379.22ff. On the subject of Zwingli's self-estimation, see, F. Blanke, "Zwinglis Urteile über sich selbst" in **Die Furche,** 22 (1936), 31-39.

If Zwingli's recollection of his initial reform efforts is correct, he, ahead of Luther, would deserve credit for having initiated many of the reforms regarding the practice and understanding of the Lord's Supper. Cf. however, Article 20, n 24 below.

20. Zwingli's correspondence reflects the friendly relationship between the two men.

21. Zwingli's somewhat ambivalent attitude to the Fathers is not a denial of their validity, but suggests critique of them on the basis of a higher norm. Cf. A. Rich, **Anfänge,** p. 50. It is not impossible, as Rich points out, that Zwingli's use of allegory continues into the early phase of his ministry in Zurich; ibid, 52, notes 24 and 27.

22. "Sophist" is a somewhat derogatory term for the scholastics of the 15th and 16th centuries whose teaching dominated Catholic theology until the humanist renaissance set in. The term is also used by Luther, Melanchthon and Calvin especially to refer to the theologians of the Sorbonne.

23. His first sermon at the Grossminster was preached on Saturday, January 1, 1519 after he had arrived in Zurich on December 27th, 1518, on St. John the Evangelist Day.

24. This significant step meant breaking with long standing tradition. Zwingli ignores the lectionary and preaches seriatim on the Gospel of Matthew. Unfortunately, the contents of his sermons cannot easily be reconstructed because of Zwingli's habit of not preaching from written notes. Cf. Z.I 133, n 2 and I 285.2ff.

25. Luther's **Ein Sermon von Ablass und Gnade** appeared in 1517.

26. Likely from his teacher Wyttenbach; the disputation may have been held in 1515 when Wyttenbach earned his Doctor of Theology degree.

27. Luther's **Our Father** published in 1519 in German was intended for simple lay people.

28. Perhaps as early as 1506 at the instigation of his teacher Wyttenbach. Cf. G. R. Potter, **Zwingli,** Cambridge University Press, Cambridge, London, New York. 1976.

29. The reference is to Luther's **The Gospel of the Ten Lepers** of 1521 (W. A. VIII.336ff).

30. Literally, "die wälschen todtenpfyffer".

31. Ein kuerpsinen–Kürbsin is something like a pumpkin; hence of little consequence. Cf. **Idiotikon** III 457. Jud translates, "infirmum telum".

32. It was erroneously held that "missa" derived from the Hebrew. Zwingli does not go beyond the understanding of his day. Cf. Z.I 555, especially note 4.

33. It was presumed that Pope John XXI (1276-1277) was identical with Peter of Spain. His **Summulae Logicales,** tractate I enjoyed wide circulation. Cf. K. Prantl, **Geschichte der Logik im Abendlande,** III, 33ff.

34. The special earlier clause is separated by the demonstrative pronoun "hoc" from the third part, "my body".

35. The term is "dapperthembder" which Leo Jud translated "plicatae stolae". This is a kind of cloak which had a long strip or tail at the back.

36. Zwingli recalls a person from Greek mythology. Thersites, allegedly the ugliest man at Ilion, was beaten by Odysseus because he had ridiculed Agamemnon. Cf. The Iliad, II.212ff.

37. Erasmus uses the saying "Asinus apud Cumanus" in his **Adagia.** It is an allusion to the fable of the donkey in a lion's skin. Cf. Wander, I 876 No. 572; 874 No. 526; 876; 570. For this and similar proverbial expressions related to a donkey.

THE NINETEENTH ARTICLE

That Christ is the sole mediator between God and us.

This Article is based on so many clear passages of scripture that I am really wondering how it happened that people looked for mediators other than Christ in the New Testament. Of these passages I shall single out some of the clearest.

Christ says in John 14:6, "No one comes to the Father, but through me." I should say here as I did earlier, "Why do the papist not turn to their logic to determine what kind of statement, "No one comes to the Father, but through me" really is. If you then point to your good works by which you intend to come to God, I will say, "You cannot come to God other than through Christ. With him alone you must find grace and mercy. To ascribe that to your own good works is to deceive yourself, for you claim for yourself what is God's only. And if you point to popish indulgences, masses, vigils, chanting [kirchengeschrei], vestments, the holiness of the Fathers, I say to you, "No, it cannot be done that way; everything must come through Christ." In this fashion you can check everything [158] the avaricious papists have taught us to be the way to God and you will find that it all crumbles, except for Christ. Whoever robs him of his honor and ascribes it to creatures, is an idolater.

Should you point to the merit or intercession of the saints who are now with God, through whom you intend to come to God, I can say only, "No one comes to God, but through Christ alone." Either God's word or the human word must fail. Since God's word does not falter, it follows that the human word is already broken. Indeed, it has never been whole, but proved to be false, deceitful and a sham from the very beginning. Therefore the only way by which we may come to God is Christ. Everyone who has ever come to God, did so through Christ alone. He is the mediator between God and us. He is the sole mediator; for no one is entitled to be a mediator between God and us, but the seed through which God has promised our salvation, Gal. 3:16.

Note at this point the specific nature of the mediator. A mediator is a referee who finds a peaceful solution for two who are fighting or at odds, thereby making friendship, because he is acceptable to both parties. Moses was a mediator of this kind through whom God proclaimed his will to the people of Israel by promising earthly gifts and through whom he was often reconciled with the people whenever they angered him. Though such reconciliation did not bring them into the immediate presence of God, it redeemed the people, nonetheless, from the punishment of God and served as a prototype of the true eternal mediator Christ who has revealed to us the will of his Father through the sure promise of grace and has redeemed us from the death of the soul. This mediator Christ is therefore not only God but also a human being; and not only is he a human being, but also God; for if he were only divine, he would not be suitable to act as mediator. For God is one. It is not fitting that he mediate in himself only, for the one who mediates must be distinguishable from those between whom he mediates. In God, however, there is nothing divisive or separated. Therefore he made his Son mediator who accepted human nature, not that he should be mediator by the sole strength of human weakness, but by the power of the divine nature which is united with human strength so that, just as human weakness was joined to God through Christ and united with him, we too may be reconciled to God through the suffering and sacrifice of Christ. Such [159] reconciliation is not proper and cannot be attributed to any creature except to the one heir to whom such was promised, Gal. 3:19f.

To what avail then was the law? I answer: It has been placed there on account of our transgressions until the heir would come, in whom the promise has been fulfilled. The law has been placed by the angels under the authority of the mediator. The mediator, however, is not the One; but God is united and the One. These words of Paul speak of the nature of the mediator, though they are short and somewhat veiled. Their sense is as follows: If faith justifies, as Abraham was justified by faith, why then do we need the law and why has God ordained it? Paul answers: Not everyone has faith like Abraham. Whoever has such faith, does not need the law; rather, as Abraham was led, directed and guided by the Spirit of God, so likewise will he be led and guided who has faith as he did. But there are many who do not have such faith and who would do nothing aright unless they be held by the chains of the law. Whoever trusts in God, like Abraham, does not need the law. Wherever this is not so, the law is needed. For where the Spirit of God is not present, there one is not informed about the will of God. Therefore one needs, without a doubt, the law which will teach us what pleases God and what displeases him so that we may be saved from transgressions.

You may still say, How could God have given the law because of transgressions? There would be no transgressions at all if there were no law, for no one would know what it is to transgress, unless the law had said, "You shall not do this or that," as Paul says in Rom 7:7, "I did not know sin except through the law. I did not know lust had not the law said, 'Thou shalt not covet'."

I answer: This is an objection to which one should simply respond in all modesty and not by sharp words, as the papists do who ignorantly throw in all kinds of objections so that I am always reminded of the proverb, "Like a pig in the poke". [1] The law is nothing [160] other than the eternal unchanging will of God which seeks only what is right and good. But how are we to know the will of God unless it is proclaimed? The proclamation thereof we call a law because it is directed against the flesh which cannot tolerate anything except what pleases it. Surely then in itself it is nothing but good news, i.e. a good and sure message of God by which he informs us of his will.

How could a faithful person not be pleased when God makes his will known? Thus the law teaches us what pleases God. If the law pleases us, the Spirit of God is in us. However, if it does not please us, then nothing good is in us, as Paul says in Rom. 7:18, "I know that within me, i.e. in my flesh, nothing good dwells." But when the law and teaching of God please us, we are spiritual and judge spiritually, for the law is essentially spiritual, Rom. 7:14, "We know that the law is spiritual and that, without a doubt, it desires only what the Spirit of God desires, from whom it comes. If then we trust in God, we do so because of the Spirit of God. If he is with us, we know all things of the Spirit and since the law is spiritual it will please us, even though it may not please the flesh. We must understand Paul's words here as follows: the law has been given so that we may not undertake anything against God.

Now you might say, "How do I know God's will?" Listen to the law, "You shall love God above all else, you shall not get angry, etc." Do you see now that laws are given so that you may learn what he demands and what he does not will to happen? Therefore it is given so that you may not transgress the will of God. Thus the letter of the law kills if we look to it only; for who can keep it? But the Spirit makes alive when you say in faith, "Though I may not be able to fulfill it, it is, nonetheless, good and just, for it has been spoken by God and revealed to us." And if you should despair of ever fulfilling the law--as indeed all creatures must despair, for what carnal being can be so drawn to God that he could love him at all times above everything else?-- you can see the need of a mediator who makes satisfaction for our weaknesses. Could the mediator be a creature? No, for a creature is unable to fulfill a single commandment of God without the Spirit of God. Hence if follows that all the elect of God are united with God by the sole grace [161] of God and since they, too, were in need of grace, they could not possibly be mediators, for they are on the side of those who have weaknesses. A mediator, however, ought not to be on the side of the weak. Therefore it follows later in the words of Paul [Gal. 3:19], "Until the son comes to whom or in whom the promise has been made, i.e. the law has been given so that one may not transgress the will of God." If then this is impossible for a person to do, yet if God is just, the righteousness of God must be satisfied before we may be reconciled. But we shall not be able to find a human being who can satisfy God's righteousness, for whoever is to make satisfaction, must be like God, Luke 6:40. The disciple is perfect only when he is like his master. Therefore God has promised an heir to the forlorn human race, i.e. a birth, a plant, by which the devil shall be overcome and we be reconciled to God, Gen. 3:15. He retained the term "heir" [seed] since he promised Abraham that in his seed all persons shall be made whole, as we have amply demonstrated above. Of this very seed he speaks here, saying, "The law has been given so that one might not act against God." If then the law makes all persons guilty, a person has no sure comfort other than in the seed in whom salvation has been promised. Thus these two things, law and seed are set against each other, not in themselves, but on our account; for both of them are of God. But one teaches us what God wills; and if we know it, we find that we cannot do it and thus we need a mediator. The seed, i.e. Christ, is the mediator.

It is not the law then which condemns. Rather, we learn from the law how impotent we are and thereafter, that we are easily rejected by God. But the seed, who is like God and able to do his will can pay for our guilt because of his guiltlessness. Therefore this one alone is fit to mediate. As the law has come to humankind through a mediator who was Moses, so also grace has come through a mediator. There was only one mediator of the law; likewise there is only one mediator of grace. According to the law [162], no person can mediate, for all humankind is on the side of sin. God did not will to mediate by himself; for he who is One cannot mediate in himself. For a mediator must be able to get in among the angered and the hurt. Thus God has arranged that his Son took upon himself human weakness so that he might be a mediator between us and God. He is not mediator as a mere human being, for we have amply demonstrated that sheer human weakness cannot make satisfaction before God, unless it be both God and Man. Since he is God, he is able to fulfill the will of God; indeed, not merely fulfill it, for God's will is none other than his own will. Since he is a human being, he can be a sacrifice which pays ransom to God on behalf of us poor sinners; for his human nature is free of all sin. O divine wisdom.

How you have considered our salvation so seriously, so wisely, with such certainty. Now the words of Paul are clear when he says in Gal. 3:19, "And the law has been placed in the hands of the mediator by the angels." But it is not the mediator who is of the One; God, however, is united and the One. It is therefore impossible for anyone other than the seed who is both God and Man to be mediator; a spotless person who is also God. Therefore these words of Christ, drawn from above, stand firmly, "No one comes to the Father but by me." They are immovable so that heaven and earth will break down before they will.

A little later John says in chapter 2 [1 Jn. 2:1], "I write these things to you so that you may not sin. But if one sins, we have an advocate with the Father, the righteous one, Jesus Christ who is the expiation for our sins, and not only for our sin but for the sin of the world." You note here that no one can be mediator or advocate except one who is righteous. Therefore he says, "The righteous one, Jesus Christ." Now, all persons are sinners except for Christ. Therefore they cannot mediate for us or stand in on our behalf; they cannot reconcile nor make recompense. He alone can be our reconciliation who himself is righteous. You also hear that Christ has made recompense not only for inherited weakness (for I understand original sin [163] to be nothing other than a weakness of broken nature), as several people dare say these days without any basis of truth, so that they might gain a great deal from the recompense which the world makes; rather, he made recompense for all sin, which I called earlier an outgrowth of sin and weakness. And not only did he do this for the Jewish nation alone or for the apostles, but for the sins of the world, provided there is faith.

After having taught in 1 Tim. 2:1-6 how one ought to intercede before God on behalf of all people, lords and rulers so that we might lead a peaceful, quiet life in all seriousness and submission to God, Paul says, "For this is good and pleasing to God, our redeemer and savior who wills that all manner of persons be made whole and come to a knowledge of the truth. For there is one God; there is also one mediator only between God and human beings, that man Jesus who has given himself a ransom for everyone." You note here, firstly, that Paul calls our redeemer and savior, "God" and shortly after, he calls him a man when he says, "The man Christ Jesus". By this you learn to know the mediator, as earlier in Gal. 3:20. Secondly, you learn that God wills to redeem everyone, i.e. all kinds of people. He wills to lead them to the knowledge of the truth, i.e. to the knowledge of the true God and his salvation. In other words, that there is only one God and only one mediator between God and humankind. Undoubtedly, we cannot achieve peace, the knowledge of the truth and knowledge of salvation with greater certainty than when we recognize in faith the only one God and the only one mediator.

As long as one person seeks this mediator, and another person, that one, we shall never become one. But when all of us have Christ alone as our mediator, it follows, since we all set our hope on the one mediator, that our minds are united in the same treasure. Finally, you hear, that Christ has given himself a ransom for us. No one but he could have done that. For other persons cannot do it, since they have become sinners and lack the honor, i.e. the grace of God, Rom. 3:23. [164] Indeed, the glory, honor, innocence and purity of the handmaiden Mary did not originate with her, but came from the grace of God. Nonetheless, she is acclaimed by everyone to be the highest and most lovely creature before God, as she herself says, [Lk. 1:48], "The Lord has graciously regarded the low estate of his handmaiden; therefore all generations shall call me blessed."

Thus all persons are by nature sinners and in disgrace. However, if they wish to become pure and to attain to a place of honor, it must happen through Christ alone who is the sole mediator. Indeed, that Mary was an undefiled virgin when she gave birth to Christ, was God's doing only who had chosen and set her aside for this purpose. If then even this exalted creature of God achieved such honor by the grace of God through the mediation of the Son of God who is her son too, how much more then must the entire human race acknowledge that it lacks the honor of God, that it cannot do anything on its own and is incapable of providing a mediator, for the mediator must be a God-Man (and no human creature can accomplish that). I have tried to translate the words, "heis kai mesites" [1 Tim. 2:5] by "single mediator" because "a" is an article in our usage and does not properly express the sense which Paul intended. Had I simply translated "a mediator", a simple person might have interpreted it to mean that Christ is a mediator after or among others, which is certainly not the meaning Paul has. He stresses rather that there is only one mediator. Similarly he said, "one only God". Everyone knows that he used the term "heis" to mean "one only God". Had he not intended that meaning, he would have used "ho", but that term would not have rendered too meaningful what follows after. This I have said for the sake of those scholars who translate my words from the Greek into German and who might have easily criticized me, had I not defined them clearly. On the other hand, these words of Paul are so strong that they are sufficient to prove that Christ is a sole mediator and that no mere creature can be a mediator. The following deliberations I shall indicate in fewer words.

Paul says in Hebrews 7:24f, "He (meaning, Christ), has an eternal priesthood, because he remains for ever. Therefore, he is able to heal for all eternity. He himself has gone to God [165], alive for ever more, to make intercession on our behalf. You judge for yourself whether these words may fittingly be applied to a creature: "to go to God", "be an eternal high priest", "to plead eternally before [God]" and "to pay ransom for the sins of humankind".

In the same context Paul also says, [Heb. 7:22], "Jesus has become the guarantor of a better testament". This means that God has sworn an oath that his Son should be our high priest for ever. One may see by this how much better than the Old the New Testament is. Our high priest is one for eternity, which certainly was not true of priests in the Old. For they were all replaced after their death. Further, our sponsor is neither Moses nor a mortal priest, nor an animal sacrifice, but the Son of God himself who is our pledge and our guarantor through whom one may come to God.

Also Hebrews 8:6, "Christ's priestly office is higher inasmuch as he is also a mediator of a better testament. You perceive unmistakably from this that there is no other mediator of the best testament than Christ. If then the testament has its foundation in him and the quality of the testament is also measured by the goodness of Christ, how then can one attribute to a creature the office (which the Son of God alone is able to administer) and the name of Christ?

Also Hebrews 9:15, "Christ has gone to heaven that henceforth he might appear in the presence of God on our behalf." Here Paul expresses the kind of work Christ the mediator is doing, as pleading and appearing in the presence of God (i.e. his righteous wrath or anger, which is what the Hebrews often mean when they use the term "presence of God"), on our behalf. Behold, Christ is our advocate and ransom for ever and ever. [166]

Likewise, Rom. 8:34, "Who is there to condemn us; if Christ died for us, indeed, was raised and now sits at the right hand of God, pleading there on our behalf?" Now you may note that the certainty of our salvation depends on the fact that the Son of God, who died for us, represents us miserable sinners for ever. I shall bring this out more fully in Article 50. At this point I have stressed sufficiently that Christ is the sole mediator between God and us.

NOTE

1. "Suw in d' praenten". "Brente" is a low trough for pigs. The image suggests a great many pigs helplessly wallowing in a small trough as they seek to feed on its contents. Cf. **Idiotikon** V 757 and Wander IV 21.

THE TWENTIETH ARTICLE

That God wants to give us all things in his name. It follows from this that we need no other mediator but him beyond the present time.

I chose to deal with the first part of this Article because I noted that the sheep of God have erred and strayed in the mountains and hills and fields, seeking food and comfort, yet were not able to find it, as is written in Ez. 34:6. For their keepers have turned them away from the door which is Christ through whom alone one is able to reach life. They did not tell them of the salvation which is prepared and made available to them solely through Christ. This has so discouraged the poor sheep that they said, "How can I, sinful person that I am, come to God? I must come through good advocates," not recognizing the sole advocate and mediator, the sponsor, pledge and recompense for our sins, and how surely he takes away all sin from us. For God wills that all things be given in his name. When we say, "In the name of Christ," we mean as much as, "for his sake, in his power, in his word," as Christ himself teaches in John 15:16, "You did not choose me, but I have chosen you and set you up that you may go forth and bring fruit and that your fruit remain; and the Father shall give you whatever you ask in my name."

Note firstly, that God has chosen his disciples and us through them so that we may be his people, his servants, and not only servants but, indeed, friends. Why should we [167] not dare come to him when he has chosen us to bear fruit? The bearing of fruit is the prerogative of those only whom God has chosen. He also elected us that we may know the Father and turn to him in all our concerns; for he revealed himself to us through his Son that he may give us whatever we desire in his name. If then he has drawn us and chosen us to come to him, why then should we not dare come to him? From the word of God alone it is certain that God gives us whatever we desire in his name, when he says in John 16:23, "Truly, truly, I say to you, the Father shall give you whatever you shall ask for, in his name." Note, in order that we may come in sure confidence, he assures us in his word that we may find whatever we ask in his name. Indeed, he suffers anguish when we do not come and ask of him everything that we need. Therefore he says, "everything or all things". And a little later he admonishes the disciples for not having asked for everything [Jn. 16:24]. "You did not ask everything in my name. Ask and you shall receive, that your joy may be complete." See, he urges us to ask, yet we reply that we dare not come to him. But he knows that our joy shall be complete only when we receive from him. Therefore he says, "That your joy may be complete".

Further, our heavenly Father has testified in his word that he is reconciled by his own Son, Mt. 3:17; 17:5, "This is my beloved Son with whom I am well pleased or reconciled--eudokesa--give ear to him." The usual rendering is, "in whom I am well pleased". The Greeks, however, use the term "eudokesa" which means, "I am satisfied" or "I am honorably reconciled", or "I have become gracious". By this word our heavenly Father intended nothing other than to show to all persons that he has now sent the very one in whom he is reconciled and pacified; him we ought to hear. Now this very same one has taught us that we cannot come to God but through him. He also taught us that everything we should ask in his name he would give us. Further, the Father bids us hear and obey him. It follows therefore that he is the sole mediator and that God wills to give us all things in his name. [168]

Further, Hebrews 5:8f, "Even though he is Son of God, he learned obedience through his suffering and, thus perfected, is a cause of salvation to all those who obey him. We note at this point that God willed his own Son to suffer and experience human weakness that he may truly recognize the same and become the more merciful and accepting and that he may become a firm cause of salvation to all those who would hear him, i.e. those who believe on him.

Further, Romans 5:15-19, paraphrased, "If by the sin of Adam all humankind died, how much richer and more plentiful for the forgiveness of everyone has been the grace of God and the gift of his grace, made available to us through the one man Jesus Christ, etc." And shortly after he says, "If because of the sin of one person death became so strong as to be master and king of the many, how much more will those who received abundant grace and the gift of righteousness reign in life through the one man Jesus Christ. Therefore, just as condemnation came to all humankind on account of the sin of one--read, Adam--so also the perfecting [rechtwerdung] of life has come to all through the righteousness and innocence of the one Christ. For as by one person's disobedience we were all made sinners, so also by one person's obedience we shall all be made righteous."

All these words of Paul teach us clearly that as infirmity has come through this one Adam, so also life, goodness and righteousness have been restored through the one Christ. And these words clearly teach that he is the one mediator and the one means through whom every good thing is given us, just as through Adam everything evil had come. I have thus sufficiently shown that God wants to give us all things through Jesus Christ.

The second part of this Article is, "it follows from this that we need no mediator but him beyond the present time."

Anyone who carefully considered the preceding two Articles may clearly see that this insight follows therefrom. Since this Article [169] then is concerned with the intercession of the saints, it will needs be important to speak of it in all seriousness. I know full well that many people hate me (albeit unjustly), because they say that I am worse than all others who write nowadays. For all the others have conceded some value to the intercessions of the saints, whereas I am the first who has dared dismiss them. Bear with me then and listen to what I do and believe.

I never thought of lessening the honor of those brave heroes who for the sake of God have overcome the world. But when I could not find anything in scripture that said we should pray to them or that they are there interceding for us, I was unable to tolerate that a person's hopes be set in them, though there is no specific reference on this in holy scripture. Therefore I had to tackle the matter after all. I did not at the very first raise the issue of the intercession of the saints, as some do now when they set out to preach. And if anyone contradicts them, they retort immediately, "Did not the apostles point out above all else that the false gods are no gods, but idols?" Hence, if I find people relying on intercession of the saints--a groundless endeavor--should I not point it out from the very outset? I answer, "No". As we shall see later there is another aspect to be considered here. Therefore I took the matter in hand, as follows: I really pointed to the true salvation, Jesus Christ, and firmly taught how one should draw from him everything good and how one should turn to him in all need. For if he endured death on our behalf when we were still his enemies, how then could he be angry with us now that we believe in him, as Paul says in Rom. 5:8f, "If Christ died for us while we were still sinners, how much more now that we have been justified by his blood, shall we be saved from the wrath of God through him?"

Thus I commended to all, the benevolent grace of God and I firmly pointed to it, knowing that God would by his word bring it about. I also showed indulgence toward the simple-minded. When they fought in an ugly manner, I said, "So be it. If you wish to take your concerns to the saints, I shall take mine to God alone. Let us see which of us is on the better road." Thus I nurtured them with milk so that several of them who once were dead set against [170] me, now cling the firmer to God alone. They found how sweet the Lord is and that everyone who gets to know him would have to confess with the disciples in Jn. 6:68, "Lord to whom shall we turn? You have the word of life. I have taken hold of you; never shall I let you go". Song of Songs 3:4, Everyone who has truly learned to know God and has been led by him, will never let him go. And though someone should, by threatening to kill him, try to turn him away from God to a creature, it will not be possible, for he cannot leave his salvation. And though he should say one thing with his mouth when tortured, his heart will never faint, for it knows that God is its sure salvation through Jesus Christ. Some four years ago I conceded to someone that he may continue to pray the prayers he vowed to say until God would give him a better understanding. But I did not allow the "Our Father" to be addressed to anyone other than the one God, lest it become heresy. For how could one say to St. Gertrude, "Our Father"? Thus it happened that the larger number reached the point where, by the word of God, they began to put their trust in God alone through Jesus Christ. He became so intimate and gracious to them through the gospel that they dropped all their prayers and their trust. They felt the sweetness of the old wine and did no longer want to drink the new wine. And once they had put their hands to the plow, they did not want to look back. Thus to this day I advise anyone who proclaims the word of God, to preach salvation truly from the clear and essential word of God. In this way, trust in the one God shall grow and the deception through false hope will fall by the wayside.

Although the human heart is to put all its hope in God, I am willing to grant that a person who has been ill advised should be dealt with leniently, lest he be frightened off the entire teaching of Christ. For there are those who are so ignorant of the truth that they will reject the teaching of Christ as soon as someone denies them their patron saints. Further, I think it is not as evil to cling to a saint as it is to worship idols, though I know it is damnable when one puts one's trust in creatures. There are some who spoke of a [171] wooden fire hook [1] when they said, "Yes, we have placed our trust in the one God, but at the same time also in the saints." The two cannot be reconciled. Those, however, who are ignorant can be forgiven easily until they have grasped the truth.

Firstly, let no one think that I have any doubts concerning the rest and peace which the saints have with God so that I may want to suggest that there is no salvation after this life. Far be this from any human being; but whoever is of that opinion--and I fear there are some such, as is evident from their behavior, their works and their words (which point to the fact that they are godless people),--is damned already. Let everyone further know that we do not speak here of the prayer which righteous, believing Christians offer on behalf of each other while they are still in the body. We refer exclusively to the opinion of some false teachers which is that the saints, who are now with God, have earned a great deal of credit with him, and are therefore allegedly more pleasing to him than we and thus able to pray to him on behalf of us poor sinners or else to offer our prayers to God, since they are given a hearing more readily than we. Some have even gone as far as to suggest that no one can possibly come to God except it be through the intercession of the saints. From this evolved the later practice of relying on their merit, or putting more trust in the creatures than in the creator, or ascribing to creatures that which is God's prerogative alone. This is nothing but pure idolatry.

In order that the truth may be clearly perceived, we shall now undertake to show on the basis of divine scripture that they have advanced such teachings without any foundation in the truth.

Since they say, firstly, that the saints have great credit with God and as a result are more pleasing to him than we--indeed, they have dared claim that the saints of God have suffered more than was needful for salvation,--therefore I think it good to begin by speaking of the merits of the saints. But before we proceed to speak of this, we should like to point out that the term "sanctus" or "holy" means as much [172] as a righteous or blessed one (as we actually showed earlier). [2] Methinks that the error of adoring the saints has received a great deal of impetus from Paul and other apostles who called the Christians "holy ones", which means "righteous people", and who afterwards urged that Christians should pray for them. From this it was concluded that such prayers referred to the blessed saints, placing them on a level with those who still walk this vale of sorrow and labor. I might readily accept that departed saints are called "blessed" and not "holy" for every good Christian who puts his trust in God is called "holy", since his name is written in the book of life. However, such a one is not yet "blessed", but becomes so only when he appears before the throne of God. The name itself does not really matter that much, as long as one understands the sense which is that we speak in this context of the merits and intercessions of departed saints and not of the intercessions of the saints who are good Christians.

Now let us discuss merits.

It is certain that Jesus Christ through his suffering has earned for all humankind access to God, peace with God and blessedness, Jn. 14:16, "I am the way." Jn. 10:9, "I am the door. Whoever enters by me will be saved." Jn. 14:6, "No one comes to the

Father but by me." Rom. 5:1, "If by faith we have been justified, we have peace with God through our Lord Jesus Christ. Through him we have been led to grace through faith. In this grace we stand glorying in the hope of the privilege to be called sons of God." Note, justification here means to follow in faith. The belief is sure that Jesus Christ has reconciled us with God by his death and sacrifice. Thus reconciliation is never ours since it is Christ's. It is actually an insult to Christ when we ascribe to any creature that which is exclusively his prerogative. For this reason he is called the healer. And if he heals, works cannot heal. We are led to the grace of peace through Christ if, indeed we believe what was earlier stated, that he is our savior. For the fact that we may boast of the honor of being sons of God on the strength of our faith is the work of the Son of God. This cannot be our own merit but solely that of the Son of God, Col. 1:20, "It pleased God to [173] reconcile all things to himself through Christ. By his blood shed on the cross, he has reconciled everything in heaven and on earth." Note that reconciliation has been wrought through Christ by whose blood God chose to reconcile all things to himself. Accordingly, peace and access to God are due to the blood of Christ; they cannot be due to human beings.

Hebrews 10:19-22, "Brothers, since we now have free access to the gates of the holy city through the blood of Christ (the new and living way which he has recently built up for us through the curtain which is his flesh and blood), and since we also have a high priest for the household, i.e. the community of God, let us therefore approach with true hearts and genuine faith, etc." Note here that the way to heaven is established through the blood of Christ and earned through him. For Paul explains his own words by saying that he built the way through the curtain of his flesh in which the godhead was hidden, yet present, revealing himself at the right time. And that we might understand what is mean by his merits, he says that we have our own high priest who by his sacrifice has earned us access to heaven; for in those days priests were designated to mediate between God and humankind through their sacrifices. Through these they made bold to forgive, first themselves and then the people. Yet this was merely a shadow of future things. Hebrews 10:1, "In the same manner Christ sacrificed on our behalf, but far more fruitfully than the priests in the Old Testament." He had no need to sacrifice on his own behalf, for he had no sin of his own. But he cleansed all believing souls and paid ransom for them. The priests of old merely cleansed the flesh; but he accomplished everything which had been prophesied. The priests of old merely were a shadow or a sign, yet he did not offer up the blood of animals, but his own, on our behalf. Thus he has definitely become our savior. We may therefore come to God with upright hearts and in confident, perfect faith, since Christ through his blood has paid our ransom.

We do not intend to bring out further evidence to prove that Christ has earned us peace with God and full salvation through his own blood and has transmitted these to us; for scripture is full of testimony in this matter [174].

Since we speak at this point of the merit of salvation which is due entirely to the grace of God and since we have shown (albeit cursorily), that Christ has merited all this, it follows then that if we figure and bank on the extent of the merit, wrought by our own works, we are complete fools and our undertaking is sheer blasphemy. For how dare we debate the worth of our own works if we can be restored by the grace of God alone? For it anyone were capable of bringing about salvation by his works and thus of reconciliation with God, Christ would not have had to suffer at all; indeed, his suffering would to this day be sheer folly and utterly in vain, Gal. 2:16-21, "If it were possible to be justified through the law (i.e. by the works which are commanded by the law), Christ would have died in vain. Far be it from any believers to nullify and reject in this way the grace of God which they received through Christ."

From this you can see that all those who have ever come to God, have come solely through the suffering of Christ. How then can one of the departed saints appropriate his merits to me if he himself has not attained salvation by his own merits and did not come to God except through Christ? It is a disgusting word which the papists have spoken when they said that whatever St. Lawrence suffered in attaining his own salvation could be of some avail to us and that the pope may appropriate this to sinners and that he has power over the treasures of the church. As if it were not unworthy of God to give a richer reward than deserved to those who suffered greatly in his warfare and work, were we to concede that human beings can be saved by their merits, even though it is clear that it ill becomes an earthly ruler not to reward according to merit. See what a poor and stingy God they have made out of the gracious and rich God, so that they might sell their merits at great enough cost, despite what Christ says in Mk. 10:29, "Truly I say to you, there is no one who has left house, brothers and sisters, father, mother or wife or child or field for my sake and the gospel who does not reap a hundredfold here in this life [175] be it houses, brothers or sisters, mothers or children and fields, through persecution and in the life to come, eternal life."

Note how Christ promises rich rewards in this life, namely a hundredfold return. This is to be understood as follows: In which way did Peter and others receive a hundredfold return for leaving their homes? I answer: In this, that although earlier they did not believe in Christ, they were turned to God by the preaching of the gospel and became brothers of Christ and of all the members [of his body], whose great number pleased Peter and all other apostles more than an innumerable number of natural brothers. From this we see why Paul rejoices so greatly when he hears that people have come to faith in Christ; and how he honestly praises them, calling them beloved brothers and children.

One then gathers in riches; should one not desire these riches, one will possess them; but when they are desired and loved, they possess us. On this point one may note in the Acts of the Apostles how the Christians gave all their possessions to be shared and used in common by the brothers. One will also find, in fact, that those who leave anything for the sake of the gospel and who plant the teaching of Christ in word and deed, shall receive from the faithful a share of their possessions. Indeed, even if God were to ordain--and his judgments are wonderful--that someone has to die because of poverty or hunger, he would then give such a one great courage not to be concerned with the gods he had to leave behind; indeed, he would instead rejoice in the freedom thus attained.

If then Christ rewards a hundredfold here in this time and gives eternal life in return for the short span of suffering which we have to endure, who then can say that he suffers over and above or more than the value of the eternal prize? And Paul says in Rom. 8:18, "The sufferings of this time are not worth comparing to the future glory which is revealed to us." Scrutinize now the Romish indulgences and what justification they have. They are built on the principle of merit which is worthless and has not brought salvation for anyone.

Now if the papists say that indulgences are not grounded in the merits of the saints alone, but also [176] in the suffering of Christ, one should retort, "What? Was the suffering of Christ in itself not sufficient to pay all debt? Did you have to patch it up to make it strong enough? You enemies of God, you negators of the eternal rock, you robbers and murderers of the soul, are you looking for support of the mighty Son of God among creatures while you still boast to be Christians?" Yes, they say, while this may be of no avail, the merits of Christ, yes, a single drop of his blood alone is sufficient to wash away the sins of all the world. I respond: that's what you say. Where then does that leave your teaching concerning merits? Why then do you go on, you robbers of God, saying that the dispensing of the efficacy of the suffering of Christ is the prerogative of the pope and his kind, thus cutting off Christ's hands and mouth? For did he not say that whoever believes, shall be saved? and whoever does not believe, shall be damned? Why do you take money for that which can be acquired by faith alone and thus falsify God's word, robbing him of his authority by your saying that no one is capable of receiving his grace but alone through you? From the entire matter we learn that no creaturely achievement which requires some repayment is to be counted as a recompense or merit. Rather, we know that all our works are a debt which we can never repay, for no one can reach the measure of grace which God demands, as we have sufficiently shown above.

Here is an example to make this still clearer to you: the giving of alms is undoubtedly good work. It is praised among unbelievers even. But step forward now, however sanctimonious you may be, and show me the donation which you have given in the right way, i.e. one by which not merely your own advantage was served, either because you were seeking thus to reduce your anticipated suffering in hell--as such it is not really voluntary and like pouring water down a well--or else, one that was given with some regret, delay or in reduced quantity. I speak very sharply here so that those who seek tó set up their own good works in their heads and in their judgment might discover the problem through their own experience; for I know [177] well otherwise, of this many people are well informed, that no work is good when it comes from or is ascribed to persons. Should you find one of these lacking, you may want to recall that your works are not good and that they merit nothing; for cursed is the one who does the work of God carelessly or who deceives in doing it, Jer. 48:10.

Should none of these faults affect you, however, which is not likely to be the case (for as long as you thus deceive yourself, you are faithful to yourself and love yourself more than your neighbor, which cannot be without sin); and assuming that your self-interest does not fool you, take heed, nonetheless, that your works are not diminished in value by excessive honor, because you are looking for praise from people or from the poor person to whom you gave the gift in the first place. But even if none of this is there, take heed then lest, perchance, you have begun to please yourself by your gift and to think of yourself as righteous because of it. And if none of these things should be present then see whether in the almsgiving you have assigned nothing to yourself but to fear God only so that you do the work as uprightly and joyously as he admonished you to do. But even if you do not find this--for those who bank heavily on their own works cannot possible avoid all these short-comings--take heed and do not bank upon your alms at all, in the hope of so and so great a reward therefrom; for it is no good if it has such flaws. For as soon as it is faulty, it is unworthy of God; how then can it earn you anything? Note then that unblemished work righteousness [werck almusen], inasmuch as it comes from humans, is worthless. How much worse will it be for other kinds of works, the devilish works, which we ourselves have invented and passed off as good. I shall say more on this in Article 22.

Note then, good Christians, for God's sake, what merit our good works have, and not only ours, but those of the saints also. For if their works are good, they cannot be their own, since nothing good comes from human beings. But if there is, as we think, any good that comes from people, it is not ours at all, but God's. Thus no human works are good unless they be of God. Why then should you want to [178] ascribe anything good to people when it belongs to God alone? The saints, i.e. the righteous ones, do not ascribe anything good to themselves, for the moment they do that, it is no longer good. In so far as it is good, however, and of God, how dare we figure out how much it merits, if it is not ours at all? The moment we make it out to be our own, we sin in the matter. To sum up: What prince will tolerate that a good deed which he prudently conceived and had also completed through a worthy servant, be credited to the servant? Or what son is there who charges his labor to the father when he is an heir of the paternal inheritance and works in accordance with the father's will with no regard to wages? Since we are children of God by his great grace and mercy, how then can we come like strange, unfree servants and calculate wages which the Lord owes us?

At this point the greedy servants who look upon their wages only shout, "Look here; they want to take away from us our just rewards and rob us of the wages of good works even though there is a good deal in scripture which indicates how God rewards our works and what they merit," Mt. 10:41f. "Whoever receives a prophet or helps him as a prophet will get the reward of a prophet; and whoever receives a good person as a good person and helps him, gets the reward of a good person, and anyone who gives so much as a cup of cold water to one of these little ones in the name of a disciple will, I assure you, not go unrewarded." Such like statements are numerous in both the Old and New Testament, promising to the children of Israel that, should they walk in the precepts of God, God would make their enemies subject to them and be their Father; on the other hand, he would make them the prey of every person, should they step away from him. God promised to Abraham that salvation would come to humankind in his seed, because he was prepared to offer up to God his very own son. Note the reward and merit. My answer: Go on a bit in the tenth chapter of Mt. [10:28-31] and you will find the following written there, "Fear not those who might kill the body, but cannot kill the soul. Fear him more who could destroy soul and [179] body in eternal death. Does one not sell two sparrows for one farthing? Yet not one of them shall fall to the ground without the will of your Father. Even the hair on your head is counted. Therefore, fear not, for you far surpass the sparrows." In these words of Christ we perceive that everything takes place under the precepts and providence of God. Had he said, "The sparrows shall not be sold without the heavenly Father", one might have been able to surmise: "Yes, indeed, God sends some things and some things he does not send." But he does say, "Not one of the sparrows falls to the ground without the directive of the Father." We cannot but admit that not even the least thing takes place unless it is ordered by God. For who has ever been so concerned and curious as to find out how much hair he has on his head? There is no one. God, however, knows the number. Indeed, nothing is too small in us or in any other creature, not to be ordered by the all-knowing and all-powerful providence of God. How much more then are all our works ordered by divine decrees? Since this is so, we cannot ascribe any credit to ourselves. Rather, we should know that everything happens by the decree of God to whom alone all things ought to be credited.

I object: Why then does God condemn us, if we do not do any good? As it is written in Mt. 7:19, "Every tree that does not bear good fruit is uprooted and thrown into the fire." Now we are incapable of doing good, yet if we do not do good, we are being condemned. From this one would have to conclude that God is unjust if he directs his wrath, i.e. condemnation toward me for something I cannot do anything about. In this fashion Paul argues in Rom. 3:5. I respond: A good tree brings forth good fruit and cannot bring forth evil fruit. By the same token, an evil tree cannot bring forth good fruit, Mt. 7:18. If then you do not bring forth good fruit, that is a sign that you are an evil tree. Therefore you will be uprooted and burned. You might say: If, however, I cannot be good of my own accord, but have to be made good by God, why then does God not make me good or else leave me uncondemned? I answer: Why God does not make you good, you have to ask him yourself. I have not been consulted [180] by him. [3] But I learned this from St. Paul in Rom. 9:20-23 that God is not unjust simply because he uses his creature according to his will, just as a potter cannot be called unjust by his vessels because he forms out of a lump of clay a vessel for worthy usage and another for less worthy usage. Does a night dish ever say, "Why did you not make an honest drinking vessel out of me?" Thus God deals with us without in any way diminishing his justice; for we are, in relation to him, lower than clay is in relation to the potter. Therefore he disposes of his vessels, i.e. us humans as he wills. One he chooses to be skilled for his purposes and use; another he cannot use. He may repair his vessels and make them whole or break them, as he wills. Thus he hardened the heart of Pharoah so that neither signs nor destruction moved him; had it not been for this, such hardness could not have been possible in view of such great signs. In the same way he hardens the hearts of anti-Christians to this day so that seeing, they do not see and hearing, they do not hear. They see that they cannot resist the teaching of God; it is forcefully brought forth; yet they still dare fend it off. They hear the truth brought out so clearly from the word of God that they cannot bring anything against it; for could they resist it, they would not hesitate to do so; yet at the moment they are not willing either to believe or understand it. This, of course, is nothing less than the judgment of God which draws some to him while rejecting others. And we shall not be able to meddle in his affairs; for who are we to quarrel or reason with God? But human wisdom concerning free will which we have acquired from the heathen has brought us to the point of ascribing to our deeds and counsel the work of God which he has wrought in us without acknowledging the almighty providence of God.

At this point unbelievers invariably shout: Now then everyone will say, "So be it. I shall not do good works any more. Let us see what God intends to work through me. If he has made me good, I should be good; let him do to me as I do to him. But if I am evil nothing I may do will be of any avail; I am bound to be damned." I respond: One [181] knows a tree by its fruit. If God has made you a good tree you will bring forth good fruit. For as little as the Spirit and power of God reneges or lies idly, but rather is eternally active in doing good works and leading toward perfection (entelechia) so little can a good tree be idle. The Spirit of God, which has made it good, moves it to do good works; its life cannot be but an active creation of God. Since it is God's nature to order and direct all things, the believer knows himself to be an instrument and vessel through which God works--he does not ascribe anything to himself but knows himself and all creation to be of God. Now again one may recognize by your works that you are a corrupt unfruitful tree if you do nothing. And even when you do something, everyone can see that you ascribe it all to yourself. Therefore your work--as you call it--serves to condemn you, for you ascribe unto yourself what is actually God's. And though God may work through you, God's work comes to its appointed end and you will falter in your high opinion of yourself and be damned, if you appropriate all this to yourself. God will make of you a vessel of wrath, i.e. of damnation, by which he shows his righteousness. Do not be concerned about how to become good or evil; God will make you good or evil, as he wills. To be a good tree is to do everything that pleases God with such eagerness that it becomes one's greatest sorrow if one is unable to do his will at all times, and to desire that such a fire be kindled in everyone.

Now I am prepared to admit that scripture contains a great deal which at first glance does look not unlike merit. This is undoubtedly so because of some little ones who do not readily come to the faith, who believe that even though the cat might have brought them a sausage, it happened as a result of divine providence. For faith, too, has its increase, as Christ indicated in the restoring of the blind man's sight, Mark 8:24, who, at first, looked upon people as if they were trees, yet soon after

[182] regained full sight. You may say: Surely faith must be meritorious; for one who believes shall be saved. For Christ often states, "Your faith has made you well." I respond: Faith is nothing other than a certain confidence by which a person depends on the merits of Christ, but it is not to be numbered among works (even though Christ calls it a work; Jn 6:29 means something else). Rather, it is confidence and assurance in the merit of Christ. This confidence and trust does not originate with humankind, but is from God; for the word of Christ in Jn. 6:44 cannot fail when he says, "No one comes to me, unless my Father who has sent me, draws him." The reason why God gives a clear and strong faith to some from the beginning while to others he gives it gradually only is in his, not in our counsel.

Consequently, to forego any claim on merit is nothing less than faith. For to ascribe nothing to oneself and to believe all things to be governed and ordered by the providence of God arises solely from a person's resignation and confidence in God; from being firmly assured that God does all things, though we may not be aware of him. This is the faith which grows and increases as soon as it is sown--but the growth is not ours, but God's. Christ teaches this in a straightforward parable in Mt. 4:26-29, "The kingdom of God is like the man who sows the seed upon the ground, then retires to sleep. And after daybreak he rises to find the seed sprouting and growing, but he knows nothing about it; for the earth brings forth fruit by itself, first the sprouts, then the ears, after that the full wheat in the ears. And when the fruit has ripened, he sends for the harvesters since the ears are full."

Take a good look at this parable. The kingdom of God is nothing less than the word of God in this place, Lk. 8:11. Where people begin to believe in it, i.e. where God sows it, there it grows by the power of God so that we can sleep, in other words, [183] we do not plant it in our own strength. And God brings about that his word increases in faith and works even though we often overlook this, unaware that God works through us. Finally, the one who sowed initially, sends for the harvesters and reaps the fruit, he himself has cultivated and planted. This faith in God which brings about all things, has its increase and growth from God alone. And the more faith grows, the more the work of all good things grows; for the greater faith grows, the more God is in you. The more God becomes great in you, the more does the good take effect in you. For God is the eternal and unchangeable power of all good things; should he ever stop being effective, he would cease being unchangeable. Pull yourself together then. The beginning and seed of faith come from God and no one comes to Christ unless he be drawn by the Father. The increase of faith is God's also, as I have shown. Faith teaches us that God effects all things, while we can do nothing. Behold what peace and quietness. Thus if follows, finally, that we credit nothing to ourselves, if we are believers. And as soon as merit comes to nought, so soon does the intercession of the saints, the hypocrisy of those who are living with which they stuffed themselves, although they do enough good works to save themselves and us.

Those who credit a great deal to free will, human wisdom and merit, cannot really escape this insight, except to say, "Yes, indeed, God is the primary cause in all things, but we too, are effective." This is little else than a subtle way of escaping God within oneself. For if God is the greater cause and perfecter of works, as the papists have to confess, I must ask whether or not God can be moved by another cause. They will have to confess that he is the first moving cause, not moved by any other; otherwise there would be an unending succession and one would have to point to a cause of each cause. Then I would ask further whether a person can be his own cause. Then they avoid answering as they twist and rhyme a great deal; yet all of it is false opinions. For note this briefly: Had a person come from himself [originated in himself], he would also have to be in himself [184] the cause of all his works. But if he did not come from himself but from God, then God is also the cause of all his works. For how can a person ascribe anything to himself if everything he is, is from God? Hence it follows that, if God, according to their own admission, is the supreme cause of works, these will have to be ascribed to him, and not to us; for credit must always be given to the greater; and here I am arguing on their own ground. We have the strong word of God on our side so that they cannot overcome us with their mighty array. In other words, God effects all things in us. We are nothing but vessels in his hand through which he works. Indeed, he himself has made them. A smithy will not credit the hammer for having made the plowshares, but himself; for he made the hammer, too, and both hammer and plowshares are the smithy's handiwork. Thus it is with the work of God. We, too, are God's who has made the work and us, his instruments. See how handsomely we stand here and give out airs like a country bumpkin. [4] He always wanted to be a knight yet never had a horse until in the end he became so miserable and sick that they carted him to a hospital on a manure cart. Pardon me, worthy Christians, for such cynical analogy; I might have omitted it, but it is so much like our wisdom that it fits rather well, at this point.

Now follows a host of proofs by which we learn that we are nothing.

Jn. 6:44, "No one comes to me unless my Father has drawn him." If he has to draw us I am right in concluding that we would never have come of our own accord. In the same context in Is. 54 [Jn. 6:45; Is. 54:13] we read, "All are being taught of God." Where then is our own advice and counsel?

Jn. 15:4, "As a branch cannot of itself bear fruit unless it remain on the vine, so neither can you, unless you remain in me." I conclude: By itself the branch can do nothing; neither can you.

In the same context [Jn. 15:16] we read, "You did not elect me, but I have chosen you to go and bring forth fruit." Do you see that it is not we who elect God but he who chooses and singles us out.

Yet again in Jn. 15:5 we read, "Without me you can do nothing." It is clear that we cannot do anything without Christ, much like the hammer (without the smithy) and the branch apart from the vine. [185]

In Lk. 17:7-10, "Who among you, having a servant out in the fields or pasture would say to him when he comes in from the fields: 'Come then and ˙sit down at the table'? Would you not rather say, 'Prepare the supper, get ready and serve at table until I have had my food and drink. After that you may eat and drink'? Will he thank the servant for having done what he was told to do? I don't think so. Likewise you. If you have done everything I have commanded, you say, 'We are worthless servants, for we have done what was our duty.'" Look well to these words. For they also cancel out our empty chatter about merit by speaking of the works only which God commands.

Paul says in 1 Cor. 3:5ff, "Who is Paul, who Apollo other than servants (i.e. hand tools), through whom you have learned the faith and that, as much as God has given to everyone. I planted, Apollo watered, but God gave the increase. Thus neither the one who planted nor the one who watered is anything, but God, who gives the growth. These words are plain enough and indicate that no messenger is anything on his own account but only as God's servant, accomplishing as much as God grants.

He speaks in the same vein in 2 Cor. 3:4-6 when he boasts of how the Corinthians came to the faith through him, and in attempting not to ascribe too much to himself, he speaks as follows, "Such confidence in God (meaning, that we may point out how we have led you to the faith), we have through Christ--not that we are in any way skilled or sufficient to think of our own ability even though it may come from us. Rather, our qualifications or skills come from God who has made us skilled servants of the New Testament which is not one of the letter, but of the Spirit. These words point out that the testament of the gospel is inscribed upon human hearts and works in us by the Spirit of God. From this follows: Where there is faith, there the Spirit of God is also, and where he is there one may find good works.

Likewise he says in 1 Cor. 12:3-6, "No one can say 'Jesus is Lord' except by the power of the Spirit. There are [186] varieties of gifts, but only one Spirit. There are varieties of service but only one Lord. There are varieties of powers which work, but God is always the One, working all things in all persons, etc." Take note, to call Jesus "one Lord" is to know him as our savior, head and Lord. This comes through none other but the Holy Spirit. Note further, that the gifts of God are available in great variety; so are the gifts or services and powers. But God who grants these, is one. From this we conclude that God effects all things in every person. Read, if you please, what follows; it will be useful.

Likewise he says again in Phil. 2:13, "It is God who works in you the will and the power of doing it according to his pleasure." Note, God is the one who moves our will to will what he wills and then provides the strength to do what he wills.

I have made this digression on the providence of God so that we may learn therefrom that God works in us everything that is good; we certainly do not do these works but act simply as instruments and vessels through which God works; for from him and through him and in him are all things. If we are aware of his providence in all things we will also discover his omnipotence and power to order all things according to his will. Thus all merit falls by the board; we cannot bank on our merit at all if every good that happens is God's and not our work. In fact, the moment we ascribe it to ourselves it becomes evil, for by nature we are evil, Gen. 8:21. "Now then, no evil tree can yield good fruit." Though God in his word promises rewards, he rewards the work only which he himself has wrought. Augustine confirms this and the Lord himself points to it when he says, "I have called you out [187] that you may bring fruit" [Jn. 15:16]. [5] He calls and orders to work in his vineyard and himself invites to his wedding feast. He it is who gives Pilate authority, otherwise he could have done nothing to him. From this we may deduce that no one has amounted to anything who on his own has sought to please God. Rather he [God] himself has allowed those to please him whom he wills. Indeed, he it was who determined the alms Cornelius [Acts 10:4] and Toby [Tob. 12:8-12] gave and he stimulated them to do so from the beginning even though the angel says, "God has seen your alms and your works." The works had to have a promise of hope to start with. Whosoever then trusts in God, is moved by God. Therefore it is good to reflect that Cornelius, though he was a heathen, was moved by God to give alms so that he may see that his false gods were nought and long for a knowledge of the true God. This is also indicated by the words in Acts 10:31, "Your prayers have been heard and your alms have been remembered, etc." Whatever God has done to these two is nothing but a reward of his own work. So rich in grace is he that he gives grace upon grace, Jn. 1:16.

Since we now have clearly disproved the theory of merit, the papists can no longer boastfully point to the intercession of the saints which has made for negligent Christians, indeed. For one could find many a foolish Christian who thought he might not be condemned if he had a patron saint who would intercede without ceasing, thus setting him free to rob, burn, wage wars, gamble, swear, commit adultery. He completely overlooked the qualities which the saint had going for him on earth--what kind of faith he had, how he loved God and how little he regarded temporal things. Indeed, he perhaps figured that he would be safe from cannons, boils and plagues just for wearing a silver or gold ornament of St. Sebastian on his hat for show; or perhaps, that he would be free of all plagues by reciting a daily Ave Maria to St. Christopher; or perhaps if he [188] had St. Barbara--delicately pictured in the shape of a whore--placed upon some altar so that the priest in reading mass may not be overly devotional, he himself might not have to die without first receiving the body and blood of Christ. And in all his vices he says--as if the saints died for these so that one could go on sinning on credit--"I know that the dear saint has earned so much credit with God that he can now give me all things." In addition, those lying tightwads have led on the evil thoughts of people with their preaching of fables; not for nothing, of course. Whenever it was St. Sebastian's Day the peasants started their dance to the altar much to the joy of the entire convent. Therefore they shout now, "Shall we no longer honor the dear saints?" or "Oh, how the Mother of God is treated with disrespect." Even if the silvery snow had fallen upon the altar as hard as it could, you would not have started to lament. Now I reply to you: You dishonest imposter. Who teaches that the saints should not be honored? But what is their true honor? Is it to sacrifice? Indeed, this may be to your advantage, but not in honor of the saints. Take note that nothing honors the saints of God more than when we proclaim their faith and bold patience--endured for the sake of God--so that we too may be drawn to such wholesome acts and learn to know him whom they all clung to also. As Peter says, we experience nothing new at all when we are persecuted for God's sake.

However, you want to speak of that only which fills your larder: This saint is good against toothache; that one, against stomachache; that one restores sight; this one helps to keep adultery secret; and yet you shout that no one honors the saints anymore just because we reject your fables. Therefore you start your lies. When you come to Zurich you say that you heard a preacher at Constance say that Mary did not remain a virgin. If you go to Constance, you say someone preached that at Zurich. [6] But if one looks at it closely, one finds that it wasn't preached in either place. But some of the big mouths carry such fairy tales back and forth, telling them with great flourish. [189] Therefore be careful, good Christians; do not believe those enemies of God, for they are as little afraid of spreading lies as a trickster would be. They do it to stir up unrest in the world. For no one is so foolish that he might not greatly admire the valiant warriors of God with the wish to be one of their companions. Through them we are shown where we, too, shall get to if we walk as they did. Therefore Paul calls them witnesses in Heb. 12:1 for they testify unto us of the salvation into which the saints shall enter which we can see with our own eyes. In short, I value the Mother of God greatly as the eternally pure, unspotted maid-servant Mary, highly exalted above those who have died for the sake of God's honor and will. Whether or not she prays on my behalf before God, of that, later.

For the sake of the papists, let me first of all give a human account by which they may discern that intercession of the saints is opposed to their own dialectic.

Thus: If the saints intercede before God on our behalf it must take place either because they are concerned with our troubles or else because they are not. If our troubles cling to them, they cannot be considered blessed, for it is the chief charac- teristic of blessedness to be free of sadness and sorrow, to suffer no want nor any other weakness. If our troubles do not cling to them, they either do not pray for us, or if they did--as you fabri- cate--it would not move God anyway. The reason: It would not come from the heart; yet God looks upon the heart alone. Thus you speak; now untie the knot.

Here is a second knot. You say: "Blessedness is given to a person when he is in the presence of God and when nothing in his own will is opposed to God any longer. Thus it must needs follow that the saints cannot intercede on behalf of anyone except on behalf of one whom they can see to be with God so that what they ask may also be granted; or else, their will is contrary to God's, should they ask something of him which is not of his will. Here a fellow objects [190] (I will not call him by name except to say that he is a first-rate papist; for he might, should God permit it, go after me otherwise, for he itches under the skin) [7], that the will of the saints is not one with God's; this is down-right blasphemy. Has not God taught us to pray that his will be done on earth as in heaven? If then the will of the saints is not one with God, we would also pray then that our will be not one with God either." See what valiant Christians these are. If they cannot support intercession with the word of truth, they begin to tell lies to the detriment of the word of God. And since they claim to save the honor of the saints, they dishonor God, his saints and all truth at the same time.

Thirdly you say: "Everything the saints know, they learn by beholding the face of God and our prayers are known to them through God. Hence it follows that God knows our prayer before the saints are even aware of it. Thus can be dismissed also what some among you say, namely that the saints transmit our prayer to God--for they learn our concerns from God.

I do not bank much on these objections even though they prove to be strong enough for the papists. But I do build on the fact that there is not a single doctrine or example in the entire Bible which says that the saints pray for us in yonder world. Furthermore, a great many important passages of the Bible, indeed, the first commandment of God, are opposed to it.

Finally, reliance upon intercession of the saints obscures, denies and rejects the wholesome suffering of Christ and is an offence to the saints. The first and foremost commandment is as follows, Deut. 6:4; Mt. 22:37; Lk. 10:27; Mk. 12:29, "The Lord your God is one God. You shall love the Lord your God with all your heart and with all you soul and with all your might and with all your mind." If a person is to direct his love toward God with all his strength it follows that he must place all his trust in him [191] also; for this is the commandment of faith which God has given the children of Israel through Moses which Christ, too, stresses in Mt. 4:10 in the words, "You shall worship the Lord your God and him alone shall you serve." Look upon this commandment as a commandment of faith and trust in God. Moses again says in Deut. 6:13, "You shall fear the Lord your God and him alone shall you serve."

Let not the papists brag of their "service" and "super service" [douleia and hyperdouleia] (what interest to us are their fanciful descriptions of these terms?): "It is true, indeed, that one ought to worship God above all and this is known as latria (the worship of God); one may call on the saints and ask for God in prayers of approach--this is dulia; one may pray to the Mother of God as the supremest of all the servants of God--this is called hyperdulia." [8] That they cannot get anywhere with this con game may be easily discerned when one realizes they they have invented the two terms dulia and hyperdulia. You will not find "dulia" in the entire Bible in the sense of prayer of approach or appeal to the saints. "Hyperdulia" cannot be found at all. But latrium is often found in the verb "latreuin" which means to serve or honor. In this manner, Christ uses the term in Mt. 4:10 when he says, "And him alone shall you serve" or "and him alone shall you honor". In this context then, latria means the honor and service which a person renders to God as the treasure in whom he trusts. Therefore Christ says, "You shall worship your Lord God and him alone shall you serve" i.e. you shall not turn in trust to anyone but God alone. You shall not direct your services to any one else to whom you may take refuge, but to him.

I give this opinion not out of my own head. It is clearly written in Deut. 10:20, "You shall fear the Lord your God and him alone shall you serve. To him you shall cling and in his name confirm truth or swear oaths. He is your praise and your God." Everyone can see [192] from this that God intended the first commandment to say that all honor, laud, fear and service is to be directed to no creature but to him alone. You must understand here that God does not intend to stop one person from serving another or from paying homage to his superiors. God does not speak of those who are still visible to each other in this world, suggesting that they should not serve each other. Rather, he says that we should not seek our comfort with anyone other than God; in invisible creatures we should have no confidence at all; we should not make of them images for our comfort.

That this is in fact the intent, namely, not to have any confidence in invisible creatures (nor) to serve them, can be seen in the words of the commandment of God in Deut. 5:8, "You shall not make for yourself any carved or graven image. Neither shall you make a likeness of anything in heaven above or on the earth below nor of the things that dwell in the water under the earth. You shall not worship them; neither shall you honor them." Do you note there that God does not speak of the living--for one ought not imitate them. It follows then that he does not forbid honoring the living with appropriate respect and serving them, as is customary among people. Rather, the creatures which we do not see, are not to be imitated, nor are we to offer them honor or services in return for assurance. For we are to cling to, honor and serve him only in all invisible things.

If then we are to put all our trust in him alone (for he is the only one who judges evil and shows mercy, which is stated soon after the above word in Deut. 5:9), it follows then that the first commandment "you shall believe" is you shall put all your confidence, trust and love in the one God only; him you shall cling to with all your heart, soul, strength and mind." Wherever all confidence is reserved for God alone there any trust in creatures comes to nought. For it cannot be that a person places his trust in God and says, nonetheless, "I trust in creatures and in saints alike." This is like children who when asked, "whom in your family do you love?" say, "I love my father." But afterwards the mother comes and says, I wish I were the dearest and the child responds, [193] "But you are the dearest, too." And after that it gives a similar reply to the maid, too. In similar fashion they speak who say, "I am a Christian and no one shall outdo me in my faith; I know well that all my confidence shall be in God; I have known that all my life; but I have confidence in the dear saints also." Can you see what children they are. They do not know what they say; they boast of their faith, yet do not understand the first commandment; for God demands the total heart. In the same way as a husband becomes angry and will not tolerate that his wife's heart is full of another man, so God cannot bear it when a human heart takes refuge with someone other than with him alone. Thus he says through the prophet Isaiah [28:20], "The bed is narrow so that the other falls out and the coat is short--it will not cover both of them." In short, God does not tolerate that confidence and trust is placed in anyone other than himself.

Accordingly, above intercession of the saints obscures the suffering of Christ. For I hope it has been shown sufficiently how fruitful and wholesome the latter is, that God in the name of Christ is willing to give us all things. Indeed, it is impossible for him to deny us anything since he has given his only Son on our behalf. Has he not promised us to find everything we need with him, as Paul says in Rom. 8:31, "If God is for us who can be against us, who has not spared his own Son but has given him up for us all. How then can he not give us all things through him?" Paul's meaning here is that God is on our side and stands by us; therefore no one can harm us. But in order that we may be sure how gracious and merciful he is and that we may be assured that he will not deny us anything, he has not spared his own Son on our behalf and given him for us. How then can he deny us anything now? Now he does not have anything greater or more precious and worthy than his Son. Why then should he deny us something? For anything that he will ever give us is bound to be less than his own Son. Therefore, since he has given him to us, we ought to come to him for all our needs since he will not deny us anything. [194]

It becomes apparent then how these foolish papists have maliciously turned God's kindness into disfavor. They have turned a kind, gracious Father into an angry judge and tyrant. For thus they have shouted from their pulpits, "Do not let yourselves be diverted from hope in the dear saints; for if anyone should go to a ruler of this world to ask for grace or anything else, he would have to have an intermediary just as if the ruler of this world had to be like that. Would not the rulers of this world be much better if they were gracious and inclined toward what is right, by allowing every poor person to come before them, listening to him graciously and as brothers and thereafter, regardless of property, favor or partiality mete out judgment and mercy? Methinks you are about to answer "yes". Then know, that our God is to be considered by us as a father before whom we may pour out all our needs; for he taught us to call him "father"; and the Spirit of God testifies to our spirit that we are sons of God, Rom. 8:16. In other words, God, by the grace of his Spirit, instructs our soul that we have a God who is kinder than a physical father. We may call him "our father" freely and without constraint and he is well pleased by it and shall be in our midst. He is so accessible that we may dare come to him. Did he not lower himself so magnanimously in order that we may reach him, as he says in Lk. 22:27, "I am among you as your servant." But now you papists--haters of truth--come along and make of him so unfriendly, unbending and frightful a tyrant, that no one dares come to him without a mediator. Why then has he taught us to come to him and say, "Our heavenly Father. Give us, forgive us, etc?" Why then does he stand with open arms which for our sake were wounded and bids us, Mt. 11:28, "Come unto me, all who labor [195] and are burdened and I shall give you rest?" Note whom he calls. He turns to those who labor and are burdened with the load of sin. Why then do you say, "How dare I, poor sinner, come unto him?" Can you not hear that he calls the sinner? Can you not hear when he says, "I am not come to call the righteous but the sinners unto betterment [Mk. 2:17; Lk. 5:32]? And when he goes on to say, "The healthy do not need a physician, but those who are sick do" [Mk. 2:17; Lk. 5:31]? Is it not, good Christian, to spoil the sweet savor of the comforting grace of God when a papist discourages the sinner, telling him that he ought not or should not come to God; that he must have a mediator? Is it not to rob Christ's honor and give it to the creatures when in fact he has given to all of us a certain surety of salvation Eph. 1? Yet you ascribe it to a creature. Is this not to turn people sour on God and to make them love a creature? What else is this but idol worship? See, how pathetic our own inventions are. We have reached the point when we put our confidence in creatures and look on the creator as on a tyrant. Thanks be to you, dear papists, for having led the world into such blindness and keeping it there in the midst of all light.

Finally, it is also mockery of the saints when after their death one treats them like God whom they had always elevated above everything else; they had gone to him because they always put their trust in him and had turned away from every creature. Indeed, the eternally pure maiden Mary cannot tolerate that all honor which rightfully belongs to her Son is placed upon her any more than Paul and Barnabas could tolerate it in Lystra [Acts 14:8-20], for if the highest righteousness is in heaven, no one ought to rejoice but be angry instead, when honor, which belongs exclusively to the highest Son of God, is appropriated to him. For Paul and Barnabas cried out when the people of Lystra took them for gods and prepared to offer up before them, saying, "We are not more than weak men, just like you" [Acts 14:15]. What do you think they might say today if they could see that people seek with them what can only be found with God? Do you not think that worthy Mary would say,

> O you ignorant people [196]. Whatever honor I may have
> is not my own. God in his grace has thus enriched me
> that I am a maidservant and a mother of all the human
> race. I am neither a goddess nor the fount of goodness;

God alone is that fountain. He permits all goodness to come to you through my son, but if you credit me with the things that are God's exclusively, the power of God and his dominion would be diminished. From the beginning of the world he did not give the kind of power to any creature in which people might put their trust except it be God's, as Nicodemus actually attributed to my Son in Jn. 3:2, "No one," he said, "can do the signs which you do, unless God be with him." He is god, therefore he can do all things. I am not God. You should not therefore, seek with me what God alone can give. While I was still on earth, my Son, for whom I was nonetheless the highest and most precious, did not give me a share in any of his wondrous works. For once, when I reminded him that the people had no wine, he gave me a strange reply, "Woman," he said, "what do I have to do with you [Jn. 2:4]?" This he said simply because the miracle was to be credited to him and not to me. Therefore leave God in his dominion and power as he has been of old. You think I feel honored when you worship me, but it is actually a disgrace to me. No one but the only God shall be worshipped. Him you should honor in the manner in which I have honored him, in faith, obedience, endurance of the unpleasant things, which I have endured with his Son, from childhood to the end, in poverty and suffering. Let me be a witness to the fact that all who are God's must suffer opposition in this age; even if you are treated badly in this age, your honor is nonetheless great in heaven. And what all did I suffer. Think then, though God chose me to be mother of his Son, he did not exempt me from agony and pain. In fact, he sent it to me in rich measure. How much less will he exempt you. But you may endure the same all the more joyfully if you have seen me bear it. I am none other [197] than a witness of my son that you may see how certainly salvation rests with him.

Something like that Mary would, no doubt, say, if she were among us. In like fashion, the faithful servants of God might speak if they could see our foolish ways,

Do you not see that we did not serve the saints nor call on them in the hour of death? We served the one God who came to our aid in the hour of need; for we put all our trust in him. Do you not see that James when being murdered, Acts 12:2 does not call on Stephen, who had gone to God before him? Neither does Peter in his affliction, nor Paul call on Stephen or James. Who taught you that you should run to us when we ourselves come to God only through Christ the mediator? While we were living, we did not want to diminish God's honor and appropriate it unto ourselves. And now when we partake of honor and joy, the like of which no one has seen or heard of, you attribute to us what belongs to God as if we should rejoice in your foolish ideas and take it to be an honor when it would be to our disgrace if we actually did rejoice. You make something of us which we are not: patrons and princes of vices. If we actually followed you or paid attention to you, we would have among us such controversies as the pagan poets imagined to exist among their gods. Just think on this: Two enemies come to the same St. George and call on him for victory. To whom should he give the victory? Or else, the Spaniards call on James and the French on Michael. Should each one go to the aid of those who call on him, he would have to oppose the other. Drop such foolishness and place yourself under the mighty hand of God. Do not judge our nature by your own ideas.

Thus it follows, does it not, that if we wish to honor the saints, we ought to do as they have done; we should take up our cross and follow Christ. [198]

Thus I have shown here and in the previous Article that Christ is our only access to God and that the hope which we were taught to put in creatures is utter falsehood and idol worship. Thus it is high time that scripture, which they have so dishonorably abused, must be torn out of their hands. They must be shown how they have misused or misunderstood it.

First of all they cited Gen. 48:16, where Jacob in his blessing of the sons of Joseph says, "They shall be called by my name and by the names of my ancestors Abraham and Isaac." In this context they say, "Do you not perceive there that Abraham, Isaac and Jacob are to be called upon?" Answer: You allow yourselves to be deceived by their arguments so that soon you won't understand either Hebrew, Greek, Latin, or German. Does "you shall be called by my name" mean "I will pray God on your behalf in the other world?" Or does it mean, "Call on me and I will pray to God in yonder world on your behalf?" Tell me, did Abraham, Jacob and others come to God before Christ came? Had it been possible to come to God before Christ, it would follow that he did not first have to prepare the way; thus he is not the only door by which one may come to God; hence it is not true either when he says, "No one comes to the Father but by me"? Far be it from any believing heart to even think that. But if they were not with God but were deprived of his presence also, how then could they have prayed on our behalf before God? When Abraham longed to see the future of Christ, he could not have been in the presence of God, or else he would have had no need of Christ. Since then he was not with God, how could he have prayed for someone else if he himself lacked something and was unable to come to God except through God alone? Look how you tear about in Holy Scripture just like a beggar in the country. Whatever place he gets to, suits him fine. You then, when you find the term, "to call on," "ask," "blessed" or such like, interpret it immediately according to your silly opinion, whether it comes close to the truth or not. Were Abraham, Isaac and Jacob to have been with God before Christ? Since that cannot have been (whatever the meaning of "Abraham's bosom" may be, I dare not say at this point), how then can they have prayed before God on behalf of the children of Israel?

Thus you turn all scripture around. More [199] dangerous enemies of God than you papists have never before been on earth. Unbelievers go to sleep with their damage; they cannot harm our faith. But you take scripture in which is contained the word of salvation and lead us therewith into idol worship just as you have done with this passage in which Jacob intends to say only that God may hear them when they call upon him in his, Abraham's or Isaac's name, that he then might remember the oath and the covenant which he entered into with them and their offspring. Thus "my name be called out upon them" means "may my name be of benefit to them." If then they call on thee, O God, for his sake, do then come to their aid. Though they may not be pleasing to thee, do remember that Abraham, Isaac and I were dear to thee and that thou hast made such promises to us." This is not my interpretation and would not prove anything according to my own reckoning if it were not for the fact that scripture gives its own illumination. Then let us see how Moses called on Abraham, Isaac and Jacob. By this the meaning of the above will become clear and we will, through one and the same effort, release yet another part of scripture from its chains [i.e. make yet another obscure passage clear].

In Exodus 32:11-13 Moses calls on God because of the evil of the children of Israel which they committed by worshiping the calf. He says, "O Lord, why art thou so very angry with they people whom you have led out of Egypt with might and a strong arm? I ask you, calm your anger and be gracious concerning the evil of your people so that the Egyptians will not be able to say, 'He led them there by stealth that he may murder them in the hills and extinguish them from the face of the earth.' Remember Abraham, Isaac and Israel, your servants, to whom you have sworn by your own being, saying, 'I shall multiply your seed like the stars of heaven, etc.' Here we actually see what it means to invoke the names of the three patriarchs over the children of Israel. It is nothing less than to have reminded God of the friendship and love which he had once shown to them and of the oath he had sworn. Thus they say, Lord, by right we should not come before you because of our evil which makes us unworthy of any good you may now do to us. But be mindful of the friendship which you had with Abraham, Isaac and Jacob. [200] They were our fathers. We are nothing, but our fathers have been dear to you. Let us benefit because of them. Be also mindful of the promise that in their seed all nations shall be blessed and that you do intend to have them multiply as the stars of heaven. How could that ever happen if you should now treat us according to our merit." Look now whether you find the words of Moses to be of similar meaning. You will see that he says, "Be mindful of Abraham, Isaac and Jacob, your servants." Note the reminder of an old friendship. After that you note that he says, "Which you have sworn by your own name, saying, etc." Do you note the reminder of an oath? From this you papists have sought to prove intercession of the saints as if it is all the same to say, "O Lord, be mindful of Abraham, Isaac and Jacob" and "Abraham, Isaac and Jacob, pray for us". Are you deaf or foolish not to understand that the one statement, namely, "Be mindful of Abraham, Isaac and Jacob" calls on God with regard to the righteous ones, but the other is to ask the patriarchs, Abraham, Isaac and Jacob themselves to pray for them. This latter [practice] cannot be found in scripture; therefore you must cut it out.

Let me recount here the words of Daniel 3 [i.e. additions to Daniel 2:11-13, the so-called Prayer of Azariah], [9] though they are not in the Canon of scripture. Nonetheless, their meaning will become clearer and they will show up how the papists dare turn scripture upon its head for their own purposes. Azariah calls upon God in this way, "O Lord, we ask you for your name's sake, do not forsake us forever and do not annul your covenant or promise; do not withdraw your mercy from us for the sake of Abraham whom you loved and Isaac, your servant and Israel, your devoted servant. With them you spoke, promising to increase their seed as the stars in the sky and the sand of the sea shores, etc." In these words, too, we find only that they called upon God in the name of Abraham, Isaac and Jacob because these were friends of God to whom God had made promises and sworn oaths. The Jews still do it to this day. They do not call on [201] Abraham, Isaac and Jacob that they might intercede for them. Indeed, were we to call on the saints to pray to God on our behalf they would ridicule us, saying that we have many gods, yet one should call on the One God only; it is right to remind him in the name of those who were dear to him. Now I do not point this out to prove something by reference to the Jews, but simply to show how they understood the first commandment and that what we use from their scriptures to confound the papists does not have that meaning even with the erring, unbelieving Jews.

Now a simple Christian may at this point think as follows:

I can clearly note from all this that the saints do no pray for me; but I may well call on God in their name, i.e. I may well say, "Lord, be merciful to me for the sake of your elect, etc." just as God was called upon in the Old Testament for the sake of Abraham, Isaac and Jacob. I respond in the negative. In the Old Testament God was reminded of the patriarchs on account of the promise he had made to them. But this promise is nothing other than the seed of salvation, Christ, who is the wholesome, saving promise by whom they have been maintained in their hope of escaping perdition and by whom they were saved when Christ actually came. Besides this they had many other promises of earthly things which were not a ground of salvation. Hence, whenever they wanted to remind God of his promises, be it with reference to the wholesome seed or for temporal consolation, they always upheld before God the patriarchs to whom he made these promises out of love. But when Christ, the seed and the promise of salvation, which has been made to them came, it required no further reminder either of the promise or the witnesses to whom it had been made; for the grace of God, Christ our salvation, has come, and has been made and given. Therefore there is now no other name by which we may come to God or for whose sake God would not give us something, but the name of Christ--as I shall show in the following Article. Therefore Peter says in Acts 4:12, "There is therefore salvation in no one else (understood is, than in Christ); for no other name is given to humankind by which we may receive salvation." Note how strong and clear these words of Peter are. [202]

They then drag out the passage, Job 5:1, "Call on anyone of the holy ones." They go on to say, "Do you not perceive how everyone is bidden to turn to one of the saints or patrons?" Answer: When are you going to learn that "sanctus" means a good person and not a saint. Or else, tell me, what saints there were with God at the time of Jacob to whom one might have turned? If people started going to God only after Christ our pathfinder and the firstborn in the resurrection was lifted up, it is worth nothing that Job does not encourage us to turn to the saints that they might intercede--because none of them was with God as yet. Rather, the meaning of these words is as follows, so that you may know the truth: When Job again and again explores in his speeches why God allows affliction to come to people, he discovers that everything happens in God's providence, that he orders all things according to his good pleasure and that he often allows labor and evil to come to the good person to test him and to make him accept the fact that God does not thrust him into such affliction because of sin but because it pleases him to do so. This of course, his detractors, notably Eliphaz, did not want to concede, arguing instead that God punishes no one but the sinner; of course, this is true, too, since all of us are sinners and none of us is clean in God's eyes. Few, of course,

will acknowledge this (he aimed this at Job in the conviction
that he did not acknowledge himself a sinner; not at all understanding Job's intention), therefore they shall be taken away in their
ignorance. To prove this to be true, Job was to name one who
did not deserve his affliction because of sin. He was to turn
to a good person and, as we would say in German, "Show me
one"; the term used here is "aliquis sanctorum", freely translated
a good person, and not a "saint". Further Eliphaz is convinced
that he cannot show him one and when he says, "Turn to some
of the saints", he does not mean that Job should do that, but
rather, that he cannot show him one who is good and who has
not brought his affliction upon himself, as if to say, "Turn around
and show me a good person" in the conviction, "you will not
[203] find him." That this is, indeed, the meaning of the words,
you may gather when you take a look at what comes before
and after this passage and at the entire book of Job.

Then they dig out some passages out of Baruch, chapter
3. This is not a canonical book i.e. the Jews do not esteem it
as highly as to count it among the books of Holy Writ and the
Prophets. Therefore I need not answer them. Indeed, I need not
answer them any more than I would answer those foolishly contrived fables which that liar of a preaching monk gathered together
in Lombardy. [10] Thick lies indeed. [11] Understand these things,
simple person, in the following manner: In the time of the new
covenant, i.e. in the new marriage, we accept all books which
God gave to the children of Israel and which are inspired. In
other words, we accept the Old Testament in its entirety which
the Jews also take to be sacred, God-inspired and worthy to
be believed. If then we do not find Baruch among the sacred
books of the Old Testament, no one can prove anything from
it which may be useful to us. Similarly, if an entire country
were to turn to the Christian faith now, we would give them
the books of the New Testament. If, however, they would want
to sneak in other books to sell alongside the books, given by
God, the number of Christian books would soon be exceeded.
Hence, those books which are not found among Christian books
would have to be weeded out and rejected. In this fashion we
have the Old Testament from the Jews. Should you try to sneak
a cuckoo into the Old Testament, I would want to see whether
or not the Jews have it and if I should not be able to find it,
I would not give any credence to it [204] nor allow it to sway
me in any way whatever. Mark this well; for we will have to
come back to it again. Therefore I shall not even reply to the
words quoted from Baruch, except when a heathen fights against
the word of God, though I know well that Baruch 3:4 speaks
as follows, "O Lord, thou mighty God of Israel, hear now the
prayers of those from among the people of Israel who are now
dead; hear their sons also who have sinned against you." This,
of course, is an expansion and must be read as follows, "Hear

all the members of the tribe of Israel of which some are dead and some are still alive. Those who are dead cried on behalf of their sins during their life time also; their prayer you should still know quite well. Like them, we also cry."

To prove that this is, indeed, the meaning, namely that Baruch begs for grace in the name of the living and the dead and shows that this was the will of the dead while they were still alive (for their cry was still well known to God), you should read what follows later, "O Lord, do not remember the evil of our forefathers, etc." Do you see then that Baruch prays for the dead; yet you are trying to convince me that they pray on my behalf. Thus the prayer of the dead must be understood simply as a prayer for the general needs and wants for which our ancestors and the dead have likewise called out; if then it has not been removed, the living still call out for it; indeed, they even call out for the dead. Note, to prove intercession of the saints on the basis of this passage is so far fetched that it would be easier to prove that no one in the Old Testament was able to come to God and it is for that reason that the living were shown to be praying for the dead. But there is no need to make this response at all; for I do not want them to get into the habit of expecting me to respond to the Apocrypha. Nonetheless, they have missed the point as badly in this context as elsewhere.

Finally, they cite what is written in the last Psalm, [Ps. 150:1], "Laudate dominum in sanctis eius" - "Praise the Lord in his saints." Here then, they say, you may perceive how we are to call on the saints. I respond: By those words you show greater ignorance than has been shown in any others. Firstly, (that I might show up your ignorance now), I will concede for the moment that "sancti" indeed means "the saints". But what follows from the phrase, "praise God in his saints"? Does it mean, "you [205] saints, pray to God for us"? Do you not even know enough German or Latin to see that it is not the same thing to say "praise God" and "O you saints, intercede before God"? Why do you not just as readily conclude from the above words that one is to give laud and thanks to God for leading people to goodness and salvation? But in order that you may fully understand these words, take note that the Hebrew in Psalm 150:1 is as follows, "Halelu el bokadscho" which Jerome translates into Latin with "laudate dominum in sancto eius", and that means, "praise God in his sanctuary". And "holy" here is the name given to the place in which God shows himself in the rejoicing in his presence. (When I call it a place, I mean to indicate the extent or form by which God reveals himself to the saints. I know well otherwise that God is not confined to or bound by place). Thus we call the heavens the seat or throne of God; and the presence of the house of God cannot be named more appropriately because of his holiness. Further, we name it thus in keeping with Hebrew practice where the temple was called "the holy place", as Paul repeatedly shows in the Epistle to the Hebrews. Accordingly, the meaning of these words is, "You ought to praise God in his sanctuary", i.e. you ought to praise God in heaven, in his holy dwelling, on his throne. The following words underline this meaning, "Haleluhu birkia uzo" which means, "praise him in the foundation of his power" which, on the basis of the Latin, we translate by the term "firmament". Thus, the thing you are arguing over is nothing other than, "Praise God in the heavens, praise him in the firmament or foundation of his power, etc." Now, if you want to understand, "Praise God in his sanctuary" with reference to Christ who is also called "the holy one" in scripture, I will not object at all; but in my opinion this is not the true meaning of these words. Thus you are wrong again. Get ready for the next shot.

Now they bring their objections by drawing on the New Testament which cannot tolerate such an opinion regarding intercession. In fact, less so than the Old Testament; for Christ the promised seed has come. The light is here. The surety has been firmly set down at the right hand of God. Yet they cite the Canaanite woman [206] in Mt. 15:22-28 who prayed for her daughter, possessed of the devil and to whom Jesus made no reply. And when the disciples asked on her behalf, he said, "I have not been sent to any one but to the sheep from the house and lineage of Israel, etc". Now they say, "Do you note that the disciples prayed for the woman?" Answer: I had in mind to reprimand you especially because of such foolishness. But there are too many errors so that I will refrain from this. I do not have sufficient words to be able to paint you in your true colors. [12]

First, we are now discussing the intercession which is ascribed to the saints in heaven. What does that have to do with the disciples who still lived in this body and vale of tears in which one is to pray daily for one another, as the subsequent Article will indicate?

Secondly, this deed suggests more likely that God did not hear the disciples than that he did. For Christ did not free the daughter from her suffering because of the intercession of the disciples. Actually, this story teaches that we ourselves should come with sure confidence into the presence of the Lord, for he desires our heart and our faith. Therefore, he did not heal the daughter of this woman until she herself came to him. I would give a similar reply to the objection they made regarding Mary, the mother of Jesus, who at the wedding feast asked the Lord to come to the aid of the people by providing them with wine. Now everyone may readily see that this passage, too, is rather against their interpretation than in support of it.

Furthermore, they fight strongly, as they think, nonetheless foolishly and in vain, when they argue that the saints are our very neighbors. Now neighbors ought to pray for one another. Hence it follows that the saints should pray for us. I answer: Whenever scripture admonishes us to love our neighbor as ourselves or to do to the neighbor as we want them to do unto us, it is intended to refer to the neighbor who in this life is exposed to all kinds of weakness. For although the saints are our fellow brothers and members of the same body, they are no longer members of the weak body; therefore they are not really our [207] neighbors. For to be neighbors in German means neither higher nor lower, but "even" as we all are in this life, on account of our creatureliness. It follows then that the saints are not our neighbors, for they are above us; they are already with God and no affliction is able to touch them any longer. It is with this meaning in mind that some have translated the term "proximus" as meaning "the person next to me". To prove that only a person who is still alive can be my neighbor whom God bids me love, I point to the Lord's own words in Lk. 10:29-37. When a scribe asked the Lord who his neighbor was, he pointed the neighbor out to him in a beautiful parable as the one who went from Jerusalem to Jericho and fell among robbers. Afterwards, neither priest nor Levite looked at him to offer assistance to him. But the Samaritan looked after him so generously, that the enquiring doctor had to admit that the Samaritan proved to be a true neighbor. This naturally pleased the Lord who said to him, "Go then and do likewise". From this teaching of Jesus we learn, on the one hand (for when one speaks of neighbor one must always understand two, since no one can be neighbor to oneself, as the sophists well know from their doctrine of relatives-de natura relativorum-), that our neighbor is any one who suffers want. Secondly, that neighbor to the needy is the one who alone comes to his aid.

Should you now say, "But what if I, too, am in need?" I would reply, "Everyone then whose aid you need, is neighbor to you. And if he does not assist you, he transgresses the law of God, just as the priest and the Levite did in relation to the victim by the roadside." Now we understand how we should interpret neighbor when scripture speaks of neighbor and that we are to see in him the one who is like us, i.e. one who is afflicted and needs us and whom, we in turn, need. From this it follows that their demand to depend on the neighbor does not hold water, for the saints of God in eternity cannot suffer want, Rev. 21:4; since they do not need us, they do not fall under the commandment concerning the neighbor either. I have not given this response because I feel that one has to make reply to everyone's battle cry or arguments which he seeks to support by improper use of scripture, but in order [208] that we may learn from this who really is our true neighbor; also in order that the naiveté of certain people may be exposed who have promised to the blessed departed that they would daily pray a certain number of "Our Fathers". But now when they are reproved by the truth, they say, "Shall I deprive the blessed departed of their prayers?" As if their prattle would increase the honor or joy of the saints. Your prayers will not gladden them; for if our prayers could gladden them, their own joy would be imperfect when it has to be increased by the prayers of the sinful people. Moreover, our prayer is little more than asking for our own shortcomings and needs. What honor to you is there in someone pressing your hand and throwing himself at you to ask for something? Note, how confused we are. Therefore, do not be overanxious on account of the passage which says, "The angels of God rejoice over one sinner, etc." [Lk. 15:10]; it is not relevant here.

Finally, they cite two passages from the Book of Revelation. The first is Rev. 5:7f, "When the Lamb took the book, the four creatures and the twenty-four elders fell down before the Lamb. Each one held a harp and a golden bowl or vessel like a drinking glass. These bowls were full of scents or odors which are the prayers of the saints." At this point they say, "Do you hear that the saints offer up our prayers to God? Or, that they pray for us?" Answer: Have they been turned into angels after their time here? (It is the office of angels to transmit our prayers to God, as you say.) You are forced to say, "No". For the angels are sent to render service to humans, but the persons who have died are not given to do such service; of that we have no reference at all in scripture, but there are plenty of references to angels. See Heb. 1:14 and elsewhere. It follows then that the sacrifice of the twenty-four elders is not the transmission of our prayers, or else you would here have to translate "sanctos" by "good Christians", which is not your custom, however; for if you did that, many of your arguments concerning intercession should fall by the board. It remains to examine your claim that the twenty-four elders offered their prayers to God on our behalf. But this is not the meaning of scripture at all, as I shall prove to you. First of all, I want to show that the Apocalypse was not reckoned by the early church to be among [209] the sacred books, as Jerome indicates. [13] Secondly, it is ascribed to John who was the Bishop of Ephesus, for it does not have the manner, heart and spirit of the evangelist. For this reason I should reject the proofs, presented to me, if I thought that they pressure me. But there is really no need to reject them. Be the Apocalypse what it may, this passage still does not have the meaning which you seek to squeeze out of it. This John sought to paint the salvation of Christ, his teaching, which God opened for us through him, the calling of all Jews and heathen, the glory and honor of Christ, the joy of the saints, several punishments and signs which God is about to send over us, in obscure words. Among other hidden things, he pointed to the joy and the pure worship of the saints (that's what "twenty-four elders" means; their prayers were symbolized by crystal bowls full of odorific savors), stressing that they were so pleasing to God in their dwelling with him now, as they are to us here on earth a well pleasing odor.

Such worship of the saints which I cannot understand as anything other than the joyous contemplation of God's face in which they were totally absorbed, John illustrated shortly before this passage in the fourth chapter [v. 9] by yet another figure, as follows, "When the beasts had paid their respects to God, etc, the twenty-four elders bowed down before the one who sat upon the throne and eternally worshipped the one who is alive forever, casting [210] down their crowns or wreaths before his throne, saying, "Lord, you are worthy to receive honor, etc." In these words you may note how John sought to express the joy and amity of the saints through the image of a royal court where such customs are used; not that the heavenly joy is poor, as we might gather, but rather that he might honor the smallness of our understanding in his own way. Thus the prayers of the saints here are nothing other than the adoration of the twenty-four elders which they make to the eternal God in all eternity, in that they rejoice forever in the rest, peace and amity in the presence of God, being eternally thankful for such grace. Now "orationes" is "proseuchai" in Greek which, according to Suidas simply means "reunion of God and humankind" or "dialogue of the soul with God"; [14] in German we would call it "a prayer"; but more of this later. That the term "the prayers of the saints" means "the grateful and joyous adoration of the saints" is shown by the subsequent words where he says in a concluding remark, "Which odors are the prayers of the saints who sing a new song, saying, "You are worthy to take the book and to open its seal, for you have been slain and have bought us out of the world, etc." Note how he expressly says what the prayers were, namely the praise of the saints which they offered to Christ, the Lamb.

The other passage in the Apocalypse is in chapter 8:3f. To get on quickly, the words would not be the same with them, though they may be translated correctly. For they could not get any other meaning than that the angels of God transmit our prayers to God; for they cannot read "sanctos" any differently here than [211] simply to translate it by the term "saints", as is their custom. The meaning would then be that the angels offer up the prayers of the saints, which is a new error. But I do not really blame them at this point; the blame goes to the translator and not to them; he added the little Latin word "de"; this distorted the meaning entirely for them, when he says, "Ut daret de orationibus sanctorum", etc. [15] The original in the Greek tongue has no "de" and goes as follows, "And another angel came and stood by or upon the altar, holding a golden censer and he was given a great amount of incense to add to the prayers of the saints upon the golden altar before the throne. And the smoke of the incense went up, together with the prayers of the saints, from the hand of the angel before God." Everyone may easily note here that John does not say anything else by the parable of the glittering court than this; When the twenty-four elders prayed, the angel, too, added pleasant odors, etc. In addition, Augustine, in his Homily on Revelation 6 turns this angel into Christ, saying that all our prayers are made pleasing to God through the Lord Christ; for he offered himself to God, a pleasing odor on our behalf.

You note here, good Christian, that those who taught intercession of the saints erred greatly when they dared use scripture according to their fancy and deceit. And though they might find other passages of scripture to twist in this manner, be unafraid, we shall rescue scripture from them, for they merely diminish and bend it. [212] This foundation is sure that the one God alone is to be worshipped and called on for all consolation. Neither angel, human being, nor devil can destroy that. After that you bring forth Jerome's **Contra Vigilantium** as if he were defending intercession of the saints. I would answer them in this way: I read Jerome's **Contra Vigilantium** long before I dared touch the issue of the intercession of the saints. [16] Yet Jerome was not able to sway me, though I relied on him as much as on any one; for he handles the matter in such a leisurely fashion that he might be called **Dormitantius** rather than **Vigilantius**. Take my meaning as follows: Whoever intends to teach a doctrine, i.e. and opinion which touches on divine wisdom and truth, will not benefit from holiness, artfulness, or much babbling if he cannot support it by Holy Scripture. Now the strongest argument in Jerome which states that the saints pray for us, is this: If Stephen prayed for his enemies here [Acts 7:20]. then he prays for them there also; for his prayers are not weakened there, if they have been strong here. If God preserved the lives of two hundred and sixty-six people in a shipwreck here, on account of Paul [Acts 27:24], would he shut his mouth now when he is in God's presence? Here then is the first dogma, in other words, an important opinion, touching upon truth, namely that the saints pray for us, therefore Jerome should have supported such opinion by reference to scripture. Since he could not do that, however, he took recourse to denunciations and he behaved so immodestly that even Erasmus should have preferred him to act more modestly in the matter (and that, on the basis of scripture and of truthful testimony from scripture). [17] Since then he cannot bring forth from scripture any evidence-- for the evidence he quotes refers to intercession by the living in this life--Jerome achieves about as much with his wise talk [213] as does the fox when talking to the rooster. [18] His arguments are so perverse that I might as well say: Paul preached here [on earth], therefore he must preach there too. Stephen chastized the Jews unafraid here, therefore he must chastize them there too. What Jerome babbles concerning miracles, I shall discuss shortly.

The papists further bring forth their canon and liturgy. Answer: God willing, I shall deal with the canon in a short while to point out of what good pedigree it is. [19] Concerning the liturgy I'll say this much: What do I care that you have introduced and invented it. It has no foundation whatever, regardless of how long you go on shouting "ora pro nobis". [20] And if you retort that Lupus [21] introduced the liturgy, I simply state that this cannot be substantiated by the truth. Even if Lupus had invented it, what do I care? People were reconciled with God before that time, without the "ora pro nobis". In short, the intercession of saints has no support in Holy Scripture; you can do what you will. Lupus apparently regarded the liturgy as one regards prayer [214] processions to this day, which are held during Holy Week and at other times. Properly speaking, liturgy is what happens when the entire congregation engages in responsive prayers. What you call a litany is false and a disgrace of Christ, a mockery of the saints and a misguiding of people.

In the same way they argue: The saints, after all, perform miracles among people; why then should one not call on then? I answer: First of all, so many miracles are done to deceive. Many of these I myself experienced. It would take me too long to tell of these. Secondly, miracles in themselves do not prove that a person is holy. Christ himself points to this in Mt. 7:22, "Many will say to me at that same time, 'Lord, Lord; have we not prophesied in your name and driven out devils in your name and wrought many signs in your name?' And then I shall reply to them, 'I did not know you. Depart from me, you evildoers'." Note, to have worked miracles does not prove holiness, but a Christian life does, which is none other than an unceasing doing of God's work.

Further, Christ says in Mt. 24:24, "There will be false Christs and false teachers or prophets. They shall do signs and wonders so great that they would, as much as in their power, deceive the elect even." Now tell me whether these deceivers are going to be holy? Indeed, there have already been and there shall be more of them yet. For what else did one do for a long time except to earn money through these invented miracles? What do they do to this day but to proclaim invented miracles? They name distant cities and then say that someone in one of these wanted to preach the new thing [the evangelical teaching] and that he suffocated instantly, or some such story. And if you investigate, you discover it to be a lie. But God he praised for their turning to lies and speaking of great things--the last refuge of all who are lost. [215]. Soon one will get to the bottom of the matter and they will kiss the ground with their fannies [i.e. they will come out losers]. Thus it will be with those who prattle about signs and wonders, as I hope to God. To wit, one drove out devils who did not follow Christ, Lk 9:49. But should there be any signs at the graves of those who died for God's sake, one must know that these happen, not because of the martyrs, but because of the power of God. Thus Christ says clearly in Jn. 14:12, "Whoever believes in me, shall do the works I am doing. Indeed, he will do greater things." This simply means that it is God who does the signs. Therefore he says in Mk. 16:17, "They shall drive out devils in my name." Mark there that he says, "in my name", i.e. in my strength, power and for my sake. Peter speaks similarly in Acts 3:12-16, when the people had gathered around them, amazed at him and John who in the name of Jesus had made the cripple walk. "Yes," says Peter, "why are you astonished by what has happened or why do you look at us as if we made him walk by our own strength and goodness, etc? God has made the one you see there strong because of faith in the name of Jesus. Indeed, the name of Jesus has made him strong; faith which comes through this Jesus Christ has restored his health in your very presence."

From these words of Peter it is clearly apparent that miracles are not of human beings, but of God who achieves them through believing people in the name of Jesus. In this then you may learn two things in one go, which we often touched on earlier. One, God works his signs through Jesus Christ; the other, that the faith in Jesus to work such wonders, is not human faith, but God's. From all this it follows that we cannot of our own strength recognize the signs when they happen, whether they are of God or of the devil. But if one recognizes them for sure, it comes from God and not from human boasting [216] which can never assure anyone. Now, confirmed signs do not effect holiness; for they are solely of God. It is not within reach of weak human strength to do what is contrary to nature; nor is it given any creature to do, but is solely in the power of the one God and creator of all things.

Thus I have clearly stated during the Disputation [22] that I could easily disprove any prattle which Jerome brought forth against **Vigilantium**. My opponents interpreted this as pride. But I will repeat it once again. In fact, I have been easy on Jerome-- otherwise I would have showed more forcefully his stubborn head which, nonetheless, delighted me somewhat. Yet though I read him diligently, I did not like many of his conclusions. But neither he nor anyone else on earth pleases me when he seeks to substanti- ate the opinions he holds by his own words or head more than by the word of God, or when, for the sake of his own ideas, he seeks to take away or change the actual meaning and strength of scripture. Unfortunately, this happens often. Therefore it is not surprising to find that one or another of the saints is not believed. God sanctifies us in such a way that we remain human nonetheless, full of error and sin. Paul has shown this by word and deed, in his teaching in Rom. 7 and in deed, when he opposed Peter to his face [Acts 15:1-21].

Then the papists also draw on the subject of love, saying, "Do the saints not abide in love? If they do, they also pray for us." This gets them nowhere. The two statements do not relate logically to each other (nego enim consequentiam). For who is to tell you what form the love of the saints takes. You are measuring it as if it were neither more lasting nor shorter than the love among those who are pilgrims, i.e. people who are now living. But I cannot make this concession to you. In short, the whole thing is a useless argument which they base on a word of Paul in 1 Cor. 13:8 and which they use wrongly, "Love never ceases" (caritas non excidet), as they say. But Paul uses this term with the implication that where God's love is, one never suffers want of anything good, never goes idly, endures all things, trusts in all things, hopes [217] in all things, etc. But he describes only the love which is appropriate to people while on earth, but not to the saints. Therefore although love never fails, their objection certainly fails badly.

Epilogue:

I do not wish to keep from you, most beloved brothers in Christ Jesus, how I have reached the opinion and firm faith that we do not need a mediator other than Christ. Some eight or nine years ago I read a comforting poem by the great scholar Erasmus of Rotterdam which was addressed to the Lord Jesus [23] in which Jesus bemoans the fact in many beautiful words that not everything good is sought with him, though he is a fount of all goodness, a savior, the comfort and treasure of the soul. I thought then: It is ever thus. Why, indeed, do we seek help with creatures? And though I found other carmina or songs by the above-mentioned Erasmus addressed to St. Anne, St. Michael and others in which he calls on those whom he addresses, as advocates, these could not rob me of the insight that Christ is the sole treasure of our benighted soul. Actually, I started to examine the Biblical and Patristic writings whether I might there discover certain information concerning intercession of the saints. In short, I found nothing at all in scripture; while with some of the Fathers I found it, I found nothing at all with others. But that did not greatly trouble me, even when they taught intercession of the saints, for in each case they had no evidence at all. And when I checked in the original the passages of scripture which they twisted to suit their case, [I found that] these never had the meaning which they sought to derive from them. In fact, [218] the more I looked upon their opinion or dogma, the less I found of a scripture basis. However, I found plenty against it as I have shown in this and in Article 19. Scripture which they have twisted to suit their own ends simply does not have the meaning which they read into it as must become apparent to all creatures through the truth. In fact, scripture speaks openly against one's turning to any creature and making an image thereof, lest these [images] should become dear to us in place of God and we should worship them. Just look at the mass of idols we have. One we dress up in a breastplate as if he were a soldier, another we dress up as a knave [buben] or keeper of whores by which the women, of course, are moved to great devotion. Holy women are shaped so attractively, so smooth and colorful as if they were placed there to entice men to wantonness. And we are pleased with ourselves as a result, thinking we have such beautiful worship when it is no more than idol worship which is clearly forbidden by God's word, Deut. 5:8ff. Yet they say, "We know well enough that we are not to worship images." What then are they doing there?

Now I know that many a simple Christian has worshipped images before one could forbid this in so many words. Are they to have no comfort in images now? Indeed, it is idolatry if they put their trust in them. And the word, "that is an image, full of grace" shows clearly that they ascribe something to images and that they account them worthy enough to place them upon the altar in front of people, even though God alone is to be worshipped. All this shows that some value is placed upon them. Likewise, the fact that in some places those were punished who removed idols from before human eyes in keeping with the divine will, shows idolatry. Indeed, if one ought to have no confidence in them, why then do they stand there? O Lord, give us a person, fearless like Elijah who would put away the idols from before the eyes of the faithful for you are one God, who is our refuge and comfort. For as Moses says in Deut. 32:6, "Is he not your father who claims you as his own? He has created you. Therefore it is an abomination to take refuge with anyone other than with him whose we are. He has no less concern for us than does an eagle for his [219] young. He takes us under his cover as a hen her young. Therefore we ought not fear him as a rough, ungracious tyrant, thinking that we are not allowed to come to him. Rather, he is to be our true inner comfort; more so than our physical father and mother."

Lastly, we should also learn in this context that everything in which one places one's trust becomes a God to the one who puts his trust in and worships it. For the term "God" means that good which is the surest refuge and help and a fountain of all good. Thus humankind has always learned from its infirmities that it requires a greater and stronger help than any person is able to give. Wherever any one looked for comforts there also were its gods. Therefore Paul calls greed an idol [Col. 3:5] in that the greedy puts his trust in money. Hence, in whomever a person puts his trust, the same then is his god. If you put your confidence in one of the saints, you have made him a god, to all intents and purposes; for "God" is the good in which we put our trust so that it may afford us the good which we need. If you consider them to be your comfort, you have made them your God. Thus it follows that you have made them into idols and that you do them the greatest dishonor by expecting anything from them. This meaning of God's name, is contained in the Hebrew terms for God by which they name him; to explain these would take too long here. Nonetheless, they name God from the [experience] of life, of strength, of wisdom, of help and satisfaction. By this they intend to teach that he alone is God who gives life to all things, who can do all things, who knows all things, who helps in all distress and who is a sufficient treasure of every good thing, who can supply all necessities. For this reason he, the only God, is alone to be called on. For the one to whom he turns for help, is the one taken to be God, even though one may say otherwise with one's tongue. God actually forbids us fathom this in Deut. 32:39, "Behold, I alone am God and without me there is no God i.e. there is no God to which one may turn for every perfection.". He also calls us in Ps. 80 [81:8f], "Listen my people, for I myself desire you to be my witness. Israel, if you are obedient and listen to me, no other God shall rise among you, neither shall you worship any strange God." In other words, you shall put your trust in none other than myself. For [220] God is ever the good in whom one ought to put one's trust; he alone knows our hearts. If he then is the only one who knows them, how then can a saint hear our prayers if he knows nothing about them. For this word in Solomon's prayer is unfailing, [2 Chron. 6:30], "You alone know the hearts of sinful people". He says, "You alone." Thus it must follow that the saints do not know anything about us, except what God reveals to them. Yet what he reveals to them or even that he reveals anything to them ahead of us has no clear support in scripture; further, this word of Solomon makes null and void the business of the intercession of saints which is advocated by the papists because we are not supposed to come to God ourselves. For we clearly perceive in this context that they [the saints] know nothing about us; and even if they did know something about us, it would have to be known to God before that and be made known to them by him. Isaiah points this out even more clearly in chapter 63 [63:15f] when he speaks with God in this way, "Look down upon us from heaven. Look upon us from your sacred dwelling and from the throne or chair of your honor. Where is you zeal and your power? Where is the multitude of your loving mercies and pardons? Oh, they have been withdrawn and stand aloof from me. But you are our Father and Abraham did not know us and Israel did not acknowledge us." If you papists are daring enough, you will take this passage of Isaiah for support. I tell you, though, in itself it is strong enough to overcome your blasphemy and cause it to vanish. It says clearly that Abraham and Israel do not know anything about us, as if to say, "Lord, we have called on you in the name of the Fathers; you are indeed the right and true Father. Though we have named the Fathers, we did so because they are pleasing to you, but they did not know anything about us. Therefore we should not really call them Fathers on our own; for if they know nothing about us, how then are they to help us? You are the right true Father in whom we are to have our refuge without any mediator." For shortly before this, [Is. 63:8] he spoke in the name of God, "My people are the sons who have not become unfaithful." Then he changes the person as he says, "And he has become their restorer. He did not become afflicted in all their affliction and the messenger of his face [221] has made them whole. He has redeemed them in his love and long suffering and has carried them and lifted them up at all times." In these words he intends to show the fatherly affection which God has shown to them in every way; therefore they turn to him without compulsion, calling on him alone in whom they are to take refuge at all times.

By the same token, every believer is to know that he has him as a God, indeed, in whom he may take his refuge even beyond this time. If, however, he takes refuge with a creature, he is an idolater, for creatures are incapable of coming to our aid. Even if wondrous signs take place, they are not of the creature but of God. Therefore we ought not to rely on creatures; for God intended to make known to us through miracles which are true and without deceit, how worthy and dear all those are in his sight who cling to his word in firm faith. And if these happen after the death of a saint they happen because God wants to indicate thereby that they are with him. Indeed, we are to put our trust in God alone which means to worship the one God; for to worship means to have confidence and trust in something ahead of time. This is indicated by the Greek term proseuchesthai. If we worship one God, we have all our confidence in one God only. Therefore let us put our trust in the one God who is our Father; therefore we can presume to come to him. For what can he deny us, if he even gave his only Son and has made him an eternal surety for the payment of our sins? He himself stands calling Mt. 11:28, "Come unto me. . ." Note how he calls us unto himself and does not point us to this one or that one of the advocates; he is the good prince who himself wants to overcome the anguish of his sheep and seeks to make them well. Therefore he took the lost sheep upon his own back and did not place it upon someone else's back; he also humbled himself so far that we may come to him in confidence. Indeed, he knows our needs and concerns before we even come to him. He also says, "I will calm you." He does not say, "You have to offer satisfaction for your own sins." Neither does he say, "Others have to make amends for your sins;" but rather,"I will give you rest." Why then would we want to go to any one other than to him? [222] Would not this mean we shun his free grace and mercy? But our resistance stems solely from unbelief and ignorance. Therefore all persons ought to call on God earnestly that he may kindle his light more and more fully to illumine human hearts and draw them into the hope of the one God. For this is certain that whoever turns to a creator is an idolater. From this stems a great deal of harm to poor human-kind. May God turn all things for the very best; to him alone I will pour out my woe for I know that he shall hear me.

NOTES

1. A wooden firehook is a plain contradiction--contradictio in adiecto-- hence, utter nonsense.

2. Cf. Article VIII above.

3. "Ich bin nit in sinem rat gsessen."

4. Guggi or Gueggi are terms used for a slow, impractical, somewhat awkward person. Cf. **Idiotikon** II 190 and 198.

5. Cf. Augustine's **Joannis evangelium,** tractatus, CXXIV and tractatus LXXXII (on John 15:8).

6. See Zwingli's pamphlet Eine Predigt von der ewig reinen Magd Maria, 17, Sept. 1522 (Z.I 385-428) and Entschuldigung etlicher unwahrlich zugelegter Artikel, 3 July, 1523 (Z.I 570-574).

7. "Ihn beisst, juckt die Haut" is a proverb found with Luther also. Cf. Thiele, **Luthers Sprichwoertersammlung,** 191 and Wander, II 440 Nos. 65 & 66.

8. According to Catholic usage of the day, latreia is the worship of God, dulia, the adoration of angels and saints, and hyperdulia, the veneration of Mary.

9. The New English Bible, The Song of the Three, verses 11-13. This addition to the Book of Daniel was inserted in the Greek Bible between verses 23 and 24 of the third chapter. Cf. R. H. Malden, **The Apocrypha,** Oxford University Press, 1936, 57.

10. The reference is undoubtedly to the **Legenda Sanctorum,** collected by the Dominican Jacob de Voragine from about the middle of the 13th century. Under the title **Legenda aurea** the fables enjoyed popularity and were frequently reprinted.

11. A word play on Legende - Luegende, familiar also to Luther. Cf. E. Egli, "Lombardick lueg gar dick", **Zwingliana** II No. 4.

12. "Ich will dich mit deiner Farbe malen" means as much as, "I will describe you as you are". Cf. Wander, I 928, No. 30.

13. Zwingli expresses a rather liberal view on the significance of the **Book of Revelation** which Luther too seems to have shared. Eusebius, **Ecclesiastical History**, VII reports the view to have been expressed as early as around AD 250 by Dionysius of Alexandria.

14. Cf. Z.II 210, n. 3.

15. Here, as elsewhere Zwingli quotes from the Vulgate.

16. Zwingli remains true to the principle which he expressed in Article 18. He reads and recommends Jerome, yet does so critically and on the basis of Scripture.

17. Cf. Erasmus, **Epistola apologetica ad Martinum Dorpium theologum,** Leiden edition IX.2.

18. Cf. Wander I 1248, No. 193.

19. Cf. H. Zwingli, **De Canone missae epichiresis,** Aug. 29, 1523 (Z.II 552-608).

20. This is likely an allusion to the First Zurich Disputation and to the exchange there with J. Faber. Cf. Z.I 539, especially notes 5-9. Zwingli himself worked extensively on liturgical reform. For a good recent study, cf. F. Schmidt-Clausing, **Zwingli's liturgische Formulare,** Frankfurt: 1970.

21. AD 814-862, Abbot of Ferrieres. Servatus Lupus was a student of Rabanus Maurus and later engaged in politics.

22. The First Zurich Disputation. Cf. Z.I 538ff.

23. **Ein expostulation oder klag Jhesu zu dem menschen,** translated by Leo Jud and published by Froschauer in 1522, **Expostulatio Jesu cum homine.** This suggests that Zwingli was led as early as 1514/15 to the recognition that Christ is the significant fount of the wholesomeness of the soul. Cf. Z.V. 721.5-724.3 in which Erasmus is credited--even before Luther--to have intellectually caused the Reformation. Cf. Art. 18, n. 21.
Cf. A. Rich, **Anfänge,** 17. There is still some controversy on the dating of Zwingli's first meeting with Erasmus. Cf. E. Egli in Z.VII 35 and 36 and Rich's own argument in **Anfänge.**

THE TWENTY-FIRST ARTICLE

When we pray for one another here on earth, we do so in the confidence that all things are given us through Christ alone.

Regarding the first part of this Article, I wanted to make clear that intercession is appropriate to us who are still on earth; whenever it is written in scripture that we are to pray for one another, it is said to those only who still live on earth. And nowhere in scripture, as far as I am aware, except in the Book of Revelation is prayer ascribed to the saints. There John takes prayer to be the adoration and praise which the saints make before God, as I have indicated in the 20th Article; however, he does not yet take it as petition or intercession, as the papists teach. That the prayer, commanded and taught by Christ applies to the living only and that they are to pray it for one another, is indicated in the Lord's Prayer, "Your will be done on earth as in heaven. Your kingdom come to us. Forgive us our debts, etc." These words are not at all suited to the saints. Likewise Mt. 18:19, "Again I say to you whenever two agree on what to ask for on earth, my Father in heaven will grant it to them." Note, he says, "whenever we agree on earth." Thus it must needs apply to those living in the body. In the same manner search all of scripture and you will not find any trace of a prayer that would be like intercession of the saints; [223] in each case such words refer only to us poor, afflicted humans. We are to pray for one another; for we are members one of the other, Rom. 12:5.

You say that there is no need either to beg or ask; everything depends on the free choice of God. He gives us what he wills, whatever I might ask for, as you yourself have shown in Article 20 with reference to merit. I respond: Yes, God gives us what he wills. He does not give us anything that is not good for us, Mt. 7:9-11. Nonetheless, he wants to be asked and admonishes us to pray. "Ask," he says, "and you shall be given; seek, and you shall find; knock, and it shall be opened." He also bids us ask without ceasing, even though nothing of what we may ask, may be given us immediately, Lk. 11 and 18 [Lk. 11:5-13; 18:1-8].

177

178

Now since the papists interpret the passage in Luke to mean that one ought to pray at all times and so sell their prayers as if these could replace the neglect of other people, I will briefly have to say something concerning prayer. Prayer is nothing other than an upturning or a looking up of the heart to God, as we have also shown above. This opinion is frequently supported from scripture such as Exodus 14:15, where Moses does not speak with his mouth, yet is addressed by God, nonetheless, "Why do you cry unto me?" Undoubtedly he cries from the heart, within which he speaks and struggles with God. Similarly, Hannah in 1 Kings [1 Sam. 1:13], who speaks in her heart and cries to God, and Eli does not hear her voice. Later on, you can also see this in the prayers of the Fathers: Where they are, there is either expression of the praise of God or else a person has spoken as intimately as with a physical father or both; but nothing is said there of the number of prayers, as our babblers have falsely stated.

In short: To pray is not to prattle. Rather, it is first of all the praise and honor of God; and this concerns faith. Secondly, it is a trustful calling on him for our necessities. [224]

Understand this as follows: When you say, "Our Father, who art in heaven, hallowed be your name," then the first part is blasphemy, if you do not have him for a Father and yet address him by "Our Father in heaven." Therefore, you require faith first of all, that you may knowingly believe him to be your Father.

Thus it follows that when a person practices faith, he actually prays when he thinks, "God is creator of all things; he is the highest good from whom all good things come. He never promises anything to humankind unless he will also keep his promise." You will want to hang on to that good for ever; it is unfailingly trustworthy. Note, the highest praise which we can bring to God is, to hold him firmly in our hearts as highest good and to have him for our Father; we will then see clearly that his name, i.e. his honor, power and praise, are to be esteemed highly by all persons when they say, "Hallowed be your name."

After this follows the prayer concerning our weaknesses: "Your kingdom come to us. Bring about that your will be done among humankind as it is done with you in the heavens, etc." Consequently there can be no prayer unless one first accepts that God is and unless one goes to him in the sure confidence of going to one's own gracious Father. And when this happens not many more words are required thereafter, for he knows what we lack before we run to him; for we have already spoken the highest prayer of faith. Christ himself teaches this in Mt. 6:7-13, "If you pray, do not aim to babble the words of your prayer often, as do the gentiles; for they think that they are heard because of their many words. Therefore do not become like them; for your Father knows what you need before you ask. But you ought to pray thus, "Our Father in heaven. Your name be hallowed. Your kingdom come, etc."

Note firstly, how he warns us of too many words, yet bids us, in Lk. 11 and 18 [Lk. 11:1-18; 18:1-8], pray without ceasing. Thus to pray cannot mean to "pour out words"; for he forbids that by the Greek term "batologia" which I have translated in German by the term "Bladdergebet" [prattle prayer]. By this I mean to prattle, regurgitate and spew out words. Note then, where are we now--you who sell the many words of the psalms as if they were of any aid to those who give us money [225]--if Christ rejects any repetitive prattle, if prayer is partly a sign of faith, but partly nothing more than a begging for our necessities? Who ever considered begging worthy of anything? Or whoever sold his faith or believed on behalf of someone else? From this you may see that our prayers are not even valued that highly, for if I constantly run to someone, "Help me here, lend me one hundred guilders there," I cannot value that as something for which people are indebted to me; for I am doing nothing more than pleading and begging.

Nonetheless, there are some who unfortunately say, "Today I have prayed one hundred Our Fathers." May God be pleased. They think God ought to reward them for this their work, for they have honored him thereby, or given him something; therefore they claim to have the right to demand something or to redress the balance of their sins as much as possible, as if their prayers are merchandise or have value which ought to be re-imbursed to them. All this is nothing but distortion and pretense. It originates with the hypocrites who took money and then immediately asked for so much or such a number, just like the spinners. Yet, it is no more than a prattling prayer which Christ rejects here in so very clear terms. Take note: When Christ had sufficiently taught his prayer, the Our Father, he did not say, "Pray it so and so often." Rather, he taught just before this that one ought not to prattle or pour out many words. I will at this point not concede to you anything when you say, "Look, that is no way to teach the world how to pray". For one learns to pray aright with the heart, not with the mouth only. This alone is true prayer, Jn. 4:24, "For the mouth utters nothing but ridicule and blasphemy of God," Mt. 15:8, and "The people honor me with their lips but their hearts are far from me," [Is. 29:13].

I shall test you thoroughly in your prayer. How did you do when you reached the mountain? Did you say, "Forgive us our trespasses as we forgive those who trespass against us?" If you found things the way I always did, you would then have had to back up. [1] For as often as I got to such a point, I could not endure the peace. [226] I had to have an advantage so that

God would not judge me according to my merit, though I recognized that he had truly and perfectly taught that in his word. And after long experience, and although I had truly forgiven with all my heart, I found by the grace of God a glad and forgiving heart. And yet in the end I always thought: "Should you not be more pleasing to God than your own enemy is to you, it would not be well with you". Thus I reasoned that God would not have to do more to me than I toward my enemy. And after a great deal of accusation and stock taking of my poor conscience I withdrew as one conquered and captured to surrender to God. "Lord, I must not presume that you should forgive me according to my own forgiveness. Lord I am an imprisoned human being. Forgive, Lord, forgive." And as time went on, I was so tired of praying that I had no will left to babble any more words. There was nothing but anxious concern that I stood so utterly exposed in the very prayer which God had commanded me. Even though I then took up a Psalm to reflect on the same, my conscience said: Look here, you armchair soldier. Here you are so courageous and pleased with yourself that you think to have taken hold of the meaning of the Spirit. If you are that refreshed, get at the word, "Forgive us our trespasses as we forgive." Thus I find that there has been no other prayer on earth which probes a person more profoundly in faith and self-knowledge than the Lord's Prayer. For I should think that no one is of such peaceable disposition that he would not know himself in light of the word "forgive us" and surrender to the pure grace of God. That is true prayer: to know oneself and to examine oneself and, having done so, to humble oneself. Which one then will lend me his prayer?

Surely no one. For there is no one who did not have to give up in face of that word so that he had to throw himself as nothing at the feet and mercy of God. Thus we discover that prayer cannot at all be counted as merit, merchandise or value. It is no more than an account of one's necessities and a calling for help to God whom we believe to be the highest good which can make up for all our weaknesses. And prayer does not count for anything, since it is only a sincere appeal in faith. For God grants that it is worthy of his grace and pleasing to his will. Now see how it is with the prayer offered up for money? It is merely sham [227] which has fattened itself on prayer. For had these hypocritical fellows known themselves, they would not have wanted to dish up their prayers for someone else, they would also have known well that all persons are their brothers and members [of the body], therefore they would have been as careful on their behalf as they ought to have been for themselves. But if they sold their prayers they sinned mightily, first because they were hypocrites and secondly because they took wages from people for their sham.

Christ says to the Samaritan woman in Jn. 4:23ff. "The

time shall come, indeed it has come, when all true worshippers will pray to the Father in spirit and truth; for the Father wants those to worship him. God is Spirit; thus those who worship him, must worship with or in the Spirit and in truth." These words of Christ alone teach us what true prayer is, namely to pray in the Spirit; in other words, to call on God with the heart [Gemuet], in truth and not through words, which are fashioned by the mouth or in outward mannerisms, saying often, "Lord, Lord." Rather [to pray] so truthfully that our heart put its trust in God alone, without presenting itself in a false light but as it is in itself, sinful, wretched, powerless, yet sure at the same time of the grace of God in genuine trust. Such true worship in Spirit and in truth God expects of us. Thus we may note that prayer is nothing other than a constant dependence of our hearts upon God, an eager going to God in truth, so that we have him as the one true good which alone may help us and of which we are made certain by him.

Now, firstly, all the babbling comes to nought which is either shouted or else droned out in temples; for whenever the human heart is truly intent on communicating with God it prefers to be alone, as Christ well knew. Therefore he pointed to a quiet place in which one could speak with the heavenly Father, saying, "Go into your chamber if you wish to pray and there ask your heavenly Father in secret and your heavenly Father who sees you well in secret will grant it, Mt. 6:6. Therefore, one can see, that shouting in front of people is utter sham.

Secondly one learns that what is found in Lk. 18:1-8 is not to be understood as referring to wordy prayers when he says, "And Christ spoke in a parable saying that one should pray at all times [228] without ceasing and without getting tired of it." There was a certain judge who, in short, feared neither God or people. He was so severely pressed by a widow who had a case to bring before him and who pleaded that he should avenge her before her adversaries that he said, "Though I fear neither God nor people, I must nonetheless mete out justice for this woman so that she may cease giving me trouble." Now Jesus spoke about it thus, "You have heard what the unjust judge said. Should not God avenge or redeem his elect who cry unto him day and night even though he may intentionally draw out the matter? I say to you he shall soon avenge her, etc." Now this teaching of Jesus is not at all to be understood as referring to the number of words. Rather [it means] that one ought to run to God for everything without ceasing and though he may draw out the granting [of the request], one should, nonetheless, run to him, not with many words but with a contrite heart, as he himself indicates, saying, "But when the Son of Man shall come, do you think that he shall find faith on earth?" Pointing out with these words that not everyone's faith is so strong that they run to him without doubt and unceasingly. Whether or not the words coincide with the desire of the heart is not a flaw; but the words are vain apart from the heart. If you are able to pray for a long time with heart and mouth, then be thankful to God; for it is not frequent that one can have prolonged worship through words only. But in the truth of the Spirit a person is able to be worshipful for a long time viz. as he thinks on the honor of God, gives thanks for his grace, rightly considers the afflictions of body and soul and throws himself at and surrenders to the mercy of God, daily getting himself up anew to live a Christian life and such like. In this manner a person may be able to pray for a long time, for that is true prayer which takes place in truth and in Spirit; but worship which uses parroted words does not last long. In like manner one ought to understand other words concerning diligent prayer in Paul and elsewhere, that one ought to look upon God always in true faith and run to him alone for help. Thus a farmer may pray while plowing if he patiently carries out his work in God's name, for the increase of [229] seed in faith, and frequently recalling that our present life is merely hardship and misery: but that yonder our gracious God shall give us rest and peace and joy. Thus he prays, though he may never move his mouth. Likewise the smith at the anvil; if he looks upon God in everything he does, he prays without ceasing.

The other Part of this Article:

That we trust that all things will be given us through Christ alone.

This part teaches us that when we pray, we ought to trust with confidence that God will look after our necessities through the Lord Jesus Christ. For we ourselves are not so good that God should give us anything for our own sake; but for the sake of his Son he gives us all things, Jn. 16:23, "Truly, truly I say to you, that everything which you shall ask of the Father in my name, I shall give to you." Do you see how he ties the desiring of a thing to his name, saying, "Everything that you shall desire, yes, 'in his name'." Hence it follows that we shall desire [everything] in the one name of Christ. He says in John 14:13, "Everything you desire in my name, I will do in order that the honor of the Father may be made evident in the Son. If you shall desire anything in my name, I will do it." In these words of Christ you perceive then that we shall be granted our requests in his name only; for by no other name have we been taught to ask. Neither does he promise to grant anything by any other name: "For there is no other name under the sun by which we shall be made whole than the name of Christ Jesus Acts 4:12." Following this you hear the power of Christ equated with the power of God the Father, when he says, "This I shall do." Thereafter you know then that he is well able to do all things when he bids us rely on his name, Rom. 8:32, "God did not spare his own Son, but gave him for us." How then should he not give us all things through him? Note that Paul thinks it to be unheard of for God not to give us all things in his Son. Peter also teaches that our sacrifices are made pleasing to God through Christ, 1 Peter, chapter 2 [1 Pet. 2:5], "Offer up sacrifices of the spirit acceptable to God through Jesus Christ." Spiritual sacrifices are none other than to surrender our hearts to God through faith, as might well be learned from Peter's words above and following. [230]

In sum: If then God will give us all things in the name of Christ, as has been shown in Article 20, it follows that we are to ask for all things in his name. Should we do that, we are Christians; for Christ is too honorable than that we should bear his name if he has not yet become the confidence of us all.

So much on this Article which is also designed to cause us to put aside idol worship of creatures. For if we are to desire anything in his name alone, and if the granting [of such requests] is vested in his name alone it would be sheer folly, indeed, idol worship, if we were to turn to any one creature.

NOTE

1. A. Rich, **Anfänge**, 143-144 gives an illuminating analysis of the twofold scripture principle found in Zwingli's exposition. There is, firstly, an Erasmian religiosity and, secondly, an experience of the text as word of God. Ultimately Zwingli has no choice but to surrender himself to God unconditionally and trust in the pure grace of God.

THE TWENTY-SECOND ARTICLE

Christ is our righteousness. From this we conclude that our words are good insofar as they are Christ's; but insofar as they are ours, they are neither right nor good.

The first part of this Article supports the above opinion concerning the worship of the saints. For if Christ is our righteousness, as he truly is, he also has been the righteousness of all the faithful who have ever come to God; thus to all eternity he ought to be the righteousness of all those who come to God. It further points to subsequent Articles which will deal with works.

That Christ is our righteousness, Paul teaches in 1 Cor. 1:30, "Christ has become our wisdom through God, and our righteousness and sanctification, our ransom [Rantzung] or redemption." For a real understanding [of this], note briefly once again what I have twice pointed out earlier regarding the law and the gospel. Therefore I shall not cite many instances now. I intend in due course, however, to write a separate booklet in Latin concerning the law and the gospel. [1] But the entire sum of it shall be contained here, God willing. God is the eternal one, unchangeable good, from whom every other good comes. Thus his will cannot be other than an eternal fount of right and good. From this it follows that everything which God reveals to us is good and right, for from that fount or tree only good fruit can come forth. [231] It follows further that the law, insofar as it comes from God, is good also; for it springs forth from the will of God who is an eternal rule or guideline of everything right and good.

If follows further: If the law derives from the will of God, it is eternally right and good, unless it be put aside by God himself; whoever does what the law calls right and good, does what God wills; and thus whatever he wills must therefore be good. I am not now going to touch on who it is who does what the law demands; this will be dealt with a little later.

From this follows further that the things were not good

which were demanded by law for a specific time, i.e. until Christ's coming; for these were parables only and served as a concession to the common folk. And if I say here that the laws which have been put aside were not good, you are to understand that they were not good as laws. Otherwise they were good in the sense in which anything, created by God is good. But a law has to be good so that those who live under it and fulfill it, become good. Thus the ceremonies [rites] and outward rituals were not good; for one who fulfilled them, did, nonetheless, not obey either the first commandment or the others and therefore did not become more like God. Also they were given to the people in punishment of their unbelief. Read Ezek. 20 and you will find it all clearly stated. If then these did not come from the will of God (which is none other than a guideline and a finger, pointing to the right) in the sense that they were to remain eternally (for he himself set them aside), they could not have been good in the manner in which the law is good. For had they been good in that form, they would not have had to be put aside. God also criticized and rejected them through Isaiah, chapter 1.

This I inserted here so that a simple person might not think those to be good laws which have been given as punishment only or those which the papists force him to keep. For in the words of the two prophets Isaiah and Ezekiel we hear clearly that as laws they were not good at all and that their works were not good either.

Now we return again to the one who does good works is he does that which the law bids him do. Not one of those born of Adam does good works, Ps. 13 [14:3]. Thus is also follows that no one [232] does what the law commands; or else he would do good works if he does what the law commands. For the law bids nothing other than what is eternally right and good; for the law is good, just and holy, Rom. 7:12. Do you want to know why? Because it is nothing less than a revelation and points to the will of God so that we may see in the word of the commandment what God wills and demands. Therefore it were better called "gospel" rather than "law". For who, wandering about in human darkness and ignorance, would not rejoice, when God makes known his will? Now would one not consider it to be good news when the will of God is made known to humankind? You will have to say "yes" if you are speaking the truth. For if a worldly ruler opens to you his silly secrets, you consider it a great privilege. For this reason I have said above that the law is gospel to him who loves God. But the fact that the law which is sacred, good and just is not popular with us and does not make us glad and happy is not to be found in the law being frightening, oppressive and saddening by nature. Rather, the sadness is rooted in our own flesh. Therefore I would really like to see that certain people who currently write of the law and who say that the law frightens and brings us despair, and causes us to hate God, would nullify [such statements] by writing more truthful words. For despair and hatred of God are not an effect of the law but are rather caused by the infirmities of the flesh which cannot keep up to the law and therefore behaves like everyone who is impotent, beginning to hate that which cannot be reached. This St. Paul has clearly expressed in Rom. 7:14, "We know the law to be spiritual; but I am carnal and sold under sin." Note, why is the law spiritual? Because it is the good, sacred and just will of God; for the divine spirit is nothing less than the highest, most just and sacred good. And we call it "law" when Moses, on the other hand, called it "teaching". For the term "torah" which we translate "law" is derived from "iarah" which among other things means, "to direct, lead or judge" because the law has been given us by God [233] that it may teach us God's will, direct, judge and guide us. See now whether it were not more fittingly called "gospel" rather than "law". This I say for the better understanding only; I do not intend to have the terms "law and gospel" mixed up so that one cannot distinguish the one from the other. For what happier things can be proclaimed to the human heart--as stated above--than to have God reveal his will? However, we call it the "law" because our flesh squirms under it and becomes restless. The law, in itself, however, is spiritual. One example shall make all this clear. "You shall not covet" is a commandment; indeed, it is the pure will of God and teaching for the ignorant person by which he is directed to know that it is not only unjust to take that which belongs to someone else; for such deeds move not only God, but human beings also to take revenge. Rather, it is unjust even to covet that which belongs to someone else.

Note here in passing the difference between divine law-- thus I should for the sake of better understanding prefer to name the will of God--and human law. Human law judges only when the evil deed is done, when the taking or robbing has happened, but it bypasses covetousness unpunished because it cannot be recognized by people. It hides in the hollows of the human heart so that no one may see it; thus it cannot be punished. God, however, who tests every heart, knows it [covetousness]; therefore he also punishes it, if it is not conformed to his will. But the human heart, to know what God wills, surely needs no one else to inform it but God alone. He says, "I am not satisfied with human righteousness, since you merely refrain from doing evil in public for fear of punishment or because you are ashamed of evil. Your hearts, however, are greedy, full of covetousness and temptation. Thus is follows that your righteousness is no more than sham; for if you dared, you would do [evil]; the temptation is there. But if you desire to dwell with me; you must also behave [234] according to my will. I am not a hypocrite but thoroughly upright and pure, good and just; thus you, too, must be just, pure and innocent from within. It is not enough therefore not to steal, rob or commit adultery in deed; for your heart would do these, were it not afraid of other things more than of me. You must be just in my sight if you desire to dwell with me. I see the inward heart, therefore no one should as much as covet even the goods or the marriage partner of another. Understand all other commandments in like manner. Note at this point whether or not the law is spiritual. For not to covet at all, is always to be upright, pure, good and just and totally spiritual, i.e. one to whom the flesh is as nothing, in whom it accomplishes nothing and whom it does not tempt. This is expected of no person as long as he is in the flesh; for whosoever lives in this world is not without desire and temptation, 1 Jn. 2 [1 Jn. 2:16], "Everything that is in the world, is desire and enticement of the flesh and of the eye, and the pride of life; these are not of God."

Now that we have actually discovered why the law is spiritual and is called so, namely, that it shows us the pattern and form of the divine will, we can easily understand why it galls us. This is so, as shall follow shortly, because we are carnal and sold under sin. But what is "to be sold under sin" other than to belong to sin and to live under the power and command of sin? This stems from our weakness into which Adam has thrust us in the beginning. Since then we are only flesh and evil, as we have shown above on the basis of Genesis 8:21, it follows that hatred of the law comes from the flesh and not from the nature of the law; for [in itself] it is good, just and spiritual, desires us to be as upright and pure as God demands. Therefore "lex iram operatu" [2] - i.e. the law brings forth wrath [Rom. 4:15] and such like sayings are to be understood [in this way]. The law shows us clearly what the Spirit of God demands, and when we see our impotence, namely that we cannot fulfill any of this, we know ourselves as deserving of the wrath or punishment of God and that we are rightly condemned. Not that the law has wrought this. Rather, it is our own evil nature, weakness and sin which has its food and supply [235] in the body--as long as it dwells therein, the body will not be without sin. Thus Paul also writes [Rom. 7:24], "Wretched being that I am, who shall redeem me from the body of death, etc?"

Therefore God has shown us his grace in our impotence and despair in that he sent us the one who is able to fulfill the law on our behalf, namely the just and guiltless Jesus Christ who does not have the predilection to sin [anzug der Sünd]; for he has not been given and sold under sin as we have. Rather, he has been sold for our sin to overcome the same that he might fulfill the will of God through the one whom sin does not even touch. For anyone who is affected by sin, cannot keep the law, for where there is sin (i.e. the weakness stemming from Adam), there also is desire and temptation. Where one finds carnal temptation there the upright, pure, spiritual law--the will of God--cannot be fulfilled. These weaknesses are not found in Christ; therefore it is he alone who can live in accordance with the divine will, reach up to it and make satisfaction. Since then Christ has taken upon himself the penalties of sin such as hunger, thirst, coldness and heat, poverty, fear, anxiety and such like penalties which cling to us because of Adam's guilt, and since he has been killed innocently on account of our own guilt in order that the righteousness of God be appeased, he has reconciled us with God; for he alone has done the will of God which no creature could fulfill, Is. 63:3, "I have trodden the winepress alone." In his human nature he is our brother. In as much as he alone has done the will of God, he is our righteousness by which we may come to God. Otherwise there is no commandment so small which we are able to keep in order to attain salvation. For where there is temptation or covetousness, there also is sin; for covetousness stems from the weaknesses of sin.

This gracious redemption by God through his Son is called "gospel". I call it thus, though the term "gospel" is not so clear that it could fully express this process. It is called a "good and sure gospel". Yet, this good news is not determined in itself, for in itself it says that the Son of God is born into the world to be a savior unto us, Lk. 2:11. Note, the words of Luke are as follows: "Today is born to you a redeemer." If he is born to us, he is our [236] righteousness, too, for he is just--even more, he is righteousness personified; therefore he is our righteousness. At this point everyone understands Paul's words which I referred to at the beginning of this Article, "Christ has become our wisdom from God" [1 Cor. 1:30]. Therefore everyone should keep to his way alone and not invent a new one. He has become our righteousness, because no one may come to God if he is not righteous; but no one can be righteous on his own account. Christ, however, is righteous. He is our head and we are his members; we the members may come to God by the righteousness of the head. He, too, has become our holiness for he has sanctified us by his own blood. He has become our ransom, for he has redeemed us from law, devil and sin.

At this point I want to speak of the way in which we have been redeemed from the law through Christ. The law shows us the pure will of God so that if we believe, we may see in it the purity and beauty of the divine will. We note in its light, however, that we cannot fulfill the will of God; for no one has ever become so righteous that he has been able to do the will of God rightly and worthily. Thus we see that we cannot after all come to God, since we are incapable of doing his will. Thus the law condemns us. In other words, we see through the law that we may not come to God and that we are therefore rightly condemned. Thus Christ redeems us from the condemnation of the law in that when we despair in the law for not being able to fulfill it, we see in Christ a certain guarantor of our salvation. For though all of us are unrighteous, he, nonetheless, is our righteousness. No longer is the law able to condemn us. Thus we are redeemed from the law; not that that which God bids and wills should no longer be done. Rather, that one is kindled increasingly more by the love of God when one discovers his great grace and friendliness. The greater this love, the more one does what God wills. Now let no one think here that one should become slothful in doing good. Whoever believes in the meaning of salvation, is illumined by God. Therefore, where God is, you need not have to worry how to do good, [237].

Those, however, who clamor loudly that we have become careless concerning grace, do not have the right faith as yet. Or else they feel in themselves that the good which God bids us do has never been more pleasing to them and that evil has never been more displeasing. Thus a believer is redeemed from the law so that he need not fear the condemnation of the law any more.

He has only to heed those works which God has commanded in such a way that they are to be done to all eternity. Ceremonies, which God has bid us do for punishment and only for a certain time, he considers to be child's play; he regards the ceremonies of the papists to be even lower. For he knows well that God has not imposed these on us in the new law; for not only has he redeemed us from the punishment of sin (which was their ceremonies), but from sin itself. So far the commandments of his will still stand firm unto eternity; for they are no less than an expression of his will. These commandments a believer does out of love; the godless hates them. The believer does not do them in his own strength. Rather, God effects in him love, counsel and works, as much as he does. In all things he knows full well that his doing and his works are naught; but that whatever takes place, is God's alone. And though he may not do the works and the will of God, or even work against God's commandments, he does not despair; for he knows Christ Jesus to be his salvation. Now the simple person will say, "Which are the commandments of God that shall not ever pass away?" Answer: Those, on which all laws and prophets depend, Mt. 22:37-40, "You shall love the Lord your God with all your heart, soul and mind. And you shall love your neighbor as yourself." Everything pertaining to these two commandments in Holy Scripture, one is obliged to do unto eternity. You may say: "Under the first commandment one might well include ceremonies, for one does these to the honor of God. I retort: No. If it were to the honor of God, he would not have rejected these through Isaiah and Ezekiel. Show me though, when he has ever let up on or placed in a secondary position the commandments of the first order. Therefore they stand firm to all eternity together with everything that depends on them.

This opinion I expressed earlier at greater length. Since I believe myself capable of saying it more fittingly and briefly, I [238] am dealing with it once again at this point. Moreover, I was not able to alter what I said earlier, since it had already gone to press. [3] Here is a summary of the matter:

1. The will of God wills eternally what is right and good. **2.** From this comes the eternal law which likewise cannot ever be put aside or changed. But we ourselves are incapable of keeping that law. **3.** Therefore the eternal will of God must remain and God's grace must come to our aid. **4.** This it [grace] has accomplished through Christ our mediator. He is our righteousness.

We have further proof of how Christ is our righteousness.

Jn. 16:8, "When the comforter shall come, he will punish the world or convict it [harfür ziehen] for righteousness sake, for I am now going to the Father, etc." In other words, the Holy Spirit shall reveal to the world that I alone am the righteous one and the righteousness which leads to God. To prove that to be true I shall ascend to the Father who is in heaven.

Likewise Rom. 3:21ff, "Now, God's righteousness has been revealed apart from the law. Both the law and the prophets bear witness to it, but the righteousness of God stands [rooted] in faith in Jesus Christ over against all persons and above all persons who believe."

If then Christ alone is our righteousness, our works cannot ever be just or good, as the second section of this Article shall demonstrate.

"That our works are good inasmuch as they are Christ's; but to the extent to which they are ours, they are not good."

This section has been proved earlier when we discussed the merits in Article 20. Therefore it does not require many words at this point other than to cite the testimonies of scripture.

Christ says in Jn. 15:4, "As the branch cannot bear fruit by itself, except it remain in the vine, so you cannot bear fruit if you do not remain in me." Thus it follows that the fruit is not ours, but Christ's. Likewise, James 1:17, "Every good and perfect gift comes from above, from the father of lights." If [329] every good thing is of God, then nothing can be good except that which comes from him. Now if our work is good, it comes from God. Thus it follows, that we should not credit anything to ourselves which is God's. Likewise in Luke 18:19, Jesus says, "No one is good except the one God." Thus it follows that the good can come from no one except from the one God. An evil tree cannot bear good fruit [Lk. 6:43]. Likewise, Job 8:15, "The hypocrite will rely on his house or his servants but he cannot stand." This is a hidden figurative speech; in fact its meaning is that those who put their trust in their own works, will be deceived.

Likewise, Jer. 10:23, "Lord, I know that a person's way is not his own. Neither is it within a person's grasp to judge his ways." This indicates that all our directives must be governed by God and not by us.

Likewise, 1 Cor. 15:10, "By the grace of God I am what I am. The same has not been idle within me; for I labored more than any of them. But it was not I who did that but God's grace which was in me." Note how Paul ascribes his works to God's grace. In short: As soon as a person credits himself with the things which are God's only, he is a true hypocrite. Though he might not ever have sinned otherwise, this would be sin enough, not to believe that God works all things.

NOTES

1. This book was apparently never written.

2. The Vulgate reads, "Lex enim iram operatur".

3. The essential elements of an evangelical social ethics, possibly referred to here, Zwingli expounded in a sermon during June 1523. In expanded form he published it toward the end of July under the title **Von göttlicher und menschlicher Gerechtigkeit** [on divine and human righteousness]. The gospel is shown to be supportive of temporal authority which is to assure that Christian citizens walk on the right path. Cf. Z.II 458-525.

THE TWENTY-THIRD ARTICLE

Christ rejects the riches and pomp of this world. From this we conclude that those who gather up riches for themselves in his name slander him greatly since they use him to cloak their own greed and wantonness.

We know that all teaching and work of Christ is for our instruction and serves as a pattern by which we are to live, for he says in Jn. 13:15, "I have given you an example that you may do as I have done." Now he despised riches and the pomp of this world. Jn. 6:15. When the people decided to set him up [240] as their king, he fled. He bids us, too, to learn from him when he says in Mt. 11:29, "Take my yoke upon you and learn from me for I am gentle and humble-hearted and your souls will find rest." It is a clear commandment of Christ exhorting us in what we are to learn from him: to bear his yoke--for he bore ours--to learn gentleness and meekness, thus we shall be at rest in our souls here and yonder.

To wit, he rode into Jerusalem upon a donkey according to the prophecy in Zech. 9:9, "Rejoice greatly, O daughter of Zion; behold your king, who is righteous, and your savior shall come. He is poor and sits upon a she-ass and upon the foal, the son of the old beast." To wit, that he himself confesses his poverty in Lk. 9:58, "Foxes have holes and the birds of heaven, nests, but the Son of Man has no place to put his head." Note the great poverty of Christ.

To wit, he says in Jn. 18:36, "My kingdom is not of this world. If it were of this world, my servants would surely fight so that I might not be handed over to the Jews; but my kingdom is not of this world."

These excerpts are sufficient proof that Christ despises the riches and pomp of this world and that he has bid us learn his manner of life.

But the second part which follows from this, requires not only strong words but the power of God so that the hypocrites might give it credence. It is this:

That those who gather up riches for themselves in his name, i.e. Christ's name, slander him greatly since they use him to cloak their own greed and wantonness.

What greater affront can we put upon Christ than for us to claim to be his servants and ambassadors when in reality we oppose him totally in all our works? Should an unbeliever listen to our alleged spiritual teaching--though we might teach it correctly--and then hear of or see our greed, wantonness, pomp and falsehood, he would have to be a dud if he should not deduce that we are utter [241] hypocrites (do not take offence if you are innocent; I know full well that there are many just servants of God who present the teaching of Christ in word and deed)--when we act totally contrary to that which Christ bade us do.

Indeed, he would say we are naughty boys and might in the end even slander Christ for having burdened simple people with such a generation, a thing that actually happened in the beginning of Christianity. Rom. 2:24, "The name of God is dishonored among unbelievers because of you, because they taught others and not themselves." What a great and most fitting word. For as long as the world has existed, there has been no holier or more comforting teaching for humankind than the teaching of Christ. There has not been a more fitting example of humility and modesty than the one which Christ has set. Yet on the other hand, no teaching has been more grievously rejected than the teaching of Christ. Neither has there been a more un-Christian devilish life lived by any people than the life of those who called themselves servants of Christ and representatives of the apostles to such an extent that if Christ had never come into this world and if the devil had decided to make himself an evil nation, he might not have accomplished this any better than had he taught to gather up riches in the name of God; subsequently, all evils would have arisen therefrom.

But since the Son of God came to annul and destroy the work of the devil even a blind person can see that deceitful and evil teaching and practices derive solely from the effect and power of error, 2 Thess. 2:11 which God sent into the world as punishment for sinful people who did not believe truth but evil. Indeed, to this day, should God send and reveal his word which points to the true anti-Christians, we would not believe it.

Observe: Christ was poor and forbade his servants to

gather riches. Yet, the anti-Christians gather unto themselves riches; they have persuaded the simple people that Christ should have riches and that these are his honor and ornament; though he cast out of the temple those who sought riches and held up to the Jews their hypocrisy for chasing after riches in the name of temple and altar. Anti-Christians act similarly to this day, thinking that accumulation [242] of riches is worship. Paul points to this in 1 Tim. 6:5, saying that, "Their hearts are broken and devastated." They say, "You do not give riches to us but to God, the saints and to the blessed Mother of God." Thus they misrepresent Christ who was poor while here on earth and though he now sits at the right hand of God, they make him out to be poor and collect in his name with such earnestness that one might think he would die unless we come to his aid with our riches. They slander blessed Mary who was poor and humble while on earth. Now when she is with God they enrich her with temporal goods saying, "she is our beloved lady." In like manner they slander the saints. For the saints neglected and despised temporal things. And after their death they do them the dishonor of claiming that they would rejoice in temporal things. Yet the sum of the matter is that they are so greedy that in the name of God they gather for themselves riches which they debauch.

Thus they are not content with lying to God as if he desires riches but vaunt themselves to be gods. For if the riches which they acquire through begging and their false pretenses are God's, why then do they themselves use what is God's? If it is God's, he shall divide it among the poor rather than stuff such lazy bellies with it. "Religio peperit divitias et filia devoravit matrem," which means, "Devotion has bred riches and the daughter has devoured the mother."

They see now how they miss out on temporal benefits; God grant that they may experience what happens to the poor in the teaching of Christ. Yet when one points up their avarice, they say, "Why should we not possess temporal goods? They have been given us willingly."

Answer: No, you are not to have these, but should give them to the poor instead without having taken them at all. Though people had not been as foolish as to take your hypocrisy for worship but had intended in good faith to give you temporal goods, you should not have accepted these but should have fled, as Christ fled kingdom and crown. Did you not know that even if you had possessed riches, you should have left them for God's sake? Yet you go to appropriate them unto yourselves. Say, with what affrontery do you dare [243] teach others to despise riches when there is no one more anxious to have them than you yourselves? And whenever there is any unrighteous property you order it brought to you and take it to be righteous. Indeed, you say it is just in the sight of the saints, thus turning the saints into accomplices of robbers, thieves and usurers. See what great wickedness is hidden behind the hypocrisy and false teaching of the papists.

Concerning pomp they know well that however anxiously the disciples of Christ asked among themselves who was chief or highest among them, Christ always humbled them by saying, "Whoever wants to be the greatest among you, ought to become the lowest." They are fighting to this day about the highest place; Turkish potentates even could not behave more effeminately and foolishly than they. A Dionysius, Nero or Ahab could not be worse than they in their fury. And to satisfy their pride, they openly fabricate lies concerning St. Peter and Constantine by saying, "Yes, the former is a representative of Christ, and they have been put in his stead." This, of course, does not tally with the truth. The other was an emperor who was to have given them the entire Roman Empire that they might take it over in time. [1] This is as glaring a lie as the broadest day. Yet they continue to show their arrogance and oppress their subjects more severely than do the landowners. I should not envy them either subjects or land or that they are considered like worldly lords and tyrants. But to say that they are bishops, i.e. guardians and preachers of the word of God without doing justice to either office, when they are mere braggards [2] who annoy everyone, start every war and are given to usury, deceit, betrayal, switch from one party to another and abuse the children of pious people; this can be tolerated no longer. And should I or someone else be silent, the rocks would sweat and cry in anguish. Christ said explicitly to the disciples, "But you are not to rule in this manner" Lk. 22:25f. Peter speaks thus in 1 Pet. 5:2f, [244] "Feed the sheep which have been entrusted unto you, not as those who are forced (in other words, because you have to), but willingly (i.e. everyone ought to be left unfettered by their laws), not from desire for gain, but with a sympathetic heart."

Neither should you be like those who boast of their territory and their people. Rather, you should be persons whom people might emulate. At the moment they do not care in the least for the teaching and the word of God. All their strength is directed against God and employed in that which offends everyone. Therefore I spoke truly when I said, "They therefore greatly blaspheme God for they ascribe to God what they abuse and they rule in this world which neither he [i.e. Christ], nor his disciples have ever done. In sum, they are godless; for if they believed the word of God, they would not commit such treachery.

NOTES

1. Zwingli means the Donation of Constantine according to which Constantine allegedly had granted certain rights and privileges to Pope Sylvester I.

2. The term is "gotsjuncksherren" which G. R. Potter translates with "swaggering squires".

THE TWENTY-FOURTH ARTICLE

Every Christian is free of any of the works which God did not command and is allowed at all times to eat everything. From this we learn that the dispensations concerning cheese and butter are a Roman fraud. [1]

The first part is easily proved. For whatever we do on the basis of human teaching and commandments is useless, Mt. 15:9, as I have amply demonstrated in Article 16. But the papists do not concede this too readily. This comes from the fact that their whole argument is built upon human prattle. But Adam was expelled from the Garden on account of no other sin than his having eaten of the fruit of the forbidden tree. From this we may conclude that he was bound to that one law only. I speak here merely of those works which are ordered in the name of Christ. I do not mean to say that one should not keep the laws of city and country which do not touch at all upon the commandments of God (though they must all be inherently formed after God's will, or else nothing but sorrow follows in their wake.).

In the first chapter Isaiah speaks of ceremonial works or humanly ordered works as follows, "Whenever you come into my presence (understood is [245] with ceremonial works), who asked you to do these things that you might dwell in my courts?" [Is. 1:12].

Jer. 6:20, "Why do you offer me incense from Sheba and fragrant spices from distant lands? Your burnt offerings displease me and your living sacrifices are not acceptable to me."

God reprimands those who put burdens upon people's shoulders according to their own judgment, Mt. 23:4. Therefore it is not a sin against God when a person does not keep a human law, as long as no one is offended (as I shall show in the 28th Article). I call that a human law which is opposed to the commandment and word of God.

197

The second part [of this Article], that a person is free to eat every kind of food at any time, I have dealt with more extensively in a separate book; from it I shall now indicate some essential directives. [2]

Christ says in Mk. 7:18, "There is nothing outside a person which could defile him by being eaten." He speaks here of food, claiming that no food is capable of defiling a person. Concerning times [of abstention from food] will follow shortly after.

1 Cor. 8:8, "Food does not make us pleasing to God." Col. 2:16, "No one shall judge you on account of food or drink." 1 Tim. 4:1-4, "The spirit shows us clearly and openly that in the last days there will be some who depart from the faith and who will listen to deceitful devils, etc." These will order that certain foods must not be eaten; yet God has created such food that it may be eaten with thanksgiving. Note that such prohibition comes from the devil. Titus 1:15, "To the pure all things are pure; but to the unclean and unbelievers, nothing is pure for their heart and conscience are defiled." The pure are believers to whom all foods are clean.

The third part of the Article which refers to the dispensations regarding bread and butter as being a Roman fraud, is evident, for they have forbidden certain foods (as they say), yet have taken money and then allowed them to be eaten. What else is this but a trick, falsehood [246] and evil? Unless it is a sin to eat every kind of food, they have no right to forbid these. Show me where they are forbidden. Since they are unable to do so, it follows that the food restrictions were issued so that they might lift them again for a fee. You foolish Christians. How long do you allow yourselves to be led about by your noses? Do you think God cares whether you satisfy your hunger with beef or with fish?

NOTES

1. Papal dispensations granted the use of milk products during fasts in areas where oil was not available. Zwingli must have in mind a letter of June 1456. For details Cf. Z.I 109, n. 4.

2. Cf. Zwingli's Sermon, Regarding the Choice and Freedom of Eating Food, 1522, Z.I 88ff. S. M. Jackson translated it in **Huldreich Zwingli**, Putnam, 1901. Excerpts may be found in B. J. Kidd, **Documents Illustrative of the Continental Reformation**, Oxford, 1911.

THE TWENTY-FIFTH ARTICLE

Times and places are subjected to Christians and not vice versa; from this we learn that those who tether times and places, rob Christians of their freedom.

The first part, namely, that times and places are subjected to a believer, Christ himself teaches in Mt. 12:6, "I say to you that he who is greater than the Temple is here already." And a little later, Mt. 12:8, "The Son of Man is lord over the Sabbath also." Thus we hear that Christ and we (who are in Christ), are lord over Sabbath and Temple, i.e. over holy days and places. There is no point in objecting. Indeed, I readily believe that Christ is above the Sabbath or the Temple but we humans are not above them on account of this. For when Christ says, The Son of Man is greater than Temple or Sabbath, he means that he is above them as a true human being. Now, he has become human that he may become our salvation; therefore his freedom over the Sabbath is ours also. For he would not need this word on his own account, since he did not transgress the Sabbath; but he said it on account of his disciples. Therefore if we are his disciples and brothers, we are above Sabbath and Temple, just as those were who were his disiples then.

To wit, he says again in Mk. 2:27f. "The Sabbath is made for humankind and not humankind for the Sabbath. Therefore the Son of Man is lord over the Sabbath." [247] Do you see then that the Sabbath is to serve people and not vice versa.

To wit, Col. 2:16, "No one ought to judge you on the basis of holy days, new moons or Sabbath days which are figures of the things that once were to come and now have come; for the body or that which is essential, is Christ and he is here now."

Thus it follows, firstly, in the above Article that no one is able to bind food to any one time by saying that one is not allowed food at certain times at all; you ought to let the disciple of Christ, i.e. the believer, say at all times, "The Son of Man is lord of the Sabbath also."

It follows, secondly, that all those who penalize someone on account of his celebrating, do him an injustice (I speak here of the celebrating which is done by being idle), for a Christian is lord over festival days. Yes, it would be better on most festival days to return to work after first having heard the word of God and partaken of the body and blood of Christ in genuine remembrance. One has rest enough when one rests on Sundays and disregards all other holy days after morning worship except for Christmasday and St. Stephen's Day on which one praises all those who have suffered for God's sake; the Annunciation of Mary, on which day one may well sing praises of the undefiled virgin; St. John the Baptist Day on which one might speak sufficiently of the faith of the ancient fathers and prophets. St. Peter and Paul's Day may be exempted, too, since it may serve to recall properly all messengers and evangelists according to their deserts. Otherwise all the celebrating we do by eating, drinking, playing, uttering lies and engaging in unnecessary talk in broad daylight is a greater sin than worship. I do not find anywhere that idleness is worship. Even if one were to go to the fields on a Sunday after having set one's house in order with God, to do some mowing, cutting, haying or whatever work of necessity may be required, I know well that [248] this should be by far more pleasing to God than sloppy idleness. For the believer is above the Sabbath.

Thirdly, one hears from the words of Christ and the works of David, which Mt. 12:3f. indicates, that all those act foolishly who bind the grace of God to specific places such as Rome, Jerusalem, St. James or any other like places. Indeed, not only do they act foolishly but also anti-Christian, for they make the grace of God more readily available in one place than in another. But this is no less than enclosing God and tying him down, i.e. they appropriate the grace of God to themselves, but do not make it known as it should rightly be [known] in this manner, namely, that in whatever place on earth he may be called on, he is there, saying, "I am here." Therefore Paul also says in 1 Tim. 2:8f, "I desire then that the men should call on me in all places etc. and likewise the women too." In other words, one ought to know that wherever God is called on, he is there and answers [prayers]. But he is not more prominent or gracious in one place than in another. Further, Christ himself calls any such worshipers of God false Christians, i.e. anti-Christians; Mt. 24:24-26, "There shall arise false Christians or imposters, etc. And if they say to you, look, God is in the wilderness, do not go out there or if they say he is in the inner rooms, do not believe them." O God, who else but the pope is the false Christ who elevates himself to the place of Christ, saying, "I have his power," and then proceeds to tie God down to Rome or to St. James or any other such place. One carries the money there in piles, erecting with it ornate houses of God (giving them those very names). And if need should arise one may draw from these. I shall not speak of the fact that in such places there is more lust and vice than in other places. If you stop the flow of money, their worship also will cease and whatever you have given toward this lust, redirect it toward a better cause. Give it to the poor and let these [people] look askance and wail as much as they want.

The other part of this Article is clear, namely, that those who tie God to time and place, rob Christians of their freedom. For they close off God from them and set up above a person the very time which is to serve him in his needs. [249]

THE TWENTY-SIXTH ARTICLE

Nothing is more displeasing to God than hypocrisy. From this we learn that everything that simulates goodness to human eyes is utter hypocrisy and infamy. This applies to vestments, insignia, tonsures, etc.

To the first, Job 13:16 says, "No hypocrite shall ever come into his [i.e. God's] presence." Now it is certain that the presence of God is denied to all unbelievers Mk. 16:16. Since it is denied to all hypocrites here, but is actually not denied any one but a blasphemer, we preceive that hypocrisy is godlessness and unbelief; for if hypocrites believed that he whom we take to be God is God, they would also believe his word and if they had ever believed his word, they would not have invented customs that contradict the word of God. Look well to yourself, you hypocrite. This judgment is not wrong. And from the work of Christ it is quite apparent that nothing was more offensive to him than hypocrisy, for he unmercifully scolded and censured hypocrisy everywhere. Whenever sinners and sick people came to him he talked and dealt graciously with them, but hypocrites he always treated roughly [saying], how they gave their alms with self satisfaction, how they distorted their faces when fasting, how they occupied the most prominent places, how they made long prayers before people so they might be fed, how they ate up the homes of widows, how they cleaned their dishes on the outside, but how, inwardly they remained full of robbery, theft and all kinds of malice, how they are like white-washed tombs, how they feed their greed at temple and altar, how they close up the kingdom of heaven yet neither do they enter nor do they allow others to enter, how they do all their works to be seen by people, how they see the splinter in someone else's eye but fail to see the large [250] beam in their own, and many such instances in all of his teaching. Observe here, in passing, the hypocrisy and the beautiful work of those hypocrites and you will note right away whether there is any difference between the Jewish hypocrites and ours. After this it will be apparent that the condemnation of hypocrites is great and serious, because, no doubt, their misdeeds are so unsavory to God; for Christ threatens the idle, unfaithful servant with the punishment of hypocrites, Mt. 24:50f, saying, "The Lord will come at an hour when the wicked servant does not suspect it, and he shall destroy him and give him his lot with the hypocrites." God is the pure and true good; indeed, he is the truth; thus it follows that hypocrisy, like all other misdeeds, displeases him.

The second part:

-

From this it follows that whatever simulates goodness to human eyes is genuine infamy.

For it is hypocrisy, and if one knows that hypocrisy is so much of an affront to God and if he lives for and clings to it, it is certain nonetheless that he is impious, godless and without faith, as has been shown before. This vice is also more dangerous than we think. And those who think they are free of hypocrisy, will be afflicted by it all the more. What did David do when Nathan the prophet came to him? He judged him who was to have done it, as if he knew nothing about it. But when the prophet pointed out to him that his number was up, he confessed [cf. 2 Sam. 12:1-14]. Note, the great murder he had committed, he had not even considered; yet he was so dear to God that he made him king in place of Saul. Therefore everyone ought to look to himself daily-- though he may be firm in his faith--whether the weed of hypocrisy has already sprouted in his own garden. For whenever the devil cannot weaken faith, he comes along with hypocrisy and rages fiercely. If he wins out, a person becomes worse than before. These are the seven devils with which he attacks us afterwards more fiercely than before [Mt. 12:43-45]. [251]

Concerning the third part:

Vestments, insignia and the tonsure are of no use here.

This is given us in the clear word of Christ in Mt. 23:5-7 in which he rejects outward appearances and insignia, sayiing, "They (i.e. the pharisees and scribes, whom in our day we consider to be the monks, priests, nuns, scholars who are as black in color as the others), [1] do all their works in order to be seen by people; they widen their belts which they call admonition of the law or protection of the law--they also make sure that the seams of their garments are prominent and they place great store by being seated in places of honor at meals, in prominent places at the synagogue and that they are respectfully greeted in the market place and addressed as "master" or "our master". Note, how nicely he pricks the boil of these Jews and alleged spirituals. He also says that they shall have their reward (here on earth) Mt. 6:2, "Truly I say to you, they have had their reward." If then God scolds such foolishness, it follows that vestments, crosses, clerical garb, the tonsure are not simply "good or evil", but they are totally evil. Therefore a Christian does well to leave them aside rather than to be stuck with them, provided this can be done without offence and uproar. Now they say that one ought to be able to distinguish an honorable priesthood from ordinary people, be it through their tonsure or else through clothes. I respond: Whoever wants to be known among his brothers through signs or clothes is a hypocrite, for we have a better way to become honorable. Christ teaches us to surpass one another in humility. He also says, "By this everyone shall know that you are my disciples, if you love one another," Jn. 13:35. If we love all persons as ourselves and if we preach the word of salvation earnestly, being concerned with the needs of everyone, and if we assist them to the best of our ability, we shall be known all right. Indeed, [252] even children will know us and that without any [outward] sign. [2] The devils, however, will not be able to tolerate us. Rather, they will shout at us like the possessed young girl in Philippi, [Acts 16:17ff]. But once we no longer have the proper dignity, the true power of God which is the bold work of the gospel; we have adorned ourselves with an untrue character such as tonsure, vestments, clothing so that even though we are of no use either to God or the world (do not pay attention to this just person), we nonetheless put on costly clothes so that people might admire us, just as the children admire the pope's golden donkey.

I have to insert yet another two-pronged objection. You papists wear gowns, the tonsure and signs. Tell me, do you wear these to please God or people? You will undoubtedly answer, "To please God." But how does that go? Could you not please him without such signs? Why did not he himself indicate [the need of] such? Or do you think that he might not recognize your worship unless you wear one of these disguises? He is not blind just because he is old. He does not look upon your outward worship; rather, he looks into the heart. But you make so much ado over your gowns and insignia that he does not have any need of the heart. He sees well by your clothing who you are, namely, mummers and hypocrites.

In the end, the first prong [of the argument] must convince you that you do not wear outward signs for God's sake, for he rejects [253] outward appearances and demands serious work without any adornment.

There would still be the second prong [of the argument] which claims that you are so full of spots that everyone knows you and your piety.

Now listen to what Christ says, "Truly, they have had their reward," Mt. 6:2. He also bids you avoid hypocrisy like an hereditary disease, Lk. 2:1, "Beware of the sour dough of the Pharisees," i.e. hypocrisy. This evil has brought all of christendom to its downfall; for it pretended to be good and holy, indeed, like a simple innocent lamb, but then tore about more fiercely than wolves. Christ, too, predicted this to be so. But we left his word and believed hypocrites. We deserve our sin and that God allowed us to fall prey to such evil. As Job says in 34:30, "He causes hypocrites to rule because of the sin of the people."

NOTES

1. The Latin proverb is Sicut lacte, lactis simile est, (They are alike, as milk is like milk).

2. Regarding the vestments worn by Zwingli, Bullinger and pastors of the Reformed Church in Zurich, cf. E. Furrer, "Geschichte des Pfarrornates in der zuercherischen Landeskirche", **Jahrbuch der historischen Gesellschaft Zuericher Theologen,** vol. 1, 1877, 211ff.

THE TWENTY-SEVENTH ARTICLE

All Christians are brothers of Christ and of one another and no one on earth ought to be elevated to be called Father. This brings to naught religious orders, sects and illegal gatherings.

That we are brothers of Christ, Paul teaches in Heb. 2:11, "The one who sanctifies and those who are sanctified are of the same origin." For this reason he is not ashamed (understand, Christ) to call them brothers, saying in Ps. 21 [22:23], "I shall make known your name to my brothers." Likewise in another passage [Heb. 2:17], "Therefore he had to be made like his brothers in all respects (understand, without the infirmity of sin), that he might become merciful and a faithful high priest before God." Likewise Christ in Mt. 12:50, "Whoever does the will of my Father in heaven, is my brother, sister and mother." [254]

That we are all brothers of one another and are not to set up a father on earth, we learn from the words of Christ in Mt. 23:8-10, "You shall not be called master, for there is only one among you who is master (understand, God), but you are all brothers together. And you shall not make anyone on earth your 'father'; for the heavenly Father is your eternal and only father."

You note here, firstly, whence come the titles "master" or "doctor"; they are certainly not of God; for he has forbidden them.

Secondly, you look upon the basis of the brotherhoods which is no more than bird-lime. If you give so much, you belong to Our Lady's or to St. John's or to the brotherhood of our order; but if you do not give anything, you cannot belong. Oh, how then might I be saved? Be strong, you poor little soul. All persons are your brothers; therefore they have to accept you whether they are favorably disposed toward you or not if they themselves want to come to God. If they have God for a father and say with me, "Oh, our Father" then they have to let me be their brother also, unless, of course, they want to withdraw from the Father themselves; for I like to have all of them as my brothers. But if they are unwilling to do so, they have to disown the Father. Indeed, if they want God to forgive them, they, in turn, have to forgive me. Therefore, wretched soul, you are everyone's brother; hold them firmly to that, even though they are unwilling to treat you as their brother. For whoever excludes you is no longer a son of God. If he should exclude you because you have made no financial contribution, he himself is excluded by God; but if he does not exclude you and prays for you without receiving any money, he does just as you do and is everyone's brother.

For this reason then, good Christians, leave the illegal gatherings of the brotherhoods and be, above all else, brother to all other believers, rather than to monks and priests, and you will be children of God with the majority of brothers. And do not worry if they prattle, "If one were not to pray for another in a special manner, James [James 5:14] would not have taught that the elders [255] are to pray for one who is lying ill." We are of the opinion, of course, that we should all intercede for one another; but you are merely intent on selecting the fat ones. You ought to pray gladly for all persons and for the weak ones, above all; without any reward; for they, too, will pray for you without any reward. Indeed, one has to pray for you more earnestly than you will ever have prayed for anyone for pay: firstly, so that you may be illumined by God to recognize your error and secondly, that he may then forgive you the same. For what a thing this would be if you have to be paid to pray for people and, yet, you in turn, do not want to pay anyone to pray for you? Yet, you need more intercession than anyone else. The more you think you are not in need of it, the more you actually need it. Note, this is the fruit of merit. It has set up for us feeble saints who sell themselves to the world as if they had already recompensed God and now work on our behalf for a wage.

Thirdly, we note, that we are not to elevate or call anyone in the world "Father"; this word is clear. Mt. 23:9, "Do not call anyone on earth father; for he who is in heaven is your only father." Christ did not intend to prohibit the calling of one's physical father by that name, but rather that we ought not set up any other forerunner, teacher or guide, except the heavenly teacher, father and guide. This is indicated by the preceding word [Mt.23:8], "You ought not be called master," which term in the same context concerns teaching as well. This is also indicated by the subsequent words [Mt. 23:10], "You ought not be called leaders, for your sole leader is Christ." Now the Latin term for this word leader is master, but the Greek term is "kathegetes" which means as much as forerunner or guide. In short, Christ does not want any other teacher for us but God and no one to be elevated as Father; for the heavenly Father alone is our Father and no one else ought to lead us but the one Christ. Heaven and earth will have to fall before this his word. This [256] he intends to have it thus eternally; for his testament is an eternal one; he has never nor shall he ever change it. From this it follows that all who have elevated themselves to be fathers, as well as all those who called them fathers and who banded together, acted against God and against the honor and order of Christ. For these words are well attested to in three places. When they say, "Yes, we know well that God is our Father, but we have a righteous, holy man as our school master and guide," their words are a contradiction of the admonition in the primary clause, "You are to have God alone for a school master; his word alone you are to know and you are not to heed any human inventions, be they ever so clever." They also contradict the subsequent clause, namely, "you are not to be called leaders; for Christ is your sole leader". After him alone we are to carry the cross without hesitation and not after Dominic, Benedict, Francis, Anthony or Bernard. I have no doubt whatsoever that none of these ever banded together or taught anyone to bear his name; for I doubt that anyone who should have done so would attain to salvation anymore than Lucifer. Rather, hypocrites who came after them called themselves the followers and disciples of such righteous person in order to be looked upon more favorably by people and as a result, take in more money from their worship. Should Francis or Dominic or any of the others be among us today they would undoubtedly say, "O you fools. What are you doing? Do you not know that you are not to have any other teacher, father and leader but God alone. Why do you attach yourselves to us who all our lives adhered to God only?"

In short, to institute any kind of order, name or sect instead of remaining with the multitude of Christians is wrong, sinful, hypocritical, fraudulent, profiteering and deceitful. This is a very harsh word and is greatly held against me when they say, "You have gone mad." There are many saints, indeed, who came to God out of the various orders and were saved. I answer: Show me testimony from scripure to prove that they have been saved. The Antichrist at Rome may well have said through his fat priests that they are [257] saved. I, for one, put more trust in the truth of the simplest Christian than in that of all those popes who followed another rule and not the rule of Christ.

But the fathers--you say--the popes and the councils have sanctioned these orders. I answer: There is a handle for every pot. Popes and councils readily endorse their wheedlers. Why did they not go by the word of Christ in Mt.23:9? They could have readily seen that they should have said, "follow the one teaching of Christ, do not set up for yourselves fathers, follow no one but the one Christ." O good Christian, do you not see what sort of testimony this is? If it were of God it would not need any endorsement, for what person can endorse Christ to be our salvation? This needs no confirmation; it is true to a believer, for God himself taught him. But the anti-Christians had to confirm their claim because it is not at all grounded in God but is totally against him.

Note the kind of foundation orders have. I shall not say anything at all about their knavery when they say that they vow poverty; yet there is no body of people on earth richer than monks and none more avaricious.

They also say that they vow obedience; yet they withdraw from obedience to God, to temporal authority and to human beings.

They do not obey God. For when he bids them have one Father only they set up for themselves an earthly father. When he bids them honor father and mother and aid them [Ex. 20:12], they say "No". You must not ever again look upon father and mother. Thus they twist the words of Christ concerning the leaving of father and mother [Mt. 19:29] in their own false fashion, as if it were for their order that one should leave father and mother. O you shameless falsifiers of God's word. Do you not understand [258] that Christ teaches to leave father and mother only if these should want to draw us away from faith and not allow us to follow Christ. But say now, when did he ever bid you leave father and mother on account of an order when he does not even permit any orders anywhere?

They do not obey temporal authority; this is apparent. Yet Peter and Paul bid us obey it [1 Pet. 2:13f; Rom. 13:1]. Indeed, ere they obey such authority, they initiate deadly wars, as has often happened. Observe now whether they love temporal things or not.

To their neighbor they do not make themselves available which is the most Christian form of obedience. They do not suffer with those who are afflicted; they do not work with those who labor; they do not mourn with those who mourn [Rom. 12:15], and when they give alms, they do so only after they themselves have had their fill. What more shall I say? The earth does not carry more useless burdens than those fattened pigs in disguise. Do not pay attention to this, righteous man of the cloth. I know well that there are many upright consciences inside a gown who actually believe and follow the teaching of Christ, whenever such befits them. But there are so many braggarts about that they may venture some day to upset the entire world, but I also know that they will have to pay up in the end. [1]

Concerning the chastity which they vow, I shall say more later. From all this it follows that everything which monks on earth have invented regarding their gowns, is sheer hypocrisy and so much wind against the word and work of God. One may readily know them by their fruits. What need is there for them to wear the mask of poverty? Many of them are actually poor, but they put on their mummers' clothes so that they might become rich. Indeed, they boast of the wealth of their monasteries, allow themselves to be made princes, while the princes stand still and allow dirt to be plastered about their mouths until the point is reached at which there are more beggar princes than true ones [259]; in fact, they now have to fear these others in part. Yet Christ says to his disciples, "You ought not to lord it over them as the princes of this world do" [Mt.20:25]. When they come together they say, "Dear sir, how is it with your house of God? Do the farmers still give you their due? [2] Mine begin to rebel against this practice." And the other one, in turn, might say, "I have a different problem. The devil has assigned a learned monk to me. I had intended to make a good administrator of him, but he showed no interest in administration." These are the fruits by which you may recognize their spirit. Whether they are born of the flesh or of the Spirit you yourself may henceforth be able to distinguish. If of the flesh, they are of the devil also; for the flesh has its infirmities from the devil. Now the apostles were able to foresee the damage such hypocrites would do and they warned in earnest words to prevent it.

Paul says in Acts 20:28-30 to the priests at Ephesus, "Look diligently to yourselves and the sheep which have been entrusted to you, etc. for I know that after my departure there will be going about among you rapacious wolves, they will devastate the herd or sheep. For there will arise among you people who will say wrong and incorrect things by which they will draw the people of Christ unto themselves." See what all this commotion about orders is: they teach different doctrines than those taught by God? And they persuade many of the younger ones to follow them and to depart from God's path.

Peter draws them in rather vivid colors in the second chapter [2 Pet. 2:1-3], "There have been among the people of Israel many false prophets, just as there will rise up among you false teachers who will introduce, on the side, harmful and destructive sects which deny him who has purchased them, bringing sudden destruction to themselves. And many will follow their destruction by which the path [260] of truth will be defiled, for they will bargain for you out of sheer avarice with feigned, pleasant words.

These words are clear and need no exposition; nor do the gowns need another wash; they have been washed clean here. Jude (not the betrayer of God), sketches them in like fashion and so that one might readily recognize them, he says [Jude 19], "Those who separate themselves off are psuchichoi, they do not have the Spirit of God."

To this end all those who are in monastic orders and all idle priests who have no offices among Christians, should firstly look upon the light of divine truth and secondly see to it that it be kindled for all persons so that no one may take offence at their deeds. Thereafter they should discard all hypocrisy and stop wearing their gowns before all else. And those who are capable of doing physical work should thus earn a living; but if they have to remain in monasteries because of poverty or frailty, they should, nonetheless, not know any other rule than that of Christ, bear no other name than the name of Christ and rather die than do; for the word of Christ does not permit them to have any other father, teacher, guide than him alone. Whoever acts contrary to this, errs and is like those who at the time of Paul called themselves "of Paul", "of Apollo", "of Cephas" whom he scolds, "Has Paul been nailed to the Cross on your behalf? Has Christ been divided?" 1 Cor. 1:3. Likewise, has Benedict been crucified for you? Or who has bid you divide the undivided garment of Christ? Why did you separate yourselves off? To worship is not to fart behind walls. [3] True worship is to visit orphans and widows (understand, all those who are in need), in their distress and to maintain oneself without blemish in this world, James 1:27. By world here is not meant mountain and vale, field and wood, water, sea, city or villages but rather, the desires of the world such as avarice, pride, impurity [261], and gluttony; all these are far greater behind walls than among ordinary people. I am not even speaking of envy and hatred, their own house companions, which are much worse than the vices which they stay clear of in the world. Simply look at their gluttony and you will soon know how pure they are; food is not without its effect on them. Everyone may see their greed and arrogance plainly. Therefore it would be better for them to lay aside their gowns, insignia and rules; indeed, they ought to do this if they want to be obedient to the commandments of God and wish to become like the Christian community at large. For they are wrong when they think that they have fled the world. Right in their monasteries they are in the world and the world is nowhere stronger and greater than in these monasteries. And let no one by fooled by their vows; I shall soon speak of this at length. [4]

NOTES

1. "Das Bad usstragen" is a proverb known in many variants. It refers to the practice in public baths to use the same tub-full for a number of clients. The last user was responsible for cleaning up the dirty tub; hence: he had to

pay up or, as we might say, "get a dirty deal". Cf. J. & W. Grimm, **Deutsches Wörterbuch** I. 1070, and Lutz Rohrich, **Lexicon der Sprichwörtlichen Redensarten.** Frieburg, Basel: Herder, 1973, 90.

2. Die fael--the share, which belongs to the lord of the manor, of all moveable property of a deceased serf. Usually, the best head of cattle or a good piece of furniture was given. Cf. **Idiotikon** I 735.

3. "Gotsdienst ist nit hinder den muren fysten". **Idiotikon** I 1123; I 1184 and V 1193. Jud translated, "pietas est religio non est, si quis intra parietes ignavus stertat".

4. Cf. Article 30 below.

THE TWENTY-EIGHTH ARTICLE

Everything which God permits or which he has not forbidden, is lawful. From this we learn that it is proper for everyone to marry.

The first part is clear, namely that everything which God permits is not sin, but lawful.

However, the other part, namely, that whatever he has not forbidden is lawful, we shall substantiate by references.

In Rom. 3:20 Paul says, "Through the law sin is known." On this, we showed earlier from Deut. 4:2 and 12:32, that one ought not add or substract anything from the law of God. From this follows that anything which God does not forbid is not sin. For if one is not to add anything, one also should not turn into a sin something that God has not forbidden; for by the law one recognizes sin. If the law does not speak of the things that are forbidden, we, too, should not add to it, since we are unable to make these into sins. No one is allowed to add anything to a person's last will and no one may take anything away either. Gal. 3:15. Likewise, no human additions can make a thing either good or evil. Only that which is against God, is evil.

Christ says in Jn. 9:41, "If you were blind, you would not sin, but now that you say, "we see", your [262] sin remains." Here Christ himself shows that if we do not know the law, i.e. the will of God (inasmuch as it has not been given; for after the law or will of God has been revealed, no one, I fear, is guiltless any longer), we are without sin.

Similarly also he says in Jn. 15:22, "Had I not come and spoken with them, they would be without sin." This word of Christ in itself is strong and clear enough to prove that in each case in which God does not speak or disallow something, there is no sin.

Again Paul says in Rom. 7:7, "I did not know sin except by the law; for I did not recognize desire. For the law says, 'Thou shalt not covet, etc'." (Ex. 20:17; Rom. 7:7.) Sin without the law was dead, i.e. it was nothing. Thus it is quite certain that whatever God has not forbidden, is not wrong. Whatever is not wrong, is not sin. Whatever is not sin, is lawful.

But we do not speak here of the right which is so right and good that it is worthy of God. We speak only of the right which is appropriate to us inasmuch as it is not forbidden by God. Other than that nothing right comes from us, for we are too corrupt.

The objection which is made here on the basis of Rom. 2:12, "Everyone who sinned without the law shall also be lost without the law" does not disturb us. For Paul's meaning is as follows: All those who do not have the Jewish law shall, nonetheless, perish, if they act contrary to it; for they are not without some law, as is about to follow. For the natural law within them accuses and forgives them. But what exactly this natural law is (it seems to me nothing other than the Spirit of God), we shall not touch on now. Up to now nothing is sin except that which God explicitly indicates or inwardly instructs to be sin. That which we do not find to be prohibited, either in the law of God or in the law of nature, is simply not wrong.

From this one may easily learn what follows now, namely, that marriage is fitting for everyone, since God does not forbid it. Indeed, he orders it. The law of nature does not forbid it; for marriage is held in high esteem with everyone, even with those who do not believe in God. God gave a help meet to Adam at the beginning of creation--the woman or wife; he did not create another man. By this we understand that all the sons of Adam are in need of the help of [263] a wife. For the sake of brevity I leave out what God has spoken to Adam and Eve in Gen. 1:28 saying, "Be fruitful and multiply". This was not just an authorization but a commandment, for those in the Old Testament who did not have children were despised.

THE TWENTY-NINTH ARTICLE

That all those whom we call "spiritual" sin when, having discovered that God did not grant them the ability to remain chaste, they, nonetheless, do not protect themselves through marriage.

To remain chaste is a divine gift and totally impossible for the flesh, as the mouth of Christ teaches in Mt. 19:11f. "Not everyone is capable of chastity except one to whom it is given." From this word flows the first part of the Article, namely, that every person as soon as he knows that God denied him chastity, etc. For chastity can be maintained by those only to whom God gives it. But how one becomes aware that God has denied one to be chaste, requires no instruction. For every person knows within himself how strongly the flesh attacks him, how strongly he burns. Without this, however, there are some, unfortunately, who sin through their deeds either by intermingling men and women or by some even more outrageous thing. Should he feel his desire becoming so strong now that it overcomes his will and captivates his thinking even, he ought to get married; for it is better to get married than to burn thus, 1 Cor 7:9. It is a good enough reason to marry when one is burning so fiercely that one's whole being burns and rages thus; then one knows well that God has denied him chastity. For those even who are already chaste do at times experience temptation, but it is not so strong and frightening that they cannot tolerate it and their soul is not so totally captivated [264]. Yet of these there are so few in the multitude of those who feign chastity that it is surprising that they are able to suffer the pain and daily torture of their conscience, since they cannot live chastely for the most part, yet never marry, thus condemning themselves in their own conscience. Therefore they should marry according to the second part of this Article, for if they don't, they sin. For unchastity outside marriage is not permitted in any of the writings of the Old or New Testament. It is distinctly forbidden, while marriage is open to everyone. Christ says in Mt. 19:12, "Whoever is able to maintain chastity, let him do so". Note how Christ recommends chastity to those only who are capable of it. Who these are, we heard earlier, namely those only to whom God granted it. He described marriage quite as clearly with its faith and commandment when he said to the Pharisees [Mt. 19:4-6], "Have you not read that he who created humankind in the beginning, made them man and woman, saying that for this reason (i.e. for the joining together and for co-creation), a man shall leave father and mother and cling to his wife and the two shall be one body. And therefore there shall be from then on not two bodies, but one. And that which God has joined together, let no one tear asunder." From these words follows not only the usual meaning, but also the following, namely, "Since God created man and woman together, let no one command them to be apart. God ordered marriage, therefore it ought not to be forbidden anyone."

That this is the meaning, Paul teaches in 1 Tim. 4:1-3, "The Spirit states clearly that in the last days several shall fall from the faith, follow erring spirits and listen to the teachings of the devils who deceivingly teach false things, yet have consciences which are branded and damned and forbid marriage. Note what fine teacher the doctrine of hypocritical chastity has; he is none other than the devil. If then the devil is the cause of illicit marriage, God, on the other hand, is the giver of legal marriage. [265]

Paul says in 1 Cor. 7:1f, "It is good for a man not to marry. But because of adultery every man should have his own wife and every wife ought to cling to her own husband."

Note how in their opening line these words of Paul are so much like Christ's teaching in Mt. 19:11, "It is good for him who has been given a purified body by God to remain without a wife." But should he ever want to indulge in marital pursuits, he should not fornicate, but take his own wife in marriage. And he specifically says, "everyone" and does not exclude priests or any other persons. Monks and nuns were not yet around in those days. They are included, therefore, along with other people, in the term "everyone", as human laws would clearly imply also.

To wit, soon after, he says again [1 Cor. 7:8], "But I say to those who are single and to widows that it is right and good for them to stay as I am. But if they are not protected from unchastity, they ought to marry; for it is better to be married than to burn with desire."

These words are clear and declare marriage open to everyone simply because they are aflame with desire. If you burn, then take a wife or, you woman, take a husband. If you fail to do so, you sin; for the servant who knows the will of his master, yet does not do it, will be chastised severely, Lk. 12:47. Now it is the will of the Lord that we should take a wife or husband, if we feel too much desire; if we fail to do so, we sin.

For to have marital relations in marriage is not sin (with moderation, of course; for even the eating of bread may be misused so that it becomes sin). The papists will pout over this, for in the matter of marital relations they have imposed strange restrictions, ties and constraints upon poor consciences. But God's word is stronger than their dreams. This is said by St. Paul in 1 Cor. 7:28, "When you take a wife, you do not sin, and when a daughter takes a husband, she has not sinned." The terms "taking a wife" and "taking a husband" do not mean here "to have a wedding", but "to have marital relations" [266] in marriage--for the term "gamein" means about what we mean by having marital relations in marriage. Therefore a virgin, maid or daughter does not sin in the first relationship with her husband; much less thereafter; for marriage is medicine and aid to all those who burn with desire.

To wit, Paul says in Heb. 13:4, "Marriage is an honorable estate among people everywhere." If marriage is honorable, it cannot be a sin. This word no one shall break.

For God again bids his servants and preachers of the word of God through the mouth of Paul to enter matrimony, understanding at all times that they would do so only if they are burning [with desire]. 1 Tim. 3:2 "A guardian, i.e. a bishop, must be without blame, the husband of one wife, etc." And that these words may not be twisted in any other way, he writes immediately following [1 Tim. 3:4], "His children ought to be obedient in all discipline and propriety." At this point I must, in passing, respond to the noise of some objectors who say, if the priests should take wives, who would raise their children? I answer: Who raises them now when they are bastards? Were it not better and more correct, since they cannot leave off producing children, to have their children legitimately, so that these might not be rejected and as a result become whores and indecent persons? Note what a clever lot of Christians we are to disgrace God's creatures by our prattle; those whom God has granted life, we do not allow to live honorably. The priests shall raise their children in obedience, discipline and propriety; however, should they fail to do this, the magistrate [civil authorities] shall deal with them as with all other disobedient elements. And if a foolish priest should object to such, he and his children will be expelled. To have priests endowed in parishes and exempt from the authority of judges, is harmful and arises from the pope's tyranny. I should like to see all priests subject to [267] the authority of the judge in whose area they live; I myself shall abide by this, for God bids me do it, as shall be pointed out shortly. To wit again, God wills that bishops, i.e. guardians or priests should have wives. Titus 1:5f,

"You ought to set up throughout the cities old and honorable men, as I have commissioned you, who are without blame, husband of one wife, etc."

From these quotations it should be apparent enough that all those who live unchastely or who are kindled with unbearable desire so that their minds are not settled within them, sin, if they do not marry; for God bids us marry, if we burn [with desire].

On this Article no more needs to be said here; the matter has been made public enough in our day. Nothing is lacking by which to stop the horrible adultery of the priests, except that the temporal authorities are so lax for the sake of temporal goods or the impotent rage of the disguised, hypocritical bishops that they do not carry out what is divine and honest. And they are not even unchaste men who may have wanted to have wives, but honorable Christians. For they know well what effort it is to be married. So far their conscience reminds them daily to live without giving any disgraceful offence and to accept the hardships of marriage. But those are knaves who cannot free themselves from the works of the flesh, yet do not want to turn to marriage.

This I shall prove to them if they wish.

THE THIRTIETH ARTICLE

Those who take a vow of chastity childishly or foolishly undertake too much. We learn from this that anyone who accepts such vows, does injustice to good people.

The first part of this Article is based on the assumption that it is impossible for anyone to remain chaste except one to whom God gives it, as has been proved in the previous [268] Article. If then chaste living depends on God and not on us, why then do we promise him to keep that which after all we cannot do? Is not this foolishness and child's play? It is as if someone were doing his friend a good turn by living at his expense. As yet our folly pleases us so much and we bank so much on it that we had rather leave the unfailing word of God than our own stubbornness, as Solomon says in Proverbs 12:15, "A fool thinks his way or designs to be right always." And later in Prov. 28:26, "Whoever relies on his own feeling, is a fool." What then is the vow of chastity before God other than trust in one's own power? Thus, those who make it are fools or children. For some have been deceived into making such vows in their childhood by those who murder the soul and are leaders of sects or orders, and when they grow to maturity we can see well how they keep these [vows]; indeed, they become twice as bad as those who led them astray, Mt. 23:15.

From this follows the second part of this Article, namely, that those who dare elicit such vows from people, sin shamefully; for they know that such vows cannot be kept by any living person; and on top of it all, they accept oaths on it. And if they do not know this from scripture, they know it on their own for they recall well what great temptation they had in their youth and how badly their consciences were spoiled. They might well have known from all this that other people fare more or less like them. Yet, they cheat these poor people, just as some disloyal carters might. They do not warn those who follow in their tracks, but they say out of envy, "let him overturn just as I did; if I have to suffer, I shall allow others to be tormented also." There is no denying or pretending that others are not equally tempted, for Christ says, Jn. 3:6, "Whatever is born of the flesh, is carnal." It follows then that they are flesh and that they have carnal tempations as ordinary persons do. And those few who on account of their works are free of excessive lust, have become so by God's grace [269] and not of their own strength. These very same people have always had the grace to thank God unceasingly for this gift; they have also been able to forgive and recognize the infirmities of the neighbor. Only the greatest of hypocrites bark most loudly against the honorable [estate] of marriage and against Christian teaching. And if one is well instructed in God's word, he is encouraged to leave all hypocrisy, but is hindered by the oath and promise which he made to God and which he feels ashamed of breaking too lightly.

Concerning Vows

First of all, everyone knows that we do not speak here of vows which promise loyalty or trust and which we humans are in the habit of making to one another. Everyone is duty-bound to keep these in faith and trust, or else, he is accounted faithless in human eyes. Furthermore, we would transgress the commandment of God. "Do unto others as you would have them do unto you" [Tobit 4:16; Mt. 7:12; Lk. 6:31], and the commandment, "Thou shalt not lie" [Lev. 19:11]. Rather, we speak here of the vows which one makes to God when promising him something.

Votum, i.e. vow, thus understood, is taken in all of the Old Testament as a sacrifice or gift, promised to God, primarily in Leviticus, Numbers and Deuteronomy, as far as I recall. But whatever is written about vows in the Psalms, Prophets or Books of Solomon is either taken to mean a gift or offering, promised to God, or else it is intended to refer to Christ who is the one true offering. Nor is it contradictory that in Numbers 6 the Nazarites were promised to God, for this too was nothing other than an offering when a person committed himself to God in his outward conduct, in what he was to eat or drink, what he was to touch, what not to cut off, etc. Therefore the vows of the Nazarites are numbered among the vows of offerings and gifts which are outward appearance and ceremonial.

Of vows in general I say that Christ has done away with them. For as the offerings which [270] referred to Christ were nullified after the promised Christ, had come, who is the one reconciling sacrifice for all eternity, so here their significance has been done away with. Likewise **vota** or vows are nullified, for they were not more than offerings and ceremonies which God did not order to last, but which were given as punishment and in order that Israel might not turn to idols, Ez. 20; Isa. 1,--as has also been shown above. [1] Therefore everything written in the Old Testament about such vows is not valid in proving the vows which we make when we promise God body and soul. For those vows pertain solely to gifts; these Christ has overcome, having made himself the surety of our salvation for the infirmities of all humankind. If then the vows concerning gifts do not touch us, we have to see wherein the vows and promises of the soul are grounded.

I hold that the three vows of obedience, chastity and poverty are grounded solely in hypocrisy and idolatry. For the outward disguise of vestments and insignia has been shown earlier to be nothing but deceit.

Concerning obedience, first of all. Of this the papists speak as follows, "Is it not a good thing for a person to deny himself and to subordinate himself under the power of someone else?" I answer: The word "obedience is better than a living sacrifice" in 1 Sam. 15:22 is to be understood only with regard to submission under God toward whom a person is to be obedient rather than to invent anything else by which to honor God when he has not done as yet any of that which God commanded. Similarly here, too. It is indeed good to be obedient, first toward God and thereafter toward those whom God commands us to obey. But whenever we deny obedience toward those whom God bids us obey by [substituting] humanly designed obedience, such human obedience is hypocrisy and sheer deception, and quite contrary to the commandment of God. When such a one subjects himself to an abbot or prior, but is not obedient to worldly authority and when he further leaves his father and mother to be obedient to the above, it is merely [271] from hypocrisy into which the sectarian leaders have drawn the simple-minded in obedience to themselves, as if obedience to them were better than obedience to the word of God. Thereafter such obedience, inasmuch as a person values it more highly than obedience to God, is idolatry. For it always means to turn away from God, when one values creatures and their words more highly than the word of God.

We must speak of avowed poverty in similar words. That it is hypocrisy I pointed out earlier. For no one seeks more boldly after riches than do gowns and tonsures. Accordingly it is idolatry, since, first of all, they consider it worship to enrich monasteries; for in such cases, riches have become their God. Secondly, they vowed poverty before God when it is not in their power to do so; for without God they are incapable of anything. All our good works are not good, if they are ours; but inasmuch as they are God's, they are good. How then can a person promise anything to God which is not his, unless it be given him by God?

We spoke of chastity in a similar vein. If God alone grants

chastity, how can anyone promise God to be chaste, if God alone is able to grant it to him?

Thus let everyone know that to promise anything to God of that which he bids us do and which he alone enables us to keep, is silly idolatry. For what God bids us do, we are to keep, because he commanded it. Or else, if we think we can keep it better when we swear or promise it, we put greater confidence in ourselves than in God's commandments; we [trust] more in our word than in the word of God, more in our own strength than in the almighty power of God. All this is no less than sheer idolatry.

God has bid us give our riches to the needy [Lk. 3:11]. At this point you need not promise God that you want to be poor; you are responsible to share your second coat with the poor, and similarly your food, other necessities and goods. For though you should promise this, it is not in your power to keep such a promise. Indeed, [272] if you trust in yourself and in your powers to be able to keep it, you are cursed, for you have made the flesh your power, Jer. 17:5. Who is still not able to see where these confused vows come from? Don't you see that they come from excessive talking, from free will which is contrary to the providence of God, that they arise from merits which are against the grace of God, and from humankind which is an evil tree and incapable of yielding good fruit [Mt. 7:18]? They arise also from ignorance of salvation. For had one put all confidence in the Lord Christ Jesus, one would know that to trust in vestments and vows is unbelief. One would also know that there is no other way to salvation, but Christ; and one would not seek other doors to enter in. Should one also know that all those who seek to block Christ's way are thieves, one would carry the cross after him alone. Otherwise a vow is nothing other than presumption, blasphemy and diminishment of God and exaltation of humankind. And people who make vows are like the son whose father bids him go into the garden to work, but who did not go, Mt. 21:30. Thus they make vain promises which they do not and cannot keep.

At this point the papists say, "Should anyone promise something to a person, he is to keep it; much more so when he promises it to God." I answer: When you promise a person something that is fitting and good for him, you are bound to keep your promise; but whatever is unfitting and harmful to him, do not keep that. You would not give a knife to a child even though you might have promised it. From this you may see that promises are not always kept even among people. But then you must not promise God that you will remain poor. Just listen to what God says and value his word higher than any person's command. I shall not speak of the fact that you promise to keep his word which, apart from his power, you cannot do, and that you promise him what you see is not being kept. Indeed, it cannot possibly be kept by common people who look only upon the things which they promise to abstain from. [273] Take the monks and nuns for an example: they vow poverty, yet no one strives more eagerly for possessions than they. They disregard obedience to God and set up their own, instead. Should an Observantine give one of his gowns to a naked person, he would act against his order, but not against the order of Christ. It thus follows that their obedience is at odds with the obedience of God. Therefore I can easily say to those who often say, "Should one not keep that which one has promised God?" as Isa. 1:12 states, "Who has demanded this from your hands?" Yes, we vowed poverty to God. But I say, who has demanded it of you?

Indeed, were you to promise God what he bids you do, you would err--as has been stated repeatedly. You would be like Peter and the other disciples who promised Christ to go with him through death and imprisonment [Lk. 22:33; Mk. 14:31]. Since it is he who works in us and not we, why then should we want to make any promises on our own? There is not a single child who promises his father to do what the father commands or else the father would say, "you need not make a vow; you ought to do it, because I commanded it or else I should force you to do it." Rather, he has the father's word before him and esteems the same higher than his own vows. In like manner we, too, are children of God and first-born sons. We ought not nor are we able to promise anything on our own account, for we are his in soul and body. What then can we promise him on our own when we belong to him from the outset? Indeed, from the very moment we promise anything to him, we indicate that we are not his. Thus, first of all, if we hold ourselves to be his, we should not make vows to him. Consequently, we are not his before we make our vows. Secondly, after having made our vows, we are not his either. For through deeds--though we might fulfill what we promise--we cannot be saved or become God's. For if our works were capable of saving us, Christ should have died in vain, Gal. 2:21. Thus we discover that [274] the making of such vows happens because of unbelief; therefore they are idolatry. For if one had faith, he would know that he is a son of God through Christ Jesus and would not want to make a vow. But if he does not have it, he would make such vows as if by them he could come to God. Whoever has faith, attains salvation; whoever does not have it, shall be condemned, Jn. 3:36. Thus it follows that since vows arise from unbelief and are rightly against God, they are also sin; for everything which does not grow out of the good tree of faith, is sin, Rom 14:23. Therefore everyone ought to deny and reject such unwise, godless, unbelieving vows, not any the less than if they had just been converted from heathendom to the Christian faith. For they know that it is wantonness, arrogance and duplicity to promise something to God which from the very outset belongs to him, as we may readily understand from Lev.

27:26 when Moses says, "The first-born which belongs to God may not be sanctified or promised to God by anyone, even if it be only cattle or sheep; for they belong to the Lord from the very beginning." Now, all believers are first-born of God, which is prefigured in the Old Testament by many terms, the foremost of which is "Israel". Therefore, no son of God may promise himself, for he is God's from the outset. "For whether we live or whether we die, we are the Lord's" [Rom. 14:8]. Anyone who does not believe that, cannot become God's, even with a thousand vows.

The objection which the papists make does not help any either, when they say that Christ himself said in Lk. 9:62, "No one who puts his hand to the plow and looks back, is fit for the kingdom of God." For this saying is more against them than for them. Christ wants to indicate clearly by this word that no one who has begun to follow God and then allows the cares and temptations of the world to pull him away again, is fit for the word, i.e. the kingdom of God. From this I might say to all who make vows, "when you put your hand to the plow, you tasted how sweet the Lord is, and trustingly depended on his grace and having done that, you did not thereafter seek after anything else which might save you [275] or else you did not trust the grace of God in the first place. But for you to have turned to groups and vows which God does not will and which he has forbidden even, on the prompting of human wisdom, shows that you have not even put your hand to the plow. Indeed, you have gone backward rather than forward; for one who becomes truly aware of the master, will no longer tolerate a servant. Indeed, should you have been believers at one time (which is not likely), you would already have put your hand to the plow. But when you turned again to your works, you looked behind and thus you are unfit for the kingdom of God.

Therefore flee this adulterous generation [cf. Mk. 8:38], all of you who out of unbelief have been led into such error, as speedily as Lot when he fled Sodom [cf. Gen. 14], and do not ever look back to your [former] orders. For to keep the order of faith is the greatest and best order which has ever come to earth. This order really knows all who are in it as children of God and as those who do the works which God commanded, not as hired servants or as day laborers, but as free sons who work in keeping with the will of the Father only, and allow him to reward them as he sees fit. Indeed, they are really heirs of the fatherly inheritance and remain forever in the household of God, not allowing themselves to be admitted to any other household. As Christ says in Jn. 8:35, "A servant does not always remain in the household, but the son remains forever." The sons are the believers; the servants, those who work for wages.

It does not help to object that 1 Tim. 5:11f. speaks of the widows who break the first faith, for "faith" there does not mean "vow" or "promise". Indeed, faith and vows are clearly distinguished. And in the same context Paul's intention is to say that a widow breaks faith, if she lives in adultery with another man, for several young widows were maintained by the goods which Christians donated. These were entitled to enjoy such goods or alms [276] as long as they remained with the church, unmarried. But then several of them were found (since women are weak and fall easily), who led unchaste lives before they were properly married. Of these Paul said that they broke their first vows, since they lived unchastely without having a husband. Yet those who took husbands did not break faith; for it is fitting for every woman to take a husband. Furthermore, they came to the church without any command or vow. Yet, since they lived unchastely without a husband, they broke faith, for they wanted to be considered honorable widows in the eyes of people and tried to cover up their dishonorable doings by pretense of being pure. And only when their disgrace was uncovered, did they afterwards think of finding a husband.

Look at the actual text and you will find no other meaning in it. "Vovete et reddite" and "vota mea domino reddam" and such like confirm this reading above all. [2] For in all of the Old Testament "vota" were either known as vows of gifts and offerings--which, however, have been made ineffective through Christ and have been laid aside--or else, as an offering of one's heart, made not with an oath, but in faith. Faith relies solely on the grace of God; an oath or promise relies on its own strength and is idolatry. I speak here only of the oath which is made in the vows of a priest. I add this so that faith and the making of vows in an oath be not considered one and the same thing, etc.

NOTE

1. Cf. The opening section of Article 22 above.

2. Cf. Psalm 75:12 and 115:14, 18 in the Vulgate (Nova Editio).

THE THIRTY-FIRST ARTICLE

CONCERNING THE BAN

No private person may impose the ban on anyone, except the church, i.e. the community of those among whom the person to be excommunicated lives, together with its guardian, i.e. the minister. [277]

Concerning this Article let us first hear testimony and then express an opinion.

Christ whom the Father attested to be truthful says in Mt. 18:15-18, "But when your brother sins against you, go to him and reprimand him in private. If he obeys or hears you, you have won your brother. But if he does not hear you, then take one or two brothers with you so that by the mouth of two or three witnesses every single word may be determined. But if he still does not hear, then report it to the church. Should he not hear the church either, then treat him as a heathen and tax gatherer. Truly I say to you, everything you bind on earth shall be bound in heaven and everything you free on earth, shall be freed in heaven."

In these words of Christ is found the entire power of the ban, and no one must understand them other than as they are stated, for God does not want anything added to or taken away from his word, Deut. 4:2 and 12:32. Even the human teachers of the law have a rule according to which the law must be understood in light of the intentions of the law maker. Therefore shall look at the sense and meaning of Christ [to determine] what sins he puts under excommunication.

Immediately preceding these words, he spoke of an offence [Mt. 18:7-9] and that no member (i.e. no brother)--be it our eye, hand, or foot--ought to be so precious to us that we would allow it to remain next to us to offend us. Rather, should it not stop

226

offending us, we are to cut it off just like a foul, rotten member which is cut off so as not to infect and spoil the entire body.

Thus Christ says, firstly, "If your brother sins against you." "Against you" means "against you, O church or community." For this is the manner in which God speaks, viz. he addresses the multitudes in the singular, Deut. 32:7 and Ps. 80 [81:9f] and in many other instances, "Israel, if you hear me, no new god shall arise in you." "In you" means as much as, "among you, O children of Israel." Similarly, "against you" here means "against the church".

He says secondly, "Whoever sins." From this we deduce that the ban is only to be imposed upon one who sins. Now you heard shortly before which sin is to be understood here, namely the [278] one which offends and infects like an hereditary disease. But of other sins, which do not offend openly, Christ spoke to Peter and through him to all of us, "You ought to forgive your brother seventy times seven" [Mt. 18:22]; indeed, we ought to forgive one who oppresses and one who is banned, should he repent and change his ways.

From this it follows that a ban which is imposed because of financial debts, is not a ban at all; since to be indebted is no sin when it comes out of poverty and when the poverty is not caused by foolishness and when the poor person repays gladly as soon as he is able to do so. But even when this is not the case at all, there are bailiffs and exactors [weybel and gyselesser] rather than bishops, who collect debts, so that the latter will not have to collect every usurer's debt. There are among Christians everywhere good courts and good laws so that one need not resort to strange judges. But any ban which they impose for monetary debts, is sheer deceit; indeed, every ban imposed apart from the community, is [deceit], as we shall show later. For the law giver does not deceive; he has ordered the ban for those sins only which give public offence. Thus the ban does not have any force, for it must be used exclusively according to the word and intention of the law giver. Therefore every creditor ought to fear the ban (provided it is imposed on him without cause), about as much as when an angry woman wishes the falling evil [epilepsy] on him or swears in Satan's name; a cat's prayer does not reach the altar. [1] Thus only those are bound by God who are bound according to his word. Otherwise they are no more bound than he is considered a murderer who kills a calf, even though he actually kills, since the law concerning murder applies to human beings only. In the same way does the law concerning the ban apply only to one who sins and offends publicly.

Thirdly, it is part of the ban that a person whom one intends to ban, must first of all be warned privately by one person. Thus if one is a known adulterer who offends, the guardian, i.e.

[279] the bishop or pastor, should, gently and in secret, admonish him to desist. Note here the fine practice of the blaspheming bishops. They have the poor fellow brought before the entire congregation for five shillings, indeed, for the tithe of a chicken [Zehenthun], since such a person when able, would often give ten times as much just to avoid a public reprimand. Have you ever in all your life heard or read of such a hard, ungracious fatherly deed? Yet these spiritual fathers do it to a poor fellow for a Shrove Tuesday chicken. [2] Indeed, they are so generous in their desire to abuse, that they will now do it with the very first warning.

Fourthly, should one be unable to move the offender by secretive and private gentleness, one ought to take along some witnesses so that he can be convicted of having been previously warned. For testimony should not be firmly believed, unless there be two or three who verify [what is said], Deut. 17:6. This, too, the worshipful fathers do not need, for they are step-fathers only; they reject the children and take their property. Though they had all the wool, milk, skin and meat, I still think that they would not tolerate the little dogs who chew on the bones. For we have many teachers, but few fathers, 1 Cor. 4:15. Many promise to be fathers, but few can show it by their works. I shall be silent here about their clerks who often suppress letters of admonition to the disobedient or else do not tend to them carefully, yet ban the poor people, nonetheless, which is contrary to their own anti-Christian law. And if some one reports this, the sanctimonious father retorts, "We really do not intend to make matters bad." Then the poor offender goes off, thinking that his gracious lord has absolved him, because he had already suffered some injustice. But after a month, the clerk comes along with a procurator, a lawyer, and all the furies of hell and creates [280] such great expenses for him, that he cannot extricate himself without being totally ruined. I have to be brief here and must see whether the "furie infernales" [the furies of hell] are likely to rave further; then only will I bring up some "juicy bits". I paid careful attention to their "honest" methods of argument and marked them well, so that at the right moment I might use them. But I had much rather that they improve, and I pray to God to illumine them so that they know themselves. Amen.

Finally, one should report the offender to the church, i.e. the community [gmeind]. He is not yet banned until the church decides to excommunicate him. Here you will see some fine things coming out of the popish art chamber [3] and tyranny. You ought to report it to the church, he says, and then the church is to reprimand him once again and only when he fails to obey the entire community, shall he be cut off. Thus the hunting dogs of the princely beggars go around and clamor before the church, "My lord official, our gracious lord of Schindberg is banning Niclas Pfrieman [4] because he has not paid the clerk in the basket. [5]

How is that? Is the bishop alone entitled to ban anyone? I thought the church was to do it. Is my gracious lord in himself the church? Christ says [Mt. 18:17], "Tell it to the church". Is a bishop, an abbot or a provost the church? Thus everyone knows well that the ban is not the prerogative of a single individual, be he pope, bishop or barber. [6] For Christ never said that a person who did not hear the first or second admonition should then [281] be shunned, i.e. that he should be banned (nor can a single individual impose the ban). Rather, he should be shunned only after he has failed to obey the church's admonition. Thus it is definitely stated that no one may impose the ban except the church, i.e. the communion in which the offender participates; it is his judge and guardian.

But which is the church to which one is to report, is disputed by the papists. They say that the bishops (now I do not mean the watchful bishops, but those who bless unleavened cakes and deface church walls), are the church; on this I shall speak only very briefly at this point (since I spoke at great length on the matter in the Eighth Article). Divine scriptures use the name church, i.e. communion, either with reference to all believers in Christ who, however, no longer gather together visibly in this our time, but are known to God. Also all those are meant whose comfort and father and confidence is God. This is the Christian Church in which we believe.

Then again the term "church" is used for every special communion which we call "parish" (that "ecclesia" is also used for every gathering, shall not concern us here). Thus we do not include here the church of the gathered popes or bishops (or blessers of unleavened cakes). Indeed, in all of Holy Scripture they will not find ecclesia used with reference to these, though they might be driven to distraction by this. Therefore these are absolutely not the church.

Now follows: To which church should one report the offender to have him banned? Answer: Christ certainly does not bid us run to the universal church with the one who is to be banned. For it is nowhere physically gathered; for who is capable of bringing together all believing people? Thus it follows that he bids us bring the offender to that church or communion which we call parish. For Christ intended with this commandment to prevent any bad sheep from spoiling all the others [282]; for nothing is more fragile than human customs. Once they start being spoiled, they spread more and more in their corruption. To prevent this from happening, no one can do better than the guardian together with the community. These are best able to judge the offender's evil deed as well as his heart and to see how he improves. Not that it ought to happen through the guardian only; everyone ought to be able to do this, should the guardian become negligent.

And note what a good and wholesome thing the ban would be, were it rightly used. For one could ban and remove from the congregation shameless adultery, open blasphemy, the deception of virgins, gluttony, evil talk, idleness, warring, procured marriages [kuplen], libel, lies and such vices that cause Christians a great deal of unrest. But these cake-blessing bishops have taken away the ban from churches and their ministers. Yet they do not ban anyone except those who speak or act against them or who do not do justice to their judgment or fail to pay their clerks. Pardon me, dear bishops in Germany and Switzerland. [7] You have seen in recent years the deadly war which these two peoples waged against each other--Christians against Christians. [8] And you know well that the same came about partly because of extensive lies and false, evil reporting. For the un-Christian crime [283] which the Swabians hurl at the Confederacy (only the gluttonous and undisciplined knaves, of course, for the upright ones, I am sure, are displeased by this), is punished more severely among Confederates than anywhere else. [9] Secondly, there can readily be found among the Confederates some who from pride or ill will tease the Swabians at carnivals or in similar places. This leads to the grave danger of wars and other disorders. Then again, the taunts of the Swabians in response cannot bring forth much good either. Should not their bishops long ago have undertaken to fight with God's word against this un-Christian talk? And anyone who might have refused to be reprimanded, should have been banned; thus the community or parish should have excommunicated and banned such knaves and a great deal of evil would have been prevented.

Now you are otherwise quick enough to send out the "exceptional cases" [10] and to collect money for Our Lady's Church, and for consolations, to hold collections, impose charity taxes [284], gather procession money, sell indulgences and the like. But by rights you should have sent out to all ministers some sound Christian instruction on how they might by the word of God have put down such foolish attacks of anger, hate and sickness of these two nations so that on both sides there might have sprung up peace, friendship and the fear of God. Don't be angry. I fear, it did not even enter your minds. How is it, however, that you did not in a single year forget to collect outstanding debts, yet never thought of such Christian admonitions in any given year? The same applies to other bishops, the world over. Know then, that I indicated this gladly, not that I expect you to take offence, but rather, because I do not doubt that the guardians and ministers will undertake to go some such path.

I shall now return once again to the topic of the ban. That the ban is the prerogative of each parish which is to ban the offender and not of a specific person, is taught in the words and by the deeds of Paul in 1 Cor. 5:1-6. When a fellow had trouble with his stepmother, he says, "It is not good that one hears of such indecencies among you which remain unnamed among the heathen even, namely that one has an affair with the wife of his father. But you flared up when, instead, you should have be-moaned the fact that the one who committed such deed is accepted among you. Yet it seemed good to me--though I am absent in body, I am nonetheless present in spirit--that the one who has done such a thing should be handed over to the devil (after you and I have come together in spirit in the name of our Lord Jesus Christ), by the power of our Lord Jesus Christ unto the damnation of the flesh, so that his spirit might be saved on the day of our Lord Jesus. Your reputation is not good. Do you not know that a little yeast affects the entire dough? Therefore remove the old yeast, so that you may be a new dough and you will then be the sweet, unleavened bread, etc." And after that, in the same chapter [1 Cor. 5:9-11], "I have written you not to get mixed up with one who may be called a brother [285] (i.e. a Christian), but who in reality is an adulterer, unclean and avaricious, an idolater, a blasphemer, a drunkard, or a thief who steals. Indeed, with such a one you must not have table fellowship."

From Paul's words it is possible to determine the many facets of the ban. First of all, the sin of the man who "deflowered" his stepmother [11] was apparent, for he says, "One hears every-where of some uncleanness among you."

Secondly, it is not enough to know such to be wrong; rather, one ought to hate and remove the vice.

Thirdly, [we note] that Paul not only bans him through his writing, but that he reports him to the church in Corinth; hence he was banned by that church only.

Fourthly, that Paul and the parish of Corinth did not do this on their own strength, but in the power of Jesus Christ which is undoubtedly the one of which he speaks in Mt. 18:18, "What we bind on earth, shall also be bound in heaven". By these words and the present deed, we can actually see that the act of binding and loosing by the parish is not the prerogative of a single person, whoever he might be.

Fifthly, that such giving over to the devil excommunicates the body only, is to be understood from, "if he confesses his evil deed and repents, there will be no harm to the soul, but rather, it shall be saved thereby".

Sixthly, that the evil deed offend as much as does sour dough which penetrates ever more deeply until it permeates the entire dough.

Seventh, that the evils of adultery, avarice, idolatry, and such like, should be banned.

Nor can anyone lift the ban except it be the church, together with the guardian, as Paul shows in 2 Cor. 2:5-8. Such an unpleasant task has been assigned to them so that the evil may not be charged against all or them or contaminate them all. The punishment has hit the sinner hard enough now; therefore [286] they ought to console him; for he pleads with them to show him love and mercy once more. From which words of Paul (I have shown them in bare outline only), we actually hear that this sinner whom he ordered to be banned, had such remorse concerning his evil that Paul was satisfied by it and then admonished the church to pardon him once again. Thus, to speak of the matter in brief, everyone perceives clearly that the ban is not the prerogative of ruling popes or bishops, but only of the church, i.e. the church together with the minister, and the final judgment is the church's, i.e. the community's and no one else's. The same applies also to the freeing from the ban.

You say: I actually perceive that the ban is used as a scourge, and when it is used other than in the manner which God has directed, I can readily see that it has no power. But how am I to act, should it be imposed on me because of a debt or for other reasons which do not conform to the practice of a Christian ban? Answer: No one is without a higher authority. To such an authority you should go and submit yourself, and, according to the authority vested in him, you should make satisfaction or else settle the disagreement, as it is the custom in country or city. Make this known to your adversary and thereafter disregard the ban (as long as no unrest arises from this), as if it were the command of a chronically ill man or the curse of an angry woman; for it really amounts to no more than feeble threats which do not harm the soul of anyone. For to bind and to loose, is the sole prerogative of the church which neither male nor female pope may break. Neither can anyone be banned, nor is he susceptible to the ban before God, except in the manner to be shown subsequently.

NOTES

1. Cf. **Idiotikon** IV 1826. "Katzengbett gat nit zum altar." The meowing of cats does not befit the altar.

2. A chicken donated to the lord of the manor, often to the priest also, on Shrove Tuesday, the beginning of the Lenten fast. Cf. **Idiotikon** II 1375.

3. Artchambers were innovations of the Renaissance. They contained artifacts and curios. Zurich's Stadtbibliothek had one such until the 18th century. Cf. **Idiotikon** III, 251f.

4. Schindberg alludes to one who oppresses heavily. A Pfriemer is a maker of leather straps, belts, etc. The names are used as sample names. Cf. **Idiotikon** V 1283f.

5. The scribe is pulled up in a basket to an illicit love affair; hence he should really be the one to be banned.

6. The saying, "Bischof oder Bader" means "Everything or Nothing". The two offices represent the extremes in the social scale as e.g. Log Cabin and White House. Cf. **Idiotikon** IV 1015.

7. "Schwabenland" is "Swabia," a territory adjacent to the Canton of Zurich. The term is often used with reference to all of German territories.

8. The so-called Schwabenkrieg of 1489 was motivated by deep-seated jealousy and long standing rivalries rather than by primarily political interests. A mild form of tension and antipathy still characterized the relationships of inhabitants in the two areas.

9. They were accused of sodomy. Among the more notorious reports were claims that every "genuine Swiss had to spend one night with a cow", etc. Cf. **Idiotikon** II 1111, 1106. See also Z II 282, n. 19.

10. "Casus reservati" are serious offences which can be dealt with by a high official of the church only.

11. I.e. one who slept with his stepmother.

THE THIRTY-SECOND ARTICLE

Only the person who causes public offence may be banned.

This Article has earlier been well enough sustained already by the words of Christ in Mt. 18 and by those of Paul in 1 Cor. 5. Therefore I admonish all ministers for [287] God's sake to consider the salvation of their soul by not abusing the useful sword of the ban among their little flock, not to have them banned for their guilt, though I know that they are not bound or banned with God if they are not banned here according to the manner, Christ commanded; still, their poor consciences are badly hurt, for they have been led astray by false teaching to think that such a ban means something important. Moreover, they are humiliated in public, which is a grave sin, Mt. 18:6 (thus Chrysostom understands the term "scandalizein" in this passage). For what sadder thing may happen in a person's heart than when in his own mind he considers himself condemned to hell? Or what is more humiliating to a person than to be humbled in the presence of the total gathered community? Do you not see, my fellow brothers, that those who misuse the ban, handle the matter much less graciously and more roughly than worldly lords? These do not punish anyone in public unless he has committed a grave misdeed. And if there is guilt involved, they incarcerate the offender without hurting his conscience (which is a most grievous offence), and without humiliating him before the entire congregation. But those others ban a poor person because he is poor. They have further invented cruel ceremonies so that they may commit the poor person to the devil, and they use such farce before the entire congregation; this should bring about laughter rather than fear. Yet it all creates such anguish and despair that I suspect many a soul to have been ruined thereby.

On the other hand, I admonish you once again to consider well the usefulness of the ban. For what, other than the ban, is better able to eradicate [288] sin and lead to improvement? Mark well. If you have a public adulterer among your congregation who offends the entire congregation, how better could you handle him than first to admonish him kindly? Should he not forsake his vice, take one or two with you to admonish him more earnestly still. Should he still not forsake his habits, have him brought before the church, i.e. the congregation. The same then will excommunicate him and re-admit him when and how it is guided by God. Do likewise in case of all open vices which are such that one cannot honestly close one's eyes to them. For we too are sinners and must be able to forgive one another, but in indecent matters which offend us vilely, one will have to use the iron rod of Christ--for it is wholesome--lest the entire body rot and be spoiled. What finer custom among Christian people could be fostered than the ban, when it is used in the manner described above?

And what I have shown with regard to the vice of adultery, is to be applied to all other vices of which I have largely spoken earlier, but from Paul's view.

At this point I can well imagine that you, dear brothers and co-workers in the vineyard of God, will want to say, "But who protects me?" I will readily concede that the ban is misused, but when I start to use it rightly, the bishop does not permit it. Answer: Almighty God who brings to nought the counsel of the ungodly, will guard you. And should he not protect you from violence, he will, nonetheless, give you skill and virtue to endure the persecution of the body with bold perseverance; it will have to be thus. Christian faith is first of all firmly established in the blood of Christ and secondly, has grown mightily through the suffering and bloodshed of those who preached. Thus, I believe that it will have to be cleansed once again through a great deal of bloodshed. Now go to it boldly and fear not those who may kill your bodies; they will not be able to harm the soul. Once you have learned to put all your trust in God, you can then show your faith first of all by having patience unto death. Then everyone will see that you despise the temporal for the sake of the eternal when you suffer death so bravely, because you [289] will soon come to the eternal, by which I don't mean to say that anyone should throw himself willfully or too early into death. For had the apostles [botten] been killed at the beginning of their preaching, how then could Christian faith have grown up? Rather, you should in all earnestness teach the truth faithfully. You preach only before those who wish to be called Christians. Thus they will also listen to the word of Christ, and God shall cause his word to grow and increase. And should you be able to make concessions to the simple-minded or ignorant, without detracting from the truth, do so and doubt not God shall direct your ways well. Do attend to his word in teaching and in deed, and thereafter let him govern. He shall ordain things well [cf. Ps. 37:5]. I say from my poor conscience that I have often been concerned that the teaching of Christ might be rejected in several places. But soon, God showed his favor and when I was not aware of any help, there the hand of God showed itself. Often he put forth his teaching through a poor woman or through unlearned, simple men. Therefore be unafraid. Do you not want to fight as valiantly as the early Christians? You say, "of course, we will take it into our hands as the early fathers". I well believe it. Do you not think God to be as strong as ever, to overcome all your enemies through your faith?

God-fearing rulers also and, ahead of them, country and cities which govern their own affairs, shall protect you with all their might, as soon as they have come to know the right ban. And as long as you teach the ban rightly and bring to light all other misdemeanors of the false priests, the pope's pomp and wantonness will have been brought down; for he shot solely with blind shells. [1] Not that anyone should take comfort in worldly power. Rather, one should rejoice that, although the truth was not allowed to break forth and could not be opposed by scripture, though they undertook to fight it with the linen harness [290] of the ban, we now can see that such shots and weapons do no harm. On the contrary, they are useful and bring honor, joy and salvation. For Christ says in Lk. 6:22, "You shall be saved when people hate you and exclude you and revile you and reject your name for the sake of the Son of Man; rejoice. . . etc". Thus everyone should rejoice, especially the mighty, when they are asked to protect the proclaimers of the word of God from the wolves who cannot suffer their song. For as soon as one stops fearing the teeth of their ban (and one should not fear any ban except the one which has been imposed by the parish because of sin), they will all soon lose their power. Therefore, let them show their teeth and roar as much as they want. You should fear them about as much as if Master Ironhead threatened you in heaven with a wooden spoon. [2]

And so that the false brothers (who are the most harmful), may not have power to teach what is wrong under your protection, you should demand of them, as Peter teaches, to give account before the church to all persons of what they have taught [cf. 1 Pet. 3:15; 4:5]. But if you let them get to the courts of the bishops, they will force the fearful and despairing to recant. Of this latter, I have seen several which were so un-Christian that I pitied the bishops for expecting such soulless recantation of a Christian person. Even a Turk could not have demanded a greater denial of God by a Christian than they did. Therefore when the bishops demand that you send your teachers to them for [291] cross examination, do not do it. But keep those who have been cited to appear before them, until the arrival of the bishops and let them be convicted through scripture in the presence of the entire parish. Thus the bishops cannot complain, and the rogues who appear in the name of the teaching of Christ can do no harm either, and the church will not be misled; for everyone will be able to see immediately who handles the word of God rightly and who does not.

And should the bishops ban you, praise God. For it is a sure sign that they cannot undertake anything with scripture. You will see then how they rot, just like pumpkins who have no fruit; [3] for all their strength is human prattle. And if one gives them as much credence as one would a gypsy soothsayer, they will soon be done in. I know well that for this kind of advice, no one who is truthful can accuse me of teaching disobedience (as the papist do); for I teach true Christian obedience which puts a stop to all vices. The word of God itself teaches how one might avoid the damaging wolves which look upon the money bag only and thus not only cheat the souls, but murder them. Would to God that the braggarts came out to fight with scripture, should my opinion displease them; I should then show up their idolatry even more. No one as yet has written quite as harshly in revealing their vices as was necessary; all these vices could be easily removed were the ban properly used. For their own ban with which they guarded their evil, would then be invalid. And to this day, anyone who is ill-informed enough as to still fear them, fears them because of the ban. If then it is cancelled out, the teaching of Christ will prosper all the more. Amen. [292]

NOTES

1. Literally, "er hat allein uss der glesinen buechs geschossen"; i.e. he used a worthless weapon.

2. "Isengrind" is a mysterious apparition who according to popular belief robbed infants of certain rights. Cf. **Idiotikon** II 764.

3. Zwingli uses the "soft" pumpkin, easily given to rot, as a symbol of the perishable. Cf. **Z.I** 173.6f or Article 18 above where he speaks of a pumpkin-like block.

THE THIRTY-THIRD ARTICLE

Ill-gotten possessions which cannot be restored to their rightful owner, are not to be given to temples, cloisters, monks, priests and nuns, but to the poor.

This Article I should like to prove over against the claim of the papists, had they hearts in harmony with their own teaching. For I well remember having read in the writings of their own systematic theologians (which it is futile to draw out now), that unjust possessions should, above all, be returned to the one from whom they were taken in the first place. [1] Should he no longer be around, then they are to belong to the poor. In case they cannot be given to them either, for one reason or another, they then are to belong to the temple. But they lost heart and now deny everything. They do not even keep to their own teaching, and do not allow themselves to be governed by the word of God. Thus if follows that they are god and those who believe in them are simply called papists, just as those who believe in Christ are called Christians. At this point we must look at the last part first, which states, that unjust possessions are to be returned, above all, to the one from whom they have been taken away.

God teaches this through Moses in Exodus 22:1, "Whoever has stolen an ox or a sheep and butchered and sold it [293], has to make amends by giving five oxen for the one and four sheep for the one". What is said of theft is to be understood of all wanton seizure or robbery. For he says again in Isa. 61:8, "I am the Lord who loves righteousness and hates robbery, even though it be offered up to me". We note from this passage that he is not about to be pleased by anything which has been taken or robbed, though it be offered up in his name. And just in passing, where now are the great robbers (I mean the tyrants), who rob their poor subjects of honor and right (apply this only to newly invented commandments. We know well what is meant by the right of rulers), and in the end endow a cloister or prebend? Do you think that they shall get to heaven? I have no doubt that the one who robs and the one who receives such goods are alike. [2] God then be merciful to them. For the robber should not have taken it away from those others and the receiver should not have accepted it, but should have said, "It does not belong to me. Return it to him from whom you took it." Take good care, God-fearing person, to accept things is full of evil consequences. Do not let the foolish pomp of this world entice you; it shall burn fiercely in the hereafter.

Christ, too, is of the opinion in Mt. 5:23f, "When you take your gift to the altar (Christ says this with reference to the time when sacrifice was still in use), and if you then recall that your brother has something against you, leave your gift before the altar and first go to him and make peace with him, and make your offering when you come back only." This reconciliation refers not only to the peace which follows hatred and enmity, but to all forms of reconciliation. [294] Now an injured person is never satisfied, unless his own goods be restored to him. Likewise, when Christ bids us to be reconciled, he bids us to restore that which has been taken away.

To wit, even the law of nature teaches restoration. For if you want to have restored what has been taken away from you, you will have to do it [to others] also.

To wit, Christ says in clear words that the clerics or Pharisees who render fathers and mothers helpless before their children by their prattle, transgress the law of God. They teach that when a son gives them something which their father or mother may ask for or need afterwards, he should say to them, "Father, I have put this into the treasury of the church, for your sake". But they actually dishonor father and mother by this [cf. Mt. 15:4-6; Mk. 7:10-12]. In this context "to honor" means not only "to give respect", but also "to help". If then Christ despised begging in the Old Testament and if he prefers that his commandments by kept, rather than that the temple be decorated, it follows also that he does not want you to take the goods of your neighbor. But should you have taken them, you must subsequently restore them also. What are all those so-called priests going to say here? Foremost among them are those who creep about in their habits, who do not go among thorns and thistles, but who much rather attach themselves to fig trees and vine branches and who grab for themselves through enticing words the inheritance of poor children. They put gowns on a dying person, but he has to pay out twenty guilders; they lead him to his cool grave with sweet incantations that one might think the [295] wasps are attacking in force. Indeed, what will they say when they hear that Christ has severely admonished the priests and pharisees because of their begging? And they take over what belongs to the poor, just as those who took unto themselves what belonged to father and mother. You hypocrites and distorters of the divine will and word.

But whether or not all unjust possessions should be returned to the one from whom they were taken, is dealt with later.

Now follows the other part of this Article: That unjust possessions, when they cannot be returned to the rightful owner, should be given to the poor.

This we support with a word of Christ in Lk. 16:9, "Make friends with the unrighteous mammon so that when you become destitute you may be received into the eternal home." These friends which we are to make, thanks to the unjust mammon, are the poor. Concerning them, Christ promises us that what we do unto them in his name, he shall reward, as if we had done it unto him, Mt. 25:40. They shall receive us into the eternal tents or homes for shelter. By unjust mammon all riches are to be understood here. However, Christ calls them "unjust" because they are seldom accumulated in the right spirit. If we understand all riches in this context, the sense does not suffer at all; rather, it is confirmed even; for actually we ought to share all our riches with the poor, but more so the riches which we know to have received unjustly. And that this is actually the meaning of Christ's word, namely, that he bids us give away our riches, the following words will show [Lk. 10:10-12], "One who is unfaithful in the smallest things, is unfaithful in great things also. If then you have not been upright in dealing with the unjust mammon [296] who will entrust you with true riches? Further, if you have not been faithful with someone else's goods, who will entrust you with what is yours? Here "the smallest which God gives" means "riches", for soon after, he himself uses it with that meaning, as follows, "If you are unfaithful in the unjust mammon, etc." meaning "if God gives you riches and you misuse them, who will then dare give you the truth, i.e. the great gifts of his word, his teaching and his wisdom? For if you draw the riches unto yourself unfairly, you will likely also falsify the goodness of truth, etc." Thus finally, "that which is yours" means nothing other than, "what really belongs to humankind", i.e. to know God rightly and to have him alone as one's treasure.

To wit, Christ says, however, in Lk. 11:39-41, "You Pharisees clean the outside of your cups and plates, but within you are full of robbery and evil. You fools. Did not he who made the outside, make the inside also? But give alms, motivated from within, and all things shall be pure." In this saying, Christ uses the first part figuratively, namely, that the Pharisees, like one who cleans his cup or bowl on the outside only and leaves the dirt inside, present themselves as good before people, yet inside they are full of robbery and evil. They actually give alms, but only for the sake of appearances; inwardly their heart longs for the stolen goods. Now they are to tear this out of their stingy hearts, and whatever they have horded they are to give to the poor in order that all things may become pure in them. It is clear enough that one shall be freed from stolen goods to the extent to which one gives them to the poor.

Lastly it follows: That whenever ill-gotten possessions cannot be restored to the rightful owner, they belong to the poor. They surely do not belong to temples, monks, nuns and priests.

One must note here that ill-gotten possessions are to be distinguished in many ways, of which to speak now, it would take too long. However, the word of God does not speak clearly of each case and there are some cases in which it would not be good to return the unjust mammon to the one from whom it has come. For instance, a captain has received from a stranger, who is not obligated to him, a great deal of property. No one forced the man, nor was it taken in an unguarded moment. Rather, he gave it willingly in return for the captain's services. For this reason the captain is not obligated to return anything. But neither is it rightfully acquired property, therefore he should give it to the poor. But there are some cases when the unjust mammon should not be returned simply because it has been accumulated by such countless numbers of people, as happens unfortunately in our day and age when those holding monopolies bewitch all of christendom and collect untold riches. This is not at all honorable, for through their financing they force great shortages; therefore they are duty-bound to return such goods. But how are they to do it? They cannot possibly reach everyone. Therefore it is needful that they return it or give it to the poor.

But whatever is clearly illegitimate robbery should be given back to the owner. This opinion of mine I cannot support by clear arguments, as I said earlier, but I interpreted it on the basis of the words [298] of Moses and Christ and also on the basis of the law of nature--not corrupt nature, but that nature which God teaches through his word in the hearts of believing people. On the basis of these three gauges everyone may carefully examine himself; should someone find clearer testimony still, I am willing to be taught. Otherwise this Article is definite in the claim that such do not belong to monasteries, temples, etc. There is no use objecting on the basis of what is written in Numbers 5:8, for the priesthood has been eliminated and transformed, Heb. 7, as I showed quite clearly above. [3] We also actually hear that Christ bids the unjust mammon to be given to the poor. Further, we showed in the twenty-fourth Article [4] above how disgraceful toward God it is when one tends to make the unjust mammon good by giving a part of it to God, as if thereby to silence him and make him a partner in the robbery.

NOTES

1. By the term "Summisten" are meant the later scholastics who unlike the "Sententiarier" attempted to provide complete theological systems. Alexander of Hales, though not the first systematician, was frequently taken as a model. St. Thomas Aquinas became one of the most prominent writers of a summa theologica.

2. "Simul colligentur aliquando et raptores et qui rapinam ab eis sub specie pietatis accipiunt".

3. Cf. Article 19 above.

4. Should read, the twenty-third Article.

THE THIRTY-FOURTH ARTICLE

CONCERNING [TEMPORAL] AUTHORITY

So-called spiritual authority cannot justify its pomp on the basis of the teaching of Christ.

I here call spiritual authority the loftiness of superiors in spiritual matters and worldly rule, as if I were to say, "The authority of clerics has no ground for boasting in the teaching of Christ". First of all, they are not to be proud or domineering in their office, though they may otherwise carry it out well and properly. This I am able to support with Christ's own words who always, when [299] the disciples spoke of pre-eminence, spoke to them of humility of the spirit in which they were to seek eminence, Mt. 18:1-3, "In that hour the disciples of Jesus went to him, saying, 'Who now is the greatest or the most prominent in the kingdom of heaven (i.e. in the church in which the heavenly Father is lord and comfort)?' And Jesus called a child unto himself, placed him in their midst and said, 'Truly I say to you, unless you change and become like children, you shall not enter the kingdom of heaven'." These words show very clearly that the disciples at that time were carnal, therefore he says, "Unless you are converted". Nothing could have been clearer or shorter than that. For his desire that they should be converted actually shows that they had often been tempted up to then. This he is unwilling to tolerate. Rather, he desires that they change their high opinion of themselves and seek as little after prominence as children who know nothing about it. Thus he says a little later [Mt. 18:4], "Whoever humbles himself like a little child, is great or the foremost in the kingdom of heaven". Nowhere in the words of Jesus do we find that Christ has given any kind of power over others to Peter or anyone else, either in the office of preaching or in the work of God. On the other hand, we do find in clear words that pre-eminence in all things is open to everyone among Christians in that the one who is the most humble, the most submissive, the kindest and the most child-like in heart and conduct, is also the most prominent. Thus it follows that whoever fights to be the foremost [300], is not at all God's own; for this prominence of humility is not known to any person, but alone to God.

This he teaches in another place when he praises John the Baptist in Mt. 11:11, "Truly, I say to you, there is no one greater among the sons of women than John the Baptist. But whoever is the least in the kingdom of heaven, is greater than he." Christ intends to show here the prominence of John by the greatness of his humility. But he did not in this saying circumscribe the extent of humility, as if no one could be more humble than John was. Rather, could someone be more insignificant or humble even than John was, he would be greater. I am not taken off the track in this because there is no one before me who shares this interpretation. You know well what is meant by kingdom of heaven in many places in the New Testament, viz. nothing other than "believing people". Thus Christ would have wanted to indicate here that God does not measure prominence by pomp or great glory or name, but by humility; in that, no one as yet born, has surpassed John. But whoever should seek to surpass him would have to do it through humility. That some of the earlier interpreters have interpreted this passage to refer to Christ or the angels seems to me to be out of place here.

In short, the prominence after which popes and bishops strive has no foundation other than in what Christ says to them through the words, addressed to the disciples, "Unless they turn away from carnal desire to gain prominence, they cannot enter the kingdom of heaven". And since almost all of them have striven for this [prominence], none of them have entered the kingdom of heaven, as a result. [301]

Peter whom the popes have made their head when they called him the prince of the apostles (which they surely do not find anywhere in scripture), says in 1 Pet. 5:1-3, "The elders or priests among you, I, a fellow priest, admonish, etc. to feed the flock of Christ's sheep which has been entrusted to you. Do not guard them because you are forced, but willingly, not for unworthy gain, but with a humble heart. Neither rule harshly over those who are entrusted to you, but rather, be an example to the flock".

These words of Peter forbid that any priest or so-called cleric should rule. Once we understand some of the terms, these words are quite clear. "Priest" means an elder, well-disciplined or earnest person. Priests are to be like that. Here Peter calls himself a fellow priest and not a ruler or pope. Then he bids them tend the sheep. After that he bids them supervise them, i.e. to be bishop, for to be bishop is nothing other than to be guardian. Then he says that they should not act from compulsion, but administer their office gladly. They should force no one under their control. Rather, they should be paternal so that everyone might obey them willingly and gladly. After that they should not look to any gain, but act with a humble heart, i.e. they should preach the teaching of God out of love toward God and people. And later, that they should not rule as harsh lords over the portion which has been entrusted to them, i.e. the church and congregation of God. Rather, they should know that they are to be an example which those who have been entrusted to them might emulate. [302] At this point, a simple person might interject this word of Peter to the papists, saying, "You say that your pomp has its justification in Peter and that Peter was to have been the foremost person in Rome; therefore your pope, too, is the foremost". But this is not in keeping with the truth; however, I shall pass it over for once. But why then do you not follow the words of Peter when he so clearly forbids all your pomp, even though it is not really Peter's word, but that of God the Holy Spirit. Is Peter the one who established you seat, why then do you not look upon his words? Note how well-founded popery is. It is built upon its own wantonness and despises God and his disciples. These two references must suffice to prove that priests should not govern at all, not even in the office which God has given them. Rather, they are to be great in humility and in Christian virtues so that they might be imitated in conduct.

Accordingly, they are to govern even less extensively in worldly matters than has been indicated above. For this reason, I shall briefly expound this matter at this point.

Lk. 12:13f, "One of the people said, 'Master, tell my brother to divide the inheritance with me'. Christ answered him, 'Man, who has set me to be a judge and divider of your inheritance'?" Note that the Lord of all things does not want to get involved in dividing of inheritances, but directs the matter to judges. Yet, those who boast of being in God's place, take over all justice and right, desire to mete out the law for everyone else, yet do not keep the law themselves.

To wit, when the disciples inquired, Lk. 22:24-26 among themselves (which they did often, but it happened for the last time after the Supper), who among them was the foremost and greatest, he said to them, "The kings of the gentiles or nations lord it over them and those who are in power over them are called benefactors. Not so with you. Rather, whoever is to be the greatest or foremost [303] among you, shall become like a disciple and the master shall be like a servant." Oh, what the papists should not give for those four words, "not so with you". Note how sharply God has denied them the right to rule. Rather, as we have shown in the first instance, they are to become great solely through humility and self surrender in the service of believers. All their pomp and power must surely come to nought in these words. Let them expound the matter as they may, there is no other meaning to be found here. God's word stands firmly; heaven and earth shall crumble before even an iota shall be removed from these words [Mt. 24:35].

To wit, he sharply forbade those to whom a portion had been entrusted to beat their fellow servants [Mt. 24:49], as we showed above.

To wit, for this reason he sent the disciples out to preach without bag, purse, or staff, so that they might not amass a pile, nor bag anything, nor beat anyone, nor rule harshly, Lk 9:10 [Lk. 9:1-11; 10:1-16].

On this foundation of scripture one should not tolerate that the priests have any kind of authority which might oppose the temporal authority or which is apart from the common government; for such separation brings about dissension. But should they insist on ruling in matters temporal, they ought to give up the office of messenger and priest of God. In such a case, one has them as superiors or tyrants or benefactors, depending on how they govern, but they cannot very well be both. Were it not better to relieve abbots or bishops who desire to rule, of their cassocks and monasteries and to let them govern, and then to use properly the temporal goods which they abused by putting guardians and not wolves in place of bishops [304] and not to create any more abbots from then on, instead of letting them play their willful games to the offence of everyone? Though a harmless Christian measure should be used here, it is nonetheless clear from the clear word of God that their stance (though they are not willing to confess to that), is directly against God in matters pertaining to vestments, sins, the misuse of riches and the exercise of power.

THE THIRTY-FIFTH ARTICLE

But temporal [authority] derives strength and affirmation from the teaching and work of Christ.

I have placed this Article next to the above so that through both we may learn to discern the papist's false interpolations. For as soon as they notice that their pomp and power are about to break when scripture shines forth so clearly and stands over against them, they want to hang on and cry to the worldly powers, "If you allow that we be suppressed, you will suffer the same fate later on". As if one were putting them down by force rather than convicting them with scripture which, in fact, strengthens worldly authority and bids us to be obedient to it. Rather, they ought to see and feel that their kingdom and authority will never be better, more peaceful and, indeed, richer than when the word of God is preached unswervingly and without ceasing, unless, of course, they are oppressors. For the latter cannot tolerate a nation to be righteous and God-fearing. Rather, the most evil and sacrilegious person suits them best. Euripides says, "The one who does no evil is considered evil by them. [305]

Christ answered the Jews when they asked him with evil intent whether one is to pay any taxes to Caesar [Mt. 22:21], "Give to Caesar what you owe him and to God what you owe him". From this word of Christ we note that if we owe obedience to the authorities, we should render such; if we owe taxes or other contributions to the authorities, we should render those; similarly, custom duties and convoy expenses, as I shall show subsequently. But the measure which is to be observed in these, we shall also see. But no one should conclude from this passage that everyone must be subject to the emperor, as the writers of **SUMMAE** have taught. For Christ never said that all the world had to be subject to the emperor. Rather, since at that time he found them to be under the authority of the emperor, he left them there and bid them render to him what they owed him. Undoubtedly, had he found them under the Babylonian king, he would likewise have said, "give to the Babylonian king what you owe him".

Christ knew well that no group of people on earth is so good as not to have at least some who live so harmfully and evilly that their evil conduct cannot be tolerated. This then has to be driven out by painful medicine, with iron or with fire, etc. This the princes and authorities are to supervise. Therefore Christ is not particularly concerned here with how to be subject to the emperor. But since he knows that punishment must be under some control and because at that time in Jewry it was under the emperor, he orders the strict physician to be given the due one owes him, because not everyone is giving to God his due. For if everyone were to give to God what is his due, there should be no need of a prince or ruler; indeed, we should never have lost Paradise. But since this does not happen in that way, one has to have rulers who prevent calamities [306] and whom one is to give appropriate sustenance, etc. in return, as I shall point out shortly.

By his deed Christ affirmed worldly authority in that he and his mother went to be registered according to the imperial command and he went to be counted as one of the emperor's people, though he was still in the undefiled body of Mary. He also confirmed this authority by giving the drachme (a penny which the emperor imposed as tax money), Mt. 17:24-27. Though he was lord and king he, nonetheless, gave the tax to the emperor to set an example for us so that we might help one another to carry the common lot. This example the priests do not want to learn. They do not help ordinary people to pay their taxes, they do not pay traditional assessments and they contribute nothing to the common weal; rather, they claim to be exempt. [1] This I might well concede when the authorities have exempted them from the duty to pay taxes without harm to the community which is not exempted. But when they defraud the poor of their goods despite their own riches and when the governments, nonetheless, want the total sum of taxes and assessments from the poor, it is considered a wrong in hell even. It is further a grave injustice when exemptions, granted by several popes, or emperors or kings many years ago, are boldly used to all eternity. Who gave him authority a hundred years ago to control the world of today? In short, on the basis of the teachings of Christ, no one is exempt from carrying the common responsibility of government [307] along with ordinary Christians. But should the authorities free one or the other, such ought to be done without disadvantage to the community whereby everyone ought to consider well what such exemptions bring with them in the long run.

NOTE

1. This so-called privilegium immunitatis is discussed in E. Friedberg, **Lehrbuch des katholischen und evangelischen Kirchenrechts**, Leipzig, 1903, and in any major Catholic Encyclopedia.

THE THIRTY-SIXTH ARTICLE

All judicial authority and the administration of justice which the so-called priestly estate appropriates to itself, really belongs to temporal authority inasmuch as it seeks to be Christian.

Let us make short shrift of this Article, though it is directed rather prominently and fittingly against the papists. For should court cases be taken from them, one would undoubtedly have to close their courts. The Article is firmly grounded in the word of Christ, also indicated earlier in Lk. 12:13ff. "When someone shouted to him, 'Master, speak to my brother that he may divide the inheritance with me', he answered him, 'O man, who has set me to be a judge or divider of your inheritance'?" Now we know well that all judgment has been given to Christ by the Father, Jn. 5:22; but he shall sit in judgment only at the end of time. But in this time he has refused to pass judgment. His word and deed is strong enough so that no pope or bishop should presume to accept any judgment. Rather, they should always say with Christ, "Who has set me over you as judge or divider of your inheritance?" Christ did not want to carry out a simple matter even, so that we might not take him as an example to do something like that too. Yet the spiritual fathers do not want to end all bloody arguments; they rather create them. Who does not know in our generation that the pope is the cause of the prolonged war in France and Italy. [1] [308] At one time he cannot stomach the emperor, then he cannot tolerate the king and he brings about all these affairs in the name of Christ and of peace. In short, sitting in judgment has been forbidden to all priestlings in Christ's word, since all of christendom has been provided with good laws and rights so that no one is left without rights when everything is done decently. But even if that were not the case, they are, nonetheless, not entitled to set themselves up as judges, for their office is to teach. Thus they should rightly teach that proper seats of law may be established, rather, than setting themselves up as judges. For Christ, who graciously hears the cry of all who call on him in need and provides them with counsel, did not want to grant to this particular caller his request, undoubtedly because he did not want to interfere with the office of the judges of this world; how much less should those interfere who are his messengers?

The fact that it is not within the realm of so-called priests to guard the law does not mean that they should not by their teaching support the process of jurisprudence. Rather, it means that they should not at all undertake by force to protect courts and the seat of justice, as do the bishops in this our time who protect their rights with a mighty hand and their own bodies with so many soldiers and fighters that even a king or emperor would find them sufficient. Yet Christ bid Peter to put his sword into its sheath; for whoever fights with the sword, shall die by the sword [Mt. 26:52]. From this we clearly learn that the two swords with which Christ contends himself after the Supper [cf. Lk. 22:38] do not indicate human power but rather the well sharpened word of God, revealed in the Old and New Testament. Had Christ wanted his teaching and himself protected, he could easily have been able to gather troops other than the twelve poor fishermen. But he says, "Put it away." If then the pope is a successor to Peter why then does he not hear Christ saying to him, "Put it away"? For if he said it to Peter, he should also accept it without a doubt, since he wants to be successor and heir to Peter. [309]

Now he wants to fight the Turks so that his household at Rome should not perish. [2] Listen to Christ, oh pope, "Put it away." The secular princes are undoubtedly quite capable of protecting their own land. But you go and preach the kingdom of God. Are we to bemoan you more than Christ, should you be knifed to death? Or does one have to fight off the Turks, who rush toward you, more vehemently than one had to fend off the Jews who attacked Christ? You may well see then, unless you are blind, that such suffering of the faithful is inflicted on us by God on account of our sin; do you want to nullify the counsel of God? Go then and call sinful Sodom to repentance, not with guns and military marches, not with riding to and fro of dolled-up bishops but rather with the word of God; preach and shout--like Jonah, John and Christ--"Repent". And take no other sword into your hand than the sword of the Spirit which is the word of God and the other weapons which Paul forged in Eph. 6:11-17, or else you shall perish. David cannot fight this in an iron breastplate [cf. 1 Sam. 17:38ff]. Or else, as long as you shout for weapons of iron, we will know that you are not a successor of Christ or Peter, but of the devil, indeed, that you are the true anti-Christ.

Do what God bids you do and rely on his word. He shall order everything well for one who depends on him. He shall find protection, though wicked Sodom shall be burned to ashes. Thanks be to God for visiting us. He reproves those whom he loves [Prov.

3:12]. He intends to pay us some day for the sake of our cunning and teach us that in future we ought not leave unpunished the great abomination which Rome dares [310] commit before all the world without any shame. And since the entire Jewish nation was extinguished for the sake of evil priests and haters of Christ, it is undoubtedly God's intention to punish us all because we tolerated the dishonorable sins of the papists without any correction, and closed our eyes so as not to see them.

In sum: Every government will be the more peaceful when it does not permit any of the chapters or conventicles to judge in any way but, instead, takes under its own purview all court matters, not allowing any chapter or conventicle to do anything in isolation except they gather together in order to learn and listen; for, in short, as much as I have seen in my days, they are always against open authority and this is against God.

Finally, the maintaining of justice belongs to worldly authority though it may affect priests, monks and nuns. For Holy Scripture places these under worldly authority, inasmuch as it aims to be Christian, as shall become clear in the next Article. This I have included here so that the papists cannot object on the ground of Paul's opinion in 1 Cor. 6:1-11, where he insists that Christians should settle their disputes among themselves and not drag them before unbelieving judges; now the papists turn this to mean that they themselves should judge among Christians and settle all disputes by their own justice. But Paul says nothing there which may be applied to the priesthood; for he says it with the following meaning in mind: Before you turn to judges who are unbelievers to settle the temporal affairs in which you are involved, you ought to seek out the poorest and most simple among you who may decide for you. But since all the princes among whom Christians live are Christians also, Christians should therefore accept judgment from them. There is, of course, the probability that they might have to suffer for the fact that they adhere to the teaching of Christ, which it must unfortunately [311] be noted, has often happened in our time. Should such be the case and should a fellow be able to go before a just temporal judge without creating any disorder, he may want to abide by Paul's word and not to go before an unjust judge. For there is no difference between those who are unbelievers and those who are Christians but do not believe and obey the word of Christ except that the false Christians are the worse of the two; Mt. 11; Lk. 10 [Mt. 11:21-24; Lk. 10:13].

NOTES

1. Zwingli refers to the War of Milan, 1499–1516 and specifically to the agreement of March 1510 between the Swiss Confederates and Pope Julius II.

2. Pope Hadrian VI tried during his brief pontificate to reconcile Emperor Charles V and Francis I that they might stand united againt the onslaught of the Turks.

THE THIRTY-SEVENTH ARTICLE

Furthermore, all Christians, without exception, owe obedience to them.

This Article shall clarify for us the foundation upon which temporal authority rests. Paul says in Rom. 13:1f, "Everyone ought to be subject to the governing authorities, for there is no other authority than the one which comes from God. And the powers that are, are ordained of God. Hence, anyone who opposes such authority, resists the order of God. And those who resist it, call forth their own condemnation."

Firstly, Paul says here, "Everyone," i.e. every living person. If popes, bishops, priests, monks and nuns are living beings, they are included here.

Secondly, he calls superiors, be they princes or rulers, "governing authority."

Thirdly, he states that all authority comes from God.

Does it follow then that evil powers, too, come from God? Yes, but in that manner God punishes our sin, Isa. 3:4. You say: Should we then be obedient to the pope also? Though he be evil, he has been hung around our necks by a commandment of God as punishment for our sins. Answer: I believe this firmly, but I also see in all this that [312] God in his mercy wills to free us again, just as he freed Israel from Egypt's power. They, too, were subject to the king of Egypt because God allowed them to be under him. But when he sent Moses among them, they tore the Egyptian bonds and walked out. Thus the objection does not hold water. For in God's providence we are not being liberated from the pope as much as at one time we were subjected to him by the same providence.

The other words of Paul are clear.

253

To wit, Paul says again in Heb. 13:17, "Be obedient to princes and authorities and obey them, for they guard your lives (here 'soul' stands for 'life' in keeping with Hebrew usage), so that when they have to give account of you, they may do so gladly and not with moaning, for such would not be good for you." The papists have interpreted these words then as referring to themselves as if they might aid them in their domination; yet the Greek "hegumeni" means "princes", "chiefs" and "dukes." Against this it does not help them that shortly before [Heb. 13:7] he called the leaders of God's word hegumenus, for he added in clear words, "those who have taught you the doctrine of God." And though it was intended to refer to these without any qualifications, they themselves cannot be the superiors of which Paul speaks in that context. For he says that one ought to be obedient to superiors in the word of God only; this to the Greeks means "peithein", etc. This meaning regarding "princes" could be supported by many another instance of which we have no need, however.

To wit, in 1 Tim. 2:1ff, Paul bids the Christians to pray earnestly for every person, for kings, i.e. the state, and for all authority, so that we might lead a quiet life in all love and sincerity. In these [313] words we are able to fathom not only the obedience which Christians were to have toward the authorities, though these were not even believers at the time, but that they were to pray to God also on their behalf so that they might lead a peaceful life in true love and sincerity. Tell me where was there in those days any sign of a disquieting Chair or the daft power of the keys and such tomfoolery? Christian teachers ought to work diligently so that everyone might pray to God on behalf of the authorities, that we may lead peaceful, steadfast and sincere lives. But when the priests themselves wish to rule, they do as if they themselves rule well and no longer need to receive anything from God; they take things into their own hands and do not lean on God.

Here you may see also what is the office of the rightful bishops, i.e. guardians, who are to see to it sincerely that all people live peaceably. With this [1] I am able to justify myself before anyone who accuses me of adhering to one or the other party for I earnestly preached peace in the good Christian city of Zurich. I testify before God and all persons [2] to have done this for no other reason than that I knew it to be my duty by virtue of my office. [3] This I feared awfully ever since I have been a priest. Indeed, I was not that young, not to fear the office of guardian more than I enjoyed it. For since I knew that the blood of my lambs would be required of me, should they perish because of my neglect, I was constrained to preach peace by virtue of my office; and when I saw that God worked through his word and inclined human hearts toward peace, I should have been a great murderer, indeed, had I not again and again led and urged them toward peace and Christian living [314] when, in fact, I could see so clearly the increase of good. But that in the midst of this my diligence the decision to fight for the pope took place, [4] no one can truthfully blame on me; for at about that time open hostility had broken out between me and the papists in the following fashion: Before that time I had already preached the gospel of Christ in great sincerity for three full years. The papal cardinals, bishops and legates, of which the city was never free at that time, [5] tried to dissuade me from this, through friendship, pleading, threats, promises of great gifts and benefices. However, I did not give in to them at all. In fact, a pension of fifty guilders, which they gave me annually, they now wanted to increase to a hundred. I did not want it and refused it in 1517. Three years thereafter, they still did not want to release me of it and in 1520 I refused it in a handwritten declaration [6] (I confess my sin before God and all people), for before the year 1516 I attached great value still to the pope's authority and thought it fitting for me to accept money from him, though I always told the Roman legates when they admonished me not to preach anything which was against the pope, not to expect me to suppress a single word of the truth because of their money. Therefore, they could take it back or leave it, as they pleased. When I refused the prebend, they saw quite clearly that I did not want to have anything to do with them. They went on and through a spiritual father--a preaching monk--betrayed my statement of rejection and the receipt, both of which were found in a letter, in the opinion that they might thus get me out of Zurich. This they did not [315] succeed in, for the simple reason that the honorable City Council knew well that I had not spared the pope in my teaching.

They realized then that money had no effect on me at all and that I did not either aid or abet them in any way and now had rejected their prebend for a second time and that with regard to any of my previous teaching, I could not be accused of any transgression either of honor or oath. In other words, the honorable Council knew me to be innocent. Yes, all this evil--it turned out to be my good--they had plotted against me at that time. I say this so that those who accuse me of having closed an eye to that very military expedition and of not having fought it seriously, might see that I could not possibly have had anything in common with the papists and that I fought them harder than I have ever fought in any war or military expedition. It so happened that the Great Council of Zurich in its wisdom clearly rejected the same military expedition. In response, that papist (you know well the fox I mean), [7] set out to make the matter rather fierce: should a confederacy not stick to the content of its agreement with the pope, they would be publicly disgraced before all people; for this particular agreement had allegedly been made with the King of France long before then. Further, the pope would consider publishing the agreement, should the contract not be kept, to make known to everyone how the confederacy behaved toward him. Now as I heard from a reliable source, he was in a great hurry in the matter, saying to several people that one would have to speed the matter before that priestling gets back into the pulpit. With this then he moved the honorable Council which had previously promised to keep all commitments, though other confederates might not want to move out with him, to agree once again to sending soldiers to him. [9] [316] Even in the streets people discussed how the fox was brewing a strange potion in his pot. [10] I did not pay much attention to this, for the wise Council looked into the matter a great deal, yet could not find anything. About our own people, I am inclined to believe the best; but to the papists, I fear, nothing is too bad. For this reason I have launched this attack which on my part shall not lack words, as long as the good people of Zurich can be aroused, though they do not really need my explanation; in fact, it may well be that I should anger them more than cheer them with this my explanation. Indeed, they were angered as I well know, for the simple reason that they still thought it a disgrace at that time, should they not honor the pope's letter and seal. And though they were then, as they are still, of the opinion that they should not enter into a supportive alliance with any secular ruler, they clung to the pope's power and authority to such an extent as to honor the contract with him. Now how they conducted themselves, I leave to them to give account of, which they are undoubtedly capable of doing. For Zurich has always conducted itself in such a fashion as to have an unblemished and honorable name even among the oldest cities. God be praised. Since, however, the promise had once again been renewed, I dared once again [317] fight it, saying among other words, "I wish one would tear a hole in the document of the contract, and pin the same on the back of the Romish legate for him to take home. [12]

Thus let everyone note that should I have wanted to get rich through the money of foreign lords, I should not have cancelled the pope's prebend, since to me, a priest, it would have been least dishonorable to receive from the pope. But I say before God, the judge of every person, that I took no prebend or bribe from any other prince or lord, and that I have been in no way obligated to anyone. And what I do to this day, is in keeping with my office; I note, too, that admonition actually works. Thus I should be a murderer of righteous people, were I not again to admonish without ceasing. I declare myself willing at all times to give account of my teaching, my writings and my deeds to everyone. And I dare say with a good conscience that when I diligently undertake to bring forth the word of God clearly, which, after all, not I, but God is doing, I do so from concern for an honorable confederacy, that it may remain true to its nature, an eternal example against despots who may see by it to what end their excessive wantonness will come. [13] Now everyone may think of me what he likes; thus far I consider myself innocent in anything I have taught or done and of which my enemies accuse me, though I surpass many a person in other vices which, however, do not damage God's truth and a righteous government. [14] For God's sake, let everyone understand, as best they may, this my simple presentation of the dealings with foreign rulers. I might, of course, have been able to present the case with much greater honor to my name, had I intended to make a name for myself. For even a few days ago I received papal letters and great verbal [318] promises, [15] which I answered, nonetheless (God being my helper), unmoved and in a Christian spirit. And I have no doubt at all that I should aspire to be great, like few others, were it not for the fact that I love the poverty of Christ more than the pomp of the papists. Indeed, let everyone understand it as best he may. For I had to do it in response to the bidding of many who pleaded with me not to carry my innocence concerning these things in my own heart, but according to Paul's example to defend it appropriately [2 Cor. 10:11], "for the enemies of Christ often harm his teaching on account of my name, concerning which they speak untruths, thus hindering the teaching of God." I followed their advice and hope not to have done the wrong thing.

Now to prove more firmly that everyone is subject to worldly authority, Peter says, 1 Pet. 2:13-17, "Therefore be obedient to all human creatures for the sake of the Lord, be it to the king as the most fitting, or to his office bearers and chiefs who are sent by him for the punishment of evildoers, or else to praise and protect those who do right; for this is the will of God that we silence the ignorance of the ignorant people by doing right and good deeds. We are free, but let not our freedom become a pretext for evil; rather, let us conduct ourselves as befits servants of God. Treat all persons with respect, love on another as brothers, fear God and honor the king or ruler."

These words of Peter are clear and apply to everyone, whoever it may be. And should those "monsters"--thus I call one who claims to be spiritual but rules in a worldly manner--say [319], "From this you may learn that you should obey us also, for it is written, "all persons", I answer, "The first word of Peter teaches that we should not refuse to obey any persons, i.e. be servants to them in brotherly service. But you priestlings are also included among those and you should actually lead the way and not set yourself up as one whom everyone ought to serve. Rather, if you are a Christian and a Christian teacher, you ought to lead the way by good deeds, obeying others and not elevating yourself above others, or else, drop the name vicar of Christ.

In short, this Article is firm in asserting that all priests and monks [kutten] are to be obedient to worldly authority according

258

to divine laws. And should someone have exempted them once, his successor may bind them again. For as no one who is dead is able to protect another, so he cannot exempt anyone beyond his death either. For freedom is grounded in the power of the protector. Thus someone who is unable to protect, cannot exempt either.

The popes themselves follow this pattern. You may also note the wantonness of the clerics in these words of Peter. They made not only Christian, but even human freedom a pretext of evil. For the great wantonness which the immunity of the priests has brought with it may be readily assessed by everyone on his own. Do not be concerned, Christian priest, when the privilege of immunity is taken away from you. When you treat all Christians as brothers, they in turn, will treat you brotherly. Only then will you be able to see rightly what a preacher of the gospel is, when you are sent as a sheep amidst the wolves [Mt. 10:16]. Otherwise you would be like a destructive wolf amidst the sheep whom no one is able to catch, yet who does not cease to destroy. [320]

NOTES

1. Namely, to have been a conscientious guardian.

2. "Allen creaturen".

3. Cf. Z.I 70ff. See also, G. Finsler, et. al. (ed.s), **Ulrich Zwingli, Eine Auswahl aus seinen Schriften,** 291ff. Strong opposition to military pursuits under a foreign flag developed in Zurich since about 1515. When the Confederacy entered an agreement with France in 1521, Zurich remained independent. Zwingli interpreted this decision as a "fruit of the gospel". However, in 1521 Zurich troops went to the aid of the pope in the Piacenca Expedition. The City Council forbade such mercenary service in 1522. Its citizens never again officially served under any foreign banner.

4. For further details on the Piacenca Expedition cf. E. Egli, "Zum Piacenzerzug", **Zwingliana** II 85ff.

5. Among the most skillful papal agents were Cardinal M. Schinner and the nuntios, E. Filonardi and A. Pucci.

6. Cf. G. Finsler, et. al., op. cit. 292, n. 3. Loss of the pension must have been hard on Zwingli's finances. He undoubtedly welcomed therefore the financial benefice of "Chorherr am Grossmünster", granted on 21 April 1521.

7. This may have been Cardinal M. Schinner, but possibly also T. Murner.

8. Meant is Zwingli.

9. Cf. Bullinger, I 53ff and G. Finsler, et. al., op. cit., 293, n. 3. The troops moved out on 16 Sept. 1521 about 2,700 men strong; their number later increased to about 6,000 men.

10. The Cardinal had secured Zurich's military aid by stating that it would be needed for protection of papal property only. In actual fact the Swiss soldiers were to be used by the pope against the French troops who held Milan (these were actually Swiss Confederates, too). When the Swiss refused to fight each other, bloodshed was averted. The pope occupied Milan unopposed. Finsler, op. cit., 293, n. 4.

11. G. Finsler, et.al, Zwingli Auswahl translates the text differently at this point; see there, 294.

12. Cf. Z.I 73.16 & Z.II 181.21f. Zwingli's recollection here is obviously correct.

13. An example of such concern is Eine göttliche Vermahnung an die Eidgenossen zu Schwyz, 16 May 1522 (Z.I 154ff).

14. Zwingli obviously refers to his ethical lapses. He was known for his "loose" moral behavior, a fair amount of pride, and excessive eating habits. Cf. Z.I 395, n. 10 and 405.5ff. In his religious conduct and convictions, however, he tolerates no slander.

15. Z.VIII 13f, Briefwechsel contains a letter to Zwingli from Pope Hadrian VI dated 23 January 1523. Zwingli did not receive the letter until May. The editors of his correspondence read it as a genuine attempt by the pope to settle the religious unrest, but doubt that the pope would likely have gone to the extent of promising Zwingli "omnia certe praeter sedem papalem" as Myconius, Zwingli's first biographer suggests in his Vita Zwinglii. For a modern edition of the latter, cf. Oswald Myconius, Vom Leben Und Sterben Huldrych Zwinglis (ed. by E. G. Rüsch). St. Gallen: Fehr'sche Verlagsbuchhandlung, 1979.

THE THIRTY-EIGHTH ARTICLE

All Christians without exception owe obedience to them, provided they do not command anything which is opposed to God.

This Article limits the tyranny of superiors so that they might not begin to act irrationally and wantonly, just because God ordered that we be obedient to them. For even though they might not be Christians and order something that is against God, Christians have been bid to obey God more than human beings, Acts 5:29. Much less ought Christian rulers order anything which might be against God.

Therefore, good Christians, when princes dare forbid you the teaching of Christ so that you neither hear, read nor preach the same, pay no heed to them. You say, "but what if they kill me?" Answer: Let it be, in the name of God. If they want to be like the Jews who have been cursed, let them be. But doubt not, your death will be a cause of excellent growth. And though you preached fervently and rightly, your innocent blood shall, just as that of Abel, preach even more fruitfully than any words can. Do you not know that in the beginning of the Christian church countless multitudes of believers were killed? Yet, Christian faith and morals were never richer than at that time. You ought to rejoice that God uses your life and blood in order to water and increase his word. For what use is your blood when it decays and spoils in your dying body, Ps. 29 [30:10]? Is it not better to be poured out as a fertilizer of the word of God? [321]

You see how the foolish princes have allowed themselves to be misled by the anti-Christian papists so that some time ago they persecuted the gospel of Christ in Luther's name by calling the teaching of Christ from then on Lutheran, by whom, after all, it was proclaimed, and by persecuting it to the best of their ability. And when one pays little attention to this (for everyone knows well within himself how he has become a believer), they begin to call the teaching of Christ a conspiracy [Bundschuh], [1] so that they may be the more justified in the eyes of people,

260

should they undertake to eradicate the teaching of Christ by murdering. For a conspiracy is invidious to everyone.

How then do you expect to act, good servants of God? Do you intend to keep silent for fear of death? God prevent that. You will have to stake your lives, otherwise you shall never overcome this insane raging. Should you retreat, you are conquered. But should you die for the sake of the teaching of God, it shall remain and yield fruit. The grain must rot and die, ere it may bring fruit. Thus Christ in his death has implanted us all and has made us children of God.

Thus you too, bold soldier of Christ, will have to expose your bodies to evil and beatings [2 Tim. 2:3]. If Nero, Domitian, Maximian and others were unable to stop the teaching of Christ with their murdering, how much less can the angry, insane princes who rage in this our time, drive it out, as long as you stand firmly and without retreating. Have no regard [322] should you be called heretics, rogues or conspirators [Bundschuher] after your death. These names cannot harm the soldier who now collects his pay from God. The more your name is rejected by people, the higher and more worthy it is with God [Mt. 5:11f; 1 Pet. 4:14]. Get up and go, everyone who is a man of God. Let us see whether God or the clowns [2] are going to be stronger.

Now I do not mean you at all, righteous rulers, but only the fierce opponents of God who dare not undertake any other courageous deed than the killing of poor defenceless Christians, the burning of books, the robbing of goods, as I hear it said of some unprincely princes who declare the property of all those free who read the teachings of Christ which they call either Lutheran or insurrectionist; this will harm no one more than themselves in the end. What sort of danger it is may be seen by every child, namely that well-fed spoiled rogues can soon bring about through false testimony the conviction of a righteous, prosperous person for having read Luther's writings when he has never read these, so that they may receive the portion, promised to informers. Now should this be recognized, the penalty for it would soon recoil on the heads of these foolish princes. Take a look, you princelings, at the ancient histories of the Romans, Marius, Sulla, Caesar and others, and you will soon find out what an informer gets for declaring a citizen's possessions "free property". Therefore, you righteous princes, do not let these soft papists become too dear to you, so that for their sake you now begin doing things which are detrimental to your office and name. [323]

Now the teaching of Christ must be examined carefully. Should it be found that one committed evil deeds under its cover, he must repay. But should he have acted faithfully in the office and affairs of God, why then do you seek to fight God? Or do you think that the world--assuming there is no God--would want to tolerate your folly any longer? If you are judges, then examine both parties. Now you see quite well that the papists do not want to dig into scripture [3] and that they cannot defend themselves with it. And yet, this entire quarrel is on account of the truth of scripture alone.

Should things go on as they are now, you will experience in your own skin what you inflict upon the skin of others. [4] If you use force, force will be used on you; for with whatever measure you mete out, with that same measure things shall be meted out to you [Mk. 4:24]. God is able to bide his time; you cannot escape him. Be wiser than to do what you now do, which looks more like might than right. Do not give heed to whether something appears great and incredible to you. Look only to whether or not it appears to be thus in itself, and you will be saved here and yonder. Amen.

NOTES

1. Since 1513 at least, rebellious peasants used the symbol of a laced shoe on their flags. The term "Bundschuh" is used since then to indicate rebellion or revolt. Cf. Grimm, **Wörterbuch der deutschen Sprache,** II 523ff.

2. A Hofdentzer is one who dances at court; hence, a fool (Latin: aulici choragi).

3. "In die gachrifft nit beissen wellend."

4. "Wirt . . . uech ouch ze huss kummen, das ir andren . . . ze huss schickend".

THE THIRTY-NINTH ARTICLE

Therefore all their laws ought to conform to the divine will so that they protect the oppressed person, though he may not actually lay a charge. [1]

Should the laws of the princes be against God then Christians will say, as we heard earlier, that one ought to obey God more than people [Acts 5:29]. Christian princes ought to have laws therefore, which are not opposed to God, or else one might evade them which brings unrest in its wake. [2] [324]

Now, should you want to know, righteous prince or ruler, how you are to know the law, whether it is on God's side or against him, pay attention to the following:

First, do not even try to change or improve anything in the commandments which God has given. You are too much of a child in his sight. Rather, be sure that the divine commandment is fully shaped according to his will, as we have sufficiently shown above. Do not criticize it; for you are not a judge over God's word and law. Rather, the word of God judges you.

Secondly, take good care that you yourself are no more than the sword with which God severs the worst members from his body. But in order that you may not ever cut off a healthy member instead of a diseased one, or leave a diseased one instead of a healthy member, you are forever in need of knowing what health and what sickness are. And this you are able to learn from the law alone, that is, from the very law which God has given. This ought to be your pattern from which you must cut; but you are not to make your pattern, but simply cut along it. Therefore, should you find that your laws are not like the divine laws at all, you must not cut according to them either. Note this: All laws concerning the neighbor are to be grounded in the law of nature. What you would have happen to you, do that to the other also, Mt. 7:12. This he expressed later in even clearer terms, Mt. 22:39, "You ought to love your neighbor as yourself". A law which is not like this word of God is simply against God. Thus you discover, first of all, that you yourself, should you be a judge who has to be maintained while others work, are acting and living against the law of nature. Do not get frightened on account of this. For you yourself would not tolerate it, should you have to work while another reaps the fruit of your labor. Thus when you do this, you live contrary to the law of nature. And if you wish to live aright [325], you will have to start with yourself first and change what is corrupt.

Now take a careful look first at the law of nature and you will discover in your own case that the natural law is against your own understanding. For a ruler cannot allow himself to be treated in the way in which he treats others, or else he is not really a ruler. From this it would follow that authority is against God; for he says in Mt. 7:12, "Everything you want done to yourself by people, do that to them also; for such is the law and the prophets." Thus it follows that no one rightly understands the natural law except for the believer. The unbeliever hears it all right, but he finds that one ought to have an authority which, however, is incapable of keeping the law of nature; accordingly, he rejects the law of nature in the opinion that it cannot be kept in any case.

I recall that I said earlier, in passing, that the law of nature is nothing other than the essence and guidance of the divine Spirit. [3] Therefore, as Paul says in Rom. 2:14ff, unbelievers have the law of nature written upon their hearts, and thus are not without a law; for God alone writes the law of nature upon human hearts. Where he teaches, there is plenty of law.

However, one ought to consider the law of nature from a vantage point other than that of a human being who is born of Adam, for it is his nature and inclination to set himself above other persons. Just as Adam wanted to be like God from the outset, so also a human being, born of Adam, measures himself by all those things in which he excels others. Is he wiser than another, he does not consider himself a member of the other, but above him. Is he rich, he thinks other persons should serve him, altogether unconcerned and undeterred by the law of nature. Thus we see that we [326] ought not to think of the law of nature as coming from us or out of our heads, which we have from Adam, but as from God, the first father and creator of all things. But how can one understand something that comes from God when he does not believe that there is a God? For this reason, one who is to recognize the law of nature as from God, the fountain of all things, must first of all believe that God has created humankind. And should he believe that, he does not do so on his own strength or understanding. Rather, as we have sufficiently shown above, faith comes from God alone who draws us. Thus the believer also knows the law of nature, for it can be known only from God. And no one can believe in him except for one who is drawn by God. Thus it follows that even knowledge of the law of nature comes from the Spirit of God alone.

Hear it as follows: That all alike are born and die naked [Job 1:21; Eccl. 5:14], is undoubtedly an image of our being brothers. After that, however, the inequality of understanding, riches, beauty, strength, misleads us and spoils us so that we become selfish and proud and raise ourselves above others.

But to believe firmly that we have come of one and the same father is clarified by the law of nature. For through it we learn that we are all brothers. And anything that we have uniquely, belongs to the community as given by God. And no one has anything unto himself, but everything belongs to the brothers in common, just as one wants to have the gifts of his brothers in common, so likewise he must recognize his own gifts to be common to all. Now look at the law of nature and you will find that "what you want to happen to you, that you will have to do to another also." This you learn solely from God. Thus the law of nature, too, comes solely from God and is nothing other really than the pure Spirit of God who inwardly draws and illumines. Therefore the gentiles, too, knew the law of nature, not with the aid of their understanding but through the illuminating Spirit of God which was unknown to them. For our flesh does not understand until it comes to the Father of all, and that can happen through faith alone. Now, had they not had faith, yet were able to understand the law of nature, it would have had to come from God alone, though I think that only a few of them actually understood it. There were a few, of course, but many only pretended to know and spoke of it beautifully.

Thus then, magistrate or ruler, you recognize the law of nature, but you observe at the same time that one does not live by the law of nature everywhere; indeed, I find that it is nowhere kept fully, although in many things we manage to keep up the pretense. For example, in giving counsel there is one or the other who advises faithfully, as he himself would want others to counsel him. But he will do this only toward a friend; an enemy he will forsake and neglect. You will also find that one cannot live better and more peacefully than when living by the law of nature; then there would be no need of you, nor would there be any quarrel, disturbance or anything offensive among people.

Thus you discover that you have been set to be a ruler because of fallen nature and because of slothful and half-baked righeousness; for such is incapable of suffering the righteousness of nature. Example: You, a ruler, cannot force anyone to give his property to the poor with whom he ought to share his goods according to the law of God and of nature. Rather, you are forced to consider him a righteous person as long as he harms no one, though he may not do any good to anyone either. But he is not really good [328] and righteous, either by God's norms or by the law of nature. For God and the law of nature (which is actually nothing other than the will of God), will that he should do unto the neighbor from within, out of his own free will, and without any diminishment, as he wants others to do unto himself. It follows then, that someone may acquire among you the reputation of goodness who is, nonetheless, damned. It follows further that you, a ruler, have power only among evildoers and among those who have been so shameless that they dared come out publicly with their undesirable lusts and temptations; for you cannot punish anyone who keeps his desires in his heart, yet is wicked. In short, you are a ruler only because of the wicked ones, 1 Tim. 1:3-11. Though you do well in protecting the righteous and though this is your duty, as we shall show later, it is, nonetheless, the wicked ones who are the reason why we have to support you, so that the righteous people may be protected from them. Which righteous people? Is there one among you who is righteous from within? No. You can protect only those who have not done wrong in outward deeds; inwardly they, too, are full of temptation. Thus you rule only among God's knaves and you yourself are one. Here I call anyone a knave of God who is not righteous before God. In other words, all persons are knaves of God, for all persons are sinners. The only thing you are able to stop is that excessive wickedness is not committed. This is God's will and he keeps you just like a strong medicine which he will use when milder medication does no longer work. Therefore you ought not to use your power on righteous people; for they do nothing against you. And as long as they do no evil, they should not fear you, Rom. 13:3f. Therefore they obey you gladly and show respect toward you, for they do not fear you and [329] contribute toward your maintenance so that they, in turn, might be protected against villains who are the ones that ought to fear you.

Why then is it that God has not ordained an authority which would look upon pure righteousness and innocence of heart and then punish the evil ones? Would we not be all the more righteous? Answer: Simply because humankind is not God; for God alone knows the human heart and we shall know them only by their fruits. And once we have seen their fruits, we then are able to distinguish between fruits and punishments.

Now such an ability to discern must have a foundation on whose basis one ought to be able to judge rightly by God's standards. For though there are many laws, the cases are so varied that some might easily elude the law. In such cases the judge will then have to judge by another standard. Now which would this be? His understanding? No. His understanding is caught up in impure temptations and does everything either from love or hatred, joy or sorrow, courage or fear.

Therefore, the judge must, above all, look upon the good from which alone we draw goodness. If he knows that, keeps it before his eyes, and desires to draw from it, he is sure not to err; for no one who seeks after it, goes away empty. But he knows that only if he is a believer; for the unbeliever does not seek it with God and therefore he does not demand it either. Therefore a ruler who desires to know what is right or who wishes to pass good laws, must, first of all, be one who loves God or who believes. Reason: He should never understand or believe rightly and surely the law of nature, as we said earlier, unless he knows the heavenly Father and believes in him.

Now he must not only pronounce judgment by the law of nature or by the law of neighbor in unexpected circumstances for which there is no law, but he must judge by the same law all ancient and former laws also, whether they are in keeping with the divine law of neighbor [330] or nature (which are one and the same), or whether they are contrary to it. Now none of them will be in conformity, for none is exactly like it; but when it approximates it or is in some sense like it we say that it is in conformity. But should these laws be contrary to the law of God, he should not at all judge according to them. From this it follows that he will have to discern the laws well by which he intends to judge. Note how risky it is to be a ruler or judge. Note, on the other hand, what a sure and beautiful thing it is when he is a believing, God-fearing person, transacting nothing according to his own whims, but in all things acting according to the word and commandment of God who alone teaches him to find the right measure. In this way, all his laws will be in conformity to the will of God, not exactly like it, but in some measure in the form of the divine law and will; for the righteousness by which a judge must walk is merely a shadow of true righteousness. Now he must still take great care not to remove healthy members in place of diseased ones and the sick instead of healthy members.

Accordingly, it is not enough that he knows good laws and understands how to judge by them. Rather, he must also have people who obey the law and give it credence and who know the right measure by which the authorities judge. Otherwise they might think injustice is done them whenever they are judged. Therefore it follows, firstly, that rulers must, above all else, bring to their people the right and true knowledge of God. This can be done only through the clear word of God which renews people; not the spoken word, mind you, but the Spirit of God who works through his word.

For what good is it to have good laws when we lack the inclination to be pleased by such laws? No setting up [of such laws] helps when the heart does not really want to [conform]. But how can the heart which by nature is evil, desire what is good, unless it be drawn by God? And how can it [331] be drawn by him of whom it does not know anything? From this it follows that good laws are usually heeded and complied with when the word of God is taught most clearly. There one knows his will best of all. There one is most eager to do it, for it is done out of love. A ruler provides good laws when he sees to it that his subjects follow simply and modestly in the spirit of such a good law. This happens best of all through the activity of the word of God. Thus it follows that no state [4] is more peaceable and God-fearing than the one in which the word of God is preached most clearly; it follows further, that nothing makes a state more solid, for the most righteous states, to be sure, are also the strongest. Hence it is also certain that those who do not want to have the gospel of Christ preached among their subjects are nothing but tyrants. They fear that one might have one's eyes opened. And this they cannot tolerate, for they are such great, greedy, wicked knaves that they fear every simpleton might become smart enough to see through their knavery, wrongdoing and wantonness. Thus they prefer to rule among blind people rather than among those who are enlightened. Yet no teaching that has ever come to earth befits a righteous, peaceful state better than the teaching of Christ. Through it a leader becomes wise and spiritual and able to discern all things; but a subject becomes desirous of what is good and peaceable and that which no one is able to make him do through orders, he will do gladly out of love.

Now if both lord and people give credence to the highest wisdom in heaven and on earth, i.e. if they believe in the word of God, only the greatest peace, friendship and love can result. The first Christians clearly demonstrated this when they shared all their possessions with one another and lived as [332] brothers. Indeed, they surpassed physical brothers even. These could not have given up their own rights quite as faithfully as the [Christians] did. By that much stronger is the work of God than the work of human beings.

Further, both people and lord will be able to administer poor human righteousness that much more intelligently inasmuch as it is possible for it to be in harmony with the law of God.

Thus all laws ought to be brought into harmony with the law of God; then a ruler will consider himself ruler over evildoers only and exercise his power on them; toward believers he will conduct himself as toward his brothers. Not only will he be concerned with how to punish evildoers, but also how he might protect and keep the righteous from any disaster, that they should not fall into unbelief and wickedness. And he will be concerned more with the souls of those entrusted to him than with acquiring temporal goods, as Paul says in Heb. 13:17. "They [the rulers] watch over your lives as those who have to give account on your behalf." For priests have no right to use force, as we showed above from Peter's writings; they are deprived of all such power. However, there are still some rams among the flock of Christ who are so bold as to give no heed either to teaching or ban. On the other hand, there are such among the flock of Christ who are so meek and humble as not to complain about every single transgression and offence. Here it is fitting for Christian rulers to act according to the words in the latter part of this Article and to protect the oppressed, though he may not actually complain. For wherever one follows laws or traditions by which one does not punish, unless a complaint is lodged, a great deal of evil is caused. The poor have to suffer abuse from the rich who are in every way too strong; and when the poor see that, they would much rather suffer their affliction than risk getting into yet other dangers. Now [333] the rich person has been victorious in his wrongs and becomes so insolent in the end that he will also resist authority; whenever that happens, a government has had it. Therefore a government has to see to it that the strong, well-fed rams do not destroy the poor, weak sheep. Now this is grounded in Paul's word in Rom. 13:3f, "The princes or rulers are not to ward off good works but evil works. If then you want to live without fear of power, you ought to do good or right, and you will be praised or supported by the authorities. For the ruler is a servant of God for your good. But when you do evil, you ought to be afraid; for he does not carry his sword in vain. He is a servant of God and an avenger of his wrath toward the one who does evil." Therefore they ought to see to it that they protect and punish. Peter also indicates this in 1 Pet. 2:14, "Officials or rulers are sent to punish the evildoers and to praise the good people, i.e. they are sent for encouragement and protection.

NOTES

1. In the **Labyrinth**, lines 218-225 Zwingli's early understanding of the gospel as identical with the law of God and with natural law is apparent. While the exposition of this Article suggests continued adherence to this principle, it would seem that there is a qualitative shift which makes an unqualified equation of the Reformer's understanding of love of God and humankind with that of the humanist and reformer of the period up to 1520 no longer possible. Cf. A. Rich, op. cit., 66ff.

2. Literally: "man tritt inen uss dem strick". Cf. Wander, IV 242, No. 17 for the related saying, "sich aus der Schlinge ziehen".

3. See Article 28 above, toward the end of the Article.

4. Regiment-res publica.

THE FORTIETH ARTICLE

They alone are entitled to impose the death penalty and then only on those who give public offence, without thereby incurring the wrath of God, unless he commands something else.

That the magistrate alone may punish and impose the death penalty within the law, Paul indicated in the very next words of the above-mentioned passage in Rom. 13:4, "He does not carry the sword in vain; for he is a servant of God and an avenger of his wrath upon the evildoer." That he carries the sword means the majesty and order of the law and that he ought not execute anyone unless the law says so. Therefore all princes and rulers who on their own kill someone in anger outside the law [334] are just as much guilty of manslaughter as an ordinary person.

I do not here give any attention to the heathen law of the princes of which they prattle a great deal, saying that this is their prerogative and that they are not to be punished like one of the people, though they might have committed murder. The devil taught them that law; they did not receive it from God; for God commands all people, "You shall not kill", Ex. 20:13. Thus a private citizen is not entitled to kill. But a prince or leader is a private citizen when he does something in the heat of his own passions. Hence it follows that he is not entitled to kill outside the law; for his passions make of him a common or ordinary person. Be it noted in passing at this point that just as the commandment, "You shall not kill" is addressed to all private citizens, but not to temporal authorities (for they are to kill according to their responsibility, as we shall show later), so all other commandments such as the one concerning forgiveness, the turning of the other cheek, etc. are addressed to all private citizens. In this wise: Are you a ruler or judge, then you are also required, as was Peter, to forgive seventy times seven, as regards your person; but with regard to the administration of public affairs, you must use the sword, though you must always stay within the boundaries which God himself maintains, who does not rush to demand the death of a sinner, Ezekiel 18:32, but rather that he might repent and live. Do likewise. Should there be hope for improvement, then mete out justice; if there is none, then remove the evildoer from among the people, Deut. 13:5.

Further, only he is to be killed who offends publicly; for you, a ruler, are not able to judge anyone by the evil of his heart until you know his heart by its fruits. And should you find him to become harmful to the body of Christ and to the community when you allow him to live, you may then put the millstone around his neck and lower him to the bottom of the sea [Mt. 18:6; Lk. 17:2]. At that point it is not you doing this, but rather his open vices which force the magistrate to do so; for should he refuse to do [335] this, it would be just as if he planted all vices himself. Whoever does not control the ever sprouting thorns with a hatchet will have to see how in the end they take over the entire field. But there is no need of any parable or admonition, for Christ himself teaches this in Mt. 5:29 and 18:8ff, "If your right eye offends you, pluck it out and throw it away." Likewise, "Should your hand or foot offend you, pluck it out and throw it away," etc. The eye is as if it were your teacher, leader and wisdom. The hand is your support and refuge. Your foot is your companion and co-worker; for one foot is the other's most faithful companion. Nonetheless, you are to cut it off and throw it away. Though these words refer primarily to the ban in the community, they are, nonetheless, a clear directive to the rulers to which they must adhere in cases which require more severe punishment. Depending on the form of the vice, they must first admonish people kindly, in case they reform. But as soon as there is no hope of improvement any longer, but only the fear that there should be even greater damage to the whole body, it is by far better that one member perish rather than the entire body. For rulers are avengers and servants of God. And God is not angry when one carries out his service. And again, should he demand something else, in other words, should he bid to kill without trial, as for example in warfare or such like, one is to obey him--not beforehand. One ought to abide by his commandments always and though he may command something else, as for example the murder of King Agag, King 15 [1 Sam. 15], one should, nonetheless, keep the commandment, "You shall not kill". From this it follows that professional warfare is inhuman, shameless and sinful. For I cannot help but judge that those who are in the army, are guilty of every murder which happens there. They are one community or multitude, all following one command, all doing one task, all taking pay, though one may sin more severely than another, should he become a greater cause of evil and wickedness. [336]

THE FORTY-FIRST ARTICLE

When they provide just counsel and aid to those for whom they will have to give account before God, these in turn, are duty-bound to give them physical support.

Everyone understands what this Article aims at, namely, that rulers who carry out the office entrusted to them, which is to administer justice, advise the simple and keep him from despair, help the weak and not allow him to be oppressed, to manage according to necessity and in earnest, are then also entitled to have their expended time and the neglect of their own affairs restored by those who thus receive their help and used it, provided, of course, that they suffered loss from this which they cannot easily absorb. However, should they otherwise be rich enough, they ought to make do with what they themselves have and, following the ways of God, should make themselves available for the common good of every person, as did Socrates, a gentile, in word and deed, who said, "The wise person is common to all", by which he meant that wisdom should commonly serve everyone.

At times you find a semblance of this among councillors in cities and towns, but not too often among the ruling nobility; these, be they ever so rich, do not make any concessions to the poor; by that much less are they like God. Of course, they are entitled within reasonable limits to collect their due according to human justice, for they have the support of scripture in Rom. 13:5-7, "Therefore it is needful that you be obedient not only for fear of punishment, but also because of your [337] conscience. For to this end you pay duty and toll; for they are servants and administrators of God so that they might be diligent in their tasks. Therefore give to every person his due. Pay duty to whomsoever you owe it; taxes or fees to whomever you owe them; give respect or obedience to whomever you owe it and honor, to whom you are bound to render it [Rom. 13:7].

Give ear here, you papists. Firstly, one owes obedience to the authority which carries the sword, not only because it forces obedience upon us, but also for the sake of conscience. Do you hear that your conscience sins when you refuse rightful obedience to the authorities which carry the sword? If you have consciences, then see to them; for should you not render obedience to above-mentioned authority, you hurt your consciences.

Secondly, you hear that you owe servants duty and protection and taxes and fees, just as if they carried out a spiritual office before God.

Thirdly, rulers also hear that they are to look after the office of the sword diligently and with attention.

Fourthly, all Christians hear that everyone is to pay the other what he owes him. From this it follows that those are mere nitwits, who say, "I am free; I shall no longer pay any rent or any other debt". Do you not hear what Paul says here and what I indicated earlier in the Article concerning unjust property? [1] Give to everyone what you owe him. It gets you nowhere to object, "We are all brothers"--miserable human justice does not go by this. It allows us to be brothers, but does not force money purses and bags to be sisters. Therefore, you must allow human righteousness to become master over you for God commands it thus. To have all things in common, is truly divine [Acts 2:44]; but God does not force the rich, but allows him to do so [338] out of his own free will. Neither can you force him or take it from him. Should you do this, you become guilty of transgressing the law, "you shall not steal."

When God illumines us so that everyone of us gladly brings his own, we then will have everything in common, as was the case at the time of the apostles, when no one was forced either, since Peter spoke to Ananias [Acts 5:3f], "Was this not in your power? Why then did you do it?" as if to say, "No one actually forced you. As far as force was concerned, you might as well have kept the total sum." Those however, who are well instructed and know that everything ought to be held in common, yet turn it all to their own advantage, should be forced by the rulers--though they may not have any property of their own--to have everything in common. They should be ordered to work for nothing in sand and rock quarries, or else they should be suspended from the gallows for a universal example. In this way they would be of some use to us; since others, led on by their example, will not commit the same felony then. In short, everyone ought to follow righteousness and cling to that which lawful rulers lay down for him, as long as it is not against God. Do not be confounded here by free will.

In this connection we ought not to forget the despots either, of whom unfortunately there are as many as there are fleas in August. They could easily put on a cloak under which to hatch all their wickedness of robbing, cheating, indeed, of murder, stealing, killing, as if thereby they are able to do justice to the office with which God has entrusted them. For so many of the temporal rulers have now gone astray that every sensible person can readily see that it would be much better were they not in office at all since they carry it out in such an inhuman manner. And there are those who impose new taxes on their people without [339] their approval, but by sheer force. That they need such taxes is true enough; but they brought such poverty upon themselves by their excessive luxury, by games, drinking, loose living, loud carousing, wars, uncontrolled cost of clothing, through servants, foreign customs and exotic cults. Not only do they rob the poor through duty, taxes, and other allocations; but in addition they have Jews and usurers sitting among them. These tax their lives so dearly each year, that neither the despots nor the Jews and usurers are worth the money. And they allow such heavy burden to come upon their people in order that they, too might get a share. Because of this they tolerate holders of monopolies among them which, according to their laws, are prohibited to operate. One has to buy spices, zinc, copper, cloth and articles of clothing from these holders of monopolies. These burden not only a princedom, but indeed the entire world. They release their goods as they please. There is not a single woman, just delivered of her baby, who does not have to pay to those wolves a farthing or more for every ounce of medicine. With this they manage to accumulate untold riches which the princes have to take away from them frequently, just as one takes away honey from the bees or else they make a deal with them on how much they are to take away from them. For this purpose they [340] have acquired a franchise from them for unspeakably high sums of money. It does not matter how much they have to give for this. For as soon as they have a monopoly, they have it made; they sell the goods as they please and thus are able to keep ahead of inflation. These controllers of monopolies, christendom should drive out and stop as one stops a conspiracy.

[It should drive out also]: everyone who protects the pomp, riches and wantonness of so-called priests that they themselves might enjoy their excessive riches which, however, belong to the poor; all who turn the hospitals of the poor into shelters for knights and soldiers--I mean the cloisters; for cloisters are the hospitals of the poor; all who allow papal indulgences among their people because they too will receive a large share thereof; all who allow these spirituals through their begging to acquire from the poor vast treasures of golden and silver images, monstrances, chalices, crosses, by skillfully devised teachings and fables (as if God is honored by these), so that they can steal these again, should they themselves be hardpressed. For whatever one gives them in times of peace that they might gather these up and thus fend off any need when such should arise, is soon spent by them. And as soon as there is some need, they go after their poor immediately. They show no compassion toward their poor and render them no help when there is a crop failure. Indeed, they would use up substantial goods in warfare against other princes rather than absolve their poor people of as much as a penny even.

Several years ago now, princes, kings and emperors used such vast sums in warfare against each other that they themselves were unable to keep track of it any more. Should their poor people have asked, however, to be relieved of only the one hundredth portion of that same property, they would have raged. But the judgments of God are such against those who cruelly exact from their poor people such incredible goods (which displeases God), that he orders it [341] drawn out again with great pain, as if God should say, "Since you do not keep peace and grace among yourselves because of material goods, your wantonness and honor, I have to make you poor, wretched and sorrowful and humiliate you before the wise and knowledgeable people, and I will have to pass on to future generations your names and deeds so that everyone may see what irrational heads you were. And whatever you have defrauded the poor of, through outrageous laws, will have to be drawn out of you with equal ferocity, because you treated the people that were entrusted to you not as human beings but as animals, in fact, worse than animals. I shall not even mention that they are actually their brothers because they share one faith, one baptism and one God with them [Eph. 4:5]. They convince themselves through their deceiving scholars that everything within the sphere of their activities is their own. As a consequence, they rob with force, ravage solid people's women and children and beat to death anyone who opposes their wantonness. See what a fine nation of idolaters this is. They daily butcher their poor people with invented law-suits so that their goods may fall into their hands. Yet these same people stand by them faithfully--soul, honor, body and goods--forever shouting, "O you God-fearing prince", though he is an evildoer (disregard all this if you are an honorable person). Those who ought to have been protectors, guardians and overseers have become bailiffs, swindlers and extortioners; in short, they are so utterly corrupted by the many countless vices that one can actually see how truly godless they are. Yes, these godless princes should not abuse their power just because God commanded [342] that they be obeyed. They knew well that God commanded obedience to be rendered to them because they carry the sword in place of God to punish the evildoer and not to bring disadvantage to the righteous person, to protect the God-fearing and not to frighten them. And no one is called on to satisfy all their whims, but only to restore to them a fair portion of that which they had to forego on our account while they were engaged in meting out justice.

"O God, grant to the poor people good pastors and pro-claimers of the word of God; that through them you princes and people may learn that an insincere, unbrotherly life will be taken away, so that your name be hallowed and praised in all the world. Preserve and strengthen the princes who give credence to your word, that they might be able to withstand the anti-christian rogues. Illumine the unbelievers. Give them understanding that they might know you and themselves. Take away their despotic hearts and give them God-fearing, sincere, lovely hearts and minds. But should you insist on leaving them in their obstinacy, we note well that you desire to punish us and them together. Grant grace then, O Lord, to your faithful people, that they may not fall from your word. And though the body must suffer, the soul cannot be harmed when it remains steadfast in the faith. Your word shall always triumph, though many may have to suffer for it. It seems to be true when we read, "The princes band together against the Lord and his fragrant smelling Son the anointed king" [Ps. 2:2]. Grant us, Lord, that their fetters break and that you and your word alone conquer. Amen."

NOTE

1. See Article 33 above.

THE FORTY-SECOND ARTICLE

Should they become unfaithful and not act according to the precepts of Christ, they may be deposed in the name of God.

Of what concern are the precepts of Christ to the princes when no one can live by these anyhow, as long as he is in the world, however holy he might be? I answer: No one can follow the precepts of God. That is certain. But we take "keeping the commandments of God" or "to be guided by them" to mean, "keeping the commandments of God as closely as is humanly possible." Understand this as follows: everyone ought to abide by the commandment of God. But if we cannot abide thereby, the ruler cannot punish us until we act publicly against it. Take an example: Should you desire another marriage partner in your heart, a ruler cannot punish you for that. But should you actually have committed adultery with someone else's partner, he can punish you. He follows the precepts of Christ when he punishes your desire which has become deed. Thus we mean here by "precept of Christ", "to follow the way of God". And one who fails to punish the sinner does not follow the precepts of Christ, but actually favors him and oppresses the innocent. This is when one protects useless bellies, lazy priests, monks and nuns in their wantonness, their adultery, chess games, greed, pride and pomp. And what they squander, they do not allocate to the poor. Rather, when one speaks truthfully against all this, they punish the one who objects. This certainly is to be outside the precepts of Christ.

But that they should be deposed in such cases, is shown by the clear example of Saul, whom God rejected, though he had earlier chosen him, 1 Kings 15 & 16 [1 Sam. 15 & 16]. Indeed, should one fail to depose extravagant kings, the entire people will be penalized on their account, Jer. 15:4. When God through Jeremiah had recounted the four plagues which he intended to send over the nation, he said [344] subsequently, "And I shall stir up all kingdoms of the earth on account of Manasseh, the son of King Hezekiah, because of all the things he has done at

278

Jerusalem". This Manasseh had committed many atrocities through all kinds of idolatry and the shedding of innocent blood, as you may discover in 4 Kings 21 [2 Kings 21:1-9]. On account of these evils, God punished the people of Israel, as is pointed out in Jeremiah and here [2 Kings 21:10-12; Jer. 19:3], "Because Manasseh, king of Judah, did these abominable things, outdoing the Amorites before him in wickedness, and because he led Judah into sin with his idols, this is the word of the Lord, the God of Israel, 'I will bring disaster on Jerusalem and Judah, disaster which will ring in the ears of all who hear of it'." In short, had the Jews not allowed their king to carry out uncensored wantonness, God would not have punished them. One must pluck out the eye, if it offends and throw it away, and cut off the hand or the foot [cf. Mt. 18:8ff].

How one is to depose the same, may be readily noted. It is not to be done with killing, war and rioting, but in a different manner altogether; for God has called us to peace, 1 Cor. 7:15.

Is the king or lord elected by the common people and should he commit a crime, then the people are also to depose him; failing this, they will be punished with him.

And if a small number of princes elected him, one is to report to the princes that his offensive life can no longer be tolerated and he should be ordered deposed.

Here the problem begins. For a despot undertakes to slaughter those who complain. But that does not really matter. It is more comforting to be killed for doing right, provided one acts in accordance with God's will, 1 Pet. 2:20, than to be destroyed by the hand of God later, because of the guilty one and his vice. But if you cannot bear going this way [345] and dare not undertake it, then suffer the wanton despot and be punished along with him in the end, for the hand of God is stretched out in a threatening manner.

Now should the despot not have been elected by anyone and, instead, have inherited the kingdom, I do not know how such a kingdom is to have any foundation at all. Then treat the born king as if he were a fool or a child. You still have to accept him as lord. But how is he to rule? It follows then, not as the popular saying goes, that a king's son is either a fool or a king, but rather that he is both at once: a fool and a king. The kingdom will have to be governed by other wise persons. It would be simpler therefore to make a wise person king; for it is an unfortunate and cursed land, indeed, whose king is a child [Preacher 10:16]. Those who define the term "despot" say that a despot is one who rules on the basis of his own power and ambition. Thus I do not know where the idea of inheriting a kingdom comes from, unless it be by the common agreement and consent of the people. But though such a one turns out to be a tyrant, not just anyone is entitled to depose him; for that leads to rebellion only, whereas the kingdom of God is justice, peace and joy in the Holy Spirit, Rom. 14:17. But when the entire populace is united in deposing the despot because he acts against God, then it is with God (or at least, in large measure), so that a rebellion may be prevented thereby. Thus, had the children of Israel deposed Manasseh in that manner, God would not have punished them along with him [2 Kings 21]. You say, when does it ever happen that the larger God-fearing part of the nation is one? Answer: When there is no unanimity I say, once again, that you ought to bear the yoke of the despot and when you are punished with him in the end, do not complain. For I, too, wondered at times why God punishes the poor nation on account of kings or rulers. Now I am [346] no longer puzzled. Why do we not act toward the neighbor according to the content of the law of nature? We would then not need any authority, since we would all be like brothers. In other words, why do not all of us love justice above all else and hate evil? Then we should certainly all be agreed in deposing the despot. But since we are so lax in our love of common justice, we allow all vices of the despots to continue and are rightly torn asunder by them and punished along with them in the end.

There is no lack of counsel or of ways to depose the despots; what is lacking is common piety. Take heed, you tyrants. The gospel shall raise up righteous people. Become righteous too, and you will be borne up on hands. But should you fail to do so and acquire unjust goods by force, you will be trampled under foot.

THE FORTY-THIRD ARTICLE

In short, the dominion of the one who rules with God alone is the best and most stable; but the dominion of one who rules by his own whim, is the worst and most insecure.

This Article is informed by the entire Old Testament. Whenever the Jews adhered to God and clung to his commandments, they fared well in temporal affairs also. But whenever they turned away from God, they brought great affliction upon themselves. This is true to this day. Our affairs of state and government remain firm when they are grounded upon the Rock which cannot be moved. Then again, when we build upon sand, i.e. upon insecure human counsel, our state of affairs shall be moved by winds and torrential waters and shall tumble down, Mt. 7:25, Lk. 6:49. For whoever puts his trust in a bamboo stick will be lost, Isa. 36:6. And again, as Solomon says in Prov. 7:2 [347], "Son, honor the Lord and you shall be strong, and fear none other, apart from him; whoever clings to God's word, shall not be moved."

Therefore, let all governments, be they ever so small, be bold and unperturbed, as long as they abide by the teaching of Christ. God will not suffer them to perish; though he might permit them to suffer tribulation, he will, nonetheless, show them a happy end so that they will be able to bear afflictions, 1 Cor. 10:13. You know well that it is not any less an effort to keep things which have been won than to win them, in the first place. Thus, believers who want to remain in the faith, cannot achieve this by sleeping; rather, they will have to stay awake and work constantly. But God be praised for ever, for using us in the service of his word by which he is always victorious in life as well as in death. The attacks of the papists will not cease, of course, but we who believe, may take comfort in the fact that they have reached the end of their rope and we must persevere like them. Should we stand upon Christ Jesus, the Rock, they may storm against it until they split their heads, but we shall not be moved. Well may they fight, but they shall not ever be able to overcome.

For Christ is higher and cannot be hit by them, though they had twice as many weapons.

Remain in the fellowship and love of God and he will remain in us and we in him, and let him finally fight out the matter. He shall give us counsel and power so that a single one of us will be able to drive away his thousands and twenty thousands, Deut. 32:30. But remain only in the liberty to which Christ has led you, and do not allow yourself to be put under the yoke of anti-Christian servitude, Gal. 5:1.

No more on this Article; I said enough on this matter in the thirty-ninth Article, above. [348]

THE FORTY-FOURTH ARTICLE

ON PRAYER

True worshipers call on God in spirit and in truth, without any clamoring before people.

Enough has been said on this Article earlier, when I stated that no prayer is more pleasing to God than that in which he is truly known and truly called upon, with a heart free of all doubt; not, indeed, in hypocrisy, but rather in true confession and knowledge. As Moses calls on God anxiously in his heart, in Exodus 14:15, yet does not move his lips at all. As did Hannah in 1 Sam. 1:13; she did not shout out loudly. As Christ, Mt. 6:7 forbade excessive prattle, and taught instead, the true worship in spirit and in truth, John 4:24, in which context he also frees us from being bound to specific places, saying that God does not desire to be called on more fervently in one place than in another. Rather, in every place where God is called upon in Spirit and in truth, he says, "Here I am".

THE FORTY-FIFTH ARTICLE

Hypocrites do their works to be seen by people, they receive their reward in this world.

So that one may recognize the hypocrisy which passes for worship, I have placed this Article right after the above. Here are the very words of Christ which he speaks about the scribes and pharisees in Mt. 23:5, "They do all their works to be seen by people". Christ paints them thus, not I. Since Christ commands us in Mt. 6:1-18 not to become like the hypocrites in the giving of alms, in prayer and fasting (they do their prayers in places where they know the greatest number of people gather), but to go into our chamber [340] when we desire to pray, and to close the door after us, and there to call on our heavenly Father in secret, it follows that now all those who do their prayers in public are like the hypocrites whom Christ scolds here. It follows, further, that we receive our reward just like the hypocrites of whom he says in the same context, "Truly I say to you; they have their reward". Accordingly, it follows that those who bring their works out in the open before the world, are hypocrites. If they are hypocrites, they do their works to be seen by people. And thus their work is nothing but hypocrisy; consequently they have their reward.

Any objection [1] with reference to the choral singing of the Psalms which the majority does not understand anyhow, is of no avail here; I do not even speak of chanting fools, those nuns, [2] who the world over do not understand a single verse of the Psalms which they drone out. Should it not be good, they say, to sing out God's praises before all people? Answer: Prove to me that it is good, and I will believe it to be good. God alone is good and the sole fountain of every good [Mt. 19:17; Jer. 2:13]. Now, if the mumbling of Psalms is good, it must needs be of God. But show me where God ordered such droning, stammering and mumbling. Look, how you stand like a cat before the furrier [3] for you actually find the exact opposite, namely, that God bid you go into your closet and there in a secret place speak with your heavenly Father. He will surely see and hear you and grant your request. If you were devout, you would be alone. Devotion diminishes in great crowds, unless, of course, one were to instruct the multitude in God's word, or else a few were to discuss among themselves the meaning of the word of God, of which Paul speaks in Col. 3:16, "Let the Word of Christ be or dwell richly among you in all wisdom, so that you [350] may teach and warn one another in Psalms, in the praise of God and in spiritual songs which you sing to the Lord in your hearts, in all love."

Paul does not teach here to shout or mumble in temples. Rather, he shows the true song which is pleasing to God and that we should sing to laud and praise God, not with the voice, like cantors among the Jews, but rather with the heart. And this happens when we discuss with each other the Psalms and the praise of God which the prophets also sang to him in their hearts and chambers, thus instructing and admonishing one another through them. Therefore, it is my earnest advice that instead of mumbling the Psalms, they might be read and expounded so that you discover the beautiful meaning of the Holy Spirit which is found in them. In like manner I also speak concerning other books of scripture. By this a person would be nourished daily and those who are called to the office of preaching would be instructed in scripture so that they do not altogether knead around in it with unwashed hands and feet.

NOTES

1. "Widerbefftzen" means literally "to bark".

2. "Sengel nurren" - a singing female fool; sengeln has a derogatory meaning; Nurr means "female simpleton". Cf. **Idiotikon** IV 786.

3. The statement is similar in meaning to the proverb "one should not take a beautiful cat to the furrier". Cf. Wander, II 1196, N. 613.

THE FORTY-SIXTH ARTICLE

Thus it follows that chanting and loud clamor, without true devotion and done for money only, either seek human praise or else material gain.

The meaning is, that chants which are performed for money and without any devotion, take place simply in order that one may be praised for one's spirituality or to make some money; both these intentions are utterly evil. And it is more evil still that such trickery is performed before people's noses taking them for a costly ride. [1] To this they make their first retort, "But when it is done with devotion, it is not evil". I answer: Did you hear that you ought not value any work too highly, be it ever so good. For were we granted to do that, we should esteem our work so highly that even God would hardly [351] be able to pay for it. Whether a work is good, depends on God only; it has to come from him. Accordingly, devotion does not parade itself before people, as a foolish paramour might; it seeks secrecy. There it is best able to pour itself out before God, for neither sight nor sound draws its attention away from meditation. It is against human reason to expect reflection or devotion amidst great clamor and noise. In addition, a person's devotion is so short and quick that one cannot be devout in heart or words for too long; in one's inward mind and thoughts, however, one may be able to prolong devotion a bit longer. From this we learn that those who greatly long for choral chants are either fools or very childish: Fools, because they have not yet learned to know what the true worship is. For had they learned to know that, they would not allow themselves to be misled by this moaning. Childish, since like children they love to sing and hear singing, though they do not understand what they sing. Indeed, I speak the truth when I tell you that I consider singing for a reward to be more evil than good. For what else do children do, who roam the streets, singing and distorting their mouths to utter strange words which neither they nor anyone else can understand? In like fashion, the majority of monks and priests sing too; they understand little of what they sing. Yet we have to reward them or else they will stop singing. On this point I have given sufficient proof earlier to show that it is not our works that save, but God's mercy with which even those funeral pipers [2] will have to be saved, not through their own works.

They retort secondly, "Is it not by far better to be like this inside the church than to be idle or occupied with playing chess? Answer: Lord have mercy. That you have come to this: comparing your beautiful worship to nothing better than idleness and chess playing. Should you put your worship on that level, I will have to reply that spinning would be better [352] than idleness or chess playing. How would it be, devout father, were you, in fact, to spin or reel? But you are actually too strong for that. How would it be were we to make you split wood or plow the fields, since you have to do something against idleness? In this way you help the common person in his work at the same time; you are certainly firm and fat. O God, how one has to entertain you in such delightful manner. Please, oblige me and read the 14th chapter of 1 Cor. [1 Cor. 14:19]. You will find there that Paul prefers to speak five words with understanding for the edification of others than to speak ten thousand words in tongues. Now I hope you will similarly work, as has been indicated above, in the spirit of scripture and leave the unintelligible words alone.

And should you insist on being joyful in the spirit, it will not last long. Therefore do it as long as heart and words are unanimous in the matter; I don't doubt for a moment that you will actually never sing in that case, for he says in the same context [1 Cor. 14:15], "When I intend to sing a Psalm with my breath, it should be from the heart," i.e. should you intend to say a Psalm with your mouth, see to it that heart and mouth harmonize in the matter. Now even in prayer, heart and mind are usually not together for long, much less, heart and song. Read the entire chapter and you will find that the highest office among Christians is to bring about a clear understanding of the word of God, so that all the multitude may be taught.

To wit, Amos in the Old Testament rejected singing in Chapter 5:23, "Put aside the mumbling of your songs, for I do not desire the song of your lyre." What would this peasant prophet do in our generation, could he see and hear the many different kinds of music in our temples, the many beats of the danse par bas, [3] trills, hops and other measures, and amidst all that see the [353] delicate choirmasters in their silken shirts, approaching the altar to sacrifice? Surely he would again shout so forcefully that the entire world could not tolerate his words.

Look at this child's play in our temples. It costs so much sweat and labor; though it does not touch anyone's heart, one has to continue, nonetheless, to nourish this hypocrisy (I almost said idolatry). And this does not happen without great sin, for it is either looked upon as excessive honor or as a sensual pleasure or else as gain, and you will not find any reference in all of scripture to worship for a fee. For the word, "the worker is worthy of his hire", Lk. 10:7 does not refer to this particular thing.

Therefore, let no one shy away from eliminating this clamor from the temples and from ordering, instead, learned persons to come and expound the word of God faithfully, and from giving the remaining goods to the poor and needy, but in such a way that no disturbance is caused by it, unless, of course, wanton priests allow no other course of action. Adieu to all mumbling in the temple. I am not at all sorry--in fact, I know well that I am not sorry at all. But welcome, oh pious inward prayer, awakened by the word of God in the hearts of the faithful. You arise as a little sigh, briefly made in self-knowledge, and then you subside to listen again. Welcome also, public prayer which all Christians render [354] for one another, be it openly in the temple or in their rooms, but free and without remuneration. I know that you are the prayer which God will grant a hearing, in keeping with his promise.

NOTES

1. ". . .zu eim geltkloben fuer die nasen usssteckt und innso tuer verkoufft." A "geltkloben" is described as a tool to catch yellow birds, which then fetch good money. Cf. **Idiotikon** III 620.

2. Zwingli means the priests who celebrate mass in return for monetary contributions. Cf. Mt. 9:23.

3. Cf. Z.II 352, note 16. Among the oldest dances preserved with musical notations are the slow "Danse par bas" and the faster "Danse par haut". Zwingli was obviously familiar with popular musical forms of the day.

THE FORTY-SEVENTH ARTICLE

CONCERNING OFFENCES

A person should suffer physical death reather than offend or disgrace a Christian.

The word "scandlizein" means not only "to offend", but also "to disgrace".

Let me speak of disgrace first. Christ does not intend to suggest in Mt. 18:6-10 that those who give public offence should then be publicly disgraced, unless they mend their ways. Rather he teaches there how one ought to exercise the ban. He also wishes his own not to be disgraced just because they are considered to be insignificant. With this viewpoint he sought to remove pride from among Christians, so that one should not set himself up above another or despise another; for whoever does so, were better off drowned. [1] Where now are those devout bishops who forbade incontinent priests to take wives and who thus turned into bastards the children who could and should have been born legitimately? And those whom God had granted life, they disgraced before all the world while they were still in their mother's womb. [355]

Indeed, no one should look upon this very grave sin as if it does not affect him. Almost every person is guilty here, for they all reject God's creatures. And yet, these innocent children have their spots only from those who disgrace God's creation, and not from God himself. Therefore it is good for everyone to give attention to the marriage of priests so that we may get out of the great sin by which we disgrace and despise God's creatures. How great this sin really is, Christ teaches us himself in Mt. 18:6f, "Whoever offends, disgraces or angers one of the little ones that believes in me, would be better off had he a millstone tied to his neck and to be dropped to the bottom of the sea. Woe to the world on account of disgrace or offence. There will have to be offences; but woe to the person through whom such offence is brought about or caused." These words of Christ teach us clearly enough how serious it is to disgrace one who is God's, according to the first meaning of offence, namely the meaning which S. Chrysostom also gives to this passage.

Secondly, these words of Christ refer to the giving of offence which is nothing other than the shamelessness of sin before people or an injury to and intimidation of the weak conscience by which it is made more evil or by which it develops disgust for the good, which it does not know as yet.

Of such shameful sinning, Christ speaks here in Mt. 18:6, saying that it is so grave a sin before God when one spoils or causes to backslide one of the little ones with shameless sins, that it were better for an offender to have a millstone tied around his neck and be drowned. Therefore he instituted the ban in [356] the same place [Mt. 18:15-18] so that the shameless sinner might be cut off just like a sick member of the body, to prevent the disease from affecting the entire body.

Further, every Christian ought to make concessions to the weak who think something (which does not really affect the faith), to be wrong which is not, rather than to intimidate them with force, because he himself is well instructed and will not be hurt, as Paul indicates in Rom. 14:[2-6]. [3] The one knows that he is entitled to eat any kind of food; he makes use of his knowledge as often as he pleases. The other is not as firm in the faith. Rather, he thinks that it is not always right. Should now the knowledgeable person eat before such a one [i.e. a weak person], the latter will show aversion and condemn the eater as if he were an evildoer and blasphemer. In such things the knowledgeable person should make concessions to the weak one, until he too becomes knowledgeable; unless, of course, it is a matter not of weakness but of stubbornness.

In a similar vein, Paul speaks in 1 Cor. 8:13, [4] "If the food offends my brother, I must no longer eat meat so as not to offend my brother". Paul means, of course, that as long as he knows his brother to be offended by his eating of meat, and provided it is an offence rather than an idiosyncracy, he is willing to protect him by simply not eating meat in his presence.

He proved this very thing with regard to Timothy. He had the latter circumcised according to Jewish custom, Acts 16:3, though he knew circumcision to be of no avail. [5] But he did this to humor the Jews, so that he might not turn them away from the faith.

Thus we have distinguished three kinds of scandals, i.e. offences. The first is to disgrace the neighbor (understood is, undeservedly).

The second is to corrupt and anger the neighbor by shameless sins which are genuinely evil and which are to be controlled by use of the ban. [357]

The third is to intimidate the weak in the faith who thinks something to be a sin which is not a sin, as for example, to eat meat on special days, to disregard feast days (which we now observe), not to buy indulgences, not having masses read for payment, marrying--though monks, nuns and priests do it,--not to fear the falsely imposed ban and such-like countless things which have been forced upon us by the hypocrites, as if God commanded all these and as if he were served through them. Concerning all these minutiae [6] the forty-eighth Article is to be heeded.

NOTES

1. Cf. Zwingli's sermon **On Fasting,** March 23, 1522 (Z.I 111ff).

2. See Zwingli's **Supplicatio** (Z.I 197ff) and his **Freundliche Bitte** (Z.I 214ff).

3. **Von Erkiesen und Freiheit der Speisen** (Z.I 114.4ff).

4. Ibid., 116.11ff.

5. Ibid., 119.3ff.

6. Guesel - trash, irrelevant matter.

THE FORTY-EIGHTH ARTICLE

One who, because of infirmity or ignorance, tends to take offence without any cause, should not be left weak or ignorant. Rather, he should be strengthened so that he may not regard as sinful what is not sinful at all.

In the first two types of offence [1] no one should be taught to tolerate injustice or to think it no sin at all. Rather, great care ought to be taken to avoid being soiled and to evade the offender. For this very offence is such an evil vice that our Lord pronounced his "woe" over it, as we noted above. Methinks that in that context Christ actually meant the first two types of offence.

Of the offence which is no more than a form of intimidation, we shall soon have said enough.

When you see that your brother is weak, and that he considers something to be a sin which you well know not to be a sin at all, you ought not intimidate him or cause him to withdraw into himself. First and foremost he is to be informed that your doings are not sinful at all; or else your knowledge in matters of faith might serve [358] to someone else's hurt and condemnation, 1 Cor. 8:7-13. Rather, you ought to teach him not to consider as sinful what is not sinful at all. But do this, not by artful schemes (for thereby you only make a person more and more doubtful and curious how such a thing could possibly happen). Rather, you ought to teach him through the pure and bold word of God and say with Deut. 4:2 and 12:32, "You shall not add or subtract anything from the word of God, doing only that which he bids you do". For this reason, dear brother, you must consider only that to be a sin which God considers to be sin and which he forbids; you must be diligent only in the works which God has commanded. But should you think it possible to honor him with things other than those which he commanded, you must know that you commit a double sin; first, by imagining everything your foolish head has invented to be pleasing to God; secondly, in that generally those who undertake such works, will leave undone the things which God commands.

Or else say to him that one does not add anything to the last will and testament of a person; similarly, no one is entitled to add anything to God's testament [Gal. 3:15]. Therefore, that alone is sin which God has forbidden and only that is right which God has commanded. Don't be so weak. God did not intend thus to scare off all his creatures. [2] This form of strengthening, Paul teaches in Rom. 14:1-3, "Help one who is weak in the faith so that he will not become even more doubtful in his mind. The one is certain in his faith about being able to eat everything, but the weak among you should eat cabbage. But one who can eat everything without fear, should not despise another who does not eat everything. But neither should one who, because of his weakness not dare eat everything, condemn or judge the one who eats, etc." Read the entire chapter.

Therefore guardians [bishops] should always seek to remove the offence, i.e. they should preach and teach earnestly what God and what human laws [359] have forbidden. They should not forever torture the poor conscience in the prison house of human statutes. It will then happen that all the world shall listen to the one word of God and pursue his works diligently and that all torturing of poor consciences shall be removed, and instead of such castigations there shall grow piety, peace and joy in the Holy Spirit [Rom. 14:17]. At this point one ought to hold up for ridicule certain fools who practice the very opposite, when they stand in their pulpits and shout, "God have mercy on us. Are we to eat meat during times of fasting? Are the priests to lie beside their wives and then be permitted to celebrate mass? How could that ever be right? They will often have hardly cooled off before they will have to get up from their beds of adultery." But let the priest preach whatever concerns him, the peasant shall not pay anything. [3] I shan't, as I ought, scold their unseemly behavior. I rather hope that they will put on a new garment which is fitted in the image of Christ.

Now the quick witted ones will say at this point, "How long do I have to show consideration for the weak?" Answer: Until he is strong and cannot be hurt anymore. You say: In his case all effort is so much wasted breath; he does not believe a single word I tell him. Answer: Then you should immediately try another tack. You will have to see whether a majority of the rest [360] of the people take offence. Should you find that the larger but more intelligent part does not take offence, then rely joyfully upon Christian freedom, provided that no more division or disadvantage to the teaching of Christ is wrought thereby. By "intelligent" I do not here mean the wise of this world, but rather those who are well grounded in the word of God. You say: But how many people or nations do I have to consider? Is it enough to take into account my parish? Answer: Yes, indeed, as long as this does not put it at a great disadvantage in relation to other people. Otherwise, everyone ought to deprive himself not only of small things, but leave father, mother, wife and child also, [Mt. 10:37] in order that the teaching of Christ be not dislodged. But those who put their trust in God, need not be anxious when they are about to break the bonds of human minutiae; for God shall lead them aright.

That one should not always make concessions to the weak person--lest one never attain to Christian freedom--but at the appropriate time should stop giving into him, Paul teaches in Gal. 2:3, in that he did not allow Titus to be circumcised when earlier he had allowed Timothy to be thus circumcised; undoubtedly he was not able to liberate Timothy, whereas he did liberate Titus. We are to do likewise with due respect of persons. Whenever we are able to exercise Christian liberty without offence to the majority of people, we should do so; whenever this is not possible, we ought to make concessions and keep on teaching earnestly. But when one single individual, who is unwilling to be guided, has all the power in his hands, I suggest that one make concessions to him again and again in the things which do not concern us that much, as long as it is impossible to extract oneself from his power. And should the parish not take offence in the things which concern the salvation of the soul (e.g. unchastity condemns us; but marital relations are not sin), one must not give in, though a despot were to look upon us with a sour mien or even kill us, for we ought to suffer death rather than offend even the least of God's children. And if the majority of the righteous do not take offence, we ought to accept responsibility. [4] [361]

NOTES

1. See the previous summary of offences in Article 47, toward the end.

2. The proverb "Einen ins Bockshorn jagen" means to force or intimidate someone.

3. "Der Pfaff las, daran im was" means "the priest read whatever concerned (interested) him most.

4. "Uff den Hals nemmen".

THE FORTY-NINTH ARTICLE

I know of no greater offence than to forbid priests to have wives, yet allow them to engage prostitutes. [1]

This Article rests solely upon my own judgment, for it seems to me that from the shameless adultery which above-mentioned priests commit, the greatest vices in all the world have arisen. My reason is as follows: The prophet or teacher who points out people's vices, should be above reproach or criticism, Tit. 1:6, so that it cannot be said to him, "physician heal yourself" [Lk. 4:23]. Why do you not punish yourself, first of all, by removing the beam in your own eye, before getting at the little speck in my eye? [Mt. 7:5]. Your vice is by so much greater and more serious than mine, by which you are a leader and I am not. Everyone looks at your vice. And the good you teach and do, shall always be measured by the evil work and the vice which clings to you. Therefore Paul, not without reason and in order to avoid such weaknesses, bade bishops or guardians to take only one wife. He knew well that to maintain purity was not given to everyone, yet that everyone would be looking to the guardian to see how he conducts himself. Therefore he tried to prevent others from taking too great an offence and ordered him [the bishop] to take only one wife. Should he not have one, however, (and there are very few, indeed, who are continent--I say nothing of those who are pure, of course), and should he not be able to live chastely, he either has his own concubine, as he sees fit, or else sleeps with the wives of others. [362] But when he keeps a concubine openly, and should then want to punish an adulterer by forcing him to return to his wife, the same might say to him, "My dear priest, are you short sighted? When are you going to recognize your own weakness?" And should he admonish the soldier, the same will retort, "May the devil get that adulterous priest." Any greedy and arrogant person, as well as every sinner who is angered by the priest, will act likewise. And those even who otherwise willingly heard the word of God whenever they heard it from the priest, will say either, "O God, he teaches well enough, but lives deplorably," or else, "He teaches well in the matter, but lives a wicked life. Therefore I consider the matter less serious than he makes it out to be. For if hell were as hot as he makes it out to be, he too would be more careful." They fall into unbelief when they see the godlessness of the priests. But when he does not have his own concubine then no one is safe from him, not even his mother or sister. I shall not speak of how they fared at times, as God well knows. In short, I know of no greater offence than the shameless adultery of priests. It has aided and abetted all other vices. [2]

The reason why this great vice is not being eradicated and why both spiritual and temporal lords allow this despicable evil to grow unchecked in their jurisdiction when they refuse the marriage of priests, must be sought in the fact that the great, wanton bishops place greater value on their money bags than do millers on their flour bags. They sold licences [2] to the powerful for such high sums that everyone had to fear not being able to raise the necessary income, should the tax on concubines ever be stopped; or else they are still so ignorant of the truth [363] that they dare not yet support it. I shall speak to you with absolute honesty. Tell these sensual priests to put away their concubines or else to marry them, lest you become guilty of their very vices. Are you blind? Don't you see why the bishops refuse to lift the vow of chastity though they see that not even a fraction [of priests] keeps this law? Yes, you say, there are too many priests. I answer: let them resign and turn their income over to the poor. Yes, and their women want to be leading ladies in the communities. [4] Then give them so much that they will be glad to be left alone, like ungracious women. But make every effort to have these shameful, horrible offences eradicated. They are nothing but fables which the hypocrites dished out who always talked of such hypocritical chastity. Chastity is readily commanded, but no one is capable of it, except one to whom God grants it.

NOTES

1. Cf. Z.I 197 and 214 for earlier expressions of Zwingli's concern on the matter.

2. Zwingli was "secretly" betrothed to Anna Reinhard since the spring of 1522. The marriage was not made public until 2 April, 1524. It is possible that his sharp attack here reflects his own inner tension on the matter. As early as the summer of 1521, reports of marriages of priests were made to Zwingli. Cf. Z.I 227 n. 2.

3. The so-called "Saeckzoll", a yearly fee paid to the bishop by priests who desired a concubine, seems to have been widely used. In the diocese of Constance alone 1500 children were born in one year to women who thus cohabited with priests. Cf. Z.I 225, especially n. 6 and 226, notes 1 and 2.

4. The term is "gnadfrouwen". A gracious woman--a woman of stature. Cf. **Idiotikon** I 1245. Zwingli raised the matter of pastor's wives as early as 1522. Cf. Z.I 245.23ff.

THE FIFTIETH ARTICLE

ON REMISSION OF SIN

God alone remits sin through Jesus Christ his Son, our only Lord.

This Article has fortunately fallen under this number which is significant as a symbol of the remittance of sin; for in the fiftieth year, all purchases and services among the people of Israel were also lifted [cf. Lev. 25:10-55].

That God alone remits sin is apparent, for nothing is sin than that which is directed against the word of God. Hence it follows [364] that he alone remits sin, since no one can forgive on behalf of another.

But the testimony of scripture will make the matter clear.

David says in Ps. 50 [51:6], "Lord against you only have I sinned." Is sin harmful simply because it is against God, it would needs follow that no one other than God alone is capable of remitting the same; for God alone is good who guides, nourishes, heals, restores and saves us.

Deut. 32:12, "The Lord alone was his leader, etc."

In Isa. 43:25-27 God speaks through the prophet, "I alone, I am he, who cancels your sin for my own sake and who will not remember your sin anymore. Remember me and let us come to terms with each other. Say, do you have anything by which you may be made righteous or innocent? Your first father has sinned and your spokesmen have acted vilely against me."

These words of Isaiah have been so well attested to everywhere that they cannot be disproved anywhere.

298

First of all, God himself shows himself a second time: I myself, I indeed, and no other God or creature am he who cancels your sin [Isa. 43:25].

Secondly, he forgives sin for his own sake and not on account of our own work. He forgives in such a way that he never recalls sins nor punishes former wrong.

Thirdly, he places humankind over against himself, bidding human beings to evaluate and judge him, calling him to remember God and then to present anything that may concern him so that he might support his righteousness; undoubtedly in the opinion that we poor sinners have nothing. [365]

Fourthly, he shows how impotent and impure we are, ever since our first father who sinned. From this it follows that he also produced sinful and dead sons.

Fifthly, that even the advocates sinned and have been sinners, though they mediated between the people and God, as did Moses and the prophets.

Now then, to state the matter briefly, there is no one who should think that sin may be remitted by anyone other than God, against whom alone it is committed. Although some of it is against the neighbor, it is, nonetheless, a sin which God who also gave the commandment concerning the neighbor, has bid us avoid. Now the papists are an exception here, for they ascribe to the pope the ability to remit sin because he is said to be a descendant of Peter and it is said that to Peter were given the keys of heaven, to bind and to free. And because of this, their opinion, they infringed on the word of God with such force that to this day there are many learned Christians who cannot get out from under the pope's power of the keys. But some in our day have written with partly a good and sound opinion that the power of the keys is not the pope's at all. But what the power of the keys really is, I have not found properly dealt with in any of them.

Now we, too, have to get at this problem and if we can get scripture to be on our side, all matters concerning the remission of sin, confession, works of penance, shall thereafter become clear.

Mt. 16:13-19 states it thus, "When Jesus came near Caesarea Philippi he asked his disciples saying, 'Who [336] do people say that I am?' And they answered him, 'Some say John the Baptist, others say Elijah, and others Jeremiah or one of the prophets.' He said to them, 'But who do you say that I am? Simon Peter replied, 'You are the Christ, the Son of the living God.' And

Jesus answered him, 'Blessed are you, Simon Bar-Jonah. For flesh and blood has not revealed this to you, but my Father who is in heaven. And I tell you, you are Peter, and on this rock I will build my church, and the powers of death shall not prevail against it. I will give you the keys of the kingdom of heaven, and whatever you bind on earth shall be bound in heaven and whatever you loose on earth shall be loosed in heaven.'" These words, the papists have taken rather clumsily into their hands because on first sight they do look not unlike their own undertakings; in fact, they deceived almost everyone through this, for they failed to fathom the manner in which Christ and his disciples spoke.

Christ often asked his disciples about things which he himself well knew. Often also he addressed all of them, though only one answered him in each case. It follows therefore that what he said subsequently was not intended only for the one who had given the answer on behalf of the others. Rather, it was intended for all those on whose behalf the speaker replied. All this shall soon be made clear through scripture.

In this connection it is essential to know that the writers of the gospels speak of all the disciples together when they refer to what has been said, since it [367] should be quite clear that they did not all prattle at one and the same time, but that one spoke in the name of the others. But as it happens, a specific writer of the gospel mentions the one by name who spoke on behalf of the others. We, too, are in the habit of doing so. If for example a council makes a reply to someone, the one might say, "mylords, gave me this answer", while another one might say, "the mayor answered", though it was not the reply of the mayor, but of the entire council.

I shall now support my argument:

Mk. 6:38, when Christ was about to feed the multitudes, writes as follows, "And he asked, how many loaves of bread do you have?" and when they checked this out, they replied, "We have five loaves and two fish". Now it is stated here that he asked them all and that they all replied, though it was Andrew who answered him on behalf of the others; now Mark does not mention him at all in this connection, but John does in chapter 6 [Jn. 6:8f], as follows, "Then one of his disciples, Andrew, a brother of Simon Peter, said, 'There is a boy here who has five loaves and two fish.'" Here, too, Andrew pointed out to the Lord in the name of all the others, how much bread they had been able to find; for he had asked them all and bid them investigate, Mk. 6:38. Here, too, Christ asked all his disciples, as the words clearly indicate, "But who do you say that I am?" Now, though Peter answered on everyone's behalf, the words are not only his; it must be noted carefully that had the other disciples not made reply through Peter, they would--much as they did at the time of the Lord's Supper when everyone for himself asked whether he was the betrayer--have had to answer, everyone for himself, whom they thought Jesus to be; for [368] this his question is a question of salvation. Whoever believes that Christ is the Son of the living God, is in God and God is in him, 1 Jn. 4:15. Therefore Peter answers on behalf of all the others. This is not my own senseless prattle or my vivid imagination. The words of Peter himself point to this meaning in Jn. 6:67-69, "When Christ spoke to the twelve, 'Do you also want to leave me?' Simon Peter replied, 'Lord, to whom shall we go? You have words of eternal life and we know that and believe it, for you are Christ, the Son of the living God'." Peter speaks quite clearly here, "We believe and know, etc" and from that it is unmistakable that all twelve disciples had the very same faith in Christ as did Peter. Now from this it follows that the power of the keys is not only Peter's, but belongs to all the disciples and to us. In other words, it has been promised to all believers through the disciples, provided we are able to say with them that Jesus is the Christ, Son of the living God.

But before we continue, we have to speak of Peter's name, upon which the papists claim the church to have been built; this is sheer idolatry. Christ said to Peter [Mt. 16:17], "Blessed are you, Peter (i.e., "good for you", according to the Hebrew), for flesh and blood did not reveal this to you, but the heavenly Father." From this we conclude that to confess Christ Son of God does not come out of the human heart, but is the result of divine inspiration.

It follows further [Mt. 16:18], "And I say to you, that you are a man of the rock and upon the rock I shall build my church." Christ says in the first instance, "And I say to you that you are a man of the rock", as if to say, "You say of me, in the name of all the others, as Jn. 6:69 [369] indicates clearly, that I am the Son of God. And I say to you, in turn, that you, the son of Jonas, shall henceforth be called Peter, as I have promised you, which means 'man of the rock' because of the firm and solid confession. This [promise] Christ made when Andrew, Simon's brother, introduced him to Christ for the first time and when Christ said, Jn. 1:43, "You are Simon son of Jonah, you shall be called Cephas, which means a man of the rock." Note in this connection, Mt. 16:18 where he gives the promised name to Simon.

With regard to this name, the pope errs in two ways.

First of all, he says that the phrase, "and upon this rock I shall build my church," refers to Peter and all subsequent popes. Yet, Christ did not say, "upon this man of the rock I shall build my church." He said, "upon the rock after which I named you,

I shall build my church." He did not stay with the man of the rock, but turned again to the very rock from which he derived the name and upon which he, along with all other believers, is grounded. For, had the church been built upon Peter, it would have tumbled at the very moment when he denied Christ by an oath.

Far be it from us to claim a creature to be the foundation of the church, i.e. of believers. Such would be sheer idolatry and definitely against the express words of Christ and Paul. Christ refers to himself the words of Psalm 117 [118:22] in Mt. 21:42, "The stone which the builders rejected, has become the chief cornerstone." This stone can be none other than the Lord Christ Jesus, as Peter himself teaches in 1 Pet. 2:6. And Paul also says in 1 Cor. 3:11, "No one else can establish any other foundation than that which has been laid, which is Christ Jesus." [370]

It follows then that Peter cannot be the foundation or ground of the church; for there can be no other than Christ. If then Christ is the true rock and foundation of all believers who assures that the house, built upon him, cannot be moved, it must follow also that everyone who confesses him (as Peter and all the disciples had done), will be named after the rock, "a man of the rock". Just as we, along with Mary Magdalene, choose the best part when we cling to Christ alone. And Magdalene did not lose anything, because Christ said of her, "She has chosen the best part" [Lk. 10:12]. Just as he also says, "Whoever does the will of the Father, is my brother, sister and mother" [Mt. 12:50]. Should anyone do his will, he does not thereby deprive Mary of any of the honor of being Mother of God.

In short, those who believe, as the disciples and Peter believed, that Christ is the Son of the living God, are built upon the Rock and are therefore called "men of the rock".

Augustine, too, is of this opinion and stated it clearly in his Homily on the Feast of Peter and Paul. [1] And the priests read this homily in all the churches of the diocese of Constance, yet they do not have ears, sufficient to perceive how Augustine understood the words "the man of the rock" and "the rock". They shout rather, heretic, heretic and pray such words, thus turning Augustine and themselves into heretics. [371]

I will now have to say a few brief words here. Augustine spoke as follows about these words: Therefore, Christ is the rock. But Peter, the man of the rock, are the Christians, for "petra"-rock is the original name. Accordingly, the man of the rock is named so after the rock and not after himself, in the same way in which Christ is not named after Christians, but rather, Christians are named after Christ, etc. [2]

Similarly, Christ built his church, i.e. the congregation, upon the rock which he himself is and not upon the man of the rock.

Now let no simple person think that there had to be something like this, after all, since Christ changed Peter's name; for the names of other disciples, too, had been changed--above all that of James and John [Mk. 3:17]. "Boanerges" they were called which means "sons of thunder", a name as much closer to that great power as thunder is heard and feared more by people.

He errs, secondly, with regard to Peter's name, not only according to what Jerome [3] teaches, but also according to what the evangelist John [372] himself indicates in Jn. 1:42. The pope claims that "Cephas" means as much in our language as "caput" or "head", by which he makes Peter and himself also a head. Yet, St. John says in chapter 1:43, "You shall be called Cephas, i.e. Peter, man of the rock," in translation. Note the holy evangelist explains this word of Christ, "Cephas" (which is Syrian), so that we might understand it. We are told that it means as much as "a man of the rock", yet the pope tells us that it means "head". What shall we do to this forger? Were one to forge papal letters, one would have to forfeit one's life for that. Yet the pope forges Christ's words and takes the lives of those who say what the evangelist John says: Anti-Christ.

Further, in the words of Christ [Mt. 16:18], "And the gates of hell shall not overcome it". Tell me, papist, to whom does this small word "it" point? You will have to say that it points either to the man of the rock or to the church. If it points to the man of the rock, then the meaning is that the gates of hell shall not overcome the rock which is Christ. If it points to the church, i.e. to the believers in Christ, then the meaning is that the gates of hell cannot overcome the believers who are built upon the rock, Christ.

By gates of hell you ought to understand the strength of hell or the devil which he calls the gates, because gates are usually the strongest part of the building, fortified by guns and armed men. And the meaning of all these words is that no one is able to overcome the rock upon which I shall build my church, [373] be it ever so great a power; no one will be able to take it by storm when it is built and founded upon me. Indeed, all power of the devil cannot harm it. The devil no longer has either right or power where Christ is believed in; and no one is able to destroy the faith of the church by which is meant all believing persons. Therefore, be unafraid all you who rightly believe. Though God should permit you to be persecuted so severely that you would have to escape into the wilderness, your faith should, nonetheless, not be diminished, let alone destroyed. For God alone gives it. And though many be killed for it, there will also be many who come to God.

Now let us turn to the power of the keys [Mt. 16:19], "And I shall give you the keys of the kingdom of heaven." The papists do not agree among themselves concerning these words. Some of them maintain that in these words Christ gave Peter the keys. Others argue that he only promised them here; these latter are right, too. But as soon as one comes to them, claiming the same power for the other disciples, they are at the end of their rope. But Christ's words are clear when he says, "I shall give you the keys of the kingdom of heaven." Had he given them at that time, he would have said, "Take them; I now give you the keys, etc."--this is merely a promise of the keys, similar to the one he made to him when he called him "Peter". And although the disciples among themselves called him either Simon or Peter ever since, he only showed on this occasion the origin of [374] his name to be in the wholesome confession which he had made on behalf of the disciples that Christ is the Son of the living God.

When later on the promised keys were given him, we shall soon find out. The keys are a metaphor of "remission, liberation and unveiling"; for Christ and his disciples freed humankind from sin by proclamation of the gospel. They reconciled him with God and opened salvation for humankind which had hitherto been closed. In other words, they clearly and certainly taught through God's word how Christ has been given us by the Father to be a savior, so that all who believe this may be saved from their sins. Those, however, who do not believe this, do not have access to salvation. "The kingdom of heaven" in this context means nothing other than the word of God, for thus also Christ calls it in Lk. 8:10, "To you is given to know the mystery of the kingdom of God", i.e. the Father grants you clearly to know the word of God. But the others he seeks to attract through parables. For he says soon after [Lk. 8:11], "The seed is the word of God, etc." Now the kingdom of God is taken to mean the joy in which those find themselves who, though dead in their faith, have come to God and who delight in his presence. Sometimes it means the word of the gospel, i.e. the good and gracious doings which God has accomplished for us through Jesus Christ; and sometimes also, the word of God in general, as for example in Mt. 5:19, "Whoever does not keep the least of my commandments, yet teaches the same to people, shall be called least in the kingdom of heaven. In other words, whoever teaches beautifully, neither doing nor [375] living in accordance with the teaching, will be the most rejected among the preachers of the word of God, as is pointed out in Lk. 8:10, here, and in many other instances.

Now the meaning of these words of Christ is as follows, "I shall entrust to you, man of the rock, the preaching of the word of God, the gospel, which shows and opens to people the way of salvation".

This meaning we shall soon place clearly before everyone.

Now these words follow right after [Mt. 16:18], "Everything which you bind on earth, shall be bound in heaven, and everything which you free on earth, shall be free in heaven."

As we showed earlier, the keys in this context have only been promised; it will now be necessary also to show how they are subsequently given.

Before we do this, however, we shall show with these words how some of the Fathers understood this passage, Mt. 16:19, so that one may see what the papists have done and how they set themselves up as gods.

Jerome [4] says with regard to these words, "The bishops and priests do not understand this passage, but use it as if they had the pride of Pharisees in that they reject or condemn the innocent or think themselves able to remit sins, though God does not call for a priest's judgment, but [376] for the life of a sinner, etc." Jerome intends to say by this that binding and loosing does not depend on priests but on the sinner. Should such a one repent and improve, the priest simply indicates to him that God has forgiven his sin. But if there is a heretic somewhere who claims that neither bishop nor priest is able to forgive, then your Jerome, O papists, is a heretic also. Far be that from you.

Ambrose says regarding Eph. 2:20, "Therefore the Lord says to Peter, 'Upon this rock I shall build my church.'" In other words, in confessing the Christian faith, I give believers their life. Note here, how Ambrose understood the remitting of sin.

Therefore they are not heretics, but Christian people who do not want to leave the binding and loosing in human hands.

However, I shall have to reveal their ignorance by an objection. You papists wish to say that you have power to bind and loose. Show me that. How ought or may you bind anyone? You will say, when one deserves to be banned, we will do it; for on account of other sins God through Peter bids you forgive seventy times seven [Mt. 18:22]. Thus you cannot bind anyone after all, except through the ban. For not even your master of high [doctrinal] opinions [6] can [377] show you any other form of binding except the ban. And since you cannot find another form of binding but the ban, you must likewise understand the remitting with reference to the ban only. Thus you cannot understand from one statement which contrasts binding and loosing that the binding refers to the ban alone while the loosing refers to other sins, as well. You must take them to refer to one and the same thing. Since you think the binding refers to the ban only, you will also have to take the loosing to refer to the ban only. Thus in this particular passage you have no more than the binding and loosing of the ban, provided you are right. But actually this passage does not bestow any authority; it only promises it. Therefore I have held to the opinion that binding and loosing here and in Mt. 18:18 refer to the ban alone.

I expressed this in my **Archeteles** [7] with reference to a quarrel I then engaged in with my skillful waylayers. But now everyone can clearly see that this passage is merely a promise of the keys and that Mt. 18:15-17 institutes the ban whose nature I have sufficiently spoken about earlier.

According to this we find nowhere that either Peter of the disciples had been given any authority until after the resurrection. Only then did Christ give the promised keys to all the disciples at once and through them to us, Jn. 20:22ff. He did not give them to Peter alone, just as he had not promised them to him alone. We want to show, rather, with the aid of Christ's word that he dealt with the disciples--in this case--as a father deals with his many [378] sons. Such [a father] might say to one who has done something pleasing and who otherwise wishes to be considered higher than the others, "Jack, you are a good fellow. I intend to give you a beautiful rich wife." Now he does not intend to treat only him like this, but will do the same with all the others by providing them all with honorable daughters. And Jack does not complain because of this nor does he set himself above the others, just because he is treated properly. Rather, he is well satisfied that his father looks after them all faithfully. Similarly, Christ acted in this context, promising Peter in Mt. 16:19 that he would entrust him with the keys, without thereby committing himself to not acting the same way with all the others. But when he made this [promise], he also entrusted them to the others, and Peter suffered no harm from it. Just as the day laborer, with whom the master of the house has reached an agreement, did not suffer any loss simply because the master gave to the last person the same pay as to the first. For the first received what had been promised and he could not on that account limit the free will of his master with which he gave to the others also what pleased him, Mt. 20:12-15.

We find similar instances quite clearly stated elsewhere also.

In Lk. 5:10 he speaks to Peter alone after the wonderful

catch of fish, "Fear not, From now on you shall catch people." Now it is not said to Peter alone to catch people in the net of the divine word and to win them for God, but to [379] all the others too. Indeed, it is promised clearly to his brothers Andrew, James and John.

Mt. 4:18-21 and Mk. 1:16-20, "Come after me and I shall make of you fishers of men." Though you may not be prepared to apply these words to James and John right away, you have to apply them to Andrew. But here you see that in one instance it was said to Peter alone, "henceforth you shall catch people," but on another occasion it was said to the others also.

Similarly, in Mt. 16:18ff the sayings of Christ, when followed literally, refer to Peter, though in reality they were addressed to all the disciples, for he asked them all and Peter answered on their behalf. Thus what Christ says subsequently must also refer to them. But this matters little. There is no need to argue over this nor do we need any defence, for the keys are given to all the disciples together in Jn. 20:22ff. This does not in any way take away anything from Peter, just as the promise in Mt. 16 does not ascribe to Peter any privilege which the others do not share.

But the fact that the power of the keys has been given not only to the twelve disciples but to all of us, I substantiate by the very word of Christ in Mk. 13:37, "What I tell you, I say to everyone." If then he promised and gave the keys to the twelve disciples, he gave them by the same token, to all believers and learners. For Luke, who supports this opinion in the twelfth chapter [v.40], but omits the words, "the things I tell you, I say to everyone", does, nonetheless, contain the question of Peter which clarifies the whole matter, viz. that Christ utters the words, "the things I tell you, etc" as referring absolutely to his entire teaching and that he addresses them not only to them, but [380] to everyone. Understand it like this: After Christ had told the parable of the good householder in Lk. 12:39ff, by which he wanted to encourage the guardians to watch over the word, as he also does in Mk. 13:37, Peter says [Lk. 12:41], "Lord, do you tell this parable to us only or to all persons?" with the intention of finding out whether he so earnestly bid them only to watch or whether he meant all persons. Now Luke gives the answer of Christ in altered form, and leaves out the clear word of Mark 13:37. Mark, however, gives the clear answer of Christ in unmistakable words,. "The things I tell you, I say to everyone." The periods in the Greek texts free this statement so that it stands on its own merit, "The things I tell you, I say to everyone." It follows then that the handing over of the keys applies to all disciples and through them to all believers in Christ.

We still don't know what is meant by the keys. Make haste slowly; [8] one at a time, like well wishers on New Year's Day. [9] The keys are none other than the preaching of the pure, undefiled word of the gospel. Whoever believes in it, is freed from sins and becomes whole. But whoever does not believe, shall be condemned. And we said above, at some length, what is the word of the gospel. Let me briefly review it here.

When a person learns of his own accord that he is incapable of doing or being good [cf. Ps. 14:3; Rom. 3:12], and when he knows at the same time that [381] he cannot reach God unless he be good and guiltless, he discovers then that on his own strength he cannot possibly come to God. Should God not come to his aid by his grace, he would have to forego being saved. Therefore God has made his Son our brother so that he might substitute for our impotence, and satisfy the righteousness of God for all our guilt; indeed, that he might become our very own brother, a surety of our righteousness and recompense [Mk. 10:45] by which we might come to God. Whoever believes in this gracious, generous deed will now depend on God's grace whose certain pledge is Christ by whom he will be redeemed from all sin. But whoever does not believe this, is caught in his sins [cf. Rom. 7:23], for he cannot make himself righteous or pleasing to God and without God's grace he cannot even trust. By this, the preacher of God's word can readily show him that he is bound and entangled in his sins so that he cannot come to God.

That this is, in fact, the case, we shall earnestly determine with diligence from the passages concerning the keys.

Christ gave the promised keys on the day of his resurrection along with the promise of the Holy Spirit, Jn. 20:20-23, as we shall show now. "On the evening of that day, the first day of the week, the doors being shut where the disciples were, for fear of the Jews, Jesus came and stood among them and said to them, 'Peace be [382] with you.' When he had said this, he showed them his hands and his side. Then the disciples were glad when they saw the Lord. Jesus said to them again, 'Peace be with you. As the Father has sent me, even so I send you.' And when he had said this, he breathed on them and said to them, 'Receive the Holy Spirit'. If you forgive the sins of any, they are forgiven; if you retain the sins of any, they are retained."

Let us, first of all, examine these words of John so that we may the better understand their meaning by comparison to the other gospel writers. For here are indicators which may be found in the other gospel writers too, who give this meaning also, but in other words. Nonetheless, it is one and the same meaning.

First of all, John indicates that this event took place on the day of the resurrection.

Secondly, that Jesus stood in their midst saying, "Peace be with you".

Thirdly, that he showed them his hands and side.

Fourthly, that the disciples were glad when they saw the Lord.

Fitthly, that Jesus gave them his peace a second time.

Sixthly, that he sent them in the same manner in which his heavenly Father had sent him. In like manner he sends his disciples that they might preach him, who is the salvation of everyone.

Seventhly, that he breathed on them saying, "Receive then the Holy Spirit. Those whose sins you forgive, shall be forgiven; those whose sins you bind or retain, shall be bound."

Indeed, by these marks and symbols we intend to show Christ's meaning to be that wherever the gospel is preached and believed [383] there the believer's sins are forgiven, but the unbeliever's sins are not forgiven; i.e. they are credited against him.

We see quite clearly, first, that the sixth point, about the commissioning, states that he sent them into the world to preach the gospel of Christ just as he had been sent by his heavenly Father to proclaim salvation. Whoever believes him, shall be free; whoever does not believe him, remains bound in his sins. Of his commissioning he speaks clearly in Lk. 4:18 in the words of Isa. 61:1f, "The Spirit of God is upon me; for he has anointed me and has sent me to proclaim to the people of meek heart and to heal those whose hearts are broken, that I might preach grace to the prisoners and liberty to those who are captives, etc."

Now let us listen to Luke and weigh his words.

He speaks in chapter 24:36 as follows, "And when they thus talked among themselves (this talking happened when Peter saw Christ and when the two spoke of the manner in which he had appeared to them on their way to Emmaus as they returned once again to Jerusalem on the day of the resurrection), Jesus himself stood in their midst." This is the first sign which John also specifies to have happened late on the day of the resurrection.

This is followed in Luke 24:36 by, "And he said to them, "Peace be with you." This is the second sign in John [Jn. 20:19ff].

Then follows in Luke 24:37, "And they were frightened and afraid, thinking that it was a ghost." This is the fourth sign in John who says, "The disciples rejoiced when they saw the Lord" [Jn. 20:20]. Now don't get upset to find that joy and fear are not the same; for Luke intended [384] to say that the unexpected appearance of Christ gave the disciples a shock--just as when someone sees or hears a desirable thing, yet dares not believe its truth for fear that it might not be thus. This doubting joy, Luke sought to express by the term "ptoethentes".

After this Luke says [24:38], "And Jesus said to them, 'Why are you confused and sad and why do you give rise to such thoughts in your hearts'?" This is a sign which Luke has in common with Mark but not with John.

After this follows [Lk.24:39], "Look at my hands and feet and see that it is I. Touch me and see. A ghost does not have flesh and bones, etc." This is the third sign in John. [Jn. 20:27].

Then this follows in Lk. 24:41, "And when they continued to doubt and wonder in their great joy, he said to them, etc." Do you see what their fear really was? It was simply an outburst through which they looked on Christ longingly and out of surprise and desire, not daring to believe that it was Christ.

After this, Luke describes [Lk. 24:42f] how Christ ate a piece of honeycomb and fish. But we shall disregard that account here, since John omitted the story. This need not surprise us, but should rather increase our faith, since the meaning of the teaching of Christ is always so unanimous, though the words or events may be described differently at times. Similarly, [385] one evangelist often tells a story which another then leaves out of the same context, but which he may give elsewhere in greater detail. For St. John says in chapter 21:25f, "There are many other things which Jesus did. Were one to describe them all, the entire world could not contain them."

After this follows in Luke [24:44-47], "And he said to them, 'These are the sayings I addressed to you while I was still with you, that it is necessary that all things be fulfilled which speak of me and are written in the law of Moses, in the Prophets and the Psalms'." Then he opened their minds so that they understood scripture and said to them, "To wit, thus it is written, in this wise Christ had to suffer and had to be raised again from the dead on the third day. And thus repentance, change and forgiveness of the sins of all people had to be preached in his name." In these words of Luke, toward the end, one finds the sixth sign of John, namely that he commanded forgiveness of sin to be preached in every nation. And this bidding is nothing other than what John calls "commissioning".

The seventh sign is the giving of the Holy Spirit. Luke calls it here, the opening of the heart; for the Holy Spirit and no one else gives understanding of his word to the human heart. It also contains the keys. Luke describes these in the following manner [Lk. 24:47], "Repentance, or change, or forgiveness of sin must be proclaimed in his [i.e. Christ's] name. Note what John calls "remitting or forgiving" and "retaining or binding", Luke here calls "preach", so that one may know oneself and repent, change for the better and believe that through Christ our sin is washed away. Just as John the Baptist did. He [386] sharply attacked the infirmity first but then he also pointed to the healing physician Christ [Lk. 3:7-17]. Christ himself did it that way. Therefore I pointed out somewhat earlier in this Article that it is essential, above all else, that a person know his sinful heart and his impotence and thereafter believe Christ to be his salvation. Christ points this out here when he opens scripture to them and how he had to suffer thus and then rise again.

Thus we also find it clearly stated in Luke that the binding and loosing is nothing other than to preach that we are impotent on our own account and incapable of doing anything. Yet against this we may point to Christ our mediator who is our righteousness. Whoever believes this will have his sin forgiven in his name; but whoever does not believe, will not have his sin forgiven.

This becomes still clearer to us when we listen to Mark. He says the following in the 16th chapter [16:12f], "After this he appeared to two of them in person, as they were about to go to the country. And they, in turn, went to tell the others. But they did not believe them either." Note first of all, that Mark sketched the same story in a few words, while Luke described in great detail the account of the two on their way to Emmaus. Note also, the first sign in John, according to whom the following story took place on the day of the resurrection.

Now follows [Mk. 16:14], "After that, when the eleven sat together, he appeared to them, reproving their unbelief and the hardness of their heart, because they would not believe those who had seen him after his resurrection. Here, all of this took place in one [387] day. The word "after this" connects the event to the preceding one, viz. "after the disciples refused to believe, Christ appeared to them and lifted their unbelief." This sign is found in Luke also and there, too, it happened on the day of Easter.

These circumstances and signs I investigate so thoroughly in order that everyone might see in them that the gospel writers describe the events of one day, but not in exactly the same words.

After this, Mark has the following [Mk. 16:15], "And he said to them, when you have gone out into all the world, preach the gospel to all creatures." This is the sixth sign in John's gospel, "As my Father has sent me to preach, [Isa. 61:2], so I send you that you might preach the good news to all creatures, that God graciously assists them in their infirmity through me, his only Son."

Then follows [Mk. 16:16], "Whoever believes and is baptized, shall be saved; whoever does not believe, shall be condemned." This is the seventh sign in John's account. Those whose sins you forgive, shall be forgiven and those whose sins you retain, shall have them retained." These words Mark expressed most clearly, saying that the sins of those who believe shall be forgiven, while the sins of those who do not believe shall be retained.

Now don't allow yourself to be misled, simple priest, by the fact that these words are read on Ascension Day; this does not mean that they were spoken on that day. For Mark treats the gospel in a much shorter form than the other gospel writers and therefore he treats all [388] things more briefly. This you can see in the short explanation to the gospel which is read on Ascension Day. In it four events are condensed. The first took place on Easter Day, up to the words which say, "And the Lord Jesus, after he had talked with them." These words indicate that Jesus was present and talked with the disciples after the resurrection and up to the ascension. Luke also mentions this in Acts 1:3, "Forty days he was seen and he spoke with them concerning the kingdom of God." This is the second event. The third is the day of his ascension when he says, "Jesus has been received into the heavens and sits at the right hand of God." And the fourth is this, "They went out and preached, etc." This happened after the first day of Pentecost, for Christ forbade them to leave Jerusalem before they had received the Holy Spirit, Acts 1:4.

This is how we understand it clearly and firmly. In fact, it is so firm with us that no wind--however strong--is able to overthrow the truth of the words in Jn. 20:23, "Everyone whose sins you shall forgive, will be forgiven and those whose sins you do not forgive, will not be forgiven." These words have the same meaning as those in Mk. 16:15, "Preach the gospel to every creature. Whoever believes and is baptized shall be saved, but whoever does not believe, shall perish." In other words, whoever believes Christ, the Son of God to be his salvation and surety by which alone he may come to God, shall be saved; whoever does not believe that, shall perish.

You say, how then were the disciples absolved? Answer: Through the word of God. Whoever confessed with his mouth that he believed Christ to be his salvation, they assured that God had forgiven his sin, and on this they baptized him. You might say again, [389] how did they bind? Answer: Whenever the word of the gospel was not believed, they went, in keeping with the word of the gospel, to shake the dust of the place off their feet, testifying that Sodom and Gomorrah would suffer less on the day of judgment than they; for the kingdom of God, i.e. the word of God, was near them, yet they did not accept it, Lk. 10:10. Paul and Barnabas acted likewise, Acts 13:46 in Antioch of Pisidia. When the Jews did not want to accept the word of the gospel, they said to them, "The word of God had to be given you, first of all; but since you disregard it and disqualify yourselves from eternal life, we shall turn our attention to the gentiles. And shortly thereafter, when the Jews, together with the authorities for the city, ordered Paul and Barnabas expelled, they shook the dust off their feet. These words stand there in such a way that one may readily see that this was a special sign to indicate how they thereby rejected unbelief and how the unbelievers remained in their sin.

No one need be greatly concerned by the fact that the words in Mt. 16:19, "Everything which you bind on earth, shall be bound, etc", are also found in Mt. 18:18, and that they refer to the ban there. They are intended as a directive [maxima] of the kind which Christ often uses, such as "nemo lucernam ponit," no one puts a burning light under a cover [Lk. 11:33]. These words, too, he uses as a great epilogue, drawing on the common practices of people, but giving them a different meaning in Lk. 8:16, Lk. 11:33 and Mt. 5:15. Similarly, [390] he uses a common saying, used by everyone, "Nothing remains hidden" on various occasions in different ways. Therefore the ban, too, is properly contained in the words about binding and loosing. For it well behooves the church to avoid the disobedient and the trouble-maker, just as the preachers also avoid those who do not want to be converted, etc.

This, too, should be noted, that God attributes to the disciples with his own mouth what he alone accomplishes, Lk. 10:9, "Heal the sick." But healing is a deed of God only, as Peter states in Acts 3:12-16, "Why do you look upon us as if we, by our own strength or fear of God, caused this man to walk again? God has done it, etc." And again, Luke says in Acts 5:12, "At the hands of the apostles many signs and wonders were done." Yet this work was the work of him who says in Mk. 16:17, "In my name believers shall drive out demons, etc." He says, "in my name" and not, "in their own strength". Yet, he is so gracious toward us poor creatures that he attributes to us what is his own domain. For a believing person knows well that the miracle is God's and not his own. Therefore he says in this context also, "Those whose sins you forgive", as if the apostles themselves might create faith in human hearts; yet no one but the Spirit of God who draws people, creates faith.

The latter part of this Article, namely, that God alone forgives sin through Christ Jesus our [391] Lord, has been amply talked about in Articles 19, 20, 21 and 22 above. In addition, a great deal is written on this in Rom. 5:19 which has been amply shown above. However, I must say one more thing here from that chapter [Rom. 5:18]. As by one man's (read Adam) unbelief all have become sinners, so by one man's (read, Christ's) obedience, we the total multitude, have been made righteous. This word no creature is able to overthrow.

NOTES

1. Cf. Augustine, sermon LXXVI (Migne, **Augustine,** 5.1). The Feast of Peter and Paul is June 29.

2. Augustine, **Retractationum,** liber 1 caput 21.

3. Cf. Jerome, **De nominibus Hebraicis** and **Commentarium in epistolam ad Galatas,** liber 1 caput 2 (on Gal. 2:11, 12ff).

4. **Commentariorum in Matthaeum,** liber 111 caput 16 (Mt. 16:9).

5. Ambrose, **Ad Ephesios** (Eph. 2:20).

6. Peter Lombard, magister sententiarum.

7. Cf. Zwingli's **Archeteles** (Z.I 249ff) and **De vera et falsa religione commentarius** (Z.III 590ff).

8. "To gemach" - Cf. **Idiotikon** IV.16.

9. The saying refers to the practice of presenting gifts on New Year's Day. In case of many callers, one would have to receive them one by one in order of appearance; hence, "Es kumpt als nach einandren, wie ein gutjare." Cf. **Idiotikon** III 58ff.

THE FIFTY-FIRST ARTICLE

Whoever ascribes this to a creature, robs God of his honor and gives it to one who is not God. That is sheer idolatry.

This Article has its roots in the former. Since God alone forgives sin, it follows that whoever ascribes this to a creature thereby robs God of his honor. For the Jews, who did not believe Christ to be true God, thought that he blasphemed God when he exclaimed, "Son, believe that your sins are forgiven", Mk. 2:5. Had Christ not been God (as they thought in their wickedness), they would have been right; on the other hand, Christ was right in punishing them, as Chrysostom held. [1] [392] But he did not say, "You err; humanbeings too, have power to forgive sin." Rather, he wanted to show that he is God, though they looked upon him as a human. And he said [Mk. 2:10-12; Mt. 9:6f; Lk. 5:24f], "That you may see that the Son of Man has power on earth to forgive sin, he said to the man who was confined to bed, 'Get up, take your bed and go home.' And the man got up and went home." He calls himself Son of Man so that one may recognize in him a true human being. Yet the miracle is of divine power only. This power he wanted to manifest among the Jews by his healing act.

Thus the remitting of sin, too, must be God's exclusively, or else he would not have been able to show through the act of healing that he is God, able to forgive sin. Both the healing and the remitting of sin are God's alone; for this reason, he proves the one by the other. Those then who ascribe to a creature the ability to forgive sin, revile God. Note what great evil it was when some people, misled by the papist's deceit, thought that a human being had forgiven their sin; because of this, God remained unknown to them. For they ascribed his mercy to humans, which is sheer idolatry. For idolatry has its name from the fact that [393] divine honor is attributed to a creature and that one gives to a creature that which is God's alone.

315

NOTE

1. Cf. **Collectio expositionum et homiliarum in psalmos,** CXLV and Homily VII, **Sermo de poenitentia;** Homily V.2 of **Enarratio in epistolam ad Hebraeos,** caput 3.

THE FIFTY-SECOND ARTICLE

Therefore, confession which is made to a priest or to a neighbor should not be advocated as the remission of sin, but simply as seeking advice.

I wrote this Article because I noticed several learned persons in our day promoting the idea that, though a priest cannot forgive sin, one should go to him, nonetheless, to be assured. Going to confession and receiving absolution is alleged to be a sign by which a sinner is assured of the forgiveness of his sin. This does not impress me, however, for it has no foundation in scripture. Now, baptism has a sign which is water; the body of Christ has a sign which is bread and wine. These signs, Christ himself instituted. But going to a priest, he did not command in any way that would make it a sign of the forgiveness of sin. The fact that Christ sent the ten lepers to the priests [394] teaches rather that one should not go to the priest if one is able to see in the light of a firm, sure faith that God has forgiven his sin. For as soon as we believe that God forgives our sin through his Son and are sure in this belief, our sins are forgiven, Jn. 6:40, "Whoever believes in me, has eternal life." And Jn. 3:18, "Whoever believes in him, shall not be judged."

Now you should understand the meaning of the ten lepers as follows: [1] In Lk. 17:14 it is clearly stated that Christ sent them to the priests before they were clean. But on the way, they were made clean. One of them, however, as soon as he saw that he was clean, returned to the Lord and glorified him, praising him with a loud voice--and this man was a Samaritan.

Note here that the one leper returned to him who was the author and donor of his health. Thus this example teaches us, rather, that we ought to thank God for the forgiveness of sin and learn to recognize him alone to be the one who forgives, and go to him, instead of running to a priest. Indeed, when we have such a faith that, as stated above, we see clearly and [395] trust that God alone forgives all our sin through Christ Jesus,

317

[we] ask God for the same in his name, "O God, forgive me poor sinner my transgression, not because of my own merit--for that is nothing but guilt upon guilt--but rather because of the merit of your only Son who suffered death on my behalf so that he might be my righteousness through which I may come to you, etc" or words to that effect.

Nor does the objection help here that Christ bid him go to the priests; therefore I am entitled to think that they obeyed him. Answer: The text does not support this objection, but states simply that the one Samaritan returned after seeing his cleanness, or rather, he returned the moment he saw it. For what else should a Samaritan have had to do with Jewish priests? He could not have offered up anything, nor did he owe them anything. He was not of their persuasion. Furthermore, Samaritans had a special dislike of Jews as also the Samaritan woman said to Christ in Jn. 4:9, "Jews have nothing in common with Samaritans."

Thus it would appear that this one Samaritan returned once again to the Lord to thank the one who healed him. Indeed, we learn from this account that we are to ascribe forgiveness of sin to God alone, and to give thanks to him; for Christ [396] praised this Samaritan for having come on his own account to give thanks. He asked for the others who did not do so, no doubt because it is wrong for us to give thanks to anyone else but God for the forgiveness of sin. Now this allegory, i.e. new understanding, cannot prove anything which is not otherwise clearly expressed in scripture.

I think, however, that those who saw in the account of the ten lepers the demand that one should in this day and age go to a priest, did so because there are still many simple folk who would take great offence were one to bar them from going to the priest. Such counsel I do not criticize too severely. But it would have been better by far, had they firmly taught faith and hope in Christ Jesus. Therein they should have found their salvation. You say, "But not everyone accepts faith that readily." Answer: Then his sin cannot be forgiven him either, though he may confess it to the priest a thousand times over. For this maxim stands unshakably firm, "God forgives sin through Jesus Christ our Lord alone." [2] What then can a priest add to that?

Going to the priest is nothing other than asking for advice in this manner: Many people are afflicted in their consciences [397] because of their sins and they do not know how these might be forgiven them. Such people might well go to the priest for medicine and help, as is suggested in Malachi 2:7, "The lips of the priest contain knowledge, and the law shall be demanded from his mouth, for he is a messenger of the Lord, etc." Now a priest must see to it that he provides the sinner with no more than the bandage which may cool and take away his anguish. In other words, he ought to teach that one must take refuge with God through Christ Jesus. He has borne our weakness, sin and wickedness upon the cross; he ought to rely on that firmly and all his sins will be forgiven. And if he believes that, he shall be liberated.

Note then what it means to bind and loose. Should the catechumen, i.e. one who is being taught by you now, believe the word of the gospel, he will be free from all sin; this you can say with confidence. Does he not believe the word, however, you can tell him with equal confidence that he has come to you for nothing. That's what is meant by binding someone.

But a Christian who had such faith beforehand [398], as has often been shown, must not come to you, for he goes to his room daily [cf. Mt. 6:6] and speaks with God there, presenting before him his weakness, knowing with certainty that everyone who calls upon the name of the Lord, shall be healed in Christ Jesus our Lord, Rom. 10:13.

Therefore confession ought to be free. Whoever is weak in the faith ought to be taught by the priest; but one who is firm, does not need him. Now there might be one on occasion who is already firm in his faith. Something may have happened to him with which he is unable to come to terms; he asks the priest for his advice, just as if he had gone to his brother, confessing his sin in the hope that he might be able to show him a way out-- for everyone is blind with regard to his own affairs--and that he might also pray God on his behalf to forgive his sins and increase his faith. This is the confession James means [James 5:16] when he says, "Forgive one another and pray for one another, etc."

The objection based on Jn. 11:44 that Christ orders the disciples to free Lazarus from his bandages is not valid either, for it, too, is only an allegory (in other words, not the natural meaning, but another, derived meaning). And allegories cannot prove anything in [399] themselves. But when something is already firm in scripture, then allegory functions like spice or salt at a meal. Should one put mustard only or such like spices on the table, one could not live from that alone. But if there are other foods to satisfy nature and hunger, then these spices are delightful additions which make the foods tasty. In like manner, allegory is a pleasing taste to a believing person in addition to that which already has a solid foundation; but on it own, allegory cannot stand. Example: Look at Gal. 4:22-31. Yet another example: to use the two wives of Jacob, Leah and Rachel, as evidence of the fact that Christ has united the Jews and us in himself, is not possible, were it not for scriptural support which states that he has united with one another and with God, Jews and gentiles in himself through the one faith. If then this is borne out in scripture and in deed (no need to dwell on that here, since all believers are informed in the matter), note how lovely thereafter the story of Jacob and his two wives sounds. Leah had weak eyes; she was the older and crankier of the two. Jacob was not as fond of her as he was of Rachel, for the latter was beautiful, happy and younger. Leah signifies to us the Jewish people who were unable to look upon the law from within because they had weak eyes; they were unable to suffer Christ, the true light, yet they clung to God from of old, etc. Rachel was [400] barren for a long time; the heathen for several thousand years did not know God, but in the end they turned to God in great numbers by faith, etc. Here too, then, where auricular confession [3] is to have been commanded by God in clear words, it would then be wonderful to cite the allegory of Lazarus, freed of his bandages. But were that not so, you could not prove anything from the unsheathing of Lazarus.

There is no use clamoring that were one to stop confessions, the world [401] would become more wicked than it was. [4] Answer: Yes, if only auricular confession could make one better. But just look at those who confessed year after year and then by comparison, [402] on those who now believe according to the teaching of Christ and who know on what salvation depends, and you will clearly see which one has improved most. Faith and not auricular confession makes a person good. Justus ex fide vivet [Rom. 1:17]. Indeed, I daresay that the greatest usurers, robbers and murderers have merely taken courage from the common auricular confession; for none of them changed for the better. But who would want to change for the better if the father confessor does not give the sinner a word of salvation, but merely asks him to perform some ceremonies and to turn over to him a cut of the robbery, teaching him further how the shame he felt against himself removes sin, and such-like empty chatter. Then he thought himself pure already and went about, incessantly ringing like the bells of the church of St. Anthony. [5] The one who is justified by faith, however, confesses daily before God in the privacy of his own home how often he has sinned. He is ashamed before God whom he has always close by and upon whom he looks in sure confidence. He fears and honors him always.

Nor does the objection hold much water which some make, "According to you one should ask a priest for counsel only in cases in which one does not know how to decide. One would then not reveal all one's sins to the priest, but only some; but this creates nothing but evildoers". Answer: You speak like one who knows no better; as if one has to reveal everything in order to dispel sin. You err in that. For no one stops sinning just because of confessions. Much rather, [403] one who sinned gravely, is more likely to cover up some sins in the confessional. And should he believe the pope's teaching that sins are not forgiven unless they are confessed, he will go away with a stricken conscience, thinking himself to be the manifestation of Satan, and thus despairing in God. All this is, indeed, the result of auricular confession.

I shall not even mention all the abuses, such as the inability of some priests to keep confidences while others take advantage of their knowledge (when the reeve entrusts them with a secret, they think right away that he has to be afraid and that, should they need his help, he will have to give it to them); or again, that father confessors are limited in their power to grant absolution, so that some sins cannot be forgiven by them, but will have to be left to a prior, superior, or bishop. And occasionally it has happened that a confessor died in the mean time.

Since then you cannot support, on the basis of scripture, that auricular confession was commanded and taught by God, you do not make matters better when you argue that it is good or may bring the soul some relief. It can, after all, not be good unless it is taught by God. But I will grant you that it has produced many a hypocrite. And what do you think was on the minds of clever "sons and daughters of the confessional" who made sweet confession in beautiful words and ornate phrases and with chewing of roots; and who in addition neatly classified all sins, though they never committed them? Surely they had no other intention than to be considered righteous and wanted to give the impression of a delicate, pure conscience, etc. In short, they soon pretended something to be good. Yet nothing is good other than that which comes from God. Surely, one honors God [404] in vain when one honors him only according to human commandments and doctrines. No amount of garrulity will help here.

Now, should you want to know and make what is the right and true confession, then do it as follows: Are you a Christian? Yes. Do you believe in the Lord Christ without doubting? Yes. What do you believe concerning him? Answer: That God made him a redeemer of our sins unto all eternity [cf. Rom. 3:25]. You have judged rightly. Have you sinned, then acknowledge your sin; for confession is nothing other than self surrender and self incrimination. And say with David [cf. Ps. 90:3; 49:16; 69:19], "Lord, my poor soul is greatly weighed down, and you, O Lord, why do you remain far from me for so long. Lord, return and redeem my soul. Forgive my sin through Jesus Christ through whom you promised to forgive all our sins." And do not cease crying until God has made it known to you in your heart and you are certain that he has forgiven you through Christ Jesus. Do not leave off until you say with joy and believe surely, "Indeed, I know well that God cannot deny me anything, since he has given his Son for me [cf. Rom. 8:32] and he has given him that he might make recompense for my sin. Therefore, he will also unfailingly forgive my sin through him; for God is truthful; he does not lie

[Heb. 6:18]. Yet, should God remove himself farther from you, so that you are unable to find rest, then seek comfort with him who can teach you God's word better than you are able to understand it. Note the keys, and he instructs you in the gospel and teaches you what hope you should have in God through the very word of God. When you believe that, you will be saved; if you do not believe it, you are bound in your sins.

Hear then an even shorter confession. Reflect often during the day on your sinful life and should it lead you to despair, say with the publican, "Lord, be merciful unto me, a sinner" [Lk. 18:13]. [405] This short exclamation is a better confession, in my judgment, than any Beguine-like prattle which takes place there [in auricular confession].

NOTES

1. See Article 18 above (Z.II 148.9ff).

2. See Article 50 above (Z.II 363.17ff).

3. Luselbycht is used derisively.

4. A variant printing of Articles 50-52 listed as F by Egli & Finsler, provides a slightly modified reading from here to the end of the Article. Cf. Z.II 400-401. See Appendix A.

5. " . . . und ist hinggangen, huer als fern, wie die toenger gloeggly singen". The likely meaning is "incessantly", always--a tongue-in-cheek reference to the constant ringing of the bells of some chapel dedicated to "St. Anthony".

APPENDIX A

(Alternate ending of Article 52, as found in Document F of Zwingli's works. Cf. Z.11 400-401)

Nor does it help much to clamor, "if we were to stop confessions, the world would become' worse than it has ever been." I answer: If auricular confessions could make people good, the world would, indeed, be quite different. But I can see quite well how good those are and become who confess and have confessed each year during Lent; how they improve and have improved. Yet, confession does not improve and never had improved anyone; but faith in Christ improves, as scripture states, "The just live by faith." I dare say that the greatest rogues have been produced by this devil's confession. They have taken courage to say, "If I give two farthings to the priest, or a sixpence, he will forgive me and the matter is settled." They have learned one thing, these studs, that the shame one did feel is the forgiveness of sin and such-like godless prattle.

But the person who is justified by faith confesses daily to God, his Lord, and acknowledges himself a poor creature unable to do anything, apart from God's grace. He speaks to God and is diligently intent on avoiding anything that might displease God. Those who confess during Lent only, do not observe this at all; they live all year long like frisky cattle and when the time of the devil draws near--i.e., the period of Lent--they go and confess because it is commanded, so that no one may accuse them of being heretics, just as used to be the custom and still is among those who had the Romish faith. For the devil and his protege, the pope, have ordered confessions once a year, and those who did not go to confession were defamed as heretics. My God, what blindness. But it is precisely this godless confession with which they have turned the entire world into heretics, unbelieving people and careless human beings, and, as far as I am able to judge, veritable cattle, unknown to God and sheer forgotten. Yet, those studs of the confessional have given it another name than it had before, calling it "the grace-ful time." Of course, it is that in the alms box and in the kitchen. Now these studs of the confession

323

and murderers of the soul come along and say, "According to your counsel, only a few should come to the confessional and then only because of certain articles on which they cannot themselves decide, that they might merely ask the priest on those matters. They are not to make confession, as the devil and his protege bid them do, lest they should turn into great rogues." I answer: You speak just like one of those evil-doers and rogues; just as if he had to say it in that way and as if you did not know better than that he had to do it and therefore be dusted off so that he might no longer sin in this matter, or at least sin less than before.

You err in that, Romanizer and disciple of anti-Christ; for no one forgives sin or avoids it on account of a confession. But this grows out of that godless auricular confession. For anyone who has sinned gravely keeps his mouth shut about it during confession. But then, since he believed the pope's teaching that sin shall not be forgiven except they are all confessed (for you godless people and murderers of the soul said when someone does not confess all his sins he is the devil), he went away with a heavy and despairing conscience, considering himself to be the devil incarnate and losing faith in God since he did not know that he could confess them to everyone other than a priest. This is the product of auricular confession. I will not even mention the fact that some give away confessional secrets and impose penalties even, so that a person is suspected and exposed and that some have even lost their lives because of such confessional, and have incurred penalties; but all this is a plague from God, because we do not now and have not before, sought him and believed on him.

To sum it all up: If one speaks long concerning auricular confession, it is in truth nothing other than a chain by which the Anti-Christ holds the world captive and in control as in a prison, so that he may be informed on all matters and assured that his kingdom might not wane. This is truly so; with this rope he has captured the conscience of people and injected the laws into them so that they have been vastly revered above the laws of God and are still held so among the godless people.

To conclude now, I say again, since I have experienced it, that nothing more godless has ever evolved in all the world than this godless auricular confession. It has corrupted so many souls, and above all the female population, that it is hard to believe. Unfortunately this is true. I know of this so well from reliable sources as if I had experienced and tried it myself. Therefore, I plead with and admonish all people who recognize such confession [for what it is] and who know what havoc and corruption it has wrought, to warn everyone and steer everyone clear of it, telling and admonishing them to seek their refuge in Christ, the Son of God, who is the recompense for our sins. For wherever this faith is found and remains in a person, that person remains in Christ eternally and lives; for the blood of Christ cleanses us from all our sin, as we may find it unmistakably clear in the divine Holy Scripture at Acts 14 and in the first chapter of Ephesians and Titus, and also in the first chapter of 1 Peter and in the first chapter of 1 John. And the Son of God says more clearly still in Matthew 6, "When we forgive, God will forgive us." John speaks of this in his first epistle in the third chapter, "Whoever says that he loves God yet hates his brother, is a liar. God has commanded and given a sign that when we fail to love our brother we cannot surely be in favor with God. For when we fail to love what we see, how can we love what we do not see?" Therefore we have to ask the Father for such love, who alone can give it; that is, God, the heavenly Father. To him be glory and praise, through his Son, Jesus Christ who illumines us by the Holy Spirit and gives us his power through his word that we may learn to know what auricular confession is, and whence it comes, and what it has brought on and accomplished in this vale of tears. May God help us out of it. Amen.

THE FIFTY-THIRD ARTICLE

Imposed works of penance derive from human counsel--with the exception of the ban. They do not remove sin and are imposed merely to deter others.

The first part is clear from the word and work of Christ; he never imposed any works on anyone whom he redeemed from sin or healed; it becomes clear from his word that he said no more than, "Your faith has made you whole" [cf. Mt. 9:22; Mk. 5:34; Lk. 8:48].

When we impose on people prattle-prayers, pilgrimages, ceremonies and the like, these invariably come from us; there is no precedent for these in Christ's teaching. Know therefore that there should be nothing placed upon you under the pretext that such things will remove your sin. However, your brother or priest should teach you how you might become whole and he should admonish you for your improvement. Concerning ill-gotten possessions, which you do not know how to handle, he should teach rather than order you how to make restitution. But should you not have the faith in God's word, by which you would do what he teaches you, all the ordering is in vain, anyhow.

With the exception of the ban.

I have excluded the ban here, simply because it has been instituted by God, provided it is used in keeping with his rule [cf. Mt. 18:15-20]. Whether or not it is a work of penance should be understood as follows: It is imposed for the sake of restoring the spirit. A person who suffers the ban, shall [406] have it lifted once again by the parish; in that case, God also remits it. However, one who fakes contrition and is in fact not contrite, cannot deceive God; he despises faked contrition [Wisdom of Solomon 1:5]. Actually, the ban is not a good work, but rather a departing from evil works. And these cannot be forgiven other than through faith.

Works of penance do not remove sin:

Earlier I said enough on the fact that no work can bring about remission of sin. For had it been possible to remit sin through works, Christ would not have had to suffer, Gal. 2:16-21, "If we are made righteous through the law, i.e. through the works of the law, Christ has died in vain."

They are imposed merely to deter others:

I made this point because of public works of penance which were undoubtedly initiated by the Fathers and regarding which the papists like to argue that they are not new at all, since the Fathers also used them. Nonetheless, they never removed sin; no one has ever been ancient enough to make good that which did not come from God. If the ancients ever intended to punish someone who had fallen from faith, they used the ban within its proper limits, as Paul used it when he chastised the Corinthian who had dishonored his stepmother [1 Cor. 5:1-5].

For it would seem to me that from the public imposition of penance, practiced by the ancients, has developed auricular confession in which the false father confessors have used their cunning according to their need. For where did they direct you to turn with your ill-gotten possessions but [407] to their own money bag? Give this much to the temple, so much for our house of God, so much for the reading of masses, so much for the brotherhood, so much for a vigil, in order that the pot of cathedrals and bishops should not ever run dry; give so much to Our Lady, and so much to every religious order; for these evil-doers (do not apply this to yourself, righteous person), are able to protect one another. In short, that which you are trying to whitewash for me again and again, turns out to be rotten inside, when looked at more closely. Secret confession turns out to be a coverlet under which all these roguish confessors were hiding their roguery, and one of their best milking cows.

THE FIFTY-FOURTH ARTICLE

Christ has borne all our pain and travail. Hence, whoever attributes to works of penance what is Christ's alone, errs and blasphemes God.

This Article has been substantiated from scripture so many times before that it needs no further proof now. For no one has been able to take away our sinful afflictions than he who is not guilty of them, yet who suffered for us as if he were afflicted by them so that by his wounds we may be healed, as Isa. 53 indicates, "Surely he has borne our affliction and suffered our pain." John the Baptist says, "Behold, the Lamb of God which takes away the sins of the world," Jn. 1:29. And Jesus says in John 6:51, "The bread I shall give you, is my body for the life of the world." In other words, the food of the soul which I shall give to people is nothing [408] other than my giving myself unto death, which shall revive the entire world.

The second part of this Article follows from the first, namely, that those who attribute to works what is Christ's alone, err grievously; indeed, they blaspheme God, as I said earlier, when they rob him of the honor of his work and of his grace and attribute it to a creature; and that which he freely gives, they allow to be sold like Gehazi [cf. 2 Kings 5:20-27], and they pay no heed to the word of Christ who says, "Freely ye have received, freely give" [Mt. 10:8].

THE FIFTY-FIFTH ARTICLE

Whoever refuses to remit any sin of a penitent person, cannot claim to be acting in the name of God or Peter, but in that of the devil.

I penned this Article to refute the so-called casus reservati. These are those cases, remittance of which has been prohibited by highly-placed bishops and ministers. But as soon as someone is prepared to pay out a set sum of money, [1] they absolve (so they claim), the one who gives money.

This misuse of the power of the keys covers such gross iniquity that one cannot speak enough against it. A while ago, several high bishops turned this into such abomination and blasphemy that I will not even relate the same at this point, in order not to offend good consciences; for it cannot be told without some damage. However, should they be unwilling to refrain from this blasphemy, we shall no longer be able to look on the mockery, nor allow it in the house of God; we would have to show it up.

But concerning the sins which are to be forgiven or retained, we may learn from the very words of Christ who says in Mt. 12:31, "Every sin or blasphemy may be forgiven a person, but blasphemy of the Spirit cannot be forgiven." These words Jesus himself explains [Mt. 12:32], "Whoever says a word against [409] the Son of Man, may be forgiven, but whoever speaks against the Holy Spirit cannot be forgiven either in this time or in the age to come." In these words of Christ we learn that all sins and blasphemy may be forgiven a person, except for the sin and blasphemy against the Holy Spirit. Now theologians ask quite seriously what the sin against the Holy Spirit is, but they speak of it as blind persons speak of colors--in ignorance, if you please.

The sin which cannot be forgiven is unbelief. This is the one sin which God shall not forgive, as we may actually determine from Luke 12:9, "Whoever shall deny me before people, will be denied also before the angels of God. And anyone who speaks against the Son of Man, shall be forgiven; but the one who slanders the Holy Spirit shall not be forgiven." You see clearly from this that to deny God or not to believe, is the sin which God does not forgive; for Luke supports the meaning of the earlier phrase, "Whoever shall deny me" by what follows, namely, "that he who slanders the Holy Spirit, shall not be forgiven."

Christ teaches this too in Jn. 3:36, "But one who does not believe the Son, shall not see life, and the wrath of God shall remain upon him." Such unbelief is called a sin against the Holy Spirit, because faith comes as a result of the drawing out by the Holy Spirit. Whoever is not drawn by the Spirit, does not believe. Hence he is under God's wrath and has become a vessel through which God reveals his righteousness [cf. Rom. 9:22].

Of the sin of unbelief or denial or falling away, you shall hear as follows. To the extent that anyone remains in unbelief or denial without repentance, the wrath of God also remains upon him. Should he repent, he is no longer held guilty. This is borne out by Peter. He repented and wept bitterly [cf. Mt. 26:75; Lk. 22:62]; as a result, his sin was forgiven him [cf. Jn. 21:15-19]. [410]

In like manner we ought to understand the word of Paul in Hebrews 10:26. If we willfully continue in sin, i.e. if we should fall away from faith once again, after having perceived the knowledge of the truth, we will have no other sacrifice for sin, etc." He means here that no one can be saved or be rid of sin through sacrifice, but only through the one Christ who, offered up once, is effective for all eternity. If one falls away from him, there is no other means or way by which one may be saved. That this is, in fact, the meaning of Paul's words, you will discover by weighing his earlier words, "habentes itaque fratres", i.e. since then, brothers we have this confidence to come to God by the blood of Christ, etc. [Heb. 10:19] and to the end of the chapter. For you will find in these words a reference from Deut. 17:5, which can be applied to unbelief and disavowal only.

I say this because there are many who do not comprehend these words of scripture properly and who tend to think that should a person sin after baptism, that sin would not be forgiven him. Yet Paul teaches the very opposite, namely, that we may eternally come to God through the blood of Christ, provided we see to it that we do not fall away from the consolation of Christ.

Hence, unbelief is the one sin in which a person may be entangled and caught up into damnation. But note, in passing, how clearly the keys stand out. In Jn. 3:36 Christ says, "Whoever does not believe the Son, will not see life and the wrath of God shall be upon him." Note the connection. Blasphemy against the

Holy Spirit is to take God's work away from him, and to attribute it instead to a creature or to the adversary of God, the devil; and such blasphemy is nothing other than unbelief. As when Christ drove out the devil from a certain person and the unbelievers said that he had [411] done it in the name of the devil. That was blasphemy against the Holy Spirit, as Mark shows in clearly stated terms in the third chapter [vers. 29], "But one who slanders the Holy Spirit shall not be forgiven in all eternity. For they said that he [Christ], has an unclean spirit which is as much as to say that he acted in the power of the evil spirit [Mk. 3:22].

Thus it emerges firmly from these words that it is through the power of the keys that all sins are forgiven the believing and penitent person and not through priests, bishops, monks or popes, but by Jesus Christ, provided one believes him to be the guarantor of our salvation who pleads with God for his sake or in his name.

Therefore it is wrong to hold someone's sin against a person except it be unbelief which includes denial and blasphemy of the work and word of God. For if a person believes, he is saved; if he does not believe, the wrath of God shall remain upon him.

Concerning this, Christ spoke to Peter [Mt. 18:22] that he should not only forgive seven times, but rather seventy times seven. With that he wanted to teach the unlimited possibility of forgiveness, provided there is contrition. Thus, no one sits truly in Peter's place who does not at all times forgive, as Peter was bid to do, even though one might concede to them the power to loose, but in the name of the devil.

But who has time enough or energy to describe here the trade in absolutions, fees of dispensations, and such like negotiations by which Rome has acquired more gold than the weight of all its inhabitants put together. I shall not dwell on the matter any longer. Let every righteous pastor do for his sheep free of charge (as long as he does not cause undue offence), what he sees others do for money, and he shall be more pleasing to God than if he allowed them to be fleeced. But let him first remove the offence through genuine teaching and by negotiating all things peacefully, as far as this is possible with God.

We owe it to one another to forgive if we desire God to forgive us. A person who truly and surely believes in God [412], shall be forgiven and he shall require no one for that task, except God. But one who is not firm in the faith, ought to go to the priest in order that he may be given food for the soul, i.e. that he may be instructed rightly. Should he give credence to the whole-some word, he will be instantly clean. Neither pope nor bishop

can refuse him this. God grant that it may be accomplished, however many cases they might prohibit to be handled.

NOTE

1. Zwingli refers to Bohemian currency which was greatly valued.
Cf. **Idiotikon** IV 1093.

THE FIFTY-SIXTH ARTICLE

Whoever remits certain sins for money alone, is fellow to Simon and Balaam and the very messenger of the devil.

Christ bids his disciples preach free of charge and to administer salvation and healing for nothing, saying in Mt. 10:8, "You have received it freely, i.e. you received it without purchase, for nothing, therefore you ought to give it for nothing too." But whoever is not willing to offer the word, unless he be paid for the same, sins against God and practices usury; he has received it for nothing, let him also give it away for nothing. Do not feel spoken to, righteous messenger of God; your master will give you food. What then shall I say of those who absolved others not by the word of God, but who said rather, that our life and death is in their hands and who condemned us to death until we would pay so and so much money?

Simon, the scholar or magician was converted (not truly; he merely pretended to be), and when he saw the Holy Spirit coming upon people through the laying on of hands by the messengers, he offered them money saying, "Give me that power also so that everyone upon whom I shall put my hands might receive the Holy Spirit." But Peter said to him, "May your money perish along with you, because you thought it possible to receive the gift of God through money [Acts 8:18-20]. Note that Peter condemns him for thinking himself [413] able to buy the gifts of the Holy Spirit with money, and the papists do not give it away without money. Now, should Peter's understanding indeed be true, as it is, it would be impossible to buy the Spirit of God; much less his gifts, which are nothing other than the presence of the Spirit of God who works effectively. Go then and give money for absolutions and you can be sure that you will not be set free; for Peter cursed this man Simon for thinking that it might be done with money. Should you too think that it can be done with money, Peter shall curse you along with him.

Balaam undoubtedly was tempted through money, as is written in Numbers 22, 23 and 24, which led him to go to King Balak; but he was, nonetheless, unwilling to falsify truth. But Peter chastises the very same trend in 2 Peter 2:15 where he accurately describes the papists' habits. Though they undertake to interpret the scripture passage as applying to other people, they do it in vain, for it cannot be applied to any other living person except the papists, as I have clearly shown in my **Archeteles.** [1]

Indeed, Peter speaks of Balaam and the papists thus [2 Pet. 2:15], "They have left the straight path and have erred, following the way of Balaam of Beor who loved the evil way, etc."

What then might Peter say now were he not only to see gifts being taken yet without at the same time twisting the truth, but also that truth is twisted while money is taken not just from a rich king, but from poor people.

Hence all who forgive sins for money after this fashion, are fellows of Simon and Balaam. For God alone forgives sin and no other person but Christ Jesus, true God and man, as I said earlier when I talked of the nature of the mediator. [2] [414]

NOTES

1. Cf. Z.I 289.14ff.

2. See Article 50 above.

THE FIFTY-SEVENTH ARTICLE

CONCERNING PURGATORY

The true Holy Scriptures know nothing of purgatory after this life.

Here I said, first of all, "The true Holy Scriptures"; from this I exclude the Apocrypha, i.e. the unknown writings.

Then I said that the untainted, sure, divine scriptures know nothing of purgatory.

This may appear strange to everyone, not to the papists alone, but to some scholars also who in our day expound scripture earnestly and faithfully. It will be necessary therefore to look, first, at the passages of scripture from which they tried to prove purgatory. And after we have shown that they always do violence to scripture with regard to this matter, we shall then state our understanding, which is, that after death we know nothing except either heaven or hell. Nor shall I be side-tracked by the fact that several prominent teachers have sought to prove purgatory by reference to their scriptures, but not from divine scriptures.

First of all, those who fuel purgatory, are trying to make a case for purgatory from the words of Christ in Mt. 12:32 when he says, "Whoever blasphemes the Holy Spirit, shall not be forgiven either in this life or in the world to come." Here they want to claim that some sins will be forgiven in a future life; but the sin against the Holy Spirit on account of its immensity, shall not be forgiven either here or there. Answer: You have forgotten your own skills again. Do you not know that you cannot raise an objection to these two contradictory statements: 1. The sin against the (415) Holy Spirit shall not be forgiven in this age, 2. The sin against the Holy Spirit shall not be forgiven in the age to come? Do you not know that both these statements are independent in themselves (particulares) and that both are negations, ad quas nihil sequitur [upon which nothing follows], and from which nothing can be deduced? And though I were to allow you to make deductions, I cannot let you deduce an affirmation when the preceding statement is a negation. Hence you cannot conclude by saying, "Yes, some sin shall be forgiven you in that age." Rather, you will have to say, "Ergo, it follows that the sin against the Holy Spirit shall never be forgiven." For this saying is "locus a sufficienti divisione", in other words, by reference to one part the entire matter is sufficiently encompassed.

Let me illustrate this by an example: We customarily say of someone who is seriously ill that "he does not sleep a wink, day and night". Here "day and night" expresses a partial time, though it encompasses the full sequence of day and night. When we say then that someone does not get any rest day and night, we mean that he never gets any rest. Likewise, when someone says that the sin against the Holy Spirit shall not be forgiven in this age or in the age to come, he means no less than to say that the sin against the Holy Spirit shall not ever be forgiven. Hence their objection is nothing but an erroneous, foolish opinion. Just as if I wanted to deduce from the statement "neither man nor woman eats strangled meat" the meaning, "someone eats it, because wolves and dogs eat it". What does that have to do with my statement, when I merely want to say that no person eats strangled meat and express "person" by the respective genders "man" and "woman"? And while I might actually say, "no person eats, etc" I actually do say, "neither man nor woman eats". And "neither man nor woman" means as much as "no person" and "no person" as much as "neither man nor woman". Likewise here, "the sin against the Holy Spirit shall not be forgiven either here or there" is as much as "never" and "never" as much as "neither here nor there".

More such examples may be found in scripture. Psalms 112 [113:2], "Blessed be the name of God from now unto eternity"; this is about the same as "the name of God be blessed at all times or eternally".

According to this then they distort the word of Christ in Mt. 5:25 by applying it to purgatory when he says, "Come to terms with your adversary promptly while you are still on the way, so that he might not hand you over to the judge and the judge to the constable and you be thrown into prison. I tell you truly, you shall not get out of there until you have paid the last farthing." In this context they translate "on the way" to mean "life in this world". And "prison" they turn into "purgatory" from which one cannot be released until oñe has paid for all one's sins; this is sheer error. For as the true meaning of that passage clearly shows, Christ there intends to warn us of all anger, hatred and quarreling. By pointing to the dangers of legal quarrels he intends to frighten us away from quarreling and legal hassles, for it often happens that a fellow thinks he can overcome his adversary when, in fact, he himself might be overcome and subsequently pursued even more strongly by his adversary--and not at all undeserved--for in his anger he was not prepared to make any concessions at all. Hence, the adversary later on is unwilling to concede anything to him either. And should he be unable to pay legal costs, he will be imprisoned and will have to pay with his skin what he was unable to pay for with his possessions.

Furthermore, legal squabbles are risky because of the judge; for should the judge not understand the matter clearly, or should he be corrupt or partial, it would be dangerous, though one might know oneself to be in the right. [417]

That this is the intention of Christ is shown in the words of Lk. 12:57-59 where this intention of Christ is described in even clearer terms as follows, "Why do you not decide and judge for yourselves, i.e. among yourselves, what is right and proper? If then you go together with your adversary on your way to the counselor, make sure that you arrange on the way to be freed from him so that he might not drag you before the judge who, in turn, might hand you over to the bailiff who might then throw you into jail. I say to you, you shall not get out of there until you have paid the very last farthing." You note in these words that Christ simply wants to discourage you from quarreling and legal squabbles, as I have said above. Paul, too, shares this opinion in 1 Cor. 6:7 when he says that it were better for a Christian to suffer harm or be cheated than to engage in legal quarrels with anyone. Christ likewise bids us give the coat to whoever demands our jacket, rather than enter into legal disputes with him [Mt. 5:40].

Thirdly, they quote in Mt. 18:34 where we find the account of the two servants of which the one, whose large debt was cancelled, did not allow his fellow servant to have a small debt cancelled. He therefore was put into prison until he himself paid the total debt. After that account, Jesus said, [v. 35], "Thus my heavenly Father will treat you, if not everyone of you forgives his brother from the depth of his heart."

At this point they say, "Do you not see that God intends to keep us in the prison house of purgatory until all our debts have been paid?" My answer: I hear well what Christ says; but I do not hear him speaking at all of any purgatory. Christ does not intend anything other than what he has already spoken in Mt. 6:14ff, "If you forgive people their sins, your heavenly Father shall also forgive your sins. But if you do not forgive people their sins, your heavenly Father will not forgive your sins either." He speaks similarly in Mk. 11:25, "If you stand up to pray, forgive whatever you may have against anyone so that [418] your Father who is in the heavens, may also forgive you." Thus Christ does not teach anything else in the three places than this, namely that if we desire God's forgiveness, we in turn have to forgive also. We may take the parable in Mt. 18:23-35 thus far. Christ still follows the custom of the people minutely. Understand it as follows: It is Christ's intention that we should forgive; if we fail to do so, we, in turn, shall not be forgiven. This is supported clearly enough in these words, "The Lord became angry with the servant and ordered him to be turned over to his tormentors." What follows after this, however, is in keeping with human practices, namely that they coerce one another with whips and corporal punishment until debts are paid off. Hence, Christ's intention does not correspond with the example cited, to the very last detail. Rather, he intends to show there what we ourselves pray when we say, "Forgive us our trespasses as we forgive those who trespass against us" [Mt. 6:12]. If we do not forgive, we in turn, shall not be forgiven. The same opinion was held by the one who prepared a harmony of the four evangelists, for he listed the three instances together. [1]

Let it be noted in this connection that not all parables may be understood to correspond to the very last detail with that which is compared, for all parables are deficient and faulty; nonetheless, they instruct well enough so that Christ taught with their aid. He said in Mt. 18:3f, unless we change and become like children, we shall not enter the kingdom of heaven. He does not intend to say by this that we should in all things become like children, otherwise we would have to ride on sticks, and would be unable to say anything about God; rather, he intends us to [419] be children in innocence and in our ready forgiveness and in humility, as Paul says in 1 Cor. 14:20, "Be children in wrongdoing." In a similar vein, Lk. 18:5, where the judge says, "I shall help the widow so that she might not scold me unceasingly." Christ intends to say here that we should not cease praying, but, like the widow, pray without ceasing. He does not, however, intend to say in this parable that one may abuse God, should he not immediately give what we desire, though the parable contains a reference to a woman who undoubtedly abused the judge often by her scolding. The parable cannot be stretched that far.

There are many such in the words of Christ. None of them lend themselves to detailed comparison, or else they would no longer be parables but the matter itself. Thus, here too, purgatory does not follow simply because Christ pursued to the very end of this parable the way people act when they do not forgive. For as we said before, allegorical meanings do not have the strength to prove anything, unless it is clearly stated elsewhere in scripture. Were we to find purgatory clearly stated in scripture, we should find this meaning expressed right to the end [of the passage].

Since this is not so, we must stay with the original meaning which is this, "Forgive and it will be forgiven you."

The fourth instance, read in the temple from the Book of Maccabees, I consider, just as it is, apocryphal; since the origin of said book is uncertain, we cannot support any argument from it. Indeed, I believe that the writer of said book did not have a clear understanding; for had he been rightly inspired he would have written the story by itself only, without introducing conclusions and dogmas, i.e. learned opinions. Since he included the same, he would have made himself suspicious to me, though the Book of Maccabees might have been found in the Canon. For of what concern is it to a historical writer to say, "Therefore [420] it is a pious thought to pray on behalf of the dead, etc" [2 Macc 12:44-46]? Indeed, how can one be without suspicion when just before that he stated how many pieces of silver Judas Maccabaeus had send to Jerusalem [2 Macc. 12:43]? Does not this sound as if he is greedy? But there is no need of this.

The Book of Maccabees has about as much authority with me as John Mandeville [2] or Hildebrand [3] [Pope Gregory]. Look at Josephus, by contrast, who also wrote a history of the Jews. Jews, Greeks and Latins use him too, though he is not canonized. You will soon see how much faith you should put in the greedy inventor of fables who rhymed together the Book of Maccabees [cf. 2 Macc. 12:38-46].

In the fifth place, they support purgatory from the words of Paul in 1 Cor. 3:10-15, "I have laid a foundation as a skilled master builder, but another builds upon it. Let everyone see to it how he builds on it; for no one can lay a foundation other than the one which is laid which is Christ [421] Jesus. Whether one builds upon this foundation gold, silver, precious stones, wood, hay or stubble, shall be made manifest, for the time or the day shall reveal it; it shall be revealed as through fire and the fire shall reveal the work of every individual as to how it is. If the work one has erected remains, he shall receive a reward; but if someone's work is burned, he will suffer damage, though he might be saved through fire." These fine words of Paul they have applied to purgatory and to good works. When one does good works, they are likened to gold, silver and precious stones; when one does evil deeds, but not too evil, they are likened to wood, hay and stubble. These are purged in purgatory; and whoever has done such works, is saved by the fire which they claim to be purgatory.

But this surely is not the intention of Paul, as we shall actually show through his own words. Paul preached Christ to the Corinthians in simple and unambiguous terms, much like one who raises a child; during infancy he will not give solid food, but milk, until the time when the child is able to digest solid food [cf. 1 Cor. 3:2f]. In his absence, however, there came to the Corinthians certain Christian teachers who in their hearts and by faith were not justified, but who were considered wise and proud according to human standards. These same people sought honor and advantage through their wisdom and eloquence, so that the simple teaching of Paul was effectively set aside by these sweet talkers: whenever people look upon the glory of this world only, they no longer like the poor Christ and his cross and the peasant band of his followers. It follows then that many people who look only to the ornate language of smooth talk, are deceived by these hypocrites. But this [422] the righteous Paul could not tolerate; for he knew well that such deception was not in keeping with the mind of Christ and that Christian life is not contained in beautiful words, but rather in a sincere and innocent life which in itself is nothing at all, unless it be firmly grounded in the faith which we have in Christ. Whoever is built up and grounded in God has rightly understood the teaching. No persecution can cause him to fall. But the one who looks to the beauty of wisdom and knowledge, stands poorly in the time of persecution; then one may see what kind of work or building everyone is, and this he demonstrates in appropriate words, as follows [1 Cor. 3:9ff].

"We are co-workers, that is, instruments in God's hand and you are the seed and the building of God; not that I have built you up, but the grace of God, which has been given me, has done it. I have done what any well-trained worker does. He sees to it, first of all, that the foundation is well laid; then only does he build upon it. In like manner, I have made the true rock, upon which all faith is built, the foundation. This rock and foundation is Christ. Him I preached, who he is and what he has wrought for us. But in my absence others also whom I do not want either to praise or to scold, built upon the foundation. Let each one look for himself what he builds upon the foundation; for no one can set up another foundation than the one which has been established already, which is Christ Jesus. Concerning the structure built upon it, I say the following: if anyone builds upon the foundation gold, silver, or precious stones, the building cannot be harmed by any fire, for the fire purifies gold and silver; and precious stones are also tested in it. If anyone builds wood, hay or stubble upon the foundation, these cannot endure the fire, though the one who built these things [423] will not be burnt unless, of course, he is wood, hay or stubble himself; he will simply suffer the loss of his building. He himself will be saved in that the fire will not harm him; for, in short, the fire must test all things, etc."

By "building" Paul here means the believers, as he himself demonstrated shortly before, "You are the seed and the building of God [1 Cor. 3:9]. And "fire" means "persecution", as in Isa. 43:1f, "Though you walk in fire, you shall not be consumed." Thus Paul intends to say in the last quoted passage, "What anyone has built upon the foundation, which is Christ Jesus, shall be revealed in the persecution. All of us may preach, but we do not all preach in the same manner. One who looks to temporal goods and appearances only, builds corruptible things. When he is afflicted by persecution, he will run away. It is just as if he had never been. And as he is unreliable, so are those whom he built up. When persecution comes, they will fall away from the faith, as quickly as fire consumes hay, wood and straw. But when the teacher has such a firm faith that he does not renege when persecution comes, though all those whom he has taught may be consumed, i.e. depart from the faith, he himself will be saved from the fire, but it must ultimately take place through persecution and suffering. For Christ predicted that the increase of God's word will bring with it persecution, Mk. 10:30. On the other hand, when someone builds up believers who do not succumb to persecution, but stand all the more firmly, these are like gold, silver and precious stones whom the fire cannot harm. Now "the work" here means as much as "the building" and "the building" means "believers" who by the preaching of the messenger of God are built up in Christ, the foundation stone. [424]

That this is the meaning of Paul in this context is supported by the following passage in which he warns them of the wise persons of the age, meaning to say that God himself does not want their buildings and that he even destroys them.

Now the sum total of this fine parable contains no less than the following: We all want to be looked upon as if we were workers of Christ; but during persecution it will become apparent by the work, i.e. by the believers, what each one built. If believers deny their faith, they are a straw building; if they remain faithful, they are like gold, silver and precious stones. But one who built the light structure will not suffer damage when his work, i.e. those who believe, flee, as long as he himself is not moved by the fire, but goes through it. This view is very much like that of Jerome on Ezekiel 3. [4]

But the entire matter becomes clear in Paul's word when one looks at it closely in its context. For the few interpreters who speak here of works done in faith as being like gold, silver and precious stones, and works not done in faith as being in vain, just like wood, hay and stubble, are undoubtedly right; yet Paul does not speak of those works here, but of the building of the preachers, as has been amply demonstrated earlier. Now go over these words of Paul and look at them once again and then judge.

They cite these words and many other similar passages, which do not have any such connotation at all, in support of purgatory (with which they warm themselves), thus doing violence to scripture. I offer to sustain my case before all learned Christians.

For these words of which they speak, contain about as much reference to purgatory as there is wisdom in an anvil. However, should they call the fire of persecution, of opposition and of the tribulations of this age, purgatory, I won't object. But that there should be another way to come to God except by way of the Lord Jesus Christ, is impossible [Jn. 14:6]. [425] He alone is the door by which we ought to enter (cf. Jn. 10:7-9); and though our own work does not merit anything, Christ merits all [cf. Rom. 11:6]. To him we want to give all honor, as we have amply shown above; and we must step back with our own merit, saying, "Lord, we are unworthy servants" [Lk. 17:10].

Whatever else they say about purgatory, how quickly or long it purges, I consider to have the value of fables. I do not care at all that they say the holy father has seen this and that. The tragic spirits themselves say how they suffer pain and we are able to aid them by celebrating mass. My answer: When the devil intends to deceive, he transforms himself into a friendly angelic being [cf. 2 Cor. 11:14]. I readily believe that the devil speaks a great deal to deceive people.

But it is impossible for souls to speak; this will become apparent shortly. For had the rich man been able to talk to his brothers, he would not have called upon Abraham to send Lazarus to his brothers [Lk. 16:27ff].

Further, how better could the devil have advanced the abuse of the mass by pretending to be a soul in need of masses. In short, whoever allows himself to be moved by dreams and winds [cf. Eph. 4:14] is not yet built upon Christ the rock.

At this point I shall indicate my own opinion also and the reasons for believing that there is no purgatory of the kind the theologians speak of.

I bank on the fact that God said nothing to us about purgatory. Indeed, he expressed an opinion which completely contradicts it, for he spoke of no other dwelling place after this world than heaven and hell, Lk. 16:22-26 when he sketched a form of departure from this world of rich and poor in the person of a rich and a poor man. God helped the latter (for he [426] had put his trust in him, as is indicated by the name "lasuriahu" which we call Lazarus). He spoke in the words of Abraham, "Between us and you a great gap has been created so that those who wish to come to you, cannot do so, and those who wish to come from your place, cannot come to us either." What more is there to say after these words? Are we not told that just as those who are in the bosom of Abraham, cannot come down, so also those who are not there (understand, the dead, for Christ speaks there of the departed only), cannot ever go up either.

Let no one object that he spoke merely of those who are in heaven or hell, but not of those in purgatory. For you are the ones who create purgatory; God did not intimate it. If you wish to object in that manner, you would first have to prove to me by reference to clear scripture passages, that there is purgatory and then how those who are in it, may be taken out. But, as I said earlier, I shall not respond to your wild guesses. [5] Instead, I shall bank on what Christ said here through the mouth of Abraham, "Those who are below, cannot come up and those who are above, cannot descend, etc."

According to this then, the purgatory of which the theologians speak is against the power of faith. For one who believes has already been saved; he need not wait for any calamity or condemnation. On the other hand, whoever does not believe, shall not be saved; indeed, it is impossible for him to be saved or to become pleasing to God, Heb. 11:6. Take this as follows: A person who dies believing, shall be saved; one who dies unbelieving, shall be damned. Beyond these two there is no third option. It helps you little to object: Yes, one who dies in faith, goes to God. This is true, but only after he has been sufficiently expurgated [6] in purgatory. My answer: Prove to me from scripture that there is such an expurgation. [427] Look, where do you stand? You say: God is merciful, but he is also just, therefore we must satisfy his righteousness in purgatory. Answer: You are not a Christian, but the pope's stoker; you heat up purgatory for him. Have you ever heard that we cannot ever satisfy God's righteousness by our own strength or by our suffering? For the sufferings of this age are not worthy of any future honor which has been revealed to us, Rom. 8:18. How can that which is finite, though it be exceedingly great, merit that which is eternal? And did you not hear that the righteousness of God cannot be satisfied by anyone except by one who has no guilt, which is Christ Jesus? How could a dead person call himself back to life? Do you not know that Christ would not have had to come into this world, were it possible to come to God through purgatory? Purgatory would have washed and cleansed sufficiently were it what you claim it to be.

Do you not know that Christ alone is our righteousness? 1 Cor. 1:30 and that we do not have any other way to God but through him? Now, is Christ called "purgatory", or the suffering of Christ, or Christ the door by which one must enter or in whom one must believe, i.e. have full confidence in the power of his redemption? Just see where you yourselves go with all this prattle. You lead yourselves away from faith and empty the cross of Christ of its power [cf. 1 Cor. 1:17]; you despise the inexhaustible grace and power of the suffering of Christ. Does Christ offer satisfaction for all sin; what then can purgatory add? Does purgatory prepare a way to God; why then do we need Christ? Woe to you blasphemers who distort all truth.

In order that you may believe this opinion, namely that believers immediately go to God and unbelievers immediately to the devil after death, I shall now give further proof. [7]

Christ says in Jn. 3:16-18, "God sent his only Son into the world not to condemn the world, but that through him the world [428] might be saved or made whole. Whoever believes in him, shall not be condemned, but whoever does not believe in him, has already been condemned; for he did not believe in the name of the only begotten Son of God." Look at these words of Christ, you soul snatchers. [8] The fire has blinded you and you cannot see well. Therefore I shall put my finger on it.

First, you hear that God sent his Son into the world, not to condemn it, i.e. judge it, according to its deeds. Where now is your opinion of the righteousness of God? For David says, [Ps. 130:3], "Lord, if you should credit our sin to us, who could endure it?"

Secondly, you hear well that he has come to save us and make us whole because of his great grace. For should he judge us according to our merit, we would not boast of much grace. But since he has not come to judge but to save, it follows that it is all sheer grace and mercy.

Thirdly, you hear well that whoever puts his trust in him, i.e. whoever believes in him, shall not be condemned. Do you hear that the believer is not to be judged? But what is your purgatory other than judgment? For you say, "Everyone must satisfy the righteousness of God--one for this long, another for that long."

Fourthly, you hear well that one who does not believe in him is already judged, i.e. he is condemned. Note, heaven and hell and nothing else.

This is made clearer still by another word of Christ, Jn. 5:24, when he says, "Truly, truly, I say to you, whoever hears my word and believes him who has sent me, has eternal life and does not come into judgment, but rather, enters from death to life." You hear that he falls into no judgment, but lives in the sheer grace of God and goes (as the Latin text puts it), [9] [429] from death to life and, as the Greeks have it more correctly,"He has already gone from death to life". [10]

What the judgment is and how frequently it is referred to in scripture, follows now.

The term "to judge" or "to sentence" and "judgment" or "sentence" are often taken to mean "revenge", Gen. 15:14,

"But I will take revenge on the nation which they serve". Then again, it is often taken to mean the arbitrating which judges undertake between two opposing parties, Ex. 18:21, "Moreover choose able men from all the people, such as fear God, and who are trustworthy and who hate a bribe; and place such men over the people as rulers of thousands, of hundreds, of fifties and of tens." Thirdly, it is taken to mean a form of sentencing, as we indicated earlier by reference to Jn. 3:16-18. Fourthly, it is used to refer to the standing and judgment which every person meets after death, as in Heb. 9:27, "And just as it is appointed for a person to die once and after that comes judgment, so, etc." In other words, just as people, immediately after death begin to live by the judgment which God has imposed on them outside the body, up to the universal judgment day, so, etc."

That this is the actual meaning, you may see by looking at what goes before and what comes after; otherwise you are unable to understand this saying properly. Fifthly, it refers to the last judgment when God shall gather all people who have lived from the beginning of the world to the end, and when he shall reward the deeds of the faithful and punish those of the unbelievers right there in the congregation, Mt. 25:31-46 and 2 Cor. 5:10, "We all have to appear before the judgment seat of God, etc." In the sixth place, it is taken to mean "select" or "segregate" which shows itself publicly as in Jn. 9:39, "I have come for a judgment into the world that those who do not see, may begin to see and those who see may become blind, etc." [430]

There are still other possible interpretations of these words, but let these suffice.

I cited them so that the words of Christ in Jn. 3 and 5 [Jn. 3:16, 5:24], may be properly understood: Christ does not intend to say there that some will not appear on the Last Day (though there will be some who come with joy to the glory of God, and others, who come with moaning for shame of their unbelief and their evil works), but rather that believers begin to be saved here in this life through a sure and undefiled faith and hope and that they shall not enter into any judgment, revenge or damnation, immediately after death, until the Day of Judgment. Rather, that they will go instantly from death to life and that they will possess and inherit what they hoped for in this life.

[I pointed out] that one might also be able to distinguish between the last judgment and the state of being which follows immediately upon physical death. For I hear it said that some want to insist on our going to sleep--body and soul--after physical death until the last judgment; then only shall we be awakened and enter thereafter into the joy and honor of God or into eternal woe. I am not at all of that opinion. For the sleep of which Paul speaks in 1 Thess. 4:13-15 and elsewhere, must be understood solely with regard to the body, as we shall show shortly. And whatever is said concerning rewards on the last day must be understood to refer to the total person--be it good or bad--and that only then a person's sentence shall be made known to all people who have been from the beginning of the world to the end; for until then our sentence will remain unknown to us.

This opinion will become quite clear when we show that salvation begins immediately after death. This we shall undertake now.

Christ is the first fruit of our resurrection, 1 Cor. 15:23. [431] Are we to rise as Christ rose, then our souls, too, will not fall asleep; for Christ's soul did not fall asleep either, but as Canticles 5:2 says, "I sleep, but my heart is awake." Though he was dead in the body, his heart was awake; for he went to the dead to proclaim salvation to them, 1 Pet. 3:18f, "In the flesh he died, but in the spirit he was alive; for he went and preached to the spirits who were kept in prison." Note how Peter seeks to show here that Christ after his death preached to the prisoners the joy of salvation. Now then, if even these were alive, how much more will the souls of believers be alive after death. "For one who remains in love, remains in God and God remains in him," 1 Jn. 4:13.

How then can we reconcile the fact that God is in us, provided we believe in him, hope in him and love him in this physical life, with the claim that he withdraws himself from us after this life, and that those who on earth begin to rejoice in the highest good, shall not rejoice anymore after death?

It follows then that just as Christ,--living and true God at his death--did not fall asleep in his human soul, but rejoiced in his manifest divinity, so we too, provided we die in faith, shall be made glad in God until the universal day of judgment of the whole world. For the birth, death and resurrection of Christ is ever an image of our birth, death and resurrection. He was conceived of the Holy Spirit; in like manner, we are made believers through the Holy Spirit. He died for our sins. So shall we, as long as we die in him, live with him in death and after death. And in the last day we shall rise--body and soul--as he rose; for he is the first fruit of our resurrection [1 Cor. 15:20].

To wit, Christ says in Lk. 20:35f, "those who are accounted worthy to attain to that age (that is, eternity), and [432] to the resurrection from the dead, will not seek marriage nor be taken in marriage; for they cannot die anymore because they are like angels and are sons of God, etc."

Here we see clearly that Christ himself uses two terms to speak of future life and resurrection and of the future state of the soul, indicating clearly that in the future age we shall be like angels, since we are sons of God. Now angels are alive. We, too, shall be alive. For children of God cannot be dead for that long. God is a God of the living, Mt. 22:32. As long as we are in this life, we alternate between sleeping and waking; there it shall be an eternal waking.

It is of no use to object that the time which is to come after this life is not to be measured by the norms of this age; for what seems long to us, appears as present to the spirits and is not measured by length of years. Answer: I mark you well. But you, too, must not speak of sleep until the last judgment which you intend to measure by our time standards; should you turn it into sleep, you must also measure their life by our time standards; for sleep means rest of those things that worked in time; after death it is applicable to the body only, but not to the soul. Do not burden yourself, simple reader, with metaphysical make-believe.

Again Jesus says to the criminal, Lk. 23:43, "Today you shall be with me in paradise," i.e. you shall be with me in peace and joy today, on account of your faith. For your asking me to have mercy on you shows that you took me to be God. Look here. Where are those who stoke purgatory? How do they intend to purge and roast this criminal? Christ took him unto himself. I am afraid they might try to tear him away once again. Did he not go instantly from death to life through faith?

If then this criminal is to be instantly with Christ rejoicing (for though Christ descended into hell, the joy of the presence of God was not diminished where he was for anyone who had been freed from the darkness of the body; for our physical eyes cannot see him in his Godhead), how much more those who served him in the faith for a long time?

This criminal provides us with two testimonies. The first is that Christ did not say to him, "This day you shall rest with me," but rather, "Today you shall be with me in paradise." From this it follows that joy or sorrow follow immediately upon this life. The second testimony is, that he did not come to this through any work or purgatory, but alone through faith. Let these sophistical mosquitoes buzz as much as they please; do not be concerned about them. [11]

Paul, too, was of the same opinion; for he says in Phil. 1:23, "My desire is to depart and be with Christ, for that is far better; but to stay alive for a while and remain in the flesh is more important for your sake." Paul shows us here that one may come to Christ without any mediation, provided one has faith. He indicated this in 2 Cor. 5:4-6 also when he says, "For while we are still in this tent, we sigh with anxiety; not that we would be unclothed, but that we would be further clothed, so that what is mortal may be swallowed up by life. He who has prepared us for this very thing is God, who gave us the Spirit as a guarantor." All this serves to show that the future state of joy or sorrow begins immediately after death. And the body sleeps until the universal day of judgment, when, with the soul it will experience joy or sorrow.

That everyone will be rewarded then according to his works, does not yet support the idea of merit; for the works [434] which happen from faith are God's and not ours. Thus God rewards his own work, as Augustine also says. [12] Whatever does not come from faith, however, will be damned; for whatever does not come from God is not good.

Thus I hope to have robbed the papists of their other milch cow through the strong word of God. [13] For by inventing the pain of the soul in purgatory, they have cashed in so much money that words fail to account for it. In this way, hypocrisy is able to find joy and profit in the suffering and pain of others. If they know that the souls suffer such great pain what great crooks are they, not to allow their works to profit them, unless they are being paid.

NOTES

1. Some editions of the Vulgate list Mt. 6:14 and 18:35 together with Mk. 11:25. Zwingli may have had in mind Eusebius of Caesarea and his **Canones decem harmoniae evangeliorum.**

2. John de Mandeville is a 14th century writer of a fascinating travelogue which describes travels in Africa, Asia and Europe. The book was originally published in French and later translated into many European languages. It is now generally held that Mandeville was not the author, but rather, the Belgian physician Jean de Bourgogne (á la Barbe). Cf. A. Bovenschen, **Zeitschrift der Gesellschaft fuer Erdkunde zu Berlin,** vol. 23, 1888, 177ff.

3. Pope Gregory VII 1073-1085 claimed an authority for the pope in his **Dictatus Papae** which had hitherto not been claimed, namely, that the pope is above any human judgment or tribunal.

4. Cf. Jerome **Commentariorum in Ezechielem,** liber I caput 4 (ad Ezekiel 3:18ff).

5. "Ueff dine blinde wuerff will ich nit werffen." Z.II 426.15.

6. Zwingli uses the vivid image "im fegfuer gnug gerollet".

7. Testimonia ex scripturis.

8. The term is "seelenbrenner" and recalls the image "des bapsts calefactor", 343 above.

9. John 5:24 in the Vulgate reads as follows: Amen, amen, dico vobis, quia qui verbum meum audit et credit ei, qui misit me, habet vitam aeternam et in iudicium non venit, sed transit a morte in vitam.

10. The Greek text reads: metabebeken ek tou thanatou.

11. "Lass hie die Sophisten schnaggen russen was sy wellend" probably means, "The Sophists buzz like mosquitoes; they are annoying but not harmful".

12. Zwingli refers to an earlier statement. Cf. Z.II 186.27ff.

13. See the end of Article 53 above (Z.II 407.9).

THE FIFTY-EIGHTH ARTICLE

The sentence of those who have died, is known only to God.

Lazarus lay in the grave for four days and God brought him to life again [Jn. 11:1-46]. The daughter of Jairus had just died, yet he recalled her back to life, too [Mt. 9:18f, 23-26]. The son of the widow he also returned to his mother alive [cf. Lk. 1:11-15]. But where and how they existed in the time between their death and the bringing back to life is not revealed to us in the words of Christ. This is a sure sign that God did not wish to reveal these things to us, but to keep them to himself alone.

Do not be deceived by the fairy tales told about Lazarus; for God does not reveal to us the time and moment which the Father has in his power, Acts 1:7. Therefore it is audacity when we want to know such things through human understanding, as shall be shown shortly. [435]

THE FIFTY-NINTH ARTICLE

And the less God has let us know about it, the less we should undertake to know about it.

Concerning this opinion we have express testimony in Jn. 21:18-22. When Christ gave Peter to understand the death he was to die and when Peter, in turn, asked what kind of death John would die, he answered him, "Should I want him to remain like this until I return, what is that to you?" We perceive quite clearly that we should not concern ourselves with the judgments of God. For if Christ did not wish to reveal to Peter the kind of death John was to suffer, how much less should we want to know the judgments of God after this age.

For in the account of the rich man, Lk. 16:29-31 Christ did not want the living brothers of the rich man to know anything of the dead, but rather that they should be content with the law and the prophets, i.e. that they should not want to know more about the dead than what scripture indicated to them.

Where then are the deceivers who condemned every mortal sin by requiring seven years of penance for it which they contrived from their open penance, which had been imposed by them on the people? Thus they interfered in Christ's judgment, for the Father gave him authority to judge everything, Jn. 5:22. In addition, they obscured his own suffering by not telling people what it is capable of accomplishing, how costly it is, namely, that it can make satisfaction and payment for the sin of everyone unto all eternity, as has frequently been shown.

Should they have done this knowingly, they are like the fellows whom Christ scolds in Mt. 23:13 and Lk. 11:52, [436] who had the key to the kingdom of heaven and to divine knowledge, yet did not enter in themselves nor allow others to enter. Did they not know this? What then are they doing in that position when they ought to know this above all else on account of their office? But now when the truth is being revealed, one may readily

351

see whether their abuse is from evil intent or out of ignorance. Those who recognize their ignorance, depart from it; those, however, who cover up, show their evil intent and hardness of heart. Their end shall be condemnation. May God illumine them so that they do not remain blind in broad daylight. Amen.

THE SIXTIETH ARTICLE

That a person, out of concern for the dead, calls on God to show them mercy, I do not disapprove. But to stipulate a time for this and to lie for the sake of gain, is not human, but devilish.

This Article I have given solely for the sake of those few who are ignorant and do not freely trust in the two truths, namely, that a person either dies in faith and then goes to God, or else that he dies in unbelief and is damned, Mk. 16:16. Yet I do not wish them to remain ignorant forever, but rather that they might be edified through the firm word of God. However, at times they still question--though they themselves believe rightly-- whether their departed have passed on in the right faith or else, whether they had a faith strong enough to suffice unto salvation. I did not really intend to overthrow their pious opinion and solicitude too quickly. Rather, I tried to show them how not to request something against God's will, such as to call on him [437] for what he knows by saying, "Lord, the sentence of the dead is known to you alone. Now you bid us honor father and mother [Ex. 20:12]. Therefore it is my anxious prayer that the state of the departed, which we do not really know, may be changed on account of our prayers and our faith. Grant that my father and mother and all believers have eternal rest. But your will be done." [Mt. 26:43] See this is what those would say who are weak and ill grounded in the word of God.

It does not as yet prove that there is a purgatory, but recalls God's mercy and his knowledge and abides by his divine will. But those avaricious people who set times and say that this one must suffer so long and that one, so long, and the sorcerers who through divinizing suggest that one may be able to help the dead through this or that work to prevent him from suffering that much longer; and the preachers of fables who say that the souls appear here and there, simply help to deceive the world which desires to be thus deceived. This is deceit and the devil is the father of deceit [Jn. 8:44]. Hence, all of it is devilish.

It does not help you to object: We priests take money so that we may pray in precisely the form you indicated. Have we not pointed out frequently, above, that mercenary worship is not grounded in scripture? Further, when you pray for payment only, you honor God with your lips, but your heart is far from him-- and that is for nothing [Mt. 15:8]. Then the heart looks upon gain only; yet, we ought to pray one for the other. And it is your office, o monk and priest, to preach the faith pure and firm so that all the world may be made firm in its faith and not remain in such debilitating doubts, and that everyone may be able to say, "My father had such sure trust in God that I do not doubt [438] his having gone to God. I also believe that everyone who has such a faith, will come to God." That is your office and also that you teach weak persons. But this nursing mother produced sweet milk from a miserable, bitter source. For had confidence in God been as truly taught as it should have been, what would it have mattered had one or the other feared purgatory or put his trust in it? But to have led everyone by such invented fear, taught you to extort riches. And as shamefully as they were won, so they were often squandered again in even greater wantonness.

Thus it is with God's judgment.

THE SIXTY-FIRST ARTICLE

ON THE PRIESTHOOD

Of an [indelible] character which priests have appropriated to themselves in recent times, scripture knows nothing at all.

"Character" is a Greek term derived from "charatto" which means "scratch," "rip," "edge-out" or "engrave". Thus "character" means as much as an edged-out mark or sign. Regarding this the hooded theologians [1] speak as follows, "When a priest is consecrated, a mark is etched out in his soul which may never again be removed or extinguished from it." This scratch or mark is nowhere to be found in scripture except in Heb. 1:3. There the Greek term "character" is found, but not with the meaning the hooded theologians have given it. [439]

And although it is true that the Apostles placed their hands upon those who were set aside to preach, this took place in keeping with the custom of those people who are in the habit of sealing faithfulness, faith and commissions with a hand clasp for greater confirmation. Yet you will not find anywhere there that they are talking of an indelible mark. [2] Rather, you will find up to the time of Jerome [3] (who reproved several diaconos, i.e. servants, and demanded that they be dismissed), that anyone who was no longer fit for the office of serving, was not considered to be a servant any more. No one had any regard for "character", but when someone was dismissed, he was no longer in office.

We may conclude from this, that the priesthood was considered an office and not a dignity or lordship. Just as one who is mayor looks after his office and recognizes it as such. That he is accorded any honor, comes from his carrying out that office properly. As soon as he does not carry out this function as he ought, he is dismissed and is no longer mayor. Thus, to be a priest means no more than to be an honorable proclaimer of the word of God and a guardian of the salvation of souls. [4]

Whoever does that receives respect as a result. But one who fails to do that, ought to be dismissed; he is then no longer a priest. Just as we have no need of a mayor who wants to be lord only and has no regard for the maintenance of public peace and justice, so there is no need of those who simply want to be priests in order that they might live wantonly while [440] having an honorable name. For Christ sent out the disciples to be messengers, giving them a commission. Whoever, to this day, faithfully carries out that commission of Christ, is like a messenger of Christ; whoever does not do so, has no such status and is not a priest. It follows then that to be a priest is an office and not a dignity and that the concept of character has been invented by false teachers [cf. Tit. 1:10]; it may be, of course, that they wish to apply to themselves the character with which the servants of the beast have been marked, Rev. 13 & 14 [13:16; 14:9].

Their reference to the laying on of hands in 2 Tim. 1:6 does not contradict what I have said. For in that passage Paul speaks of the sign or custom which the apostles followed at the time when they transmitted the Holy Spirit through the symbolic laying on of hands. But this transmission was not the apostles' prerogative, but that of the one God, as we have amply shown above. God may be gracious enough to credit us with his work, but he does not think of an indelible character.

NOTES

1. "Kappentheologi". Elsewhere Zwingli uses the term "Kappenfritzen" (Z.I 381.2) and "Rappenzipffel der theologen" (Z.II 48.29ff). The origin of these derisive terms may be traced through **Idiotikon** II 155, 156; III 384 and through Grimm, IV 220.

2. For details of the development of the concept "character indelebilis", cf. **The Catholic Encyclopedia.** See also E. Friedberg, **Lehrbuch,** 26f, 157.

3. Z.I 231.26f especially, n. 7. See also Jerome, Epistola 52 ad Nepotianum, cap 5-7. In his pre-Reform writings Zwingli often notes Jerome's opinion. Cf. J. M. Usteri, **Initia Zwinglii** 685.

4. Cf. Z.I 231.20ff.

THE SIXTY-SECOND ARTICLE

It [scripture] knows of no priests other than those who proclaim the word of God.

Properly speaking, a priest is simply someone who is old, honorable or zealous. Therefore, one ought to select the most senior and zealous persons in all parishes and ecclesiastical communities, as Paul teaches in Tit. 1:5-9. [1] While it is true that seven servants were selected at the time of the apostles [Acts 6], it should be noted that these were not called priests, unless they proclaimed the word of God. Paul also says this in 1 Tim. 5:17, "The elders who set a good [441] example, ought to be rewarded in a twofold manner." This does not prove either that there were no other priests except those who preached. For there he speaks of old men who were to be maintained by the parishes. Of these he says that they should be given a double portion for the simple reason, no doubt, that old age is helpless. He further states in the same context [1 Tim. 5:17], "Foremost those who work in proclamation and teaching." I will gladly concede that the term priest in this context is used for those who teach in the church, who proclaim the word of God, who translate Greek and Hebrew, who preach, heal, visit the sick, give help and alms to the poor and feed them; for all these tasks belong to the word of God.

But of those others who act like lords [gotsjunckeren], divine scripture knows nothing at all, regardless of their claim, except to say, "Their God is their belly," Phil. 3:19. They are like drones in a bee hive who consume leisurely what others gather in toilsome work.

NOTE

1. Cf. Z.I 239.22f.

THE SIXTY-THIRD ARTICLE

To them [who proclaim God's word], scripture bids us show respect by giving them physical sustenance.

Christ allows his messengers to eat with those to whom they proclaim the gospel, Lk. 10:7, "Live in the same house, eat and drink what they set before you (ta par autōn), for a laborer is worthy of his hire."

Paul is of the same opinion, 1 Cor. 9:13-15, "Do you not know that those who serve in the temple are fed by the temple's food and that those who serve at the altar, eat the food of the altar?" Thus God [442] commanded that everyone who preaches the gospel is to live by the gospel, though I myself made no use of it."

Here several slaves of the mass use the first part of the parable to their advantage saying, "You may see from this that we who are servants of temple and altar may live from our service."

Answer: Dear slaves of the mass, look into the matter more carefully. It is a "blockhead". [1] The first part does not concern you at all, for it is an introduction to the parable. It is derived from the Old Testament traditions which in those days were still adhered to by several of the Jews, though they had become believers. This is evident from the word which he says immediately following, "Do likewise". For whoever says, "do likewise" has earlier used a pattern or an example, [2] but does not intend to prove or praise the example.

Christ uses the image of the manager in that same way [Lk. 16: 1-9], who before his dismissal came to an agreement with the debtors of his master in a subtle manner. Now Christ does not want us to act dishonorably toward our neighbor. Rather, he wants to show that people are so wise in preserving their physical lives that they seek to prepare for themselves where they want to be. Much more ought those, who desire eternal life, take care not to become indebted to temporal, perishable goods, but to give the same over to the poor in his name; thus they will be received into the eternal dwelling place.

Similarly, Paul does not intend to teach here that one should fatten the slaves of the mass. Rather, his meaning is as follows, "Look to the Jews who still use the law of ceremonies (later in chapter ten [443] he calls them the "Israel after the flesh"); they follow the custom that those who serve at the altar, receive their food from the altar also. Thus (you see here the other part which he intends to teach and introduce), God ordered that those who preach the gospel, should live by it.

Again, Paul says in 1 Tim. 5:17 that the priests who attend to the word and teaching of God, should be doubly rewarded, as we said earlier. But these fat, lusty bulls chased the poor working oxen away from the trough. Just look at the wealthy abbots, priests, deans and canons and you will find out many a pretty thing. They take away from the pious shepherds and watchmen of God contributions of the tenth and of their fruit and then burden the poor farmers with them by giving them either nothing at all or so little that one could hardly feed a pig with it. What is the poor parish priest to do (of course, such obligations are usually accepted by those who can neither carry burdens nor pull any loads)? He begins to look to seasons, funerals, exemptions, penances, masses, sacrifices, altar and church anniversaries, collections for the poor, the reading of masses and the like, whether he might find his food in such stooks, for he is not allowed to get into the harvest. [3]

Out of this, all ceremonies have come. Those who do not work, are filled. Those who work, have to earn their living with lies [444] to prevent death by starvation. We have unearthed here such grievous abuse among clerics that one should really write a special book on the matter, for the wanton, fat priests do not live by their rightful income and engage in such vile abuses through incorporations--and pope and bishops allow them to do all these things--that God even could weep.

But, worthy Christians, maintain the proclaimers of the gospel without such patchwork arrangements and many of them might cease their abominable practices and take the pure word of God in hand, for many of them say, "O God, what shall I do? If I do not get that offering, I am lost."

I say further, that whenever a priest does not have sufficient food, he is entitled not merely to offerings, but to decent support. And when there are other gifts available, it is wrong to hold offerings up to people as if these are of any use, just because they are offerings. For an offering is not more than a gift to those who teach. Whenever such gifts are available, apart from offerings, it is wrong to burden parishioners with a double load. In all things one ought to avoid offence and keep from destroying the work of God for the sake of food or temporal goods, Rom. 14:20.

Let these examples suffice.

NOTE

1. Stockfisch. The meaning is "a stupid person", or else, one who, by groundless chatter reveals his ignorance. Cf. **Idiotikon** I. 1104.

2. The term used is Anbild which is weaker than Abbild. Cf. Grimm, I.295 and **Idiotikon** IV. 1198.

3. For further, more detailed, discussion of the problem of the remuneration of priests and related matters, cf. Zwingli's **Vom Predigtamt** [on the preaching office] of 1525—Z IV.369-433.

THE SIXTY-FOURTH ARTICLE

CONCERNING THE REDRESSING OF ABUSES

All those who acknowledge their errors, should not be forced to make amends, but are to be allowed to die in peace, and their endowments are then to be administered in a Christian spirit. [445]

Since the kingdom of God in this age and in the age to come is piety, peace and joy in the Holy Spirit, Rom. 14:17, and since Christ, too, at all times earnestly desired peace for his own people, after his victory and resurrection from the dead, as an example to us, so that we, too, when we triumph by the word of God in all places and when the once rejected Christ rises again, may be peaceful, it is not fitting therefore to undertake anything wantonly and by force. For whoever does so, is not a Christian, but a baseless enemy of the teaching of Christ. For every wanton theft involves tumult and rioting, Isa. 9:5. Whoever wantonly or by force undertakes anything, incites rioting and uprising; he is intent on destroying the teaching of Christ. For wherever it becomes evident that uprisings may result, one should shy away from them as from poison.

I know well that Christ says, "I have not come to bring peace upon earth, but separation, Lk. 12:49. I also know, on the other hand, that he said in Jn. 16:33, "These things I said to you that you may have peace through me." The unrest which Christ causes is not in connection with temporal goods. Rather, it is a means of separation in cases where some of our own people seek to stop us from adhering to Christ. Christ does not rob, nor does he engage in warfare, nor does he kill anyone. He would endure all things rather than use any of them.

You say, That is exactly what the clerics do. Answer: They are not spiritual but carnal, yes, even devilish persons. And when you do what they do, you are like them. Therefore, every government should see to it that all abuses are quietly removed. For when it becomes apparent that the greater number of clerics are idle without having them reduced in number by peaceful means of elimination, then in the end the impatience of ordinary people will become so great that it must find a vent. There is not a single master strong enough to imagine himself [446] in control of such situations. If reports are correct, it is more likely that a person will lose his entire kingdom before he will be able to protect these useless bellies. For what is a state other than the totality of all who live in it? And should these be of a different mind from the protectors of the papists, how then are these to protect?

Nothing will come of it except unrest, disobedience, and all kinds of evil. No one is able to fight God in this way. But should one take the matter in hand thoughtfully and in peace, an impatient person is much like an ugly animal. As soon as he sees, however, that one acts in a Godly fashion and reasonbly he calms down.

Now, whenever it becomes apparent in a chapter, order and sectarian grouping that some of said clerics are obedient to God's word, though this may be of temporal disadvantage to them, one ought to see that those same people teach the word of God faithfully and earnestly, admonish others to maintain peace and order; and the authorities must earnestly see to it that abuses are done away with. In this way it can be done orderly.

Of this we have a very convincing example in Acts 15:1-21. When several of the Jews, who had become converted to Christ, thought that one should keep not only the ceremonies of the law, but circumcision also, Paul and Barnabas opposed them and made this known also to the congregation and the apostles in Jerusalem. After a great deal of talk they agree not to eat meat offered to idols nor to drink or shed blood, not to eat anything strangled and not to be unchaste.

Here everyone may see clearly that the congregation in Jerusalem forbade several small matters only in order that circumcision, sacrifices and other great matters might be done away with.

I consider the eating of meat offered to idols to be a small matter; for Paul, too, allows it as long as no one is offended by it and as long as the one who eats has no part in the sacrifice or in the idol [cf. 1 Cor. 8:1-7] [1] "Small" is the eating of blood; for it was a Jewish commandment, too. "Small" is the [447] eating of strangled meat, for this too was a Jewish commandment. Both these were not kept by any of those who had come to Christ from among the gentiles. But they were conceded to the Jews for the sake of peace. Thus it is right and proper to this day to make concessions to above-mentioned clerics for the sake of peace, allowing them to die in the manner in which they were raised, but assuring in future that such abuse should never again grow up.

Here we must say a word concerning councils; for the papists support their councils with reference to this passage; yet, the passage is against their prattle in every way.

First of all, Peter clearly stated that it is tempting God to impose the yoke of ceremonies on Christians [Acts 15:7-11].

Secondly, James spoke with equal frankness in the congregation [Acts 15:13-21].

Thirdly, Peter does not attribute anything to works, but ascribes everything to the grace of God; he makes no reference in his speech to sacrificing to idols, to the eating of blood or of anything that has been strangled. James only introduces it, which is directly against the pope. Had Peter had the power among Christians which the papists ascribe to him, his counsel should have had greater weight; indeed, he should have ordered it to be followed; yet he did not win. One may clearly see from this that he did not have any such power.

Fourthly, the apostles on their own accord never gave answers like those of the bishops in our day, but always in consultation with the entire congregation. From this it follows that every parish should deal with the matters which arise and which are contrary to the word of God.

Fifthly, the congregation in Jerusalem did not have the authority to give orders to other congregations. Hence the three commandments are friendly advice and not laws at all. For they do not say, "We order this," but rather, "Should you keep these things, you would do well". One may actually see from this that they advised on these matters so that peace might be kept between the quarrelsome Jews and the gentiles; for these matters are long outdated. One no longer eats meat offered to idols among Christians, for there is no one who sacrifices to them any longer. However, blood and strangled meat we do eat. [448]

Concerning councils, the learned papal lawyers talk more than frogs in a river: Who is to call a Council; who is to preside in the assembly; might a Council err; is all the world duty-bound to keep what it decides; whether its decisions have to be as firmly obeyed as the gospel, etc? And in our age, when they see that they are losing out, [2] they cry, "Who is entitled to let anything go without a Council? We shall hold a Council within a year.

Answer concerning the first: Who bid you hold a council by yourselves without the congregation? But when you begin a council at the grass roots and develop it to the very top and then deal therein with temporal human affairs only, nearly reaching agreement, we will be delighted with the holding of such a council. But when you boastful bishops [3] gather and decide against the word of God, as has frequently happened, and when you rape it according to your own good pleasure, God will not tolerate that.

Secondly, almost all papists, as God well knows, kept their oaths for a while, concerning councils, ever since the Council of Basel [4] by promising councils again and again yet not calling them; but even if they had called such a council it would have been of much the same color, I fear, as all previous ones.

Therefore the pure teaching of Christ is counsel enough for all the world; it stands out as clearly now as it did thirteen hundred years ago. For though one were to hold councils and discover during these, something which is opposed to the word of Christ, no one would stand by it. And when they say, "Who is going to decide the arguments which we have to this day?" I answer [449] "The word of God and no other judge at all."

Here is an example: The papists sell the mass as a sacrifice. Those who adhere to the teaching of Christ do not allow this to be so. They then insist: This will have to be decided by someone. Answer: Indeed. The word of God alone must decide in the matter. Do you wish the mass to be a sacrifice, then you will have to prove it from the word of God. Look then how you stand, like a ram before a butcher. You then start shouting, "The Fathers held it to be so." I say to you, "It's neither fathers nor mothers, but the word of God alone that counts."

Thus, good Christians, one needs no council, but only the pure word of God; in it all things become crystal clear. For as soon as one attempts to distort that, all faithful servants of Christ will stake their lives to preach it freely, according to its own course and nature. God preserve us from that which popes, emperors, bishops and kings will have to say; for the last error will then be greater than the first [Mt. 12:45]. Can they not see that the word of God has gained preeminence everywhere and that it remains unconquered? To call for councils is as much as to demand that the word of God be chained once again and placed in the hands of boastful bishops.

Therefore, each [temporal] authority on its own, inasmuch as it promoted peace and tranquility, must govern with God and assess the inordinate number of clerics rightly.

And their endowments are then to be administered in a Christian spirit.

Here the simple people are frightened off, because they think it improper to change someone's last will and testament; this, however, is as great a deception as all other abuses. Consider what those were guided by who made endowments? They had no guide other than the false [450] teaching that the mass is a sacrifice. Yet, they should have distributed their possessions to the poor instead of making endowments. Now when one recognizes the deceit, namely that the mass is not a sacrifice but food to the one who partakes of it with spiritual hunger, it is far better to give the endowments to the poor than to stuff these useless bellies--only after their death, of course.

At this point they object again: Look, how they dare invalidate the last will and testament. Answer: This is where deceit lies in ambush. Does not every [temporal] authority have its ways and means to decide how last wills are to be executed? Who says anything against such wills? Who would want to falsify them? You papists falsified them more than anyone else, for you sneaked yourselves into the last wills and testaments so that you were given what should have belonged to other rightful heirs; and you have done this with your deceitfulness and your false teaching. And that which was a temporal law you turned into a divine law. The last will is not at all grounded in Sacred Scripture in the form in which you use it. But you have taken it from secular law and have gone into the pulpits shouting how sinful it is to disregard a person's last will. This is true, of course, inasmuch as a last will is upheld as firmly by a worldly authority as a testament. This, however, is not customary in a number of places; whatever is not backed by a testament is simply not kept. What business did you have in such places to speak of last wills? It was really none of your business.

Here you say: It often happens that someone keeps unlawful property until his death; then only does he order it returned or given to the poor. Answer: In that case, too, you should have simply said to him, "This belongs here and that there, as we stated earlier about unlawful property." [5] But you turned such advice into a special law, called it the last will and in the process you falsified the last will. If one was to return unlawful property or give it to the poor, why then did you order it to be given to temples, your monasteries, for endowments, [451] vigils and masses, etc, for which you had no support at all in the word of God? For that which belonged to the poor and to rightful owners, should not have been stolen by you. Can you see how one detects here the real falsifiers of last wills, who in pretending to do things for the benefit of human souls, allowed their greed to get the better of them.

Again they say, "When, however, a person gives us something in his death of his own free will and accord, is it not fitting for us to take it? Answer: No. For you should have instructed the giver in true Christian understanding, somewhat as follows: You should not keep temporal possessions unto yourself, since you are only a steward of the same. You are to distribute them among the poor, which is pleasing to God, and you should not give them to those who do not suffer want. Can you not see that such goods are often used in the temple simply because of pride or greed, though they may not be squandered wantonly? For this reason, God ordered these things to be given to the poor and you should do likewise.

Therefore let no one shy away from turning once again to the Christian care of the poor, which thus far has been misused. If they were here who unknowingly distributed these goods to the bellies, they would now tear them from their hands once again. Let no private citizen appropriate these things to himself either; whoever does so, is a thief and robber. The magistrate must wait until endowments are freed up and then administer them in the name of God. Thus common justice is maintained and no one is tempted to do evil.

NOTES

1. Cf. Z.I 93.21ff.

2. "Das inen der seyten abgat" – that the string breaks on them.

3. Bochbischoff.

4. The Council of Basel opened in 1431. It held forty-nine sessions until its close, May 1443.

5. Cf. Z.II 292ff.

THE SIXTY-FIFTH ARTICLE

Those who are unwilling to recognize their error, will be dealt with by God. Therefore, no violence is to be done to their bodies, unless, of course, they behave in such an unseemly fashion that one cannot do without it. [452]

I wrote this Article in order that it may be seen that God does not intend to advance his teaching by the force of arms. For he said to Peter [Mt. 26:52], "Put away your sword. Everyone who fights with the sword, shall die by the sword." For it would not be right at all, were one to reprimand the enemies of God because they acted by force and not in response to scripture, when afterwards we should become exactly as they are. One should stand by and uphold the word of God alone; it will be effective, indeed; for Christ shall destroy his enemy, the anti-Christ, by the breath of his mouth, 2 Thess. 2:8. Should we be persecuted for this, it were better had we to endure everything, than to be forced away from it. And let no private citizen take revenge. The magistrate alone is to silence the enemies of God, but only after it is clear that those who cannot oppose the truth with valid arguments, continue, nonetheless, to hinder the teaching of God in clandestine gatherings, by riots and through common denunciations.

There are many, unfortunately, who would not stop short of murder, poisoning, denunciations, if only they had no fear for their skin. Whenever such persons can be stopped by peaceful means, one should do so in all earnestness; for we are not to fight with such tricks, but with scripture alone. If they were allowed to carry on with their own schemes, they would unsettle the entire world. To this they aspire--let everyone take heed, therefore. Several of them in addition, speak so abusively of scripture, God and truth, that it would be good to have some of them silenced. They can do nothing that is borne out by scripture. Yet they always bark against it. None of this, however, is to be done by force. Rather, after having discerned their ignorance, one should then order them to learn silence in the manner of Pythagoras. [1] [453]

NOTE

1. Adherents of Pythagoras allegedly were given a trial period of between two and five years during which they had to observe silence.

THE SIXTY-SIXTH ARTICLE

All clerical superiors are to humble themselves instantly and erect the cross of Christ only and not the money box. Otherwise they will perish; the axe is laid to the root of the tree [cf. Mt. 3:10].

This is a sincere admonition to leave off quarreling and to surrender to the cross of Christ, i.e. to humble oneself and to believe the word of Christ in all things, rather than to fortify oneself daily in new lies. For anyone who thus fortifies himself, is unable to escape in the long run, Prov. 19:5. Force is useless here. Nor does it do to say that the princes will not accept the word of God, in any case; for the greater number of them have accepted it lately; after all, the teaching of Christ does not grow from the [temporal] heads downwards, but it grows rather from the small, insignificant people upwards to the heads so that the power of the word of God may be known; against it the strong and powerful have not been able to do anything; they have been overcome in their sin so that the divine wisdom and power of God may become apparent. It won't help anymore either to spend money and to refill the coffers by begging through the sale of indulgences. [1] The matter has been found out and no one gives a farthing for it any longer.

The axe is at the root of the tree, according to John's word, Mt. 3:10, i.e. where the light shines, there the darkness disappears; where the truth appears, there the untruth flees; where God appears, there the devil has to give way; where the word of God appears, which does not come under false colors, there all hypocrisy has to vanish. Therefore the word of God threatens all hypocrisy. For wherever it is accepted there the meekest proves to be strong when it comes to dispelling hypocrisy. And though for a time they may be able to fight [the word of God], there is no escaping in the end. I do not say this in view of the flood (as some might think), which [454] no one ought to fear; they should simply say, "Your will be done". [2] I do not fear such a flood and do not believe that it will come, as the astrologers predicted; for thus far they have always missed the truth by a long shot. Whenever they predict cold weather, one almost suffocates from the heat and when they predict heat, we have to sit beside the fireplace. I hope they will miss it this time, too, and learn [as a result], that God is lord.

NOTES

1. Es wird hie nit helfen gelt ussgeben und widrumb mit ablas erbetlen.

2. Astrologers had predicted a flood for the year 1524 on the basis of unusual constellations. Cf. J. Kessler, **Sabbata,** 136. Zwingli and Kessler must have drawn on the same source; their wording is in part identical.

THE SIXTY-SEVENTH ARTICLE

Should anyone wish to discuss with me interest rates, tithes, unbaptized children or confirmation, I declare myself willing to respond.

I am prepared to talk here about interest, on the basis of Christ's teaching: whether it may be charged, in keeping with the word of God, and whether it is legitimate or not. I do not intend to prove (for this is impossible), or state that a moneylender should not be paid interest, for as long as temporal authorities tolerate money lenders, [1] a debtor is duty-bound to pay interest on the loan with which he burdened himself. However, I do want to point out here to those of good conscience how they might conduct themselves in such matters, so as not to arouse God's wrath.

Concerning laymen's tithes, which come from them rather than from the church, I did not want to get involved. For these arise from the fact that the entire land was theirs at one time and that they rented it out in return for a tenth and for slave labor, so that whoever made his living from the soil became bound [2] to him, whom he wed tithes.

However, concerning tithes, imposed by sanctuaries or churches, I intend to respond, whether one is bound to pay these on the basis of divine or human [455] rights. In this connection, I intend to show the great abuses concerning tithes, so that the poor parish priests who have been deprived by force of their food, may have it restored, not in its entirety, but an honest, fitting portion of the same. For there are quite a few among them who say, "Were I to speak the truth, I would have to go a-begging. But I did not intend to do this on my own behalf, as some claim untruthfully. By the grace of God I am content with so very little that I can readily testify that should I ever be found to desire more than what is needed to feed the body and to take care of reasonable necessities, I must not be given any further aid. But I am not overly anxious in the matter and have never been all my life, knowing myself to be freer of greed than of any other vice (praise be to God), for the entire world cannot satisfy a greedy person. I cry then on behalf of poor, simple clerics only, so that they won't have to feed themselves forever with the aid of invented fables such as how St. Wendelin had to nourish himself by taking care of sheep, [3] but that they might be able, instead, to take the pure and undefiled word of God to hand.

Concerning unbaptized children I preached somewhat as follows: It is more likely that they will be saved than that they should be damned. For this the wearers of cowls [4] tried to eat me alive. For I placed an obstruction in their way which they were unable to scale. For I spoke only concerning children born to Christian parents, and then I simply said, "it would appear more likely" and not, "it is certain that they should be saved". For God's judgments are not known to us. There are, however, some dastardly people who are so unskilled that they cause grief by their disdain [456] to poor parents who are hit by some accident; they do not allow them to bury their children in consecrated ground and penalize them with public shame and penance; thus they pass judgment on the judgment of God. Actually, I had no intention of speaking on these things at this point for the simple reason that the whole matter has been drawn out enough and it is high time for me to come to an end; enough therefore.

Apology and Protestation

I can easily see that my reprimands will greatly displease many, but only those who cannot tolerate any admonition, and are unprepared, at the same time, to change their ways in the least; they care for the word of God about as much as the Jewish priests and Pharisees cared for the teaching of Christ. Their self-willed ignorance and boastful behavior affects every writer when he sees how shamefully the wholesome teaching of Christ and his ordinances are disregarded and despised, so that he cannot be without severe anger and displeasure toward the godless people. This is likely what happened to me also. It would seem, however, that these adversaries of Christ, who do not allow themselves to be bent or circumcised, but who blaspheme God without ceasing, have not ever been touched by anything (though they deserved to be). But if there is anyone who feels that I shortchanged him in this writing, let him inform me. Should it be found then that someone has been hit too hard or that I have spoken too sharply, I am willing to correct the matter. For as little as I desire the teaching of Christ to be violated, so little do I wish, God being my helper, to do violence through it to anyone. [457]

Now, as far as the opinions are concerned with which I dealt in this writing, I can testify before God and our Lord Jesus Christ, that I handled them in this way, as may be readily seen, because I found scripture to be of that opinion; and I did not allow any human prattling or opinion to dissuade me whenever I realized that God spoke differently.

Should I have erred regarding the meaning of scripture, and should this be demonstrated here and there on the basis of scripture, I offer to be corrected--not by human teaching and statutes, of course, but through scripture which is theopneustos, i.e. inspired by God. [5] Further, the meaning of scripture must be verified, not from the writings of the Fathers, but from scripture itself. I, in turn, offer to clarify the dark passages of scripture, not from the top of my head and through useless prattle; the meaning I elicit from scripture, I shall also support from scripture. Scripture must be my judge as well as the judge of everyone else; but no person must ever be judge of the word of God. I hope that Christ who is the truth, will not allow his word to be suppressed, but rather, that he will reveal to us poor sinners more and more fully the glory of his grace and honor. To him, together with the Father and the Holy Spirit, be praise, honor and thanksgiving for ever, Amen.

NOTES

1. The singular is "faenerator-foenerator." It describes a money lender (capitalist), but has a pejorative connotation of "usurer". Zwingli's use of the plural suggests that he had a derogatory meaning in mind.

2. Eigen - leibeigen-hoerig. Cf. **Idiotikon** I 145.

3. For details about this saint of Scottish ancestry, cf. J. E. Stadler & J. N. Ginal, **Vollstaendiges Heiligenlexicon**, Hildesheim/N. York, 1975.

4. Cf. Z.I 381.2; Z.II 48.29ff.

5. Cf. Z.I 458.3ff. In the brief preface to the 67 Articles Zwingli used these very words.

SCRIPTURE INDEX

Old Testament

Apocrypha

SCRIPTURE INDEX

New Testament

382

384

GENERAL INDEX

388

394